69 A.D.

ALEXIS AQUINO PEREZ

69 A.D.

The Year of Four Emperors

Gwyn Morgan

OXFORD
UNIVERSITY PRESS

Acknowledgments

Over the years many friends and colleagues have given me help, advice, and encouragement. So too have many students, graduate and undergraduate. To single out individuals would be invidious, but to all of them I express my deepest appreciation. There are three people, however, to whom I owe particular debts: Chris Williams for drawing the maps that will, I hope, make the narrative easier to follow; Thomas Le Bien, formerly of Oxford University Press, for his help in getting this project launched; and Susan Ferber, his successor as my editor at the Press, for suffering so much with such equanimity during the book's lengthy and often painful gestation. Finally, there are the three men to whom the book is dedicated. To them I owe the profoundest gratitude for having pounded into me, many years ago, the need to develop at least some feeling for literature to balance my fascination with history.

Contents

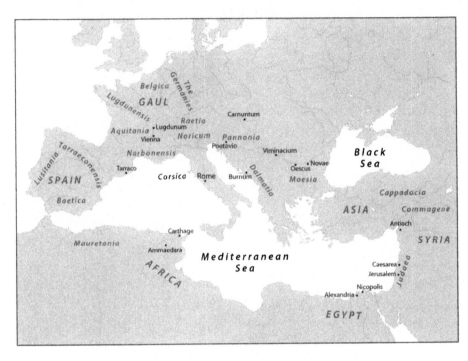

The Provinces of the Roman Empire in 69

Introduction

The Year of the Four Emperors is the label we attach to the 18-month period that opened with the suicide of Nero in June 68 and closed with the triumph of Vespasian in December 69. In the interim three other emperors held power, if only for a few months. There was Galba, officially declared emperor in June 68 and assassinated on 15 January 69. There was Otho, the man responsible for his murder. Having seized power by a coup in Rome, he committed suicide on 16 April, in the vain hope that his death would end the bloodshed. And there was Vitellius, hailed emperor by his troops on 3 January 69, recognized by the senate in Rome once they heard of Otho's death, and cut down by Vespasian's partisans on 20 December. Galba, Otho, Vitellius, and Vespasian were usurpers, of course, whereas Nero had been the legitimate emperor, the last male member of the Julio-Claudian dynasty established by Augustus a century earlier. In retrospect it is easy to make Vespasian's victory look inevitable. In fact, it owed an enormous amount to accident and luck. But Vespasian was a practical, hard-headed man, disinclined to look gift-horses in the mouth, and his dynasty, the Flavians, would rule the Roman world for 27 years.

Why write a book about all this, especially when, in the past century, there have been three full-length studies in English, by Henderson, Greenhalgh, and Wellesley? The answer revolves around the conflict between what the evidence says and the conclusions we can legitimately draw from it. It is a conflict that has bedeviled historians ever since the events took place. Tacitus, for example, our fullest source, had no qualms about denigrating his predecessors' works on the Year of the Four Emperors and the Flavian dynasty. Even as he plundered them for material, he asserted that they were all unreliable because written from a faulty perspective, and that the record needed to be set straight. One can still claim to be trying to set the record straight, since any new study of a period should rest on the proposition that previous works on the subject are flawed by shortcomings of some kind. It would be inexcusable as well as unjustifiable to dismiss the work of earlier scholars in the Tacitean manner, but Henderson, Greenhalgh, and Wellesley—for all their many virtues—failed to handle the evidence adequately.

Bernard W. Henderson's *Civil War and Rebellion in the Roman Empire* was published in 1908, when Europe was awash in studies of the changing nature of warfare in light of the Franco-Prussian War of 1870 and the Russo-Japanese War of 1904–1905 (the significance of the American Civil War was largely missed or ignored). So Henderson set out to reconstruct the military history of 68/69, to make sense of the confused and contradictory narratives of the ancient sources, and to introduce the latest insights into the study of Roman campaigning. The results varied. His interpretation of the war between Otho and Vitellius proved to be overcomplicated and anachronistic, and was criticized savagely by his peers. But as they also observed, the rest of the book is much sounder. It has the comic-opera air of a work composed by "a very modern major-general," referring as it does frequently to the long-forgotten little wars of the Victorian period. Yet its author was no fool. On many points Henderson has proved a more incisive critic than his successors, and his book deserves a better fate than to have become a collector's item among military buffs, as eager as are their detractors to believe that military thinking has stood still for two millennia.

Since the fascination exerted by one period of history or another waxes and wanes according to the temper of the times, nearly 70 years elapsed before two more studies appeared. Both were published in 1975, and both focused on the overall picture, as Henderson had not—but to very different ends. P. A. L. Greenhalgh's *The Year of Four Emperors* was an overtly popular study, told almost as if it were one of the "ripping yarns" on which British schoolboys were reared in the days of Empire. Stitching together a lively and seamless narrative on "one of the most exciting, bloody, colourful, critical, absorbing, best documented and least well-known episodes in the whole of Roman history," Greenhalgh drew his material principally—and as a rule uncritically—from Tacitus' *Histories*. The results are eminently readable, but they do little to advance our understanding of the realities of 68/69. Tacitus is too difficult and demanding an author to permit our taking his narrative at face value. Much as there is to be said for the machete-wielding popularizer who hacks a path through the jungle of academic theories, interminable discussions, and innumerable footnotes, the path tends to lead nowhere or back to its starting point.

Kenneth Wellesley's *The Long Year: A.D. 69*, conversely, has proved the most durable of these monographs, to judge by the number of times it has been reprinted. Wellesley was a scholar who devoted much of his life to the study of Tacitus, and his book was preceded (and followed) by a long string of learned papers in which he addressed specific problems raised by our sources. The result was a more comprehensive narrative, even if overly preoccupied with matters of topography (apparently Wellesley had served in Military Intelligence). Some also find it less reader friendly. But the real problem lies in the fact that though Wellesley dedicated his book to the shades of Tacitus, his study of the *Histories* convinced him not merely that Tacitus could seldom be trusted, but also that he went out of his way to distort the evidence. Hence *The Long Year* rests on an interpretation in which the Tacitean evidence is regularly doubted or dismissed in favor of material from our other sources, Plutarch above all (hence a portrait of a kinder, gentler Galba). So Wellesley went to the opposite extreme from Greenhalgh, in method and in results: Greenhalgh trusted Tacitus too much, Wellesley too little.

As a first step, therefore, let me say that one overall aim of this study is to offer an account of the Year of the Four Emperors that rests on a fresh scrutiny of the evidence and, in particular, steers a course that grants Tacitus more credit than Wellesley allowed him but less than Greenhalgh accorded him. This is important, because it is not just Tacitus' evidence for the upheavals of 68/69 that cannot be taken at face value. None of it can. The most eye-catching artifacts to have come down to us, for example, the coins struck by the emperors, remain our least helpful guides to specific events despite all the work devoted to them by numismatists. For a start, Roman coinage was not struck on any systematic basis at this stage. There would be a flurry of issues at the start of a new reign, but then the flow tapered off. Again, it was usual to strike in gold, silver, and bronze (for small change), but Otho issued only gold and silver coins, since Nero and Galba between them had pumped huge quantities of bronze into circulation. Then there is the fact that we cannot prove that the emperor in whose name a coin was minted was the person who picked the design. And finally, while it would make sense to assume that Vitellius, say, personally chose the legend for an issue honoring "the loyalty of the legions," we cannot always determine whether such a legend referred to past events, present concerns, or hopes for the future. Obviously, the minting authority was conveying some kind of general message, and apparently the consumer was supposed to swallow this message without demur, but that is about all we can say.[1]

Rather more can be gleaned from archaeology, epigraphy, and papyrology. In 1887, for example, archaeologists recovered the bronze facing to the military chest of the Vitellian legion IV Macedonica, the container for the troops' savings. Found some 50 meters outside the walls of Cremona, the chest must have been dropped or abandoned during the Flavian assault on the Vitellians' position in October 69. Then there are inscriptions, ranging from dedications to the gods made by two soldiers who took part in Caecina's march through the Alps in March 69 all the way up to the so-called law on Vespasian's powers (*lex de imperio Vespasiani*). A large bronze tablet found in Rome in the fourteenth century, this preserves the concluding sections of a law passed once the fighting had ended. Not only does it spell out Vespasian's rights and prerogatives for the future. Its final clause also legalizes every action taken by him and his subordinates between 1 July 69, when he was proclaimed emperor by his troops in the eastern provinces, and 21 December, when his claim to the throne was officially recognized by the senate in Rome. As for the papyri, the most important of these is the text of an edict issued in Alexandria on 6 July 68 by the prefect of Egypt, Tiberius Julius Alexander, to announce his acceptance of Galba as the legitimate emperor.

Important as such documents are, they tend to create as many problems as they solve. Tiberius Alexander's edict, for instance, has prompted an inordinate amount of speculation, because it throws a flood of light on one matter, and yet raises a series of questions about the relationship between that matter and other events. Besides, these are random discoveries, and so do not and cannot give us the material to construct an account that ties together all the bits and pieces of information. For that kind of framework we must turn to the surviving literary sources, of whom there are five, two Roman (Tacitus and Suetonius), two Greek (Plutarch and Dio Cassius), and one Jewish (Josephus). I have relegated to appendix 1 the questions who these men were, when they wrote, and what they wrote about. The point to be emphasized here is that each of the five provides only partial coverage, since each chose to write what he wrote from a particular perspective, in a particular manner, to suit a particular purpose.

A good illustration is provided by the tale of what happened when Galba left the palace on 15 January 69, the last day of his life, to confront the usurper Otho. On his way out he ran into a ranker named Julius Atticus, who was brandishing a bloody sword and claiming loudly to have killed Otho. Galba responded by asking Atticus who had given him his orders. The story was undoubtedly told to highlight Galba's question, since he was a notorious martinet, who deplored any sign of initiative or independent thinking by others. Yet there are four different versions of the incident, from Plutarch, Tacitus, Suetonius, and Dio. None of them is much interested in Atticus' motives for lying, but they take Galba's question in four different ways. Plutarch, the best disposed toward the emperor, misses the point or deliberately defuses the effect of the question by having Atticus respond that he had acted "out of loyalty and the oath he had sworn," a declaration greeted with applause and shouts of approval from the bystanders. The other three writers focus on Galba's question and, as Philippe Fabia put it, for Tacitus, the emperor's behavior illustrates his intransigence when faced with a breach of military discipline; for Suetonius it exemplifies his misplaced confidence that Otho's coup was a tempest in a teapot; Dio sees only his credulity in swallowing the tale without demanding corroborative evidence like Otho's head.[2]

With a minor incident like this, we could argue that it does not matter which version we prefer or, less convincingly, we could combine all four into one by the judicious application of scissors and paste. Neither method works when the point at issue is the interpretation of the period as a whole. Here we face a double-barreled question, what exactly it is that the evidence says and just how much weight we should give to the different pieces. Can we and should we, for instance, continue to accept the widespread view, derived from Plutarch, that during the Year of the Four Emperors the Roman armed forces went berserk? As he puts it in the preface to his *Life* of Galba, "many terrible events, especially those that befell the Romans after Nero's suicide, . . . show in exemplary fashion that a state should fear above all armed forces subject to untrained and irrational impulses. . . . The Roman empire was overtaken by disasters and upheavals like those caused by the Titans of mythology, at one and the same time being torn into many pieces and collapsing in on itself in many places. This came about not so much because of the ambitions of the men who were proclaimed emperor, as because of the greed and indiscipline of the soldiery . . . who ushered one emperor into the palace and another out just like characters in a stage play."

Plutarch's interpretation is a wholly artificial construct. It rests, first, on his own admission that his work was not a detailed, formal history of the period, only biographies of individual emperors. This is what allowed him to get away with the wild claim that the empire was "torn into many pieces." Second, he granted that it was his duty to include peripheral incidents "worthy of mention," but in order to decide which incidents these were he used the criteria of a philosopher drawing general lessons from the study of history. Third, and most important, his scenario turns on a specious antithesis between the supreme commander on the one side and the "soldiery" on the other. In a piece of rhetorical legerdemain that too few have challenged, Plutarch declared the emperors largely ciphers and their ambitions inconsequential, and he lumped the rankers together with the officers between them and the emperor. However we view the rankers, their officers were no more brutal, mercenary, and licentious than their emperors.

Why, then, has this vision of the brutal soldiery so captivated succeeding generations? In part, it is clear, this presentation has always struck a chord with readers in countries where people suspect—justifiably or otherwise—that the armed forces are not wholly under the control of the civil authority. But it owes most of its strength to the failure of our other sources explicitly to provide an alternative conceptual framework in which to set the story. Suetonius and Dio explain Nero's suicide simply as the consequence of his own misdeeds, and view subsequent developments as results of that suicide. Tacitus prefaces his narrative with a short survey of what he saw as the moods prevailing at the start of 69 in Rome and the provinces, of those high on the social scale and those in its lower reaches, of civilians and soldiers, enough to show that he refused to limit himself to the relationship between emperor and troops. But because he also states that events now revealed "a (*not* the) secret of empire, that an emperor could be made elsewhere than in Rome," this remark has been ripped out of its context and used to support Plutarch's scenario. In fact, Tacitus did not specify by whom any such emperors were made, clearly because he expected his readers to grasp that the process was far more complex than Plutarch would have us believe.

Like Plutarch, Tacitus held that authors and readers could and should draw lessons from history, this being a vital function of Roman as it was of Greek historiography. Nor was he averse to fitting incidents into larger themes, the luck that attended Vespasian's bid for power, for example, or the irresponsibility of the senate, or the mutinous spirit of armies, or the general decline in people's respect for laws and gods—provided that the similarity of the events or their progression in one direction, more often than not downhill, permitted it. But he presented his case studies (*exempla*) as the particular and specific results of the individual behavior of individual men or women on individual occasions. It was their uniqueness that justified describing them, and he refused flatly, and rightly, to force them into some kind of preordained, theoretical construct warranting the sweeping generalizations that so entranced Plutarch.

If we take Tacitus as our guide, therefore, it emerges that the soldiery played a significant role in the upheavals of 68/69, but not in the simplistic manner that Plutarch champions. As Tacitus tells the story, for example, rankers gave their emperor loyalty far deeper and more enduring than their officers were ever able to develop—no small thing, in that this tended to prolong both the fighting and the bitterness that went with defeat. Similarly, military discipline was obviously undermined by these civil wars, and the men were perfectly capable of picking and choosing which officers to obey and when to obey them. Much depended on the respect they felt for their commanders. But the results could vary.

In Otho's case the consequences were dire, since his troops did in fact help usher him off the stage, albeit not by design. In the concluding stages of the campaign against Vitellius, on the other hand, the Flavian commander Antonius Primus exploited the troops' mutinous spirit in order to nullify the other officers' opposition to his plan of campaign. So rankers were normally the raw material used by emperors or officers to get their own way, and it was certainly not rankers who set in motion the events that put Galba, or Otho, or Vitellius, or Vespasian on the throne.

Once we recognize that we can give less weight to the soldiery and more to their officers, we can restore a political or, better, a personal dimension to these struggles that permits a more rounded explanation of what was going on. Like Tacitus himself, for example, all these officers accepted the principate. None had ideas of restoring a republic. But their aims tended to be self-serving and immediate. The loyalists who defended the status quo wanted to preserve or raise their status within the political élite. And those opposed to the reigning emperor hoped to accelerate their own advancement within the élite as they helped set their own candidate on the throne. In both groups the overriding consideration was fear or ambition, not principle. This is the basis for Tacitus' assertion that only one of the officers who took part in the war against Vitellius "brought good qualities to this campaign." And whether fear or ambition animated these men, they expressed these drives almost invariably in what may well seem an incredibly shortsighted manner. Academics, unfortunately, have tended to discount this opportunism, perhaps because—like conspiracy theorists—they prefer to assume that only planning could have produced the results for which shortsightedness, inadvertence, or downright incompetence were responsible. But when Tacitus talks of the "madness" of civil war, it denotes the loss of any sense of proportion among the officers as often as it does the loss of any sense of discipline and decorum among the men.

To this view of the situation, it can—and no doubt will—be objected that we should not trust Tacitus. This is reasonable, up to a point. As recent events have shown, it is not enough merely to assemble information or to pick out only the bits and pieces that happen to agree with opinions we have already formed. We have to evaluate all the evidence before us, and that evaluation requires that we start from the proposition that all information is suspect until proved otherwise. Yet over time we must rank the sources of that information according to the quality and the coherence of the material they provide. We have to allow for bias, conscious and unconscious, on our part as well as on that of our informants. And we should strive to ensure that no misapprehensions cloud or distort the picture as the result, say, of a failure to recognize that the

informant is in every sense speaking a different language than the evalu-
ator. Nobody today can hope to get inside the head of an ancient writer,
since different languages are the products of different thought patterns
and different value systems. But this does not absolve us from trying.
And in Tacitus' case much of the criticism rests on a misunderstanding
of his aims and methods, on an inability to come to grips with the quirki-
ness of his syntax and style, and on an almost Pavlovian refusal even to
consider the possibility that he was as conscientious in the evaluation of
his material as he was artful in its presentation.[3]

Since it is precisely the artfulness with which Tacitus presents his
material that has proved the greatest stumbling block to any understanding of his aims and methods, it will be as well to make a basic point here,
that in Greece and Rome history and biography were regarded as branches
of literature. In the scale of values that went with this approach, the
writing of history belonged on the highest level, since it dealt with the
great deeds of great men, and qualified as the prose equivalent of an epic
poem (one reason why Tacitus' narratives are suffused with diction from
Vergil's *Aeneid*). Biography belonged further down the scale. Though it
too dealt often enough with great men, the biographer was allowed to
use trivial incidents or apocryphal tales to characterize the man he was
describing (hence Suetonius' delight in the rumors that are too often
taken by moderns as hard facts). Still, one rule applied to historians and
biographers alike, that the medium must match the message, that the
writer must aim at literary artistry in the presentation of his material. As
a result, it was accepted practice for a historian or a biographer to lift
huge slabs of material, without acknowledgement, from an earlier writer,
usually the earlier writer who was thought to have given the most au-
thoritative account to date (for the events of 68/69 the so-called common source). The later writer could abridge this material, as did Plutarch,
or he could expand it, as did Tacitus. He could alter its arrangement,
and change the emphasis and the interpretation to suit his own purposes, as did Suetonius, above all in his *Life* of Vitellius.[4] And none of
this qualified as plagiarism, because the later writer recast the story in
his own way and in his own style. The ancients' definition of originality,
in short, was not unlike the modern justification for remaking a movie.

What set Tacitus apart from our other four sources is that an unusual and arresting style was considered essential for a first-rate historian from Thucydides' time onward, both to hook the audience and hold
its attention, and to reassure it that the author had taken the same immense pains with the evaluation of his subject matter as he had with the
creation and application of his style. Tacitus carried this approach to
extremes. Since he lived in an age when brevity was prized and long-

windedness suspect, his Latin exhibits a terseness that even headlines in a modern newspaper cannot match. And since it was an age that esteemed epigrammatic turns of phrase, sound bites with real teeth, he obliged with gems like his six-word "everybody agreed that Galba would have made a great emperor, if only he had not become emperor" (*omnium consensu capax imperii nisi imperasset*). This jibe, moreover, encapsulates another weapon Tacitus used to achieve his effects, antithesis or the juxtaposition of opposites. This turns up constantly, not just in individual sentences or chapters. So Tacitus constructed his account of Vitellius' march to Rome after the defeat and death of Otho (a process that occupied the four months between mid-April and mid-July 69) as a series of episodes grouped by category and contrasted with one another by juxtaposition. The account may look linear, and it has been interpreted as such, because there is little in the way of overt comment. But there is little overt comment because Tacitus was a subtle writer and the arrangement made his point.

This has caused enormous problems. For a start, these are all rhetorical techniques, and these days the term "rhetoric" raises suspicions, even hackles, implying deception, exaggeration, and spin. And this is the basis for the widespread assumption that Tacitus is out to hoodwink his readers. For a Greek or Roman writer in any genre, however, rhetoric provided the means of approaching a subject, of arranging the material, and of presenting a case or reaching a conclusion (Plutarch's on the soldiery, for example). All five of our literary sources used the techniques listed in their handbooks—the other four less competently perhaps, less often, and less overtly than Tacitus—to organize everything they had to say. And the original audiences for whom they wrote had no objection to this. It may be arguable whether any but the smartest among them were able to deconstruct a speech or a narrative as fast as its author constructed it. Nonetheless, literate Greeks and Romans were not merely trained in rhetoric. They lived and breathed it. For them it was a way of thinking, a way of speaking, a way of writing, and a way of acting.

Now, in the nineteenth century Leopold von Ranke proclaimed it the historian's function to write history "as it actually happened" (*wie es eigentlich gewesen*). Although still quoted with approval by nonspecialists, this dictum is little honored in academe. Since Ranke's day the study of history and literature has become immensely more sophisticated. This has had its advantages, among them the realization that no matter how reasonable Ranke's aim may look, it is impossible to achieve: history is only a record of the past, a historical fact only something historians think important. But there have been disadvantages too. This specialization has been carried so far that there is now a massive disconnect between students of history and students of literature. The historians seldom pay attention to the literary rules that guided Tacitus, and the students of literature ignore the historical matter he presents. So Tacitus, who saw himself simultaneously as historian and as literary artist, now falls between two stools. Modern historians of Rome distrust or dismiss his style, taking it for granted that whenever he says anything they find incomprehensible or unacceptable, he is guilty of inaccuracy, carelessness, or bias. Modern students of Latin literature discount the historical content of his work and talk, usually in the abstract, of his exploitation of irony and innuendo, or the way in which oddities in his vocabulary supposedly reflect the Roman political unconscious or his delight in ambiguity. Both schools emphasize analysis, rightly, but the result of both approaches is to tear down his narrative and to find fault with almost everything it contains.

It would be absurd to claim that Tacitus makes no mistakes, but how many and how serious they are is another question. There are occasions, for example, when he sacrifices substance to style, but they are far less frequent than it has become fashionable to claim. His epigrams certainly qualify, since they rely on overstatement for their effect. His descriptions of battles may fall into this category too, since they resort sometimes to formulaic modes of expression, but most ancient battles followed much the same lines anyway. He certainly refused to fuss about terrain, but why should he have, when most of his readers were likely as ignorant of the area being described as were the troops trudging or fighting their way across it, had no atlases to consult, and almost certainly did not care anyway? He credits characters with speeches they may or may not have delivered, but in antiquity these served as the equivalent of a modern analysis of the situation or as the presentation of the speaker's assessment of it, accurate or not. And despite his claims to be writing without partiality, some hold that he shows bias in his readiness to think the worst of just about everybody. But one can also argue either that civil wars seldom bring out the best in people, or that Tacitus—like Galba— held his subjects to standards they simply could not reach.

How, then, are we to approach our subject? I have made Tacitus' account the framework within which to describe the military and political history of the Year of the Four Emperors as best it can be recovered. To that extent this book may be able to function as a kind of companion to the *Histories*. But at the same time I have tried to indicate, more often than is customary in a book like this, which material is being drawn from which author. This, I hope, will allow my readers to make their own assessment of the quality of the informant as well as of his information, and so to decide for themselves how well founded any particular interpretation, ancient or modern, may be.

I

The Fall of Nero and the
Julio-Claudian House

Tacitus opens his account of the Year of the Four Emperors on 1 January 69, with the entry into the consulship of the emperor Servius Sulpicius Galba and his henchman Titus Vinius. Though he offers a brief survey of the overall situation, he refers to earlier events only in flashback, and as infrequently and tersely as possible. For what happened in the earlier year we must turn to Suetonius for the fullest account of Nero's last days, to Dio for the only surviving narrative of the revolt of Julius Vindex, the man who set off the events that led to Nero's fall, and to Plutarch for the most comprehensive report on Galba, the man who harvested the fruits of Vindex's endeavors. So why does Tacitus write as he does? Because he was following—and exploiting—the rules for writing history in Rome. An account was organized around an annalistic or year-by-year framework (how smoothly the narrative flowed over or around these breaks depended on the literary skills of the writer), and it was taken for granted that the reader was familiar with the years prior to the chosen starting point or else knew where to find the details. From the starting point onward, each year began with the entry into office of the new consuls on 1 January, since they were—in theory—the highest magistrates or chief executives in the state. And using their names to mark the year had been the custom since that formative event in all Roman history, the foundation of the republic (509 B.C.).

There was another method of indicating the passage of time, reckoning from the year when Romulus supposedly founded the city (753 *AUC* B.C.). This was less common and more cumbersome. But it could be used to remind the reader how long the city had lasted, especially as there had been occasional predictions that Rome would fall in such-and-such a year. That is why Tacitus brings it up next. The consulship of Galba and Vinius, he says, was the eight hundred and twenty-first year of Rome's existence, so that he can add "and very nearly its last." In one sense the comment is obvious exaggeration, but every historian was expected to open with dramatic claims to justify his choice of theme and capture the readers' attention. In another sense the remark is highly misleading.

Whether or not the troubles of 69 nearly brought down the empire and warranted Tacitus' plunging immediately into what he considered the year of crisis, they had not come out of nowhere. As we know from Suetonius, Dio, and Plutarch, the previous year had also seen revolts and civil wars, riots and massacres, murders and suicides. But it had seen only two emperors, Nero, a suicide, and Galba, now shrouding beneath his consular robes the fact that he was a usurper.

So why did Tacitus pick 69 rather than 68 as his starting point? All sorts of explanations have been offered, but he had no real choice. As Nero's reign ended in June 68, it could not be fitted easily into an annalistic frame. Tacitus had either to go back to the start of Nero's reign, when Nero could not be separated from his predecessors, or to move forward to the start of 69 and the last two weeks of Galba's reign. This was not the tidiest turning point either (hence the opening survey of the empire), but it served his purposes better. Since Galba was in his early seventies and childless, even his few ardent supporters recognized that his rule would be brief and, unless he named an acceptable heir, would precipitate another, still more massive storm. Besides, the city of Rome had suffered little in the upheavals of 68, whereas in 69 it was to see the deaths of two more emperors (Galba and Vitellius), and become a battlefield itself. When its inhabitants were brought up to believe that Rome was both the center of the empire and the one place where important events could occur, their historians naturally shared this viewpoint. This is another key to Tacitus' observation that in 69 "a secret of empire was disclosed, that an emperor could be made elsewhere than in Rome." The point being made is geographical as well as constitutional.

To understand how this situation came about, we have to go back a century, to Augustus, the first emperor of Rome. Most of the problems that came to a head in 69 can be traced back to the arrangements he made. The Roman state was never a democracy, and it was never a despotism. From start to finish it was an oligarchy. Much was made, before and after Augustus' day, of the rival claims of "liberty" and "tyranny," but this was rhetoric. During the republic's last century it was prompted by the endless factionalism within the governing class. Once Augustus had created the principate, a settlement that took its name from the claim that the emperor was merely "first among equals" (*princeps*), it reflected the constant tensions between the emperor and his governing class.

The title *princeps* applied to Augustus only in the civil sphere, that is, in Rome and Italy. Outside these limits he was the commander in chief (*imperator*) of almost all Rome's armed forces and of the provinces where they were stationed. The vast bulk of the troops, some 25 to 30 legions of Roman citizens (the number varied) and an equivalent number of auxiliary, non-Roman soldiers, were organized on a permanent basis and stationed on the frontiers, facing out. Though the ancient sources and modern writers play up the importance of these troops, they were seldom prime movers. When Tiberius succeeded Augustus in 14, there were mutinies in the units on the German frontier and in Pannonia (more or less modern Hungary). These, however, were triggered by the men's justifiable discontent over conditions of service imposed on them by Augustus, and both were settled fairly easily once the men's immediate needs were met. Without officers to give them a strong lead and point them in a predetermined direction, angry soldiers tended to stand rooted to the spot, or to mill around in confusion, or to do something even more shortsighted than the actions of which their officers were capable. What made the situation so dangerous in 68/69 was precisely that the discontent of the troops was combined with the audacity and unscrupulousness of officers willing to back this or that contender for the throne.

So the real problem lay in the city of Rome itself and, more particularly, in its form of government. Augustus started his career at the age of 19 as the warlord Octavian, and it took him 15 years of civil wars to win the empire. Fortunately for him, the last of these wars—against Antony and Cleopatra—could be represented as a foreign war against an "evil empire" in the east. Just as fortunately, the empire's population as a whole, perhaps 50 million people, was prepared to settle for what was close to one-man rule, if only that put an end to wars, civil or foreign, that had been fought inside the frontiers on and off for half a century. In this sense the principate was every bit as much a military monarchy when Augustus created it as it was in 68, when Galba took over from the last of his descendants. But since Augustus had neither the wish to share the fate of his adoptive father, Julius Caesar, nor the strength singlehandedly to run the empire he had won, he had to come to terms with the two small segments in Roman society that constituted its upper classes.

First, there were the senators, the members of the old governing class lucky or skillful enough to have survived these wars. They had not run the government as senators. In the republic the senate had been by design an advisory body, and though it was influential and prestigious, we talk of senators *doing* this or that for convenience. The executive was made of a series of annual magistracies, to which aspirants were elected by the people. The lowest, the quaestorship, gave its holder membership in the senate after he had laid down his office. The highest, the consulship, was the ultimate distinction. As consul, a man could run the government. And since only 2 consuls were elected a year, there could be only 60 in a generation, with the result that about 10 percent of late republican senators exercised disproportionate influence as ex-consuls and, supposedly, elder statesmen. To placate all these men, Augustus tried consistently to preserve as much as possible of the appearance and, once in a while, of the substance of the republic he had overthrown. This would persuade them that he was sharing civil and military power with them. In fact, it was the work, not the power, that fell to the senate. Although the magistracies retained their prestige, they became much less important, and there could be 12 or more consuls in a year. In effect, the consulship became a diploma in government, and men held it in their thirties instead of their forties.[1] With this requirement out of the way, these men could be sent out to govern Rome's provinces. But it was the emperor who picked the ex-consuls to govern the provinces in which armies were stationed, the senate only the men who were to govern provinces without troops.

The emperor was backed up in Rome itself by the praetorian guard, a force originally of 9 cohorts, probably of 500 men apiece, who served mainly as his honor guard. To this he was entitled as commander in chief of Rome's legions, but Augustus and his successors took care not to offend senatorial sensibilities. No guardsmen was allowed within the city's limits except in civilian dress. No doubt they carried concealed weapons, but the weapons *were* concealed. No legions were stationed in Italy in normal circumstances (the situation in 68/69 differed markedly). And the senate could lay claim to a guard of its own, the (originally 3) urban cohorts, also of 500 men apiece, who were commanded by one of their own, the prefect of the city (*praefectus urbi*), chosen by the emperor and senate in consultation. And as a senator, the prefect of the city outranked the prefect or prefects of the praetorian guard, who were merely knights.

This brings us to the other, much larger segment of the upper classes that Augustus had to consider, the equestrian order, equites or knights. The basic requirement for membership was a total worth of 400,000 sesterces (many had fortunes in the millions), but though they counted as an upper class for this reason, they were never regarded as senators' equals. When Suetonius reports that an emperor had such ancestors, it is because they were thought blots on the escutcheon. The knights were also much more heterogeneous. Some were entrepreneurs in the private or the public sphere, men whose interest lay in making money (they it was who gave the order a bad name). Then there were the men forming the governing class of any Roman city except Rome. The equivalent of senators in their hometowns and likewise landed aristocrats, they shared the attitudes of senators, but they could not be categorized as such because they had not held magistracies in Rome itself. Men of this kind might serve for a time as junior officers in the new standing armies, for example, as military tribunes of individual cohorts in a legion. (This is how Suetonius' father became a tribune of legion XIII Gemina in 69.) Then they could return to their homes, with enhanced prestige and boring tales of their exploits, or they might continue on and join the handful of men who took posts in the minuscule civil service Augustus created. The emperor's appointees, this group included procurators (his financial agents in senatorial provinces and actual governors in unimportant districts like Judaea) and, at the summit, four or five prefects. These were, in ascending order of importance, the prefect of the watch (the fire service in Rome), the prefect of the grain supply for the city, the prefect of Egypt, and the one or two prefects of the praetorian guard.[2]

Augustus had virtually no trouble getting the knights—of whatever category—to accept his new settlement at face value. Unless they developed ambitions to enter the senatorial order, as did Tacitus himself, they were usually happy to pursue their own interests, oblivious to or even welcoming changing conditions in the world in which they lived. With the senators, on the other hand, Augustus had to strive constantly to paper over the gaps between appearances and realities, and above all, between the illusion that they were his peers and the fact that he meant to establish a dynasty. As it happened, Augustus was able to persuade many senators to see things his way. Partly, this was due to his own prestige. He had ended the civil wars that threatened to destroy them, and he brought peace to an empire that not only prospered but continued to grow under his guidance. Partly, it was skill. Augustus was by far the smartest politician of his day (his wife Livia was smarter still, but never in public). Partly, it was self-control. Augustus never flaunted his powers in Rome, preferring to play the simple citizen there. And partly it was luck. When Augustus died in 14 at the age of 78, there were few still alive who could remember the old republic.

It proved more difficult to conceal the gaps between rhetoric and reality after he died. His four successors, known collectively as the Julio-Claudian dynasty, lacked his prestige, his abilities, and above all, his self-control. So, under Tiberius (14–37), Caligula (37–41), Claudius (41–54), and Nero (54–68), the situation was bound to deteriorate. It did this not so much steadily as in fits and starts. To give himself room to maneuver, Augustus had spelled out a minimum of rules and regulations (this was not to change significantly till the "law on Vespasian's powers" was passed). So the workings of his unsystematic system depended heavily on the character and caprices of the ruler. Each of his four successors undertook on his accession to fulfill the hopes of the senators that a new princeps would bring with him a new beginning. Each in turn failed sooner or later to live up to these promises, to the sorrow and—more often than not—the suffering of the senators. The only variables were how long it took for disenchantment to set in, how widely it spread, and how deeply it penetrated.[3]

This disenchantment made senators much touchier about their rights and privileges, and steadily more insistent on their social distinction as they watched their political power fade. It seldom led to conspiracies against the emperor, however, and when it did, they were small. There were few active participants, because senators spent more time jockeying for position among themselves than they did complaining about or plotting against the emperor (this nursery-level behavior pattern dominated every level of the society). Again, these conspiracies were usually attempts to assassinate the emperor and replace him with a senator more congenial to the plotters and—in theory—to the rest of the governing class. Only on two occasions were legions involved. There was a conspiracy against Caligula in 39, which included among its members Gnaeus Lentulus Gaetulicus, commander of the troops stationed in Upper Germany, and that ended the moment Caligula appeared on the scene and ordered Gaetulicus' execution. And in 42 there was an uprising against Claudius by Furius Camillus Scribonianus, governor of Dalmatia. That collapsed within five days, because the troops had second thoughts. Suetonius avers that they believed the omens unfavorable, Dio that they were unimpressed by their general's announced intention of restoring the republic. These explanations are not mutually exclusive, but the latter highlights a more basic reason for the troops' refusal in both cases to follow a rebellious general against an established emperor. From Tiberius' time on, the armed forces renewed their oath of allegiance to the emperor on 1 January each year. Taking the sanctity of this oath seriously, they remained true to him whether others thought him mad, incompetent, or vicious. The praetorian guard were equally loyal. A detachment murdered Caligula in January 41. Yet while the senate debated who should succeed him, the guard as a whole applied the rules of dynastic succession and proclaimed the late emperor's uncle, Claudius, their ruler. A guardsman had found Claudius hiding behind a curtain in the palace and had carted him off to the praetorian camp. From any point of view, this was not kingmaking as it is commonly understood.

Even so, senators probably imagined that the situation looked rosier than usual at the start of Nero's reign. Whereas his three predecessors had been adults when they took power, Nero was only 16 in 54. Suetonius catalogues the iniquities of his ancestors, since Romans believed that in diseased stock evil would out. But those who put their faith in education could believe that there was a chance of schooling Nero to run the state in something like the manner required by the ideology of the principate.

And the first five years of the reign were relatively tranquil, thanks largely to the fact that control lay in the hands of the two men appointed as Nero's tutors by his mother, the Younger Agrippina. One was the senator and supposed philosopher Seneca, the other Lucius Afranius Burrus, prefect of the praetorian guard. Unfortunately for his tutors, however, and for the senators, Nero used this period to indulge a temperament as sadistic as it was artistic. His passions were for acting, singing, and chariot racing, not for learning the duties of an emperor. Much could be forgiven an adolescent, since Romans also believed that boys would be boys— until they reached the age of 25 or so. But once Nero became master of the world, he saw no reason for self-control. And because he would brook no challenge even in his early years, they too were marked by murder, of his stepbrother Britannicus in 55, and of his mother Agrippina in 59.

The killing of Britannicus, innocent though he was of anything but being Claudius' son by his first wife Messallina, was seemingly regarded as the price to be paid by somebody whose claim to the throne was as strong as that of the incumbent—and it could be blamed on the domineering Agrippina anyway. Agrippina's murder was probably greeted with sighs of relief by most, though it became fashionable later to dwell on the horrors of matricide, and even to allege that this cast a shadow over the emperor's mind. Still, the situation continued to deteriorate as the years went by, and in 62 Nero engineered the exile of his wife Octavia (Britannicus' sister) on a charge of adultery, to clear the way for marriage to his mistress, Poppaea Sabina. Since Octavia was palpably innocent of any wrongdoing, the common people demonstrated noisily, as prone then as they have been recently to fits of unwarrantable sentimentality. The senators bore Octavia's exile, and her death a year later, with equanimity. Whatever they thought of Nero's actions, little was to be gained by quarreling with an emperor intent on destroying his own immediate family.

The year of Octavia's exile, however, also saw the revival of the trials for treason that had been the most objectionable feature of the reigns of Nero's predecessors. Designed to counter any perceived threat to the emperor, these were subject to abuse because, without an official mechanism like a prosecutor's office, they relied heavily on informers among whose motives were usually self-advancement and malice. So whether the charges were dismissed (as often by Tiberius), or led to a full-dress trial, conviction, and enormous rewards for the informer who had brought the charges, senators were able to persuade themselves that each victim was an innocent member of their order, who had fallen foul of the emperor for no good reason. Nor, incidentally, did this viewpoint change from reign to reign, even when these trials steadily wiped out the older aristocratic families and injected equestrian "upstarts" into the order. New senators—like Tacitus, when his turn came—proved their worth by embracing fervently the thought and behavior patterns of the men whose misfortunes had created the vacancies they were filling.

The revival of these trials in Nero's reign did not indicate that he was taking a more active interest in the running of the state. It was due to the intrigues of the two people who had secured—and meant to keep—the greatest influence at court, by playing on the emperor's fears. One was Ofonius Tigellinus, who became one of the prefects of the praetorian guard when Burrus in 62 seems—remarkably—to have died a natural death. Although Tigellinus had already served as prefect of the watch, he owed his promotion and his grip on Nero largely to his having been a breeder of race horses. The other was Poppaea, now the emperor's wife. The most beautiful, or at any rate the most seductive, woman of her day, she was also one of the most power hungry in the brief span left to her (Nero killed her in 65, allegedly kicking her in the stomach in a rage, although she was pregnant at the time). Encouraged by these two, Nero turned his attentions to the senatorial aristocracy, all the more so because he needed to raise money for the rebuilding of Rome in an appropriately grandiose fashion after the Great Fire of 64.

The result was a series of conspiracies against him between 65 and 67. These were invariably as unsuccessful as they were small. But the repercussions were widespread, or so the sources assert, echoing the claim that birth, wealth, and ability were criminal charges in Nero's eyes, and fatal to their possessors. At the start of 68, nevertheless, there was little to suggest that he would be overthrown. In Rome the senators may have been depressed by the thought that the pattern had been set for a long and eventful reign, but they were too cowed to do anything about it. The important posts in the provinces, the military posts above all, were held by men appointed specifically for their mediocrity, governors and military commanders who would never dream of challenging their emperor, as they proved in the winter of 67/68. And the troops on the frontiers remained as steadfastly loyal to Nero as did the praetorians in Rome, *because* he was their emperor. The fact he was young and (in their view) good-looking, as well as lazy and vicious, may have lent him additional charm in their eyes. But it was by no means the entire explanation, even if favored by the ancient sources and by moderns equally disposed to draw moral lessons from history.

The man responsible for bringing down this house of cards was Gaius Julius Vindex, a romanized Gaul in charge, probably, of the unarmed province of Gallia Lugdunensis (central France). His rallying cry was "Freedom from the Tyrant," enough to prove his wish to rid the world of Nero, but not enough to establish what he had in mind by way of replacement. This vagueness may have owed something to his need to rally support first among the Gallic tribes, since they had no reason to look beyond the confines of their province or to care about conditions elsewhere in the empire. But the speech or speeches that Dio puts in Vindex's mouth denounced neither the principate as an institution nor Roman imperialism, only Nero's inadequacies as emperor and the abuses of government to which his personal vices had led. So Vindex almost certainly planned to set up a new emperor, a step that would establish his own reputation and satisfy what Dio terms his vast ambition.

According to Plutarch, Vindex's first move, during the winter of 67/68, was to send letters to neighboring governors and military commanders, to win their support for an uprising. In these too he avoided naming a candidate to be set in Nero's place. Perhaps he thought that for him, only a first-generation senator, to nominate somebody would be considered presumptuous by the men he contacted. It is more likely, however, that he wanted to avoid alienating them by suggesting a specific person. No matter how unhappy they were with Nero, they could not be expected to give up jockeying for position among themselves, or unanimously to accept one man unconnected with the dynasty in his place. But just as we are not told explicitly why Vindex omitted to name names, so we are not informed what responses he received. There should have been some, but if so, they look to have been equivocal or misleading. Apparently the respondents were willing to sit on their hands while Vindex went ahead with his rebellion. What we are told is that these governors and commanders turned the letters over to the authorities forthwith. There was only one exception, Servius Sulpicius Galba, governor of Hispania Tarraconensis (the largest of the three provinces into which Spain was divided, it comprised the northern, eastern, and much of the central parts of the peninsula). He did nothing, neither replying to Vindex nor reporting the matter to Rome.

We know, again from Plutarch, that Galba had decided that inaction was the best way not to attract Nero's attention. Nobody, he supposedly declared, could be called to account for things he had not done. It was a reasonable plan if, like other senators, he believed that birth, wealth, and ability were criminal charges in Nero's eyes. He had the birth and the wealth, and he was not alone in thinking that he possessed the ability. But we should probably add pique to the mixture. Insofar as his inaction rested on the belief that he was an obvious target for Nero's attentions, and his self-esteem would scarcely have let him think otherwise, he should also have resented Vindex's not inviting him to head the movement from the start. Plutarch, however, asserts that Galba put no trust in the letters. This cannot mean that Galba imagined the letters to be forgeries, put out by Nero's agents to tempt him into a fatal indiscretion, because then his failure to pass the correspondence to the authorities makes no sense. It is more plausible to hold that he rated the rebel's chances of success so small that it was not worth taking the matter seriously. As Suetonius reports, Nero had a similar reaction when he heard that Vindex had come out openly in revolt against him.

Since Vindex was supposedly an intelligent man, he must have suspected that some of the officials he contacted would inform Nero, and that even if nobody took the uprising seriously at first, this state of affairs could not continue indefinitely. Realistically, therefore, Vindex had either to go ahead with the revolt or to commit suicide. Since Dio asserts that his audacity was as vast as his ambition, he picked the first option. Supposedly experienced in military affairs as well, Vindex seems not to have expected armed opposition from Verginius Rufus and Fonteius Capito, the commanders of Upper and Lower Germany respectively, the two military districts that lay along the western bank of the Rhine and housed no less than seven legions. Hence the likelihood that one or both of these men had given equivocal or misleading responses to his original letters. Whatever the case, Vindex raised the standard of revolt in mid-March 68, only to find that his support was limited to ill-armed levies, drawn mostly from but 3 of the 64 tribes in Gaul, the Aedui, the Arverni, and the Sequani. Nearly 100,000 men are said to have joined him, with the prospect of thousands more, but this gave his revolt the appearance of a Gallic insurrection against Rome. And this ruled out all prospects of help from the commanders on the Rhine frontier. Their function was to defend the empire, not only against attacks by German tribes east of the river, but also against uprisings by Gauls to its west. Within two weeks Vindex was driven to the conclusion that the only way to put the revolt back on track was to interpret Galba's silence as tacit approval of his aims, and to invite him to become its leader.

At the start of April Galba decided to accept the offer. He did this on the urging above all of his associate Titus Vinius—or so Plutarch says. In this case he may be right, even though Plutarch does everything he can to save the reputation of the emperor by casting Vinius as Galba's evil genius. According to Suetonius, however, Galba had another incentive, the discovery that Nero had sent secret instructions to his procurators in Tarraconensis, ordering them to assassinate its governor. This story is probably untrue, since it looks like an attempt by Galba to justify his actions by posing as a victim of Nero's tyranny. That accords better not only with the emperor's failure to take the revolt seriously until Galba publicly announced his decision to become its leader, but also with the carefully orchestrated scene in which Galba made the announcement. Hailed emperor by a crowd assembled for the occasion in Nova Carthago (Cartagena), he denounced Nero, stressed the number of prominent men murdered or exiled by him, and declared that he himself was acting as "lieutenant of the senate and people of Rome." Then he proclaimed a suspension of public business, to signify that this was a time of crisis, and to enable him to drop everything else and strengthen his own position. As one of his first moves, we are told, he assembled "a kind of senate" from the oldest and most experienced of the local dignitaries. Since we never hear of this body again, and Galba at his age was in any case disinclined to listen to the advice of others, this was probably a way of guaranteeing—or compelling—their support and of satisfying appearances.

This may explain also why there is no evidence that he dispatched anybody to sound out members of the senate. His freedman Icelus was in Rome when the news arrived that his master had accepted Vindex's offer to head the revolt. Suetonius tells us that Nero threw the man in chains for that reason. But even if the emperor suspected Icelus of acting as an intermediary between Galba and any senators he could contact, his suspicions were probably groundless. Icelus was rounded up the moment news of Galba's announcement of support for Vindex reached the city, and Galba's announcement—according to our sources—followed almost immediately on his decision to rebel. Either the freedman was arrested before he could carry out his mission or, more probably, he had been sent to Italy on other business, to check on Galba's family estates for example. Besides, no prominent senators seem to have boasted of their early support for Galba once he had become emperor, though they could then safely have done so. Nor, for that matter, do such senators figure among his choices for important positions in the new regime. In short, Galba may very well have taken it for granted that he was the best replacement for Nero, have refused to believe that senators could or would think otherwise, and have dismissed any who did as fools and traitors. This interpretation fits best with the way Galba behaved in his province and during his journey to Italy. It was conduct, as Tacitus puts it, that turned his progress from Spain to Rome into "a long and bloody march."

Before Galba set out, Suetonius reports, he "sent out proclamations to the provinces, urging all collectively and individually to join his movement and aid the common cause in whatever way they could." More specific appeals for help were sent to officials in the two other provinces into which Spain was divided, Lusitania (Portugal) and Baetica (Andalusia), and from them he was able to raise some of the money he needed to fund his activities. The rest he secured by appropriating the revenues from all imperial properties in Tarraconensis. With this in hand he was able to take care of the most important business of all, raising troops. To begin with, he had at his disposal only one legion, VI Victrix, three auxiliary cohorts, and two squadrons of cavalry (one squadron, interestingly, tried unsuccessfully to desert). So Galba conducted a levy and put together a second legion, VII Galbiana. Another levy was held in the territory of the Vascones (Basques), and this raised two more cohorts of auxiliary infantry. On paper Galba almost doubled the number of troops under his command.

What Galba most certainly did not do was march to the aid of Vindex. Quite possibly his preparations took well over a month to complete. Or he may have fancied that Vindex could be left to his own devices. If so, he was wrong. The revolt in Gaul was characterized by one farcical episode after another, and this may not be the result solely of the inadequacies of Dio, our main source for the details. Vindex had to begin by laying siege to his own provincial capital, Lugdunum (Lyon). There is nothing to indicate whether he had expected the town to shut its gates against him, but its resistance is unsurprising. For a start, its citizens were particularly devoted to Nero, since they had contributed four million sesterces to help rebuild Rome after the Great Fire of 64, and Nero had returned them the same sum when Lugdunum was devastated by fire in the following year. Again, inscriptions suggest that some of the inhabitants were veterans who had served with the legions stationed along the Rhine frontier, and they had no reason to turn on Nero. And finally, Lugdunum housed the imperial mint that struck some of the bronze issues used to pay the troops stationed in the west, and so housed an urban cohort too, *cohors XVIII urbana*.[4] On its face, this was a negligible force, only 500 men strong, but it was an organized unit and still more likely than the veterans to remain loyal. One might imagine that Vindex, aware of all this before he began his revolt, would have taken steps to seize the city by trickery. But perhaps he thought that his own audacity would carry the day, gambling that the townsfolk would never refuse entry to their own governor. Or perhaps he deliberately gave Lugdunum the chance to display its hostility, in order to broaden the base of his own support elsewhere. The attack on the town won him the enthusiastic support of the people of Vienna (Vienne) some 20 miles further down the Rhône. The other major town in the province, Vienna, had been feuding bitterly with Lugdunum for over a century, and each seized every opportunity to score off the other. Provincial towns were as prone as senators in Rome to jockey for position, no matter whether that jeopardized any larger aims they entertained.

While Vindex laid siege to Lugdunum, the governor of Upper Germany, Lucius Verginius Rufus, mustered the forces to put down the revolt. From his own district he took the two legions stationed in Mogontiacum (Mainz), IV Macedonica and XXII Primigenia. To these he added detachments from the four legions in Lower Germany. This yielded some 20,000 legionaries, and auxiliaries—probably as many in number—accompanied them as a matter of course. This was ample for the task, since Romans were convinced that a legionary was worth ten or more of any enemy, and none would have been alarmed by reports that Vindex had collected 100,000 rebels. Why Verginius drew troops from both military districts is another question. It might seem tempting to argue that it would have been foolish for him to strip every soldier from the frontiers of his own, and so leave it exposed to attacks by the German tribes beyond the Rhine. But pulling the two legions out of Mogontiacum left a gaping hole in the defenses anyway, and this hole could be plugged neither quickly nor easily by his third legion, XXI Rapax, stationed miles to the south at Vindonissa (Windisch in Switzerland), near the river's head waters. More likely Verginius thought it simpler and faster to assemble detachments of V Alaudae and XV Primigenia at Vetera (Xanten), XVI at Novaesium (Neuss), and I Germanica at Bonna (Bonn), than it was to summon XXI Rapax to his aid. This proved to be a mistake, however, or so Tacitus says. Contacts between the legions stationed in the two Germanies had been few and far between. Each unit nursed its own grievances, whatever they were, unaware that others had just as many. Not that Verginius' troops were especially unhappy—as yet. But many of the men in the drafts from Lower Germany were dissatisfied with their governor, Fonteius Capito, and Tacitus seems to have concluded that they spread this disaffection throughout the ranks of Verginius' force.

How long Verginius needed to make his preparations we do not know, but it was apparently toward the end of March that he began his advance southwest through the Belfort Gap to Vesontio (Besançon), tribal capital of the Sequani. He seems throughout the campaign to have been reluctant to fight a pitched battle, but whatever caused this, it was neither reluctance to crush the revolt nor respect for Vindex. Initially, he may have hoped to intimidate the rebels into surrender. Or perhaps he was more concerned about what would happen if he let his own men off the leash. By now the legionaries had worked themselves into a rage over a rebellion they saw as an affront to the honor of Rome. They were eager to fight too, because they anticipated an easy victory and vast amounts of plunder. As Gaul was the richest province in the west, it promised them loot in quantities they could not hope to amass by ordinary means, no matter how many punitive raids they made against the German tribes in the forests and swamps on the far side of the Rhine. So when the inhabitants of Vesontio refused to open their gates, Verginius had to put the

town under siege, Vindex to come to the aid of his allies. Vindex may
have left behind a force to mask Lugdunum, but the prospect of serious
fighting caused many of his followers to desert. He made his way to
Vesontio only with some 30,000 men.

Vindex reached the area around the end of April, seemingly a week
or so after Verginius, and according to Dio another fiasco ensued. Finding that Verginius and his troops had drawn lines around Vesontio,
Vindex opened parleys with his counterpart, and eventually the two conferred without witnesses. At this meeting they agreed, "so it was conjectured," to join forces against Nero and, on this basis, Vindex ordered his
men to march into the city and take possession, presumably to indicate
that the siege was over and to reassure the town's inhabitants. Dio, however, does not specify what purpose this move was to serve. Instead, he
presses on and, hard as it may be to believe, reports that Verginius' legionaries interpreted the Gauls' marching toward them as a sign that
battle was imminent. We could assume that the legionaries were not
told of the agreement, or that they refused to believe that it had been
made. Then too, the commanders could have reached different conclusions about the points on which they had agreed, or Verginius could
have had second thoughts once he returned to his camp. Unfortunately,
we are not told what his officers thought. No matter how we explain it,
Vindex's men acted as if an agreement had been reached, Verginius' as if
it had not. "Without waiting for orders," the legionaries attacked the
rebels before they could deploy into a battle line. Plutarch tells a similar
story, but predictably he stresses the helplessness of both commanders.
Likening them to charioteers who lose control of their horses in a race,
he has them driven by their troops into the collision of a great battle. In
fact, it was a massacre. Some 20,000 Gauls are said to have been killed,
Vindex committed suicide in despair, and Verginius was allegedly as dis-
consolate over the result as were the surviving rebels.

The victorious legionaries now took it into their heads for the first
time to proclaim Verginius emperor. This has provoked endless speculation, including Machiavellian theories to the effect that Verginius had
led Vindex on and then destroyed him to ensure that he alone would
determine who the next emperor should be. This is fantasy, not even
palliated by claims that the skullduggery was covered up later by spin
doctors who put Verginius' conduct in a much better light. Inability to
control his troops was not something a Roman general would care to
have said of him. No doubt Verginius' interpretation of his own behavior varied according to the audience to whom and the date at which it
was voiced. (He was to live for another 30 years, and when he died in 97,
he received an official eulogy from none other than Tacitus, consul at

the time.) It signifies little that the troops retained some admiration for
Verginius, since that could have been won by laxity like that shown by
Lentulus Gaetulicus in 39. What counts is that Verginius had been appointed to his command because he was a mediocrity, and that he was to
be so treated by Galba, by Otho, by Vitellius, and by the three Flavian
emperors who followed them. This suggests that Verginius found himself out of his depth in May 68, caught off guard by a situation outside
his imaginings and his experience, and neither crafty enough to ma-
nipulate the troops, nor enterprising enough to play the cards they had
dealt him.

If we look first at his rejection of the troops' offer, Verginius—like
Vindex—was a first-generation senator. He really should have known
that he would be unacceptable to the governing class as a whole. The
premium on ancestry, as Sir Ronald Syme put it, would fall sharply over
the next 18 months, but an aristocratic pedigree had not ceased to count
just yet. Besides, there was already another, better qualified candidate in
the field, Galba. Yet Verginius showed no greater eagerness to endorse
Galba's claims, be it by choice or of necessity. So if he was playing
kingmaker, it is hard to discern for whose benefit he took on the role.
There is nothing against the idea that Verginius had doubts about Nero's
fitness to be emperor, or that his reluctance to make common cause with
Galba stemmed either from reservations about the latter's chances of
success or from his own troops' hatred of Galba (this was pronounced, as
we shall see). But there is also nothing against the simpler idea that
Verginius never even contemplated turning on Nero. He was one of his
protégés, and many more senators remained loyal to the emperor than it
was prudent to admit later. True, Verginius asserted that only the senate
and people of Rome could pick a new emperor, but this was the standard
phraseology for such occasions. Galba had said the same when he accepted Vindex's offer to lead the revolt at the start of April. There seem
to be only two realistic choices. Either Verginius' response to the soldiery was a case of strict constitutionalism or he was temporizing. It
comes to the same thing: Verginius was trying simultaneously to blunt
the clamor of the troops, to sidestep their anger at his rejecting their
offer, and to bring them back to their allegiance, all this in a way that
precluded charges of disloyalty to Nero.

More important than Verginius' refusing the title of emperor, however, is the troops' making the offer in the first place. It is unwise to
assume simply that the men had fallen victim to a fit of kingmaking.
Although they may have taken the lead (this is the impression Plutarch
tries hard to create), all the instances for which we have detailed information suggest strongly that it was their officers who were primarily

responsible, capitalizing on the troops' anxieties in order to advance their
own careers. In either case, however, we have no warrant for believing
the rankers disenchanted with Nero. He is often criticized for never visiting his troops, but it may have been as well, given the figure he would
have cut. One of the more bizarre plans Suetonius has him consider after
hearing the news that Galba had accepted leadership of the revolt was to
appear unarmed before the troops and just weep. This—he declared—
would induce them to repent, and he would then be able to lead the
celebrations by singing paeans of victory that he ought at that very moment to be composing. In any event, the sources state explicitly that the
men returned to their allegiance after Verginius refused their offer, and
their readiness to do so suggests that their prime motivation was hatred,
not of Nero, but of Galba. Nor is this so strange, when Galba had served
for two years as commander in Upper Germany, and had spent his time
on restoring discipline after the conspiracy for which Caligula had executed Lentulus Gaetulicus. In other words, the troops seem to have
thought, or to have been persuaded, that if there was to be a new emperor, they would be better off with Verginius than with Galba. So while
they were angered by Verginius' refusing them, they were reassured when
he too declined to support Galba. They could safely return to their allegiance to Nero. It was not a ringing endorsement of the incumbent emperor, but—to reemphasize the point—it was a long way from kingmaking
for its own sake.[5]

This interpretation may seem far-fetched because, by mid-68, there
can have been few, if any, rankers or junior officers still in service who
had experienced Galba's severity. But any such objection assumes that
neither the Rhine legions nor Rome's armed forces in general possessed
a corporate or collective memory. A story in Suetonius undermines the
supposition. Originally, so he declares, Otho planned to murder Galba
on the evening of 10 January 69, "but he was checked by consideration
for the praetorian cohort on duty at the palace at the time, not wanting it
to be burdened with still more infamy. For that same cohort had been on
duty when Caligula was assassinated and, again, when the guard deserted
Nero." This is not all. As Otho himself was hardly the type of person we
would expect to have a detailed knowledge of such matters, before or
after he decided to murder Galba, it is worth wondering how he developed this consideration for the troops, legionary or praetorian. An answer can be found in another story Suetonius tells, this time about Otho's
father. He had been made governor of Dalmatia by Claudius in 42, immediately after Camillus Scribonianus' revolt. There he had publicly
executed some soldiers who had attempted to make up for their own
momentary defection by killing their officers, alleging plausibly that the

latter had led them astray. Since Otho's father had done this, though he knew that the men had been rewarded with promotion by Claudius, his foolhardiness cost him the emperor's favor for a while. Suetonius does not report the troops' reaction, but it is by no means fanciful to conclude that they were angrier still. Against this background, we can see Otho's consideration for his supporters as the result of a wish not to repeat his father's mistake and add another error of judgment to the troops' collective memory.

There is a more serious objection to this explanation, however. So far as we can tell, the four legions in Upper Germany that had been subjected to Galba's severity between 39 and 41 were XIII Gemina, XIV Gemina Martia Victrix, XVI, and XXII Primigenia. Of these only one was still in the district in 68/69, XXII Primigenia. But another, XVI, was practically next door, in Lower Germany, and that adds another dimension to Tacitus' comment about the folly of bringing together legions from different areas. If one unit complained loudly about Galba's shortcomings, it might be ignored. If two different units from two different areas complained, their claims tended to confirm one another. Besides, while XIII Gemina was miles away in Pannonia now, XIV Gemina Martia Victrix was stationed in northern Italy, and though Tacitus never explains why, XIV Gemina Martia Victrix was of all four legions the most loyal to Nero, up to the moment of his suicide.[6] And this is before we add that many veterans from the Rhine legions settled near their old camps, to be with their friends. It would be unwise to assume that old age diminished their long-term memory.

Whatever the case, Galba possessed the trappings of an emperor by the time Vesontio was fought, even if he persisted in terming himself the lieutenant of the senate and people of Rome. He still lacked significant military support, however, and he was shattered by the news, not of Vindex's defeat, but of Verginius' being proclaimed emperor by the Rhine legions. He wrote to Verginius immediately, inviting him "to work with him to preserve both the empire and the liberty of the Romans," but Verginius ignored or rejected these overtures. So, says Plutarch, Galba withdrew in despair to Clunia, a small town in the inmost recesses of his province, and was persuaded only with difficulty not to take his life. In Rome, conversely, people may have been disquieted by the conduct of the Rhine legions, especially as Verginius made no attempt after the battle to return them to their billets. Instead he and his forces lay encamped somewhere in Gaul, perhaps at Vesontio, but more probably in the neighborhood of Lugdunum. This was just the kind of situation to encourage gossips to theorize that he was planning, not to pursue Galba, but to turn on Nero. In all likelihood, Verginius was intent only on pacifying

Gaul, and there was no reason to despair. Besides, Nero had bestirred himself at last.

Nero had treated the news of Vindex's revolt with <u>indifference</u>, still flushed with the success of his pilgrimage to Greece, home of all the arts. During his tour every single Greek city had obligingly staged its every festival and had ensured, just as obligingly, that the emperor won first prize in any athletic or artistic contest he entered. According to Dio, he won a grand total of 1,808 victories and besides this Vindex's revolt was small beer. <u>To the news that Galba had accepted leadership of the movement, however, Nero responded vigorously</u>. He recalled forces earmarked for the eastern campaigns he was contemplating; he mobilized units waiting in Italy to take part in those campaigns (XIV Gemina Martia Victrix among them). He probably attempted to bring troops across from Africa. He set about forming a legion from marines of the imperial fleet stationed at Misenum in the Bay of Naples. And in Rome he called for volunteers from the citizenry. Unlike Vitellius a year later, he was unable to mobilize the citizens, but he extorted huge sums of money from the wealthy with which to pay the forces he did raise. The bulk of them were placed in the Cisalpina (Italy north of the Apennines) under a known loyalist, Publius Petronius Turpilianus, and the rest were assigned to another commander, Rubrius Gallus.

Although Suetonius gives the fullest account of Nero's last days, he no more than hints at this. Instead he expatiates on a series of bizarre plans Nero allegedly contemplated (to poison the entire senate at banquets, for example, or to turn loose on the citizenry the wild beasts being held in Rome for the games). He also dwells on the comic-opera aspects of the emperor's more realistic preparations, among them his procuring wagons to carry his theatrical equipment and his fitting out his concubines with Amazonian axes and shields. This is scandal mongering, but Suetonius for once is on the right track. Nero's grip on reality was little stronger now than it had ever been. In the 30-odd days left to him he swung from overconfidence to a total failure of nerve. What caused this it is impossible to say. But since Tacitus attributes his overthrow more to messages and rumors than to force of arms, it looks as if the emperor was unnerved by news, false as it turned out, that he had been deserted by all his commanders. One key figure, Rubrius Gallus, certainly went over to the rebels, and Petronius Turpilianus appears to have been deserted by his troops or, more probably, to have been unable to lead them against the enemy. Although one of the legions under his command was XIV Gemina Martia Victrix, it was stalemated by the eight cohorts of Batavian auxiliaries attached to it. Yet Verginius Rufus still held firm to Nero, and he could have disposed of all the dissidents easily. But perhaps his

motives, not to mention his ability to resist temptation, looked questionable in Rome. What is certain is that by the end of May Nero was contemplating flight. He was unsure of his destination, but his first choice
was Alexandria in Egypt.

At this point a new player took a hand, Nymphidius Sabinus. Of his
earlier career we know only that he had been prefect of an auxiliary unit
in Claudius' reign and in 65 had been appointed Tigellinus' colleague
as prefect of the praetorian guard. By June 68, however, he was effectively the only prefect. Once again the evidence fails to explain how this
came about. Perhaps Tigellinus lost his nerve as badly as did the emperor whose creature he was. He was certainly not committed wholly to
Nero's cause. Tacitus reports that Tigellinus saved the life of Titus Vinius'
daughter, probably during the roundup that ensnared Icelus, and that he
did so to protect his own position in the future. Perhaps too Tigellinus
was seriously ill; he was certainly so by January 69. Whatever it was that
disabled Tigellinus, Nymphidius seized the opportunity to put Galba in
his debt by bringing the praetorian guard over to his side. In return, he
seems to have thought, Galba would make him sole prefect of the guard
for years to come and so sole arbiter of Rome. For Plutarch has Nymphidius imagining that if the aging Galba survived the long and arduous
trek from Spain, Nymphidius would be able to lead his new master around
by the nose.

Plutarch makes Nymphidius the villain who first demonstrated to
the brutal *Soldateska* the power they could exercise over events. Not only
is this incorrect chronologically, in that Plutarch sets Verginius' being
hailed emperor by his unruly troops earlier. It is misleading too, since
subverting the guard proved far from easy. Nymphidius made his move
on the night of 8/9 June. He was able to loosen the bond of the praetorians'
oath of loyalty, to a large extent, by alleging that they were not deserting
their emperor. He had deserted them and embarked on a ship bound for
Alexandria. The allegation was premature. Suetonius reports that Nero
had just sounded out tribunes and centurions of the guard about accompanying him to Egypt. Even so, the prefect had to promise the men, in
Galba's name, a donative of 7,500 denarii (30,000 sesterces) apiece, a
gigantic sum, ten times their annual pay and twice the amount Claudius
and Nero had each distributed when they became emperor.[7] Insofar as
this proved a conclusive argument, it may have done so largely because
neither the prefect nor the men considered how so vast an amount was
going to be raised—unless they imagined that Galba would find it out of
his own pocket. This goes well with Plutarch's statement that Galba was
the richest private citizen ever to enter the house of the Caesars. Once
the guard had been persuaded to abandon Nero, the senate plucked up

the courage to declare him an enemy of the state and formally to proclaim Galba their new ruler.

Nero fled to the country villa of his freedman Phaon some four miles from Rome and, after much hesitation, steeled himself to commit suicide by driving a dagger into his throat. It was a singularly inartistic end for the last male member of the Julio-Claudian line. When the Rhine legions heard the news, not just of Nero's suicide but of Galba's recognition by the senate, they made one more attempt to put Verginius on the throne, and this time we are told explicitly that an officer threatened him with a drawn sword if he declined the offer. Yet decline it he did. Since the senate had ratified Galba, and since Verginius had asserted all along that it was for the senate and people to choose an emperor, he could hardly reverse himself. And so, after the lead had been given to them by Fabius Valens, legionary legate of I Germanica, the troops accepted Galba, and even Plutarch concedes that this was carried through "only with difficulty."

Tacitus sums up Galba's reign in his epigram that everybody agreed that Galba would make an excellent emperor, until he became emperor. Like most good epigrams, it is an overstatement and a misstatement. Suetonius puts it more awkwardly but more accurately, when he states that Galba enjoyed greater popularity and respect when winning the empire than he did when running it. But even this does not capture the essence of the situation in the second week of June 68. Apart from the fact that not everybody could be brought to agree on Galba at first, it was by default, almost by a chapter of accidents, that he became emperor. Yet this may explain why he succeeded where previous attempts to displace the Julio-Claudians had failed. Had Vindex's uprising not looked like a Gallic revolt, the legions would not have been drawn from both Germanies to crush the insurgents, nor would Vindex have appealed to Galba. Similarly, had Galba not assumed the leadership of the uprising, the legions from the Rhine frontier would likely not have tried to make Verginius emperor. And had there been less uncertainty about the motives and prospects of Galba and Verginius alike, Nero might still have panicked, but Nymphidius would have been much less tempted to take the action that completed the ruin of the imperial house.

2

The Reign of Galba
(June 68 to January 69)

The moment Galba was recognized as emperor, people began dusting off stories to prove that he had long been destined for the principate. Suetonius has several examples, among them claims—liberally sprinkled with circumstantial detail—that Augustus and Tiberius had each foreseen this outcome. The reality was more prosaic, but Servius Sulpicius Galba was justly proud of his ancestry. The Sulpicii, a patrician clan, had held office in Rome since the early republic, and as Suetonius observes, to give a detailed account would be a long and tedious business. The branch that bore the surname Galba came to the fore during the Hannibalic War, and was the dominant line thereafter. Its members were some of them heroes and some of them scoundrels, some of them gifted and some of them mediocrities—like Galba's father, Gaius. He reached the consulship in 5 B.C., but spent most of his life as an industrious but ineffective advocate. What people remembered was his being a hunchback. This fascinated his second wife, Livia Ocellina, more rather than less "after he responded to her repeated advances by taking off his robe in private and revealing his physical disfigurement to her." It also elicited jokes from Augustus and other prominent men. Having developed an aesthetic that regarded physical defects as fit subjects for ridicule, Romans readily made fun of the handicapped. This indeed is why Suetonius reports that Livia Ocellina was beautiful as well as rich, leaving his readers to draw the appropriate conclusions about what an ill-assorted couple the marriage produced.[1]

Over the years dynastic marriages must have produced links between the Sulpicii Galbae and other leading families, but the value of these alliances faded as each generation passed. Galba himself prized only two. First, through his mother Mummia Achaica, there was the relationship with Quintus Lutatius Catulus, the consul of 78 B.C. and grand old man among the politicians of the late republic. Galba apparently saw him as a role model, especially in his own old age. The second was his relationship with his stepmother, Livia Ocellina. In her will she adopted Galba as her own child, leaving him considerable wealth so long as he took her name. From then on he styled himself officially Lucius Livius Ocella Sulpicius Galba. Unofficially, he probably kept his original name, just as Marcus Brutus the tyrannicide became Quintus Servilius Caepio Brutus by adoption, but was rarely so called in nonofficial contexts. When Galba became emperor, he reverted officially to his original name. By reminding people that he belonged to a family glorious in the republic, it seems, he imagined that he could render his elevation more acceptable, and create the impression (it was never more than an impression) that he would respect the rule of law as his Julio-Claudian predecessors had not.

As emperor, according to Suetonius, Galba displayed in the atrium of the palace a family tree that traced his ancestry back to Jupiter on his father's side and on his mother's to Pasiphae, the mythological wife of the equally mythological King Minos of Crete. It would be easy to see this as part of a plan to credit him with origins as illustrious as those of the dynasty he supplanted. But Caesar had claimed descent from Venus long before there were emperors, and such claims were all the rage among the aristocrats of his day.[2] So it is much likelier that one of Galba's ancestors grafted this genealogical fantasy onto the family tree, and that the matter came to public notice in Galba's reign, because that was when the family tree was first displayed for all to see. But no matter how we explain it, the detail is significant, because Galba was obsessed with bloodlines, his own and those of others, ultimately to the point where it cost him his life.

Galba was born on 24 December, in either 3 or 5 B.C. (The sources contradict themselves as well as each other.) He had one elder brother, Gaius, ten or more years his senior, but Gaius proved to be a "bad lot." Although he reached the consulship for 22, he squandered his estate, withdrew from Rome, and, after falling from favor with Tiberius, committed suicide in 36. Galba himself married around 20 A.D., taking as his wife Aemilia Lepida, a patrician lady with an ancestry even more illustrious than his own, and by her he had two children (we are not told whether they were boys or girls). Since he lost them and their mother in the early years of Claudius' reign, apparently to illness, it may seem odd that he never remarried, though he lived for another 30 years. But Suetonius describes the union in terms suggesting that it was hardly more than a formality. And if Galba's obsession with ancestry was matched by a concern for descendants, he may have decided that when the need arose, adoption would provide him with more satisfactory offspring and conserve his own energy in the meantime.

Galba's entire early career fell within the reign of Tiberius (14–37), and it was not distinguished. He worked his way through the assortment of offices a senator was supposed to hold, at more or less the ages he was

supposed to hold them, and the process culminated in the consulship for
33.[3] Another six years had to pass before he got a chance to make his
mark. In the summer of 39 Caligula uncovered a conspiracy against him
in which one leading figure was Gnaeus Lentulus Gaetulicus, the popular but lazy commander of the legions in Upper Germany, the military
district closer to Rome. Disposing of the plotters, the emperor installed
Galba in Gaetulicus' place, and Galba lost no time in displaying qualities
that endeared him greatly to his master, though not at all to the troops.
Less a disciplinarian than a martinet, he reintroduced the men—veterans
as much as raw recruits—to constant exertion, and in military maneu-
vers showed that he was as tough as he wanted them to be by running for
20 miles behind the emperor's chariot. This may be an impressive tribute to the physical endurance of a man in his early forties, but it also
illustrates that Roman generals could be valued for their physical prowess more than their mental capacities, and not only under a Caligula.

Galba was still the governor of Upper Germany when Caligula was
murdered in January 41. Suetonius asserts that "many now urged him to
seize his chance," that is, to bid for the throne, but he rejected their
advice. The tale cannot be taken seriously. Claudius' accession followed
so closely on his nephew's assassination that news of both events should
have reached Germany almost simultaneously. It may even be fiction,
intended to foreshadow Galba's later elevation and to explain the favor
he enjoyed under the new emperor. In 43 Claudius made a whirlwind,
16-day tour of his latest acquisition, Britain. Yet, according to Suetonius,
he was so set on Galba's accompanying him that he delayed his own
departure until the latter had recovered from a sudden illness. The emperor showed the same trust in Galba when he intervened in the alloca-
tion of senatorial provinces in 44 or 45, insisting that Galba be made
governor of Africa (coterminous more or less with modern Tunisia) for
a two-year term. His assigned task was to restore order within the province and on its frontiers. As Suetonius' report is limited to anecdotes, it
is certain only that Galba campaigned successfully against nomads raiding across the southern frontier. For this he was given "triumphal ornaments," the substitute in imperial times for a triumph, or victory
procession, through the streets of Rome that had been awarded to generals under the republic.

At some point after this Galba retired into private life. As our sources
offer no explanation, it is usually assumed that one reason for this was
Claudius' deciding in 49 to marry his niece, the Younger Agrippina. The
sister of Caligula and the mother of Nero, she took more delight in carrying grudges than did most Romans of her day, male or female, and she
nursed one against Galba. She had made a dead set at him while he was

married. Not only had he rejected her. His mother-in-law had also slapped Agrippina's face publicly, a major scandal since aristocratic women were even less prone to physical violence than their menfolk. Galba gave up living in Rome and, says Suetonius, "whenever he went out for exercise in his carriage" (*sic*), he took care to be accompanied by a second carriage loaded with a million sesterces in gold. Whether he envisaged using the money to buy off potential assassins, or to purchase a refuge beyond their reach, he clearly fancied that his life was at risk.

From this well-insulated obscurity Galba emerged in 59 or 60, when Nero sent him to govern Spain (Hispania Tarraconensis). Plutarch sees the appointment as a tribute to Galba, observing that Nero had not yet learnt to fear citizens of high renown, but high renown was what Galba had been shunning for a decade. Besides, Nero and his advisers probably expected little from a man in his sixties (even Plutarch allows that Nero thought Galba's age would render him cautious). It would be better to link his reemergence with Nero's murder of Agrippina in 59. Since others who had fallen foul of her also reentered public life then, Vespasian amongst them, Galba's appointment suggests that the court began recruiting personnel who were neither friends of the emperor's late mother nor troubled by her demise (she had remained a formidable personality to the end). Not that Galba recognized this. At first he imagined that energetic administration would win him plaudits in Rome. When he found the reverse to be true, he let inertia take over. As Tacitus says, to defend his own father-in-law Agricola, "in Nero's times inertia passed for wisdom." But advancing years also played their part. Suetonius reports that Galba's hands and feet were crippled by arthritis, and Galba spent eight years in Spain. So what started as a plan hardened into habit.

In person Galba was nearly six feet tall, with blue eyes, an aquiline nose and a jutting chin. His coins depict a man with a full head of hair, probably because baldness was another defect to ridicule and Galba was almost completely bald. But if he looked like an emperor in most respects, his character traits undercut the image. Grim and humorless, he made a fetish of being old-fashioned even in his youth, and he not only clung to such behavior patterns, but carried them into his public life too. The Romans, for example, had always considered frugality a virtue—unless it was carried to extremes, and even Plutarch concedes that Galba went too far. Such behavior was not entirely irrational. Rich as Galba was, nobody accused him of gaining his fortune by illegal or immoral means. And whatever he thought of his elder brother's behavior, Galba was swindled out of 50 million sesterces by Tiberius. According to Suetonius, this enormous sum had been left to him by Livia Drusilla, Augustus' widow, when she died in 29. Tiberius, as her son the executor of the will, first chopped the figure down to 50,000 sesterces and then neglected to hand over the money. Dio, it is true, asserts that when Caligula succeeded Tiberius in 37, one way in which he marked himself off from his predecessor was to pay the bequests Tiberius had not honored, among them those made by Livia. So Galba should have received his money eight years later, and that may help explain his readiness to work with an emperor who, by the summer of 39, was behaving somewhat erratically. Yet this windfall could not undo a marked tendency to penny-pinching. Though emperors were expected to be generous with money as a matter of course, Galba—to quote Tacitus' backhanded compliment— "coveted nobody else's, was sparing of his own, and was miserly with the state's."

This refusal to part with cash was to hurt Galba most in his dealings with the soldiery, but he could hardly have acted differently in the face of their demands, when he was also such a martinet. In saying that "he selected his soldiers, he did not buy them," Galba evinced a harshness as well as a parsimony deeply ingrained in his nature. He expected rankers and officers alike to do neither more nor less than they were told, and he considered disobedience and discontent unacceptable challenges to his authority—and not only when they came from the military. The biggest problem, however, was the isolation created by the combination of Galba's behavior patterns with his age and position. To have survived the reigns of five emperors unscathed was a feat almost none of his peers had matched. In effect, he was the last member of his generation, one reason probably why he idolized Lutatius Catulus. Even had he not undergone ten years in retirement from public life, and another eight in semi-exile in Spain, he would have found it difficult to relate to the men who had risen to the top in Nero's reign. And since, in his estimation, these men could have advanced their careers only by truckling to the emperor, he had no more reason to respect or trust them than they had to admire or support him. As a result, he put his faith only in three immediate associates, Titus Vinius, Cornelius Laco, and Icelus. Derisively nicknamed his "pedagogues," since they never left his side, these three feuded among themselves constantly, but they were united in their determination to ensure that nobody else gained a hold over their master. And that set the seal on Galba's isolation, since he turned a blind eye to the faults all three possessed in abundance.

Vinius was the most influential member of this cabal, predictably, when he was a senator and in 68, despite a career beset with scandals, commander of the legion stationed in Tarraconensis, VI Victrix. He was also the most energetic of the three, although he exerted himself above all to amass a huge personal fortune and, well aware of his master's age, did so as if there were no tomorrow. Laco, a knight, held the lowly post of Galba's legal adviser, until the emperor took it into his head to make him prefect of the praetorian guard. To this post Laco brought no military and little administrative experience, but unlike Vinius, he appears to have been honest. His principal vices, as the sources put it, were intolerable arrogance and unbelievable laziness. As for Icelus, Galba's minion as well as his freedman, he was promoted to equestrian status when he brought the news of Nero's suicide from Rome to Spain in a mere seven days. He would spend the rest of his short life, like Vinius, trying rapidly to accumulate the fortune appropriate to his new status. According to Suetonius, he also intrigued to secure appointment as prefect of the praetorian guard with Laco, one more reason perhaps why he tended to side with Laco against Vinius whenever the pedagogues fell out among themselves.

So tight was the circle the "pedagogues" drew around Galba that not even the two men who did most to help him while he was readying his revolt in Spain were able to break through. The younger of the two, Aulus Caecina Alienus, may not have been interested at this stage, since he had a career to make. As quaestor of the senatorial province of Baetica in 68 his job was to control the public monies of the province. These, or—more accurately—much of these, he turned over to Galba, as soon as the latter appealed for help. His reward was promotion to the command of a legion stationed in Upper Germany, probably IV Macedonica at Mogontiacum (Mainz), and with this he ought to have been well pleased. It was a position he would not normally have reached for another five to eight years. Before the end of 68, however, Galba was informed that Caecina had diverted funds into his own pocket, and ordered that the young man be brought to trial for embezzlement. His principles were to cost him dearly. Rather than submit, Caecina would use his forceful personality to make himself one of the leaders in Vitellius' revolt.

The other, far more important person was Marcus Salvius Otho, governor of Lusitania (Portugal). Born on 28 April 32, Otho was determinedly untypical, as a senator and as a governor. The family came from Ferentium in Etruria, a town about 40 miles north of Rome. Otho's grandfather was the first to acquire senatorial rank, but his father Lucius was far more successful. A close friend of Tiberius, he became consul in 33, and despite a falling out with Claudius in 41/42, the latter raised him to the patriciate in 47/48 for his conspicuous and unshakeable loyalty. By his wife, Albia Terentia, Lucius had three children, a daughter of whom almost nothing is known, and two sons. The elder, Lucius Salvius Titianus, followed dutifully, if uninspiringly, in his father's footsteps. He became consul in 52 and governor of Asia (western Turkey), probably in 63/64, a post in which he distinguished himself mainly by his avarice, or so Tacitus asserts in the biography of his own father-in-law Agricola, Titianus' quaestor at the time. Otho, the younger son, took a different route. Gaining entrée to the court in his early twenties, he became Nero's boon companion, rivaling him in wildness and surpassing him in extravagance. But they fell out over Poppaea. The dynamics of this triangle remain controversial, but according to the story told by Plutarch, Suetonius, and Tacitus' *Histories*, Nero coveted the woman, and persuaded Otho to marry her as a stopgap while he himself disposed of his wife Octavia; Otho had the audacity to fall in love with Poppaea; and when Nero failed to persuade Otho to honor the terms of their agreement, he got his own way only by inducing Poppaea to repudiate her husband. Not that she seems to have needed much urging. Nero then removed Otho from the scene in 58 by sending him to govern Lusitania. In one way this counted as a promotion: Otho had held only the quaestorship, and Lusitania was normally governed by ex-praetors. In another, it amounted to exile, since Nero had no intention of recalling Otho to Rome, ever.

To everybody's surprise Otho proved a good and responsible governor. But since he had made his name at court as a young man about town, he was probably desperate to return to Rome and civilization long before 68. When Galba accepted Vindex's invitation to head the revolt against Nero, therefore, Otho was the first to support him. He handed over all the gold and silver on which he could lay his hands, giving Galba the specie he needed to coin the money with which to pay his troops. With firm ideas about fashion and taste, Otho also presented Galba with those of his own slaves he thought qualified to wait on an emperor's table. Neither gift inspired gratitude in their recipient. The slaves could be regarded as needless refinements at this stage in the proceedings, as potential spies for Otho, and as an indication that Otho thought Galba's lifestyle less modest and sparing than tasteless and uncouth. The specie Galba no doubt took simply as his due.

To explain Otho's behavior, Suetonius talks of a wish for revenge on Nero, and this was probably his original motivation. Romans believed in repaying bad turns as well as good, with interest too. But there was another factor at work. Otho had picked up a taste for astrology, seemingly from Poppaea, and one practitioner of the art, Ptolemy, had accompanied him to Spain. To ease Otho's fears that he would be spending the rest of his life in the backwoods of Lusitania, Ptolemy had predicted that he would outlive Nero. Once this came to pass, Otho was ready to take as fact anything else Ptolemy had to say, and Ptolemy announced now that Otho would become emperor "soon." Buoyed up by this prediction,

Otho decided that the easiest way to achieve this objective would be to secure his adoption by the childless Galba. This would subordinate him legally to Galba, but the price was worth the prize, and nobody thought Galba long for this world. But in following this course Otho manifested a talent for self-deception no smaller than Galba's. As Tacitus remarks later, Galba had not rescued the empire from a Nero to entrust it to an Otho. So even as the latter did all he could to make himself indispensable to Galba, he set himself up for disillusionment great enough—in his own mind—to justify violent retaliation when his hopes were crushed.

Since Galba had to secure Spain before he left, he took nearly a month to quit the peninsula, but we have few details. Suetonius offers a generalized picture, applicable to Gaul as well as Spain: according to him Galba raised the tribute to be paid by towns that had hesitated to join him, and lowered the figure for the towns that had declared for him. He adds that Galba put to death governors and procurators who equivocated, and their wives and children too. This last detail Galba's apologists have tried to explain away, but stray hints tend to confirm its veracity. When even vicious emperors found it expedient not to molest the wives and children of their victims, Galba's action justified the reputation for savagery he acquired. For the rest, nobody disputes that he executed Obultronius Sabinus, probably the governor of Baetica whom Caecina had sidestepped, and Lucius Cornelius Marcellus, another senatorial functionary in Spain. As it turned out, killing two senators was killing two more than the senate thought right and proper, and these two only led off the list of illustrious casualties. Heads would continue to roll, as in Nero's later years, with little semblance of due process.

In middle or late July Galba completed his preparations. After installing the ineffectual Cluvius Rufus as his replacement in Tarraconensis, he set out for Gaul, escorted by his newly recruited legion, VII Galbiana, and wearing a general's cloak and a large sword at his side. The sword was meant, it seems, to proclaim his determination to deal harshly with all opposition, and to bolster claims that his every exercise of summary judgment was justified by military emergency. But initially, says Dio, it provoked "a good deal of laughter." Neither by age nor by physical condition was Galba suited to play the energetic military leader he may once have been. Though we cannot reconstruct his itinerary, he must have made his way first to Narbo Martius (Narbonne) on the southern coast. Here, early in August, he was met by an embassy from the senate that begged him to hurry on to Rome, since all awaited his arrival eagerly. This was probably conventional courtesy. Tacitus stresses the senators' delight in being able to discuss any subject they liked without an emperor presiding over the session and inhibiting debate. Then too, the senate had sent a similar message to Caligula in 40, when they were in such bad odor with him that he allegedly contemplated slaughtering them all.

Yet there is another possibility, that the envoys were attempting tactfully to indicate concern about the conduct of Nymphidius Sabinus, the prefect of the praetorian guard. Plutarch, our primary source on this, gives a detailed account of Nymphidius' fall, but nothing he says correlates the prefect's activities with Galba's. It is impossible to say what contacts Nymphidius had made with Galba's supporters in Rome before Nero's suicide. And Icelus—whoever released him from confinement—left the city immediately after the emperor's death, to carry the news to his master. Perhaps Galba imagined that Tigellinus would keep his colleague under control, not only as the senior prefect, but also because he had hedged his bets in Nero's last days by saving the life of Vinius' daughter. But Tigellinus had withdrawn from public life, and that allowed Nymphidius to seize sole control. Emboldened when magistrates and senators rushed to dance attendance on him, Nymphidius gratified those who wanted reprisals by letting them kill any of Nero's ministers they could find. And he redoubled his own efforts to win friends among the leading men and women in Rome.

According to Plutarch, Nymphidius' ambitions grew apace. But he received no word from Galba, even when he sent furnishings from the palace to Narbo Martius. Galba did not appreciate this finery, at first anyway. Why Galba did not respond is another question. He may have planned to give Nymphidius enough rope to hang himself. Or he may have wanted to avoid alienating a convenient helper by divulging that he meant to install Laco as prefect of the guard. Leaving somebody unreliable in control of Rome was better than having nobody at all in charge. Or Galba may have thought the situation in Rome the least of his worries. He certainly seems not to have envisaged the possibility that a prefect would engage in kingmaking on his own account. Nymphidius tried to clarify the situation by sending one of his friends, Gellianus, to act "as a kind of spy on Galba," but from him he was to learn only that the emperor was impervious to his charms. Gellianus had been kept away from Galba by Vinius, while Laco had been appointed prefect. Overwhelmed by the injustice of it all, Nymphidius summoned the officers of the guard, informed them that he had no objection to Galba, a wellmeaning old man, but stressed his concern that the emperor was putty in the hands of Vinius and Laco. They should send a collective letter, he suggested, urging Galba to give up his friendship with two men who bid fair to exert the kind of baneful influence on him that Tigellinus had on Nero. Whatever the officers thought, they replied that it was not for them to dictate to a man of Galba's years, as they would to a youth, who should or should not be his friends.

Forced to use different tactics, Nymphidius tried to provoke a response by sending Galba a string of alarmist messages: there was unrest
in the city; the legionary legate of III Augusta, Clodius Macer, had seized
control of Africa and was withholding grain supplies from Rome; the
legions in Germany were still mutinous; and bad news was coming in
from Syria and Judaea.[4] So far as we can tell, this was supposed to induce
the emperor to speed up his march to Italy, and so expose himself to the
prefect's personal influence. But Galba disregarded these tidings of woe.
Perhaps he did not believe the reports. Perhaps he did but, being disenchanted with Nymphidius, imagined that the troubles would add more
to the prefect's unpopularity than to his own. So Nymphidius decided
that since he could not control the emperor, he might as well become
the emperor.

This was a suicidal move. Nymphidius held the highest position to
which a knight could aspire, but for all his power he was still a knight,
and no knight would become emperor for another century and a half. If
this helps explain why Galba may have underestimated Nymphidius,
however, it does not account for the prefect's behavior. We cannot accuse him simply of *folie de grandeur*. He seems to have realized that while
knights could seek promotion into the senatorial order, they did this
customarily at the start of their careers, not at their peak. So, apparently
to surmount this hurdle, he fabricated an imperial ancestry for himself
and claimed to be a son of Caligula. Actually, says Plutarch, the prefect's
mother had had an affair with the emperor, but after Nymphidius was
born. He was thought to be the child of a gladiator named Marcianus.
Possibly Nymphidius imagined that the end of the Julio-Claudian dynasty marked so vast a dislocation that new rules could be invented for
the game of politics. His more sycophantic senatorial associates certainly
encouraged him to bid for the throne. And though one friend warned
him that neither dissatisfaction with Galba nor Nymphidius' record could
justify such a step, the rest kept silent. As for the praetorian guard,
Nymphidius fancied that he could rely on their loyalty, and so decided
to enter the camp after midnight and stage-manage his own proclamation as the new ruler of the Roman world.

Unfortunately for him, one of the military tribunes, Antonius
Honoratus, showed unexpected initiative. Assembling the cohort under
his command, he pointed out the shamefulness of their changing allegiance once again, especially as they could not charge Galba with the
crimes they had used to justify deserting Nero. To kill Nymphidius, he
continued, would avenge the death of Nero (clear proof that the guard
was not as venal as is sometimes imagined), and it would confirm their
loyalty to Galba. This convinced the men under his command and they

scattered to win over their comrades. The resulting uproar, says Plutarch, convinced Nymphidius either that the soldiers were ready to proclaim him emperor, or else that he must intervene before those opposed to his elevation gained the upper hand. So, accompanied by a crowd of hangers-on, he made his appearance at the gate, carrying in his hand the script of the speech he meant to deliver.[5] At first, he was refused entry. When he demanded to know who had given the order, the men shouted that they were true to Galba. Responding that so too was he, Nymphidius was admitted with a few followers. Once he was inside the gates, however, they were shut behind him and somebody hurled a spear. Although it missed its mark, it spurred the men to draw their swords and close in. Nymphidius fled further into the camp, hotly pursued by the guardsmen, and was cut down. His corpse was dragged out, surrounded with a paling, and exposed to public view for a full day.

Whether or not the senate's anxieties about Nymphidius prompted their envoys to request that Galba hasten to Rome, he had no intention of complying. Plutarch reports that Galba impressed the envoys with his kindness and modesty. He invited them to dinner, something members of the senate always appreciated as a sign of an emperor's approachability (*comitas*), no matter how bad the meal. And since he ignored the furniture Nymphidius had sent from the palace, he gave them the idea that he was a man of exalted spirit, averse to vulgar luxury. Such conduct, Plutarch adds, he would abandon under Vinius' tutelage. Nonetheless, he turned north into Gaul, traveling perhaps as far as Lugdunum. There he seems to have installed as governor of the province Junius Blaesus, an aristocrat known for his breeding and his loyalty. Galba must also have been responsible for stationing legion I Italica in the town, along with its associated cavalry squadron, the *ala Tauriana*. Though this legion had been raised by Nero late in 66, and had been quartered in northern Italy, as part of the force assembled to oppose Vindex, Galba apparently took it for granted that the troops were loyal to him, or—at the least—that the new governor would not use them against him. So the unit could perform useful service holding down the city that had been the first stumbling block to his erstwhile associate. Besides, Lugdunum housed an imperial mint, and Galba mobilized its workshops to add to the flood of his own coinage.

Elsewhere in the area, with less wisdom as it turned out, Galba began to settle accounts with other friends and enemies. He rewarded the Aedui, Arverni, and Sequani, the tribes that had supported Vindex, with additional territory and remission of tribute. And he punished correspondingly the two tribes that had cooperated closely with the Rhine legions, the Treveri and the Lingones. But the legions, especially those of Upper Germany, he appears to have left well alone. He may have recognized that visiting the troops would only upset them, but his later conduct suggests that he failed to appreciate how deeply the Rhine legions hated him and, taking their allegiance for granted, moved on to the next item of business. This left the legions with no reason to be thankful. They were probably relieved that he neglected to punish them for having crushed Vindex, but they never shook off their fear that there would be drastic reprisals one day. And they must have persuaded themselves that such punishment would be unjust. They had suppressed what they saw as a provincial rebellion, and they should have received rewards, decorations, promotions, even new postings. Galba's failure to reward them merely increased their animosity.

In Gaul, Galba is said to have put to death only one man of note, Betuus Cilo, the governor of Aquitania who had had the temerity in 68 to request auxiliary troops from Galba when Vindex's rising first broke out. But there were to be two more casualties. The first was Verginius Rufus. Galba could not execute a commander who, like himself, had stated publicly that only the senate and people of Rome could choose an emperor. But apart from Verginius' having given Galba a bad fright when the two of them were feeling each other out after Vesontio, he had been hailed emperor by his troops. Since it was obvious folly to leave Verginius in command of men who had believed him worthy of supreme power, Galba replaced him with somebody safe, Hordeonius Flaccus. Tacitus describes Flaccus as old and disabled by gout, irresolute, unimpressive, and so incompetent that he could not control the soldiery when they were quiet, let alone restrain them when they mutinied. Verginius waited for Flaccus, handed over the command without demur, and set off to join his emperor. Whatever reception he expected, he was treated with studied indifference. Perhaps leaving Verginius in suspense was Galba's way of repaying him for the uncertainty he himself had suffered in Clunia.

The second casualty was Fonteius Capito, commander of the legions in Lower Germany. The circumstances are obscure. Tacitus reports that he was killed by two legionary legates, Cornelius Aquinus and Fabius Valens, and that they acted without orders around the time when Galba was nearing Rome. Some people, he continues, believed that while Capito had led a thoroughly disgraceful life, he had never contemplated revolt. So he was killed by the two legates for rejecting their proposal to mount a conspiracy against Galba and, once dead, was accused of the crime of which his subordinates were guilty. This may be true. Fabius Valens had persuaded the troops to swear the oath of allegiance to Galba, a success achieved "only with difficulty," and he must have been incensed when he was not rewarded. He seems not to have appreciated that Galba let the matter go. Whether Galba feared what an inquiry would unearth, or decided that an investigation would change nothing, he countenanced the murder, and by so doing accepted responsibility for it.

The names of four more prominent men were added to the list of the dead before Galba reached Rome, and another one after his arrival. Strictly, Galba did not order the execution of Nymphidius Sabinus. But after he heard of the latter's fate, he gave instructions that those of Nymphidius' associates who were still alive should be put to death. This took care of two men, Cingonius Varro, one of the consuls designate for 69 and author of the speech Nymphidius had meant to give to the guard, and Mithridates of Pontus, once the client-king of the Bosporus but a resident in Rome since 48, and at this stage given to joking publicly about Galba's bald head and wrinkled face. Galba also gave specific orders for the assassination of Clodius Macer, the legionary legate of III Augusta in Africa, for preventing the grain ships from sailing to Rome. And finally there was Petronius Turpilianus, the consular Nero had put in charge of the troops concentrated in northern Italy in his last days. Though he had achieved nothing and had returned to Rome "a helpless old man," he was unswervingly loyal to Nero, and for that he was made to pay.

This did not close the list of victims. Next came an episode Galba's apologists have done their utmost to minimize, the massacre that attended his arrival at the Milvian Bridge on the outskirts of Rome, sometime in the first half of October. Though Nero put together an impromptu legion from the marines of the imperial fleet stationed at Misenum, he had not the time to constitute them formally. So a sizable number of the men, perhaps between 1,000 and 2,000, gathered at the bridge, and pressed Galba obstreperously to confirm their status. Outraged, he refused to hear their requests. Ordinary people, however, expected an emperor to deal with their problems at once. So the demonstrators rioted, some even drawing swords. Galba's response was to turn his infantry and cavalry loose on the rioters and "many thousands" were killed. Though a fitting conclusion to the "long and bloody march" from Spain, it was a terrible start to the new reign. Small wonder that Suetonius characterizes Galba's principate as one that alienated every order of society, though "the soldiery detested him above all."

Not that this ended the slaughter. The fallout from this affair illustrates three of the character traits that made Galba so poor an emperor. First, deciding that the survivors deserved exemplary punishment, he demonstrated his love for ages past by reviving the custom of decimation. This required that one (*not* nine) in ten soldiers of any military unit guilty of cowardice or insubordination be put to death by their peers, while all the other armed forces at the commander's disposal were paraded to witness the ceremony. On this occasion the citizenry also watched the carrying out of the sentence. To justify his action Galba could appeal to the military code, in which death was the penalty for numerous offenses. But the code went back to the republican period, when the state had been protected by a citizen militia and exemplary punishment served what was considered a useful purpose. Under the principate most generals shunned rigorous enforcement, probably because they recognized how unrealistic it was to apply such rules to an army of long-term professionals. As a result, decimation had not been used to punish cowardice since early in Tiberius' reign, nor to punish insubordination since 49 B.C. But Galba was not to be deterred. He took pride in his severity.

Second, there is Galba's legalistic turn of mind. In his youth, Suetonius tells us, Galba had made a special study of the law. What this produced ever after was a devotion to literal meanings and pettifogging attitudes. In Spain, as a result, the legion Galba began raising in April, VII Galbiana, was constituted formally on 10 June, not coincidentally one day after he had been proclaimed emperor by the senate. In the same way Galba seems now to have granted the mutineers' request, and to have given Nero's marines formal recognition as legion I Adiutrix. In part, this may have been the result of the men's wishes. When Caesar had faced down mutinous troops in 49 and again in 47 B.C., they had acknowledged their guilt by offering to suffer decimation to prove their loyalty. But on the second occasion Caesar had not taken the men up on their offer, and there was no more need for Galba to do so. That he went ahead anyway suggests a wish to satisfy the letter of the law. Because decimation was a punishment inflicted by legionaries on legionaries, legionaries the mutineers and the more obedient of their comrades had to become. Hence the creation of I Adiutrix probably in October, between the massacre and the decimation.

Third, there is Galba's savagery. To decide who would die, it was customary to throw lots, and if the lot fell on the innocent as well as the guilty, that was the will of the gods and, at the same time, one of the most frightening aspects of the process. Caesar had recognized the possibility that the ringleaders of a mutiny might escape both the initial suppression of trouble and the workings of the lot. In 49 B.C., therefore, he had rigged the results to ensure that the guiltiest perished in the ceremony. Galba was too legalistic to engage in sharp practice, and yet refused to let the ringleaders go unscathed. So, after the ceremony, he rounded up the surviving troublemakers, a handful of men, and threw them in chains, intending to finish them off later. This combination of massacre, decimation, and refusal to accept the results of the decimation did untold damage to his reputation. The ex-marine members of I Adiutrix felt no gratitude to the emperor for their promotion to legionary status, given the circumstances in which it had come about. The morale of Galba's other troops plummeted when they were made to watch the spectacle. And the people of Rome were horrified by the slaughter. There had been nothing to match its ferocity for a century or more.

This episode illustrates one more aspect of the way emperors operated in Roman times, that is, their habit of reacting rather than acting. Even if we had fuller information on Galba's brief reign, it would be doubtful whether we could talk of his pursuing specific policies. Scholars used to take an emperor's various actions and extrapolate programs from them. At best, this made some kind of sense out of the reign; at worst it sorted those actions into categories to which they may or may not have belonged. These days it is agreed—and it is much more likely—that an emperor reacted on an ad hoc basis to whatever problems arose. He seldom initiated policies as we understand them, and on occasion he failed even to deal with the problems with which he was confronted. This is not all. There are also entire areas of Roman government on which we have no worthwhile evidence, taxation for example. So what may look to us like a new approach by one emperor could easily have been established practice, unattested earlier precisely because the documentation is so random and so sparse.[6]

With Galba, we can go on a little further by taking into account the legends emblazoned on his coinage. But though coin after coin insisted on the Augustan nature of the quality advertised, this served to attach the usurper, not to the dynasty he had supplanted, but to its founder, a ruler whose virtues were accentuated by his successors' failings. Besides, the qualities on whose Augustan nature Galba's coins dwelt might be eminently laudable, but they were unspecific: peace, liberty, harmony between citizens (*concordia*), safety, and so on. And some issues may have raised wry smiles, those advertising Galba's "equity" (*aequitas*) for example. Whether this "equity" denoted activity in the judicial or the monetary sphere, it was belied by Galba's behavior and, still more, that of his entourage. And the issues that credited him with saving the lives of citizens, likewise based on Augustan models, must have looked positively bizarre. Whoever selected the legends on these issues, Galba's conduct proved that he did not regard them as parameters within which to operate, let alone as announcements of any programs he would implement.

What made the emperor's behavior especially unpredictable was the hold exerted over him by his pedagogues. Tacitus comments merely that the evils perpetrated by the new court were as bad as those of Nero's reign and much less excusable. Suetonius, however, states explicitly that Galba was wholly under the thumb of Vinius, Laco, and Icelus, who moved into the palace with him and never left his side. "To them he surrendered himself so completely that he was hardly ever consistent, being one minute more rigorous and frugal, the next slacker and more careless than was appropriate in an emperor who [unlike Nero] had been elected to his position and had reached so advanced an age." We have seen examples of Galba's rigor and frugality already, and there are more to come. The emperor's negligence Suetonius illustrates with the claim that "there was nothing he did not allow his entourage to knock down at auction or to grant as a favor, the imposition of taxes or remission from them, the punishment of the innocent or the pardoning of the guilty. Why, when the Roman people demanded the execution of Tigellinus and Halotus, he saved the lives of these two alone out of all Nero's agents, even though they were perhaps the worst of the lot. What is more, he gave Halotus an important procuratorship, and he issued an edict that censured the people for their savagery toward Tigellinus." In fact, Halotus was a minor player; as Claudius' food-taster he had helped Agrippina poison her husband. Tigellinus, on the other hand, had been exactly the kind of minister Galba should have exterminated. That he survived was due partly to his own inaction in Nero's last days, but mainly to Vinius' intervention on his behalf. Vinius acted partly out of gratitude, because Tigellinus had saved the life of his daughter (Tacitus' version, supported by Suetonius), partly because he was able to extort large sums of money from the ex-prefect (Plutarch's version).

As a result, there are only three areas in which we can maintain plausibly that the emperor had definite, if at times inconsistent, ideas of his own. The first of these, the question of a successor, is best postponed. Galba almost certainly formed his own views on who that successor should be early in the reign, although he declined to publicize them until January 69. This left everybody else, from his own advisers down to the ordinary man in the street, to speculate in a vacuum, and so provoked a flood of gossip. Yet his reticence was not as foolish as it may look. The moment Galba announced his choice, there was bound to be so much intrigue that the court's attention would be diverted from everything else. And since the announcement of that choice actually set in motion the events leading to his own assassination, as well as that of his designated heir, the topic can be left for the next chapter. What we need to consider here are Galba's attempts at retrenchment and his dealings with the armed forces.

When Galba arrived in Rome, the various treasuries should have been nearly exhausted. Nero had wasted huge sums in pursuit of his pleasures. More had been expended during the brief civil war that precipitated his suicide. And though Galba had no intention of paying the praetorians the donative Nymphidius had promised them (for that he would have had to find—at an absolute minimum—135 million sesterces), it made sense to try to rebuild the state's finances. The means he used, however, produced little money and created more unrest. He set up a 30- or 50-man commission of knights, a committee as unprecedented as it was unwieldy, and entrusted it with the task of recovering from Nero's favorites as much as possible of the 2,200 million sesterces the late emperor had allegedly squandered on them. This turned out to be a two-stage affair, though Plutarch and Suetonius alone mention the second. In the first stage, Nero's favorites were to be allowed to keep one-tenth of the proceeds, but would be required to turn over the other nine-tenths to the state. Since they had long since disposed of the bulk of the money, whatever they had left was concentrated in items with no resale value. This triggered the second stage. If the original recipients could not come up with the cash, the commissioners were empowered to recover it from those who had acquired items from the favorites, even if they had done so in good faith. This may not have seemed quite as iniquitous to Romans as it would to us, but it was sharp practice. In Roman law, plaintiffs were entitled to recover illegally acquired funds from a thief or from those to whom he passed those sums. So Galba decided to treat Nero's giving the money away, retrospectively, as a criminal offense.

The seizure of goods therefore went ahead all over Rome, along with auctions at which anything recovered was put up for sale, but to little avail. The auctions brought in hardly any cash, people not being prepared to lay out large sums in a depressed and uncertain market. They provoked apprehension among those who thought themselves likely targets of the enquiry, and intrigues between the people already targeted and the commissioners whose attentions they wanted to evade. And they benefited the bulk of the population not at all. Nero's victims, according to Tacitus, were given the malicious pleasure of seeing imperial favorites who still had money reduced to the same penury they were suffering. But Plutarch asserts that the only person to enrich himself was Vinius, snapping up valuable items at a fraction of their worth (in fact Plutarch credits him with inspiring the process). This may be why the commissioners went after beneficiaries outside the city too. Dio states that they recovered 40,000 sesterces that Nero had handed over to the priestess of Apollo at Delphi, but this sum—a drop in the bucket—may have been their most noteworthy achievement. Dio mentions too that the judges of the Olympic Games had been given a million sesterces by Nero, but he says nothing to indicate whether they complied with a demand for its return.

The entire operation was not merely disruptive. It was futile, in the sense that Galba had no intention of using any of the money raised to pay the troops even a fraction of the donative they had been promised. Nor was this the only example of Galba's economizing, both at other people's expense and without material benefit to the community. An inscription set up in the fall of 68 has been taken to suggest that the emperor made repairs to the *Horrea Sulpicia*, the largest granary in Rome and—as its name shows—not just a family monument but his own personal property. He certainly advertised his concern for the grain supply on his copper coinage, the small change people used everyday. Yet he either refused or decided that he could not afford to restore the *frumentationes*, the allocations of free grain to adult male citizens resident in Rome. Suspended by Nero after the Great Fire of 64, these were reinstated only when the Flavians had taken power. Ineptitude like this could not fail to make Galba unpopular with the citizenry, and Suetonius illustrates this with a story that picks up all at once on the emperor's penny-pinching, his old-fashioned ways, and his isolation.

At the first games held after Galba's arrival in the city, in November it seems, the actors were performing an Atellan farce, an ancient form of drama going back to the period before Latin playwrights began adapting Greek originals to their needs. When the actors reached a song the first line of which was "Onesimus is back from the country," the entire audience not only joined in but sang the whole thing several times. Although this is the only reference we have to this particular play, Onesimus was undoubtedly the traditional, hard-lining, stingy parent we find ridiculed elsewhere in Roman comedy, while his implied preference for the rough life of the countryside over the softness of city living was clearly taken as a jibe not only at Galba's general behavior but also at his eight-year term in the wilds of Tarraconensis. Such demonstrations in the theater were traditional, it is true, and they seldom produced significant results. But sensible emperors valued them as a guide to the mood of the populace. Galba, in his isolation, showed no signs of caring what the people thought.

On his dealings with the senate during this same period we have very little information. As he had killed individual members of the order out of hand during his march to Rome, it would have been wise to show the survivors collectively more respect than he had given to the "kind of senate" he had recruited in Spain. That he did so seems unlikely. Tacitus, for example, tells a story involving Helvidius Priscus. He was the son-in-law of Thrasea Paetus, a prominent senator and supposed martyr to free speech whom Nero had forced to suicide in 66, on the basis of charges laid by Eprius Marcellus (his reward was five million sesterces). Galba not only recalled Helvidius from exile but also made him praetor designate for 70. No sooner had Helvidius returned, however, than he took advantage of a senate meeting to try to settle scores with Marcellus. In later days Helvidius too would be idolized by supposedly freedom-loving senators, but he must have been almost impossible to deal with in person. On this occasion his conduct split the senate. The possibility of Marcellus' conviction carried with it the frightening prospect that "a whole host" of lesser senators would be charged with similar offenses. And so the matter was dropped, not least "because Galba's wishes were uncertain." Here it does not matter if Galba reserved to himself the right to settle scores, if he preferred to let sleeping dogs lie, or if his concern was that senators not waste his time with their squabbling. The important point is that he gave the body no guidance and took no account of matters it thought vital.

The same high-handedness shows up in another story, though this time it is unclear whether it deals with facts or perceptions. To document Galba's rigor and frugality, Suetonius asserts that the emperor "was thought to be contemplating" a plan that would have limited to two years the military and administrative posts allocated to men of senatorial and equestrian rank, and even then would have assigned these posts only to the men who did not want them. The underlying idea, of course, was that the posts would go to senators and knights who viewed their appointments as something other than routes to power and wealth. But most senators approved of efficient and disinterested administration, if at all, only in the abstract. Attempts to put such a novelty into practice, whether championed by Julius Caesar or by Domitian, were invariably met with passive resistance, grumbling, or abuse. This is not all. If Galba actually assigned any such posts to men who did not want them, he may have been making a virtue out of necessity. The evidence suggests strongly that few senators were willing to take service under him anyway.[7]

With the armed forces, the legions especially, Galba showed a degree of self-confidence the situation hardly warranted, and a concern for discipline that might better have been imposed on his own entourage. Since he recognized Nero's legion of ex-marines as a regular unit, I Adiutrix, probably in October, and since he had brought to Rome the legion he had recruited in Spain, VII Galbiana, there were now two full legions in the city, that is, two more than were usually stationed there. So Galba decided, apparently in November, to reassign one of them to Carnuntum in Pannonia (Hungary). His choice fell on VII Galbiana, not on I Adiutrix. Although VII Galbiana ought theoretically to have been more devoted to him, he appears to have thought that it was a new unit in need of discipline and some experience in warfare. The same could be said of I Adiutrix, of course, but it looks as if Galba also believed that the new recruits of VII Galbiana would succumb more readily to the temptations of the big city than would the ex-marines of I Adiutrix. The latter had had the experience of serving in Rome in Nero's reign, and so should have been more inclined to resist temptation. And their loyalty could be taken for granted, because they had been cowed by the harsh punishment Galba had inflicted on the disaffected among them.[8]

This contrasts strongly with Galba's treatment of some detachments of soldiers from Germany. They had fallen ill as a result of being sent to and then recalled from Alexandria in the first half of 68, as part of the troop movements for Nero's planned eastern expeditions. The nature of the illness is unknown, but Galba nursed the men back to health with unusual care. So devoted were these troops to Galba as a result that they were the one organized force to try to help him on the day of his murder. But they were either too ill to move (Tacitus), or too unfamiliar with the city's layout to arrive in time (Suetonius). And that is why the story is told, to underline that even when the emperor inspired loyalty in his men, it bore no fruit. True, we have no information on the urban cohorts, except that Galba placed them under Aulus Ducenius Geminus, whom he apparently recalled from Dalmatia to become prefect of the city. But it is unlikely that these men were any happier than the praetorian guardsmen. Them Galba kept firmly under his own thumb, since Laco was installed as their prefect more for his dependence on the emperor than for any ability to win the men's loyalty, let alone their affection. And all requests for the donative promised by Nymphidius were met with Galba's most notorious saying, that he selected his troops, he did not purchase them. As Tacitus puts it, it was "a statement which reflected well on him as emperor but was dangerous to him as a person, since nothing else came up to these standards."

Still, it was less the rankers than their commanders with whom Galba made grievous mistakes. It has been suggested that he tried to place able officers in intermediate positions, to keep the men under control and to report back on the doings of their superiors. Marcus Antonius Primus, appointed commander of VII Galbiana despite his spotty record under Nero, fell into this category. So did Manlius Valens, the aging legate of I Italica at Lugdunum. And so too did Aulus Caecina. But Caecina was soon to be ordered to trial on charges of embezzlement, and there is no evidence that the other two ever rendered Galba worthwhile service. Nor did one other man known to have been among the emperor's early partisans, Cornelius Fuscus. He was appointed procurator probably of Dalmatia and Pannonia, but Tacitus describes him as a man who reveled in the perils of civil war rather than the rewards to be gained from it. So in all four cases there are enough oddities in the record to suggest that it was not their abilities that won them their appointments, but their readiness to work for an emperor under whom more conventional and circumspect men hesitated to serve.

Where the high commands were concerned, Galba continued Nero's practice of appointing nonentities. He had certainly installed Cluvius Rufus, "a good orator and a man of peace," in Tarraconensis, and he probably made the urbane Junius Blaesus governor of Lugdunensis. It looks too as if he appointed Marcus Pompeius Silvanus governor of Dalmatia and Lucius Tampius Flavianus of Pannonia. Tacitus dismisses these two as "rich old men," adding that the latter, apparently a kinsman of Vitellius, was "a procrastinator by nature." And just as Galba had replaced Verginius Rufus with Hordeonius Flaccus in Upper Germany, so he appointed Aulus Vitellius to replace Fonteius Capito in Lower Germany. Widely considered the worthless son of the most illustrious senator of the previous generation, Lucius Vitellius, Aulus was a threat only to his own reputation. A notorious glutton and spendthrift, Aulus had to finance his journey to Germany, so Suetonius says, by moving his wife and children out of their house and into an apartment, and by stealing a pearl earring from his mother, while Dio reports that he was besieged by his creditors when he tried to set out. According to Suetonius, Galba commented that nobody was less to be feared than a man whose every thought was of eating, and that Vitellius' insatiable appetite could feed on the resources of his province. As told, the story is probably fiction, but Tacitus' one brief and elliptical comment on the subject confirms that the emperor felt only contempt for Vitellius.

When Vitellius reached his new command, in the last days of November 68, discontent had been brewing for some time. In both Upper and Lower Germany, the troops were no more reconciled to Galba now than they had been at the time of Vesontio, and there were seven legions stationed in these two military districts. Tacitus declares that the troops loyal to Galba were about as numerous as the malcontents, but that the latter were far more active. He also gives a lengthy description of their state of mind. They were elated by their victory over Vindex and the loot they had won without effort or peril. They were eager for more campaigns of this kind, a refreshing change from the endless exertion, harsh discipline, and minimal reward they endured along the western bank of the Rhine, a terrible land with a terrible climate. Thanks to the fact that the forces that defeated Vindex had been drawn from both military districts, they were conscious of their strength as they had never been when they were kept separate. They were furious that their defeated foes, the Aedui, Sequani, and Arverni, were not only prospering again but boasting about it. And they were disquieted by a rumor inspired by Galba's punishment of the marine demonstrators at the Milvian Bridge. This rumor, "craftily manufactured and readily believed," put it about "that legions were being decimated and the most active officers dismissed," clearly with the implication that the turn of the Rhine legions would not be long delayed.

What Tacitus does not develop here, though it becomes more prominent later, is the "Germanic" character of the Rhine legions. Whenever he can, he seizes the chance to blur the distinction between these troops and the German tribesmen who accompanied them on campaign, as auxiliary troops or as native contingents. But though this is an exaggeration to suit his own purposes, it contains more than a grain of truth. These legionaries seem to have been recruited primarily from Italy and southern Gaul, but they had to acclimate to service on the German frontier. This affected their dress (hence Caecina's taste for a parti-colored cloak and Gallic trousers), their diet (they became meat eaters to a far greater extent than was usual in other areas where legions were stationed), and even their weaponry, in that they appear to have adopted nonstandard equipment from the enemy (long spears for example), in order to combat that enemy better.[9] All this created a striking paradox. These men were widely considered the flower of the Roman army and yet they neither looked nor behaved like the ideal, parade-ground legionary.

This is part of a larger issue. It has long been recognized that an army unit tends to become a world unto itself, a "total institution." As a result, it marks itself off from other elements in the population, draws sharp lines between soldier and civilian, and so reinforces its isolation still more. This behavior pattern is found just as much among Roman legionaries as it is in later forces for which we have better documentation.[10] The detail that needs stressing, however, is that the intensity of this isolation could vary from unit to unit, and from province to province. The legions in Syria, for example, were billeted in the towns and were not only much less disciplined and combat-ready than they should have been (a point Tacitus makes in the *Annals* of Corbulo's campaigns against the Parthians), but also formed closer bonds with the civilian populace (a detail he stresses in the *Histories* for its role in the Flavian revolt against Vitellius). With the Rhine legions, by contrast, the isolation was all but complete. The camps in which they were based and the shantytowns occupied by their camp-followers were set pretty much in open country. The one site along the river that qualified as a town at this stage was Colonia Agrippinensis (Cologne), the administrative center of Lower Germany. And none of the seven legions was quartered there. So, to put it invidiously, with no local culture to leaven the mix, the legions were forced back on themselves and, in the absence of alternative perspectives, could form their own opinions and nurse their own grievances, however distorted, with little likelihood of contradiction.

Tacitus is our primary and our best source for what follows. According to his account, which alternates between Upper and Lower Germany in a way that will confuse or annoy the modern reader, what happened was this. In Lower Germany, Vitellius' command, the situation was complicated by the troops' feelings about his predecessor, Fonteius Capito. Some resented his murder, though they placed the opprobrium for that, not on the perpetrators, Fabius Valens and Cornelius Aquinus, but on Galba for condoning it. Others were angered more by Capito's sneakiness and avarice. Even before Vindex's revolt, he had granted or withheld privileges and promotions as a way of enriching himself. Vitellius showed quite uncharacteristic energy in remedying these abuses during his first month as commander. Even though it was winter, he made a careful tour of inspection immediately after his arrival. He restored their ranks to men who had been demoted, struck down the dishonorable discharges that had been given to some, and cleaned up the records of others who had been officially reprimanded. To an extent, Vitellius wanted to ingratiate himself with his troops, but he was also determined to redress injustices. Lower Germany was his first military command and he reveled in it.

This was not the result of any wish to use the command as a stepping stone to the principate. That interpretation was put on his actions by his officers and men. They could not conceive of a commander's showing such consideration for any but ulterior motives, in itself an interesting insight into the thought patterns of the time. Vitellius, however, genuinely delighted in the company of ordinary people and cared for their welfare. Suetonius illustrates his "common touch" with reports that as Vitellius made his way to Germany, "he confirmed his reputation for an easy-going and open-handed nature; he embraced even the common soldiers he met en route, and he was unusually affable to the mule drivers and travelers at the inns and taverns along the way, asking each of them of a morning whether they had breakfasted yet and belching to prove that he had." Tacitus more primly—and more revealingly—declares that talk of his affability was misplaced; respectable people thought him coarse.

The situation in Upper Germany was just as volatile, but for different reasons. Here the troops were angry, first, that Verginius Rufus had been stripped of his command. Their attitude toward him from now on would be ambivalent, partly because he had refused their offer of the throne, and partly because he had submitted tamely to his own supersession. But the enthusiasm he had aroused, not so much for kingmaking as

for finding somebody—anybody—to replace Galba, needed only a cata-
lyst to erupt again. Yet the troops were hardly ready to cast their new
commander, Hordeonius Flaccus, in the role. For him they had only
contempt, one reason why Caecina gained so much influence in the camp
at Mogontiacum. To complicate matters further, this widespread disaffection was fostered sedulously by the Lingones and the Treveri, the
Gallic tribes that had suffered at Galba's hands. They sent representatives into the legions' camp to stir up trouble. Wherever they found a
receptive audience, they made much of the state funeral given to Vindex
by Galba and of the rewards Vindex's allies had received, and they be-
moaned the injustice with which they and the legionaries had been treated.
This aroused so much ill will that Hordeonius decided eventually to order them out of the camp. To avert an outcry, he made the tribesmen
leave by night, but this produced the opposite effect. A rumor was quickly
manufactured and spread that Hordeonius had murdered the men. Angry meetings followed, and first the legionaries, then even the auxiliary
troops encamped with them, took up the cry that they must not only
look out for themselves but, what made this a conspiracy in the eyes of
officialdom, swear oaths to support one another too, in case Hordeonius
attempted to kill off the most active agitators.

The sources agree that the two men who did most to fan this agitation were Fabius Valens, probably legionary legate of I Germanica at
Bonna in Lower Germany, and Aulus Caecina, legate of IV Macedonica
at Mogontiacum in Upper Germany. Of the two Valens figures far more
prominently in the record. He may well have been behind the troops'
offering the throne to Verginius at Vesontio. He certainly took a lead in
the attempts to persuade them ("with difficulty") to accept Galba, after
Verginius refused the offer made when the news of Nero's death arrived.
He was, again, one of the legates responsible for Fonteius Capito's murder. And now, according to Tacitus, he did most to urge Vitellius to bid
for the throne. Dwelling on the governor's ancestry, so much more illustrious than that of Verginius Rufus, he emphasized the strength of
the forces Vitellius could call upon if he made such a bid, and did all he
could to discount any opposition they might encounter. Vitellius' enthusiasm for playing a vigorous army commander, however, was not
matched by a desire to become emperor. Aware of his own limitations,
something for which he is rarely given credit, he responded to this mis-
judgment of his capabilities only to the extent of wanting to be emperor,
not of doing anything about it. As a result, the agitation hung fire. When
the legions in Lower Germany were called upon to renew their oath of
allegiance on 1 January 69, they did as they were told. There was delay,
there was grumbling, there were threats, and even the men in the front

ranks—directly under the eyes of the officers—showed little enthusiasm. But as Vitellius made no move, nobody else had the nerve to give the lead for which all were supposedly waiting.

In Upper Germany things went differently. Aware that he was to be tried for embezzlement, Caecina had nothing to lose by stirring up trouble on a grand scale. So, with his encouragement, the two legions stationed in Mogontiacum refused to take the oath on 1 January, smashed Galba's statues, and—to give their actions a semblance of legality—declared that they were placing themselves at the disposal of the senate and people of Rome. Four centurions from XXII Primigenia who tried to protect Galba's statues were thrown in chains, and the other officers did nothing until the demonstration was over. Then, says Plutarch, they began pondering whom they could make emperor in Galba's place. To their own commander, Hordeonius, they paid no more attention than the troops had done. Caecina must have played a leading role in these deliberations, whether or not he was the unnamed officer who, according to Plutarch, declared Vitellius the obvious choice. This is no proof that Caecina had been party to Valens' plotting, however. Since their later dealings indicate that Caecina could not stand Valens, he would never willingly have subordinated himself to the other. Caecina was intent on saving his own neck and advancing his own career, aims he could fulfill by grabbing a leading role for himself. And that is why his second-in-command, the standard-bearer of IV Macedonica, was the officer sent to Colonia Agrippinensis that evening to inform Vitellius of what had happened.

Even to Vitellius it was clear that in swearing allegiance to the senate and people the two legions in Mogontiacum were playing for time. But since he had no great ambition to become emperor, despite the pressures to which he was being subjected, he decided to observe the proprieties and, at the same time, to test the feelings of his underlings. So messages were sent to the commanders and troops in his own province, to inform them officially that the two legions had refused to take the oath to Galba. They must either suppress this revolt, he said, or "if they preferred peace and concord, support a new emperor." The answer was not long in coming. On 2 January Fabius Valens rode into Colonia Agrippinensis from Bonna with an escort of legionary and auxiliary cavalry (to show that Roman and non-Roman forces were equally enthusiastic), and hailed Vitellius emperor. The two legions in Mogontiacum followed suit on the next day. And the third legion in Upper Germany, XXI Rapax at Vindonissa (Windisch in Switzerland), presumably did likewise or, if it did not, everybody else must have taken it for granted that its officers and men would bow to a *fait accompli*.

We have two versions of Vitellius' response to this turn of events. While neither flatters the new candidate for the throne, it needs stressing that Suetonius has an ulterior motive for devoting his more circumstantial account to the events of the evening of 2 January. As he tells the story, Vitellius was taken from his bedroom without the chance to dress. Instead, wearing his informal house-clothes, he was carried around the town by his troops, holding in his hand a sword of the Deified Julius that someone had taken down specially from a shrine of Mars. By the time they returned him to his headquarters, a neglected stove in the winter dining room had set fire to the place. Although the troops took this as a bad sign, Vitellius was able to reassure them: "do not lose heart," he declared, "to us light is given." But the point of this story is not Vitellius' quick-witted response. Suetonius focuses on the events of 2 January, because the second day of any month was regarded by Romans as an unlucky day on which to start something new, like hailing Vitellius emperor. And evening was considered the least appropriate time of any day to engage in public business, new or not. Suetonius is picking up on the theme that dominates his *Life* of Vitellius, that the emperor must fall.[11]

Plutarch's version, like Tacitus', focuses on 3 January, when the news arrived that the legions in Upper Germany had accepted Vitellius. Since they need not have followed the lead given them by the troops in Lower Germany, and since the latter could have backed down (*they* had taken the oath to Galba), both writers correctly see the agreement reached between the two army groups on 3 January as the decisive moment. Vitellius, says Plutarch, was so overwhelmed that he was able to handle the situation only after bracing himself with a massive lunch and heavy drinking. As well he might. What had started as a mutiny by two legions had been transformed inside 48 hours into a full-scale rebellion by seven.

3

Adoption and Assassination
(January 69)

Since Galba was old and childless, everybody recognized that if he was given time to pick a successor, he would have to adopt the man of his choice. Even when Romans appeared to abandon dynastic succession, they believed in grafting the next emperor onto the family tree of the incumbent. When Galba began thinking seriously about the matter is uncertain, since Tacitus states only that it was "some time before" he announced his choice on 10 January 69. But as he had not pursued the idea of adopting an heir in the years immediately following the deaths of his two children in the 40s, it seems likeliest that his proclamation as emperor on 9 June 68 was what started him thinking about the issue, and not solely because he had achieved the traditional aristocratic aim of surpassing the achievements of all his ancestors. This timing suggests that we should give him credit for worrying about the welfare of the state as well. He may not have cared who inherited his personal effects, but he recognized that he could not show this indifference when it came to the question who would succeed him as emperor.

Galba's refusal to name that heir publicly for another six months was smart politically, in that it limited the intrigue bound to swirl around the man he picked, and it foreclosed discussion on the wisdom of his choice. But it was ill advised, in that it did nothing to limit gossip. It was in the nature of Roman society that prominent senators would each consider themselves an ideal choice for heir, and that their friends and dependents would seize every chance to talk up their man. And nothing fascinated the people more than trying to identify whom Galba would choose. Under the young and childless Nero it had been unsafe as well as unwise to discuss so sensitive a topic in public. Galba's old age made speculation inevitable, and the sheer delight of being able to gossip generated still more talk. Yet since our sources name only two men as the objects of this chatter, Otho and Cornelius Dolabella, it looks as though every other potential contender failed to break through the lines drawn round the emperor by his pedagogues.[1]

Otho was the obvious candidate from the start. He was a senator, if only a third-generation senator, and at 36 he was a relatively young man. As the governor of Lusitania, moreover, he had done all he could to help Galba from the moment the latter accepted Vindex's offer to lead the revolt against Nero. Otho had not acted out of altruism, of course. He wanted to ingratiate himself with Galba, with his henchmen, and with his troops. So he made himself affable to the men of VII Galbiana as they trudged from Spain to Italy. Of Galba's henchmen he won over Vinius, supposedly with hopes of a marriage alliance: Otho, a bachelor, would marry Vinius' unattached daughter once his ambitions had been fulfilled. But he could make no impression on Laco and Icelus. And whether he failed or refused to recognize it, he had no more success with their master. Otho had once been Nero's boon companion, and as almost everybody viewed him through that lens, it was easy to discount the sterling job he had done as governor of Lusitania and the help he had given since. This is how Galba arrived at the conclusion that he had not rescued the empire from the clutches of one playboy to hand it over to another. The other alternative, Dolabella, was a relative of Galba's, perhaps his great-nephew, and like the emperor, he came from a family prominent in the republican period. But he seems to have had nothing to recommend him except that he was a senator and an ex-consul. If Laco and Icelus supported his cause, it was not because they thought him a good choice. They were merely united in their opposition to anybody Vinius supported. As for Galba, whatever his reasons, he seems to have been no more impressed with Dolabella than he was with Otho.

Whether or not Otho considered Dolabella a serious rival, he continued his own efforts to win favor, no longer with the legionaries he had cultivated on the march from Spain (Galba had shipped them off to Carnuntum in Pannonia), but with the praetorian guard. We need not consider this sinister. Talking of the brief lapse of time between Galba's passing over Otho and Otho's murdering him, Plutarch observes that loyal troops could not have been corrupted in a mere four days. His remark is not very perceptive in fact. Even if Galba had chosen Otho as his heir, Laco was prefect of the guard, and he was hostile. Lazy and incompetent as he was, he could have made things awkward for Otho if he chose. So it was in Otho's best interests to take precautions as early as possible, to circumvent Laco and the senior officers he might be able to influence, and to build a following in the lower ranks, among the men who would be susceptible to his blandishments. We have two stories to indicate how far he went. When the emperor dined with Otho, Galba was attended—as was customary—by a cohort from the praetorian guard, and to each man in the unit Otho gave 100 sesterces, a gift of phenomenal size for one night's work. More striking still was the help he gave the "speculator" Cocceius Proculus.[2] Proculus was entangled in a dispute with a neighbor over the property line separating their farms. Offering himself as arbitrator, Otho purchased the neighbor's land and presented it to the guardsman.

It was the way events played out that enabled Otho opportunistically to find another use for the guardsmen he had been cultivating. By the close of 68 Galba had settled on another prospect altogether, Lucius Calpurnius Piso Licinianus, a young man of impeccable ancestry. Born in 38, Piso could trace his lineage back to Caesar's two colleagues in the First Triumvirate, to Pompey on his mother's side, and to Crassus on his father's. His own immediate family had not fared well under the Julio-Claudians, however. His father had been cosseted and then, around 45/46, executed by Claudius. Of Piso's three brothers, one died with his father, the second was executed by Nero, and the third would suffer the same fate in 70, by order of Vespasian's coadjutor, Licinius Mucianus. Piso himself had been scarcely more fortunate. He had spent much of Nero's reign in exile. How much we do not know, but six years is a reasonable guess, since Piso seems to have held no public offices before he was recalled. Apparently to excuse this, Suetonius asserts that Galba had long admired Piso, and had made him his heir in the wills he drew up before becoming emperor. This is very improbable. It is hard to see how Galba could have gotten to know Piso, before or after the latter was sent into exile, when he himself had spent the last eight years in isolation at the western end of the empire. Though Galba was responsible for recalling Piso from exile, there is more to be said for the view of Tacitus and Plutarch, that what recommended the young man to the emperor was his ancestry, his being a victim of Nero, and his temperament, which—by the time he returned to the city—was old-fashioned, austere, and humorless.[3]

Tacitus, to anticipate a little, develops these points in the speech that Galba supposedly delivered to Piso when he told the young man of his decision to adopt him. According to the *mise en scène* nobody else overheard what was said, and the two principals were dead within a week. So the speech must be an invention, by Tacitus or by an earlier historian. Hence, like other similar speeches in the *Histories* and the *Annals*, this fiction has been hailed sometimes as evidence for Tacitus' own views on the succession, sometimes as evidence of his unreliability. It is neither. It was a convention of ancient historiography that important figures in the narrative give speeches. Written in the historian's style, albeit with touches of the speaker's mannerisms to lend verisimilitude, these speeches represented perhaps the substance of what was said, perhaps the substance of what should have been said, or perhaps the reasoning behind the speakers' actions, whether they said anything or not. So the speeches served the same purpose as modern scholars' speculations about the motives of their subjects, and we can take this example as a distillation of Galba's principal concerns as best Tacitus was able to reconstruct them.[4]

Galba stressed three themes. There was ancestry, regularly considered synonymous with ability by Roman aristocrats. Galba would have worried about this aspect anyway, since there was no value in grafting inferior stock onto his own family line. As it was, Piso's ancestry far surpassed that of any other claimant to the throne, and it ought to have won the respect of the senate. At the same time, since Galba was adopting his heir, senators would not conclude, as they had under the Julio-Claudians, that they were being inherited like pieces of furniture. Second, there was Piso's age. He was old enough to have left behind the irresponsibility of his twenties and young enough to have many years ahead of him—years in which he and his wife Verania might yet produce sons. This promised a long and stable reign, for Galba clearly a major consideration, since his aim was not to placate his enemies but to preempt their activities by presenting them with an heir they must accept. And third, there was Piso's experience of exile. As he had been tested by adversity, so Galba supposedly thought, he would be less inclined to abuse his power, and less likely to be corrupted by it. So long as he kept the example of Nero before his eyes, he would be a ruler of the highest moral caliber. And if that proved to be his only qualification, it was not one lightly to be challenged or set aside.

Galba delayed announcing his choice until his hand was forced on 9 January, when he received a dispatch from Pompeius Propinquus, procurator of Gallia Belgica and paymaster to the legions stationed along the Rhine. This gave him the hard, if unwelcome, information that the two legions stationed in Mogontiacum had refused to renew their oath of allegiance to the emperor on the first of the year. Since the dispatch said nothing about developments like Vitellius' proclamation, this seemingly persuaded Galba that he was faced only with a mutiny, and with grievances that would subside as soon as he announced that he had chosen an heir. On 10 January, therefore, he summoned his closest advisers to the palace. Those present, we are told, were Vinius, Laco and Icelus, of course, Marius Celsus, a loyal supporter of the emperor, and Aulus Ducenius Geminus, prefect of the city and so commander of the urban cohorts. Plutarch adds Otho to the roster, but he seems to have done this, wrongly, to intensify the humiliation Otho suffered as a result of Galba's unexpected decision and the anger it sparked in him.

Tacitus calls the meeting an "imperial election," but he is being sarcastic. For one thing, those present hardly constituted the semiofficial circle of advisers with which an emperor surrounded himself, the so-called *consilium principis*. This was a kitchen cabinet. And there was no debate or discussion. Galba announced that Piso was his choice, called the young man in, and then—according to Tacitus—took him off to one side to deliver his homily. When they rejoined the group, Piso expressed his gratitude to Galba and spoke modestly of himself. None of this made a favorable impression on the others present, any more than it did on the rest of the populace later. Galba's entourage was quick to congratulate Piso on his new status, but they were disquieted by his impassiveness. He showed no emotion, as if to be emperor was more a penance than a prize, a chore to be undertaken rather than the fulfillment of any right-thinking senator's ambitions.

Though Galba denied his supporters the right to debate his choice of heir, he allowed them to discuss a question the answer to which should have been a foregone conclusion, whether they should announce the adoption first to the people, to the senate, or to the soldiery. Since the emperor plumed himself on his respect for constitutional proprieties (no matter how often he flouted them), the senate should have been the first to hear. Yet the upshot of the discussion was to pass over both senate and people, though a large crowd had gathered outside the palace. Instead, the announcement would be made in the praetorian camp. Purely practical considerations played some part in this. The guard could be paraded far faster than the senate could be called into session, and there was nothing to be gained by delay. But Tacitus declares that the decision was justified with the specious argument that the guard would appreciate the compliment: "it was wrong to court the soldiery with bribes and flattery, but their support was not to be despised when gained by honorable means."

The weather was terrible: the skies were dark, there was torrential rain, and there was much thunder and lightning. In the old days, says Tacitus, this would have been considered an evil omen, justifying the cancellation of any public meeting. If we were to believe Suetonius' stories of the omens that affected Galba, for good or ill, the emperor would have called off the meeting. But since he was not to be deterred, it seems better to accept Tacitus' explanation, that either Galba thought such phenomena natural (it was a warm winter), or he was a fatalist who believed that there was no avoiding what fate had in store. The emperor certainly made his way to the praetorian camp, the troops were paraded in the pouring rain, and he addressed them in a brief, soldierlike manner. He informed the men that he had adopted Piso as his heir, after a precedent set by Augustus, and in a manner that seems to have been used in the distant past to raise recruits for the army (the troops probably had no idea what he was talking about). Then, to prevent the spread of rumors that problems in Germany were getting out of hand, he admitted that the two legions in Mogontiacum had mutinied. But he attributed this to a handful of troublemakers, and added that since there had been no violence so far, it would be easy for the legions to return to their allegiance. And that was that. There was no flattery. And there was no mention of money, either the donative Nymphidius had promised the men six months before or a new one, to mark a supposedly festive occasion like the announcement of an heir.[5]

Brusque as the speech was, the tribunes and the centurions, along with the men in the front ranks, raised a cheer. The rest of the guard maintained a sullen silence, angered by the non-mention of a donative. It is generally agreed, says Tacitus, that even the smallest concession would have won them over, but Galba's old-fashioned rigor and his excessive harshness damaged his cause irreparably. This is an oversimplification, to cue the epigram that nobody else could come up to Galba's high standards. For a start, Otho was already working hard to win the favor of the rankers, and they must have been disconcerted to learn that Piso was to be the next emperor. Then too, there must have been problems with the officers, since Galba cashiered four of them in this same period, Antonius Taurus and Antonius Naso from the praetorian guard, Aemilius Pacensis from the urban cohorts, and Julius Fronto from the cohorts of the watch. The fact that the last two would be reinstated by Otho cannot prove that they had been agitating on his behalf. They may simply have failed to deal with the unrest among their men. But Tacitus states that dismissing these four solved nothing, as it induced all the others to believe that they were suspect in Galba's eyes. And the fear that kept them loyal led them to crack down more harshly still on the discontented rankers.

From the camp Galba and his associates made their way back to the senate. Here the emperor gave another speech, as brief and brusque as the one he had delivered to the troops. This time, however, Piso spoke too and—in the one and only official act he took as emperor designate—he won favor with his courtesy. The senators, of course, felt it incumbent upon them to respond, and one by one they declared their delight at this turn of events. As Tacitus puts it, some genuinely liked Piso; those who did not were correspondingly more effusive; and those who cared neither way, the majority, acquiesced easily. They were more preoccupied with their own futures under the new dispensation than with the question whether the adoption served the best interests of the state.

By the time all who wanted to speak had had their say, it must have been relatively late in the day, but the senate took up the question of sending an embassy to the mutinous legions. There were endless revisions, as senators' names were added to or removed from the list. Those who wanted to go were motivated primarily by ambition, says Tacitus, those who preferred to stay in Rome by fear. Finally, the task of picking the envoys was turned over to Galba and with that the session came to an end. For Tacitus talks next of a private meeting, held perhaps that same day, in which emperor and advisers discussed whether they should send Piso on this mission as well, to represent the emperor as its other members represented the senate. Tiberius had done something of this sort when he sent his son Drusus to quell the Pannonian mutiny of 14, but he had been accompanied by two cohorts of the guard and the prefect Sejanus. Yet a proposal to send Laco was met with the prefect's flat refusal to put himself in harm's way. Just as absurdly, there was no agreement on which senators were to serve, since Galba changed his mind on the embassy's composition as often as the senators had. All in all, it is remarkable that a delegation ever set out, or so the reader is supposed to conclude. Tacitus delays reporting that it did until much later in his narrative.

When and where Otho heard that he was not to be Galba's heir we are not told. But it is unlikely that he learnt of it only in the senate meeting of 10 January, a meeting he must have attended despite the humiliation it brought him. More probably, he heard of Galba's decision almost as soon as it was announced, perhaps from Vinius, perhaps through his contacts in the praetorian guard (they must have been ordered to get ready for the parade at which Galba revealed his choice). His initial reaction was rage. Suetonius reports that he thought of seizing control of the praetorian camp that same day, and of killing Galba while he dined in the palace. The story illustrates how desperate Otho's situation had become. Aside from the disappointment of his hopes, the waste of eight months of effort, and the humiliation of being passed over, Otho had run up enormous debts, according to Plutarch in the neighborhood of 200 million sesterces. What had kept his creditors at bay was their belief—which he no doubt fostered assiduously—that he would settle up with them once he was designated Galba's heir.[6] Hence the joke he made as he calmed down, that he could not keep his feet unless he became emperor, and it made little difference whether he fell at the hands of his enemies on the battlefield or of his creditors in the Forum. Luckily, he had laid hands on a million sesterces a day or so before, and with this war chest he launched a plan to assassinate Galba and Piso. He left the details to Onomastus, the most talented of his freedmen, and the latter latched onto two noncommissioned officers,

Barbius Proculus, a "tesserarius" in charge of the password for the emperor's bodyguard (more or less a corporal), and Veturius, an "optio" or second-in-command to a centurion (in modern terms an adjutant). After sizing them up and finding them as crafty as they were daring, Onomastus promised them enormous rewards and gave them enough cash to recruit a few accomplices meanwhile. As Tacitus puts it with a mixture of indignation and incredulity, "two noncommissioned officers undertook to transfer the empire of the Roman people from one man to another and, what is more, they did."[7]

Barbius and Veturius let only a handful of praetorians into the secret, but they took every opportunity to stir up the rest of the men. To those who had been promoted by Nymphidius they pointed out that this alone rendered them suspect in Galba's eyes. In the rest they rekindled anger and despair over the oft-promised donative. Some they reminded of the good old days under Nero, when much less stress had been placed on discipline and duty. And all alike they terrified by emphasizing that there was no remedy for their grievances. Those who complained would be demoted or dismissed by Galba, and those who hoped for better days under his successor were deluding themselves now that he had settled on Piso Licinianus.

The conspirators' first plan, says Tacitus, was to grab Otho under the cover of darkness as he returned home from a dinner party on the night of 14 January, and to rush him to the praetorian camp. They had to abandon this idea, because the unrest among the praetorians had spread to the legionary detachments and auxiliary units scattered around the city. There was a real risk that somebody else would be seized and rushed to the camp by legionaries from Pannonia or Germany. These men had not the least idea what Otho looked like, and since they would probably be drunk into the bargain, it would be difficult even to get them to follow the plan. As it was, there were plenty of indications that a conspiracy was being hatched. The plotters did what they could to hush it up, but what saved them was Laco's discounting the rumors that reached Galba's ears. He had no idea how deep the disaffection of the troops went, but he refused to support any action he had not suggested himself, and he was relentless in his opposition to those who knew or claimed to know more than he. Whether or not the conspirators were aware of this, they recognized that further delay would lead to their betrayal. So the decision was made to go ahead on the morning of 15 January.

For Galba that morning opened with a sacrifice for good omens in front of the temple of Apollo attached to the palace. He was attended not only by his leading associates but also by Otho, who had come—as was customary—to pay his respects. The ceremony ran longer than expected. The priest in charge was Umbricius, supposedly the best seer of his day, and he announced that the signs were bad: there was a plot under way and an enemy within the walls. None of this disquieted Galba (so Tacitus states), since he was contemptuous of such matters. But as emperor and head of the official state religion he could not walk away. So the search for favorable omens had to continue.

Otho, standing next to the emperor, was more inclined to believe in heavenly signs. But rather than being dismayed by Umbricius' apparent knowledge of his activities, he took the announcement of evil omens for Galba as proof that his own plans were destined to succeed. So he was ready to go ahead with his coup when he was joined by his freedman Onomastus. The latter had come to inform him that it was time to meet with the master-builder and the contractors about an old house Otho was buying. On its face, the message was innocuous and plausible: Otho was so penniless that he could afford only a tumbledown place bound to need major repairs. At another level, it told anybody who inquired that Otho had accepted Galba's adoption of Piso, since he had obviously abandoned any hopes of moving into the palace. And at base it was a message in code: Onomastus (the master-builder) and the guardsmen he had suborned (the contractors) were ready to make their move.

To calm suspicions that there might be more here than met the eye, Otho still took his time about leaving the sacrifice and made his way by a circuitous route down to the Forum. He had arranged to meet his accomplices outside the temple of Saturn, and since the praetorians wore civilian dress inside the city even when on duty, a large body of men would not be recognized for what they were amid the hustle and bustle of the busiest spot in Rome. As it happened, there were only 23 guardsmen at the rendezvous. Perhaps because this unnerved Otho, perhaps because his leisurely stroll had put them behind schedule, the plotters quickly hailed him emperor, bundled him into a chair, and with drawn swords rushed him off to the camp well over a mile away. They were joined by another 20 to 30 men along the way. Some, says Tacitus, were already in the plot and brandished their swords with noisy enthusiasm. Others were merely curious, not loyal to Galba but unwilling to commit to Otho. Yet when this group reached the camp, the tribune on duty, Julius Martialis, was so taken aback that he made no attempt to stop them entering. People thought later that he was in the conspiracy, but more probably he was shocked by the small number of plotters and by their audacity. Unable to imagine that 50-odd men would try to seize the throne, he refused to risk his neck in case the conspiracy was more widespread. The other officers showed no more initiative. Tacitus asserts that they preferred dishonor to danger, but as Laco was at the palace, nobody may have taken the lead because Laco was no keener than Galba on displays of initiative by his subordinates.

The manner of Otho's departure from the Forum was too unusual not to be reported back to Galba. So he, still intent on his sacrifice—to gods of an empire, as Tacitus puts it, that belonged now to another—was told first that an unidentified senator had been hurried off to the camp and, later, that the senator was Otho. After a hasty consultation it was decided to test the loyalties of the cohort of the guard on duty at the palace. Neither Galba nor his advisers seem to have grasped how serious a problem they faced. So their decision that the emperor be kept in reserve, in case the situation deteriorated, may in fact have been a diplomatic means of ensuring that he not make matters worse by alienating the troops with another of his brusque, even brutal, speeches. Instead, the task was given to the heir designate, Piso.

According to the speech Tacitus wrote for him, Piso seized the moral high ground and made much of honor and shame. There was the honor of the imperial house that—he told the guardsmen—rested now in their hands. There was the honor of the guard itself. Although legions had mutinied, the guard had never abandoned their duly constituted emperor. Nero had deserted them, not they him. There was the disgrace they must all endure if an extravagant and effeminate playboy like Otho became emperor. And there was the shame of letting a handful of renegades and deserters set up an emperor, when they were men who could not be trusted to choose their own junior officers. Yet in his peroration Piso came down to earth. If the cohort followed Otho, the only result would be a war they would have to fight. And there was no point in that when Galba would give them a donative as large as any sums they could expect from the usurper.

Tacitus obviously constructed a speech he thought appropriate to Piso's character. How successful the reader is supposed to consider it is another matter. It is full of incongruities. A long-time exile addresses praetorians as "comrades"—and for the emperor or his heir to address soldiers as comrades was itself a sign that civil war impended. Piso tells an audience of soldiers that good men think to kill is as terrible as to be killed. Piso claims disingenuously that Galba had gained the throne not only legitimately but without bloodshed, reviving the legalism with which Galba himself had justified his usurpation. Piso depicts Otho as another Nero, not the best tactic when the guard was still devoted to Nero's memory. And Piso promises the men the donative for which they have been waiting so long, without indicating why they should believe that he had the influence to deliver on his promise. We know that Galba and his entourage thought Piso had done a good job (it was one reason why they sent him to the praetorian camp later in the day). But their judgment need have been no sounder on this than it was on any other matter. In fact, the heir designate managed only to delay the inevitable. The cohort gave Piso a hearing, but he may not have aroused much enthusiasm. Tacitus states that the men milled around in confusion rather than doing anything in particular. And whatever enthusiasm they mustered evaporated in a matter of hours.

While Piso addressed the cohort, emissaries were also sent to other forces scattered about the city. There is no mention of any appeal to the urban cohorts, probably because their loyalty was taken for granted. (They had been placed under Galba's own nominee, Ducenius Geminus.) But since they were quartered in the praetorian camp, they must have made common cause with the guard, and so do not appear as a separate entity. Similarly, the idea of appealing to the men of I Adiutrix was mooted, but no action was taken, this time for the opposite reason, the recognition that these troops still resented the treatment Galba had meted out to their former companions at the Milvian Bridge. But Marius Celsus was sent to a detachment from the Illyrian legions quartered in the Vipsanian Portico; two senior centurions approached the German troops in the Hall of Liberty (*Atrium Libertatis*); and three military tribunes hurried to the praetorian camp, in hopes of bringing the guardsmen around. It would be some time before Galba heard that none of these efforts had borne fruit. The three military tribunes were sent about their business; Marius Celsus was driven off at spear point; and though the German troops were well disposed toward Galba, they never turned up.

By this time a large crowd had gathered outside the palace, calling for the execution of Otho and his accomplices. None of them preferred Galba to Otho, says Tacitus. They were simply following the traditional pattern of flattering the emperor because he was the emperor. Inside the palace there was less unanimity. Vinius urged Galba to fortify the building, block the entrances, and arm the palace slaves. This, he is supposed to have argued, would give loyalists time to assemble, the plotters time to rethink—and abandon—their plan. The emperor could always venture forth when the situation improved, but he risked getting caught out in the open if he left immediately. It is uncertain if Vinius was involved in Otho's plot, but even if he was not, his advice now lent credibility to that interpretation. The rest of Galba's entourage took the opposite line: they must move at once to crush the conspiracy, before it could grow larger, and before Otho could find his feet. Better to go meet the danger, even if it meant their deaths. That was their duty and, if nothing else, it would make Otho an assassin as well as a usurper.

When Vinius persisted in his opposition to this plan, Laco—
encouraged by Icelus—nearly came to blows with him. Violence in the
upper reaches of Roman society being normally verbal, this breach of
decorum, combined with the mention of duty, drove Galba to a decision: they would take the more honorable course and sally forth. But
again there was a delay. As a first step Piso was sent, with an escort, to
the praetorian camp, to reinforce the efforts of the tribunes sent off earlier. (It was not known that they had failed.) His speech to the cohort at
the palace was judged a success, and it was thought too that his being the
emperor's son would win him a more favorable hearing than that accorded to junior officers. But no sooner had he left on this mission than
a rumor circulated that Otho had been killed in the camp. Whatever its
origins (some thought it invented by Othonians who had mingled with
the crowd, to draw Galba out of the palace), the rumor was readily believed. In fact, some claimed to have seen the killing, some to have taken
part in it. And since it looked as if the danger had passed, the common
people were joined now by senators and knights, and together they broke
open the doors of the palace, surrounded the emperor, and loudly proclaimed their loyalty to him and their disappointment at being robbed of
the chance to take revenge on Otho.

So great was the confusion that Galba hesitated again. Apparently
unconvinced that the danger was past, he put on a breastplate. But before he could do anything else, the crowd swept him off his feet and
hoisted him into a chair, intending to carry him to the Capitol so that he
could give thanks to Jupiter Best and Greatest for his preservation. He
may have been reassured to some extent by meeting a guardsman, Julius
Atticus, as he left the palace. The latter was waving a bloody sword about
and claiming loudly to have killed Otho. It would be easy to assume that
Atticus was an Othonian, trying to throw the emperor off his guard and
ensure that he left the palace. But it is just as likely that this was an auda-
cious piece of self-advertising, designed to win its author immediate promotion and a large monetary reward. Atticus received neither. Never
one to pass up the chance of playing the disciplinarian, Galba inquired
who had given him his orders. Even imaginary displays of initiative were
not appreciated by an emperor inflexible in the face of threats and flattery alike.

Otho meanwhile was being given a tumultuous welcome by the rankers in the praetorian camp (their officers they kept well away from him).
Carried around on the men's shoulders, he was set down eventually on
the raised mound in front of the HQ building, amid the standards of the
cohorts and on the spot occupied previously by a statue of Galba. The
enthusiasm of the guard was so great that his partisans had no difficulty

persuading the rest of the men to declare their allegiance. Then the oath was administered to the former marines of I Adiutrix, who by now had joined the praetorians in their camp, and they took it without exception. At this point Otho must have made a speech to the assembled soldiery, but we have only Tacitus' version. The original was probably neither as carefully organized nor as eloquently expressed. Yet the historian's version may preserve the themes Otho chose to emphasize.

According to Tacitus, Otho's main goal was to induce his audience to take the next step and kill their legal emperor. So he pointed out, first, that the welcome they had given him bound them together indissolubly. Now they must finish the job or submit to punishment by Galba, when his record proved that there was no hope of leniency. The emperor had put to death men of high rank and low, soldiers and civilians, individuals and groups, not only in Rome but in every camp and province of the empire, and each time he masked his ferocity with claims to have "restored discipline." Although Icelus and Vinius in a mere six months had managed to amass fortunes larger than those accumulated by all Nero's favorites put together, Galba prated about "economy" to cover up his tight-fistedness, and refused to pay the troops the donative promised by Nymphidius. Nor, finally, was the situation going to change for the better. Galba had picked as his successor a young man embittered by exile, a man who, in the emperor's opinion, best matched his own grim disposition and meanness. And the gods had shown their displeasure with the storm that attended the announcement of the adoption.

The senate and people, so Otho supposedly continued, were as unhappy with this as the troops were, but only the troops could act. There would be no fighting and no danger. All the armed forces were with them, and the cohort on duty at the palace was not so much protecting Galba as detaining him. It too would swear the oath to Otho, the moment it caught sight of the rest of the guard (this at least turned out to be true). The only contest then would be to see who could put Otho under the greatest obligation. But they had to begin at once. They must not delay carrying out a plan that was honorable enough, but would only be perceived as such if it succeeded (Otho's variation on the dictum that if treason "prosper, none dare call it treason"). Having roused his audience to a fever pitch, Otho ordered the armory opened, and the men rushed to grab whatever items of equipment came to hand. Nobody waited for tribunes or centurions to give them orders, says Tacitus, and Otho's keenest supporters were delighted by the distress they saw in the faces of the officers still loyal to Galba.

Piso heard this uproar as he approached the camp and, turning on his heel, caught up with Galba in the Forum. Since the emperor had learnt by now that his other emissaries had been no more successful in their appeals to the soldiery, there was another discussion. Some of his entourage urged a return to the palace, some that he should take refuge on the Capitol (Brutus and Cassius had done that after murdering Caesar), and some that he occupy the speakers' platform in the Forum, presumably to try to rally the people behind him. The argument these suggestions provoked added to the confusion, and Tacitus claims that Laco considered killing Vinius out of hand, "perhaps to placate the soldiery with his death, perhaps because he believed him a member of Otho's conspiracy, or perhaps just because he hated him." The story points up the disunity prevailing in Galba's following, and explains why many of the more prominent lost heart and began to slip away. Galba was unable to regain control. Still in his chair, he bobbed about above the heads of a crowd that ebbed and flowed this way and that in the center of the Forum. Meanwhile the citizenry gathered in the porticoes and temples around its edges, as silent and yet as keyed up as they would have been at the start of a chariot race. They cannot have imagined that Galba would be murdered, but they could not resist waiting to see what happened next.

The cavalrymen whom Otho had ordered to carry out the assassination now galloped into the Forum. Waving their swords over their heads, they trampled down any who got in their way. For Galba's escort, the praetorian cohort from the palace, this was enough. They threw down their arms, and as Galba's bearers panicked, he was toppled from his chair. He was killed on the ground, before he could get to his feet, but he met his end bravely. As Roman aristocrats considered a man's last words *the* index of his character, Galba's were reported variously. Some alleged that he asked what wrong he had done and begged for a few days to pay the overdue donative. A majority asserted that he offered his throat to the soldiery, telling them to strike and be done with it, if they thought that best for Rome. As Tacitus puts it, his killers (rankers all) did not care what he said, and admiration or hatred of the emperor determined which version members of the upper classes preferred. There was also a dispute over the identity of his killer, but this rested on practical considerations: the soldier actually responsible could expect a huge reward from Otho. All we know for certain is that Galba's head was cut off, to be carried to Otho, and that the body was left lying where it had fallen, in the middle of the Forum.

Of the others in Galba's party, Laco and Icelus got away. Vinius too turned and fled, but he was cut down from behind. He tried to evade his fate by insisting that Otho had not ordered his death, but it is uncertain whether he invented this claim on the spur of the moment or was admitting complicity in the plot (Tacitus prefers the second explanation). By contrast, a centurion of the praetorian guard showed real bravery. Sempronius Densus, leader of the men assigned to escort Piso, drew his dagger and rushed to meet the enemy. It cost him his life, but it gave the wounded Piso time to find refuge in the nearby temple of Vesta. Sheltered by the slave in charge of the building, he must have remained hidden for some time. When Otho was brought Galba's head, he told the men that it was Piso's he wanted, and two soldiers were detailed to find and kill his rival. One was a *speculator*, the other an auxiliary soldier only recently given Roman citizenship by Galba and, apparently, more determined on that account to prove his devotion to the new emperor. The two had little trouble in locating Piso, and since Romans (unlike Greeks) did not recognize the right of sanctuary, they dragged him from his hiding place and murdered him before they even got him out of the temple.

Whatever Otho's feelings on being presented with Galba's head, it was Piso's that delighted him and the sources say that he feasted his eyes on it, as if free of all anxiety now that the business was concluded. Alternatively (this is Tacitus' less plausible suggestion), he was so overcome by the memory of his treachery to Galba and his friendship with Vinius that he could justify what he had done only by putting the emphasis on the murder of the hated Piso. The troops found their satisfaction in sporting with Galba's head. Because he had been bald, so the story goes, the soldier who cut off the head either wrapped it in his cloak or stuck his thumb in its mouth and carried it that way (these details come from Plutarch and Suetonius, neither of them concerned to preserve the decorum appropriate to a narrative of high events). Since this made it difficult for others to see the head, the soldier impaled it on his spear and brandished it down the road from the Forum to the camp. There it was paraded around like a trophy, along with those of Piso and Vinius, amid the standards of the cohorts and the eagle of I Adiutrix. Meanwhile, the troops tried to top each other's stories. Some claimed to have done the killing, some to have participated in it, and all—truly or not—to have carried out some memorable deed. More than 120 petitions for rewards would be handed to Otho, and discovered in the palace by Vitellius. As Tacitus says, Vitellius ordered every last one of the men hunted down and executed. It was not that he had any respect for Galba or any concern to highlight Otho's failure to punish the murderers. He wanted to deter future assassins.

Otho, by contrast, shunned reprisals, except in two cases—Laco and Icelus—and only in one did he act openly. Plutarch reports that Laco was killed in the Forum and his head taken to Otho. This is probably wrong, since Tacitus declares that Laco was rounded up later and led to believe that he would be exiled to an island off the coast of Italy (the standard punishment for those of the high rank Laco now enjoyed). Once he reached the island, however, Laco was killed by a veteran whom Otho had sent on ahead to take care of the matter. Since there was no reason to deceive Laco (he was in no position to protest), this trickery was probably designed to appease public opinion. Laco had never been hated like Vinius, only despised as an incompetent buffoon. But as Otho called a halt to the killing immediately after the slaughter in the Forum, he could not afford to execute any of Galba's free-born associates later, no matter when they were caught. Icelus, on the other hand, was crucified openly, wearing the newly acquired rings that marked the equestrian status that should have saved him from an ignominious death. But he was a freedman, and persons of quality lost no sleep over the death of an avaricious ex-slave.

Otho showed similar restraint in his dealings with those whose kinsfolk had been murdered in the Forum. The bodies were left lying where they had fallen till late in the evening, when Otho permitted the relatives to take care of their burial. They had to ask permission, because the corpses were viewed as those of executed criminals, and permission could be refused if the emperor wanted to inflict more infamy on his victims. However, Otho left the relatives with the task of redeeming the heads the killers had retrieved after the parade through the camp, in order to realize a tidy sum of ransom money on them. Piso's corpse was cremated by his wife Verania and his brother Crassus Scribonianus, Vinius' by his daughter Crispina. (His ill-gotten gains were seized by the new emperor.) Tacitus asserts that nobody had the desire or the nerve to claim Galba's corpse that day, but this need not contradict Plutarch's assertion that the insufferable Helvidius Priscus undertook the task. All we have to assume is that Helvidius acted on the next day, partly out of gratitude to the emperor for recalling him to Rome, and partly out of disgust at the failure of anybody else to come forward. It was certainly on the next day that the head was recovered, from a group of soldiers' slaves and sutlers. They had been amusing themselves with it in front of the tomb of Patrobius, one of the Neronian freedmen Galba had executed after his arrival in Rome. And so the man who had given Vindex a state funeral at last received burial, though it was one of his own bailiffs, a former slave named Argius, who carried out the task.

The sources themselves found it hard to summarize Galba's character and achievements. He had enjoyed a long and relatively distinguished career, but his ancestry and his wealth seem to have cloaked a certain lack of ability, and this is the point behind Tacitus' comment that everybody agreed that he would make an excellent emperor until he took on the job. Nor was this lack of ability counterbalanced by a winning personality. In a private citizen, a preference for old-fashioned ways, a frugality scarcely distinguishable from miserliness, and a blind insistence on discipline were all unfashionable in a permissive age. Such traits could not be considered vices, when they recalled the heroes of early Roman history, men long since elevated into role models for later generations. But they were not virtues either, especially in the eyes of a populace schooled by Nero's 14-year reign to expect bounty at every turn. As Tacitus put it, Galba lacked vices rather than possessed virtues. In Rome, again, old men were expected to be wise, like Augustus, or at least crafty, like Vespasian. But they were also supposed to be authority figures whose sternness was tempered by a readiness to forgive human frailties, a role Augustus and Vespasian played to perfection, each in his own way. Although Galba had been out of circulation for nearly 20 years, or perhaps because of it, people seem to have expected him to live up to this stereotype. As emperor, however, he demonstrated neither wisdom nor craftiness, let alone forgiveness. He deluded himself about the strength of his own position and the best means of reinforcing it. And his integrity could never compensate for his failings, especially when he surrounded himself with rogues whom he trusted to excess. Since he had never enjoyed as much support as he fancied, his defects and the delinquencies of his entourage combined to ruin them all. Plutarch may sum up the situation best: Galba left behind none who wanted him as their emperor, but many who pitied the manner of his death.

4

The Opening of the Vitellian Offensive (January and February)

While Otho horrified people by murdering Galba, Vitellius outraged their sensibilities by omitting to proclaim his respect for the constitutional proprieties. Whereas Otho called a senate meeting to secure legitimacy for his coup within a matter of hours, Vitellius and his supporters dispensed with appearances. So far as we can tell, there was no dispatch to the senate. There was no justification for his being hailed emperor by the armies on the Rhine. There was certainly no claim to be saving the state or ridding the world of a tyrant. And on his earliest coinage there was scarcely a reference to the senate and people of Rome. Some issues bore conventional legends like "Liberty restored" (LIBERTAS RESTITVTA) or the "rebirth of Rome" (ROMA RENASCENS). But these were outnumbered by those advertising the "agreement of the armies" (CONSENSVS EXERCITVVM), the "loyalty of the armies" (FIDES EXERCITVVM), or—whether an example of wishful thinking or an attempt to reassure Vitellius' own legions—the "praetorians' readiness to make common cause" with the rebels (CONCORDIA PRAETORIANORVM).[1]

This indifference to decorum is better attributed to inadvertence than to policy. Whether we call it an unconventional, even self-destructive streak, or an ongoing failure to grasp the importance of observing the usages of polite society, odd behavior shows up in every generation of Vitellius' family. As Suetonius tells us, eulogists had equipped them with a pedigree stretching back into mythological times. Yet the first Vitellii in the historical record are supposed to have been two patrician brothers who led an unsuccessful conspiracy to restore Tarquin the Proud to his throne in Rome, even though their sister Vitellia was married to the virtuous Lucius Brutus who had driven out the tyrant (Plutarch is our source for this snippet). In fact, of course, there was no link between this trio and Vitellius' family, but there might as well have been. Though they were five centuries apart, the same kind of behavior resurfaced from the start. So the emperor's grandfather Publius Vitellius, a knight from Luceria (or Nuceria) in Apulia in southern Italy, was put in charge of Augustus' purse for a time. But if Dio is to be believed, he had a brother

Quintus who reached senatorial rank and yet had the bad taste to fight as a gladiator at games given by Augustus in Rome in 29 B.C.

Publius fathered four boys, Aulus, Quintus, Publius, and Lucius, but though all four reached senatorial rank, three of them negated this achievement. Publius began well but never reached the consulship, and when he died in 31, it was amid allegations of complicity in Sejanus' conspiracy against Tiberius. He need not have been guilty, but he was probably guilty of something. At the time he was prefect of the military treasury (*aerarium militare*), as Tacitus tells us, and he tried to commit suicide before dying of an illness brought on, apparently, by this bungled attempt to kill himself. Quintus was one of the six senators expelled or asked to resign from the order in 17, at the urging of Tiberius, for having bankrupted themselves by their extravagance. Aulus was almost blameless. He earned notoriety for the lavishness of his banquets, a detail preserved no doubt to indicate another genetic flaw inherited by his nephew to go along with the spendthrift ways of Uncle Quintus. But by dying of natural causes in the consulship he shared with Nero's father in 32, the elder Aulus avoided further indiscretions. Lucius, the emperor's father, alone showed outstanding ability and achieved outstanding success, not only overshadowing his brothers but also making his an impossible act for his sons to follow.

Consul for the first time in 34, Lucius was appointed governor of Syria with extraordinary powers, to conduct delicate negotiations with the king of Parthia, who was then threatening Rome's eastern frontier. So successful were his efforts that Lucius endeared himself both to Tiberius and, no mean feat, to his successor, Caligula. He found another use for his diplomatic skills when he returned to Rome in 40, the most notorious instance being his response to a question few others could have fielded. When asked by Caligula if he could see the Moon in the emperor's company, Vitellius replied promptly that "only you gods, Master, can see one another." Still, Lucius reached his apogee under Claudius, being consul ordinarius with the emperor twice (in 43 and 47), serving as his regent during the months Claudius was away on his British expedition, and holding the censorship with him in 47/48. Last heard of in 51, Lucius died soon after, of a stroke according to Suetonius, and was honored by Claudius with a state funeral and a statue bearing the inscription "of unshakable loyalty to his emperor."

Lucius married Sextilia, a woman of indifferent ancestry but monumental virtue. She needed the latter during her husband's life and she refused to forsake it after his death. Though Lucius was honest and energetic in his public life, he had no qualms about currying favor in the most outrageous manner, not only with the freedmen but also with the womenfolk of the imperial house. In Tiberius' reign he cultivated Antonia Minor, the mother of Claudius; and in Claudius' reign he charmed each of the emperor's wives, first Messallina and then Agrippina the Younger. Indeed, he played a major role in smoothing out the legal and religious problems created by Claudius' decision to marry his niece. Besides this, says Suetonius, he acquired a terrible reputation as a result of his passion for a freedwoman: "he even used to take her saliva, mixed with honey, as a soothing remedy when he had a sore throat, and this he did, not se- cretly or rarely, but openly every day."

Sextilia bore Lucius two sons, Aulus and Lucius. Of Lucius, the younger, we know only that, before 69, he usually followed in his brother's footsteps: they held the consulship for 48 one after the other (Aulus as ordinarius, Lucius as suffectus), and they governed the province Africa in sequence in the early 60s. Lucius made a good first marriage, to a great-great-granddaughter of Augustus, but that ended in divorce in 49. Subsequently, he married the less well born, if far more formidable Triaria, but they had no children—a nondevelopment for which those who knew Triaria should have been profoundly grateful. Lucius came into his own only in 69, and then because he was the emperor's brother. So he was "invited" to join Otho's entourage because he was too danger- ous to be left in Rome while the emperor conducted a campaign in north- ern Italy. And once his brother had won that war, he became his most stalwart defender.

The date of Aulus' birth is disputed. Suetonius reports that he was born, in Rome no doubt, on 7 or 24 September. The biographer prefers the later date, but the earlier is commonly held to be correct, largely because it provides what is thought a more satisfactory chronological datum for the campaign that began soon after his birthday in 69 and ended with his overthrow. There is similar uncertainty over the year, 12 or 15. Again Suetonius opts for the later date, but this time the earlier must be right if the emperor died at the age of 57, as a majority of our sources report. (One possible solution to the conundrum is to hold that the brothers' birthdates were confused, Aulus being born in 12 and Lucius in 15.) This kind of detail fascinates Suetonius anyway, even when he gets the answers wrong. But in Vitellius' case much more is involved. As Suetonius goes on to say, when the infant Aulus' horoscope was cast, his parents were appalled. The astrologers predicted that if Vitellius was given command of an army, the result would be disaster. Now, Suetonius is not above ridiculing astrologers, but he no more doubts astrology than those who sue doctors have lost faith in medicine. So he tells this tale, with an excess of circumstantial detail and—it appears—after consulta- tion with a friendly astrologer, because he has a very specific purpose in mind, to set the tone for a *Life* that must end badly. Like his placing Vitellius' proclamation on 2 instead of 3 January, this is one of the signs he attaches to his account at moments of crisis, to remind the reader that this emperor is doomed.

The story of the horoscope is probably true. It looks very much as though the emperor's father did all he could to prevent Aulus' being assigned a military province, and his mother gave him up for lost when he was sent to Germany in 68. It is also a fact not only that Aulus developed a strong dislike of astrologers (when he needed a prediction in later days, he called on a German prophetess), but also that he held no military post before 68. His duties as consul in 48 were civil and formal (and his father, as censor with Claudius that year, was able to ride herd on him). His proconsulate of Africa in the early 60s involved no formal links with the military forces stationed in the province. And the one other official post he is known to have held before going to Germany, that of curator of public works, also kept him firmly in Rome (the year for which he held this office is uncertain). Yet here too the contradictory nature supposedly innate in Vitellii came to the surface, if we believe Suetonius. His administration of Africa was distinguished by flawless integrity (a detail confirmed by Tacitus), but his curatorship was allegedly a scandal: "he was said to have stolen some of the offerings and ornaments from the state temples, and to have exchanged others, substituting tin and brass objects for the gold and silver originals." If the story is true, incidentally, he must have run through the money almost at once. He was already penniless when he set out for Lower Germany in the autumn of 68.

The same contradiction shows up in Aulus' marriages. In the mid-30s, when his father was governing Syria, out of sight but scarcely out of mind, Aulus married Petronia, a woman of prominent family whose father was to become another boon companion of Claudius. This marriage broke up around the time that Aulus' father died, coincidentally or not, and Petronia went on to marry Cornelius Dolabella, the kinsman of Galba. By Petronia, anyway, Aulus had a son who was blind in one eye and whom he subsequently poisoned. According to Suetonius' account, Petronia died fairly soon after she remarried, and in her will she left the boy some property on condition that his father emancipate him (hence his being named Vitellius Petronianus). Since this property would go to the father so long as the boy died without issue, Vitellius charged his son with an attempt to kill him, and the boy swallowed poison, according to Aulus a draught he had planned to administer to his loving parent. Whatever the truth of this tale, Aulus also remarried, taking as his wife Galeria Fundana, a relative of Otho's alleged speechwriter, Publius Galerius Trachalus. By her he had two children, a girl who was born first though we cannot establish when, and a boy who was six years old in 69. And he seems to have loved all three deeply, perhaps because his was a changeable nature, perhaps because this time he chose his partner.

As if this were not enough, Aulus is said to have been tall, a good thing, but out of proportion, a very bad sign. By the time he died, after 12 months of unrelenting self-indulgence, his face was flushed with his drinking and he had developed a potbelly. And he limped, another bad sign in the eyes of aristocrats who held strong views on the need for graceful deportment no less than a well-proportioned physique. Yet despite the maneuvering of his father, his mother's disapproval, an undistinguished career, one misadventure in matrimony, and off-putting looks, Vitellius found a way to reach the top. According to Suetonius, he became one of Tiberius' minions on Capri (this is a certainly untrue, and not merely because it is attached to a claim that his physical charms advanced his father's career). But to Caligula he endeared himself by sharing the emperor's passion for chariot racing (this was how he acquired his limp); to Claudius by showing the same enthusiasm for dicing; and to Nero by acting as a leader of the claque whose function it was to applaud the emperor's acting and singing.

None of this proves that Vitellius was unversed in the etiquette expected of senators, although a few anecdotes we have about his conduct in senate meetings before and after his elevation suggest that it was so. There is no evidence that he developed a contempt for the senate and senatorial values to match that the senate showed for him, the contempt that induced Galba to make him governor of Lower Germany in the first place. Rather, he seems to have been as awkward in his dealing with his peers as he was ungainly in his appearance and, for that matter, clumsy in expressing himself (Tacitus never gives him a speech). Nor would the snooty upper reaches of Roman society have been reassured if, like Claudius, he compensated for this with the "common touch" so evident in his journey to and his first month in Lower Germany. All in all, it seems reasonable to argue that despite the gusto Aulus displayed during the first month of his new command, he soon found—and knew—himself to be out of his depth. Overcome by the troops' hailing him emperor, a step he had neither sought nor anticipated, he may even have gone into a kind of fugue. It is as good an explanation as any for his falling into what Tacitus calls a torpor, in which, day after day, "he anticipated his elevation to the principate in luxurious idleness and lavish banquets, tipsy by noon and stuffed with food."

Even if Vitellius paid insufficient attention to the proprieties, his personal failings alone do not explain this disregard for decorum. We must also take into account his two self-appointed lieutenants, Caecina and Valens, both largely unconcerned with gentlemanly behavior. Normally, the position of legionary legate was given to men who had held the praetorship, that is, to men who were launched on their political careers but not yet assured of high office, provided always that this is what they sought. If things went well, they held the post normally for two or three years, in their early to mid-thirties, when they were thought old enough to be aware of their duties, but too young and, perhaps, too "unsocialized" to be entrusted with a major command or another senior position, one more reason no doubt for making them answerable directly to the governor of the province in which their legion was stationed. But the system was not yet set in stone, and there were two types of exception to this rule, both likely to involve misfits.

The first category was represented by men who reached this post much earlier in life, as did Caecina—and as did Vespasian's son Titus. Josephus tells us that Vespasian had frequently to rebuke Titus for his rashness. Caecina was even more of a handful. From Vicetia, a small village north of Verona, he was a good-looking young man, probably around 26 years old (as quaestor of Baetica he should have been 25 in 68). He must have been over six feet tall, as his height is said to have been as enormous as his ambitions, and the latter were fanned hugely by Galba, when the latter rewarded him for his services in Spain by making him a legionary legate. In Germany his temperament above all endeared him to the troops. Fast-talking and impetuous, he was open, generous, energetic, and undeniably charismatic. He was also an adventurer. The moment he was threatened with indictment for embezzlement, he concluded that he had nothing to lose by encouraging Galba's overthrow, and everything to gain from a display of military prowess on Vitellius' behalf. Glory, high office, and influence at court would all be his at an impressively early age, he seems to have believed, so long as he seized every opportunity for deeds of derring-do.

The second kind of misfit was represented by the men who received the appointment later in life. Two who clearly fall into this category, Titus Vinius and Marcus Antonius Primus (Galba's appointee to VII Galbiana), had suffered setbacks in their career, and were impatient with or contemptuous of a system they could blame for holding them back. Fabius Valens apparently fell into this category too, for all that he traveled a different route. Tacitus tells us that he was born of an equestrian family from Anagnia (Anagni) in Latium and spent his youth in poverty. Completely immoral but by no means unintelligent (Tacitus' wording), Valens caught Nero's eye at the "Festival of Youth" in 59. So he decided to win himself a reputation as a man of the world by his rakishness, and then parlayed this somehow into a senatorial career and an appointment as legionary legate of I Germanica. Since Tacitus states explicitly that Valens was "an old man" in 69, he should have been in his forties. The troops found him too crafty to trust and too tight-fisted to like, but his skills and his delight lay in intrigue and manipulation, as is evident from his dealings with Verginius Rufus, Fonteius Capito, and now Vitellius. And Valens saw a war against Galba as a way of taking revenge on an emperor who had treated him shoddily, of gratifying his taste for plunder and satisfying his varied sexual appetites, and of securing entry into the upper reaches of the senate by gaining high office.

Even a strong-willed commander would have found it difficult to control Caecina and Valens. Vitellius never stood a chance. So the uprising was masterminded by two men who never considered playing by the established rules. One reason for Tacitus' almost unremitting contempt for Vitellius, in fact, seems to spring from the conviction that he allowed these two to run wild. And it is for the same reason that Suetonius' *Life* of Vitellius lacks much substantive detail. Under the rules laid down for biography, the writer omitted matters handled by the friends or subordinates of his subject. So Suetonius ignored almost every action taken by Caecina and Valens, and could capture the tenor of the new administration only with the vague assertion that Vitellius conducted his eight-month reign "largely according to the whims of actors and charioteers."

Once Vitellius had been proclaimed emperor, there could be no going back. So long as Galba held power in Rome, there was no hope of negotiation, and the Rhine legions would not learn of his assassination until the last days of January. Now Tacitus, for much of the time our only guide to the opening moves in this campaign, brings out the enthusiasm of the soldiery at the start by drawing a vivid contrast between the urgency with which they demanded action and the lethargy of their commander. Making his point in a manner worthier of Plutarch, he declares that the soldiery would brook no delays: "winter was no obstacle, nor hesitancy about breaking a peace only cowards would observe; they must invade Italy at once and seize control of Rome itself." The contrast between emperor and soldiery has tended to overshadow the implications of the phrase "hesitancy about breaking a peace only cowards would observe." We could dismiss it as a rhetorical flourish, or see it as a reference to Vitellius' reluctance to take action. But as Tacitus revels in conveying important information obliquely, the remark probably reflects a disagreement, not between Vitellius and his troops, but between his officers, a disagreement similar to the one that would preoccupy the Flavian commanders in September.

The basic point is simple. Given a choice, Roman armies tended to avoid campaigning in winter. So it would not be surprising if some—a majority even—of the Vitellian officers argued for delaying the start of their campaign until the weather improved. In Germany they would not have suspected that the winter of 68/69 would be unusually mild. The counterargument, that neither winter nor delay would serve their purposes, can be attributed to Vitellius' two henchmen. Caecina must almost certainly have thought that to launch an offensive forthwith would get things off to a dashing start befitting his self-image. Valens may have been less enthusiastic, but he could not afford to let himself be outshone by Caecina, an interloper who was taking advantage of the plotting Valens had fostered for so long. This could even have been the spark that ignited Valens' dislike for Caecina and prompted him to engage in the feuding that would continue almost unabated until his death. So even if their motives differed, these two probably urged immediate action, because that alone could bring them the immediate advancement they coveted.

It was by no means unrealistic for the Vitellians to imagine that they could win a victory in any war they fought. The Rhine legions were considered to be, and may have been, the finest troops in the empire. They quickly won important support too. Although governors and commanders in the nearby provinces had no choice but to join them, their first supporters seem to have been genuinely enthusiastic. They included the governor of Belgica, Valerius Asiaticus, whose reward was briefly to be Vitellius' son-in-law; Galba's choice as governor of Lugdunensis, Junius Blaesus; and the commander of I Italica in Lugdunum, Manlius Valens, probably 63 years old and apparently a career military man. There was the promise of aid from Britain as well, but as the governor, Trebellius Maximus, was feuding with his legionary legates, detachments from the British legions would arrive only after the campaign against Otho had been won. Meanwhile, the resources to fund the war were volunteered not only by the Lingones and the Treveri, but by the leading men of nearby communities, Roman and indigenous, and even by the troops themselves. Of their own accord they contributed their savings and their decorations of gold and silver.[2]

The plan of campaign, surely worked out by Caecina and Valens in the headquarters at Colonia Agrippinensis, was straightforward, to dispatch two columns to Italy by two different routes, and to crush any opposition. Henderson claimed that behind this there lay an ambitious two-pronged strategy, designed sooner or later to envelop the enemy in a pincer movement. Such interpretations are anachronistic. Strategy as we understand it had not been invented, and Roman generals, like Roman military manuals, seldom functioned or needed to function at anything above the tactical level. And the Vitellians' plan was based on sound

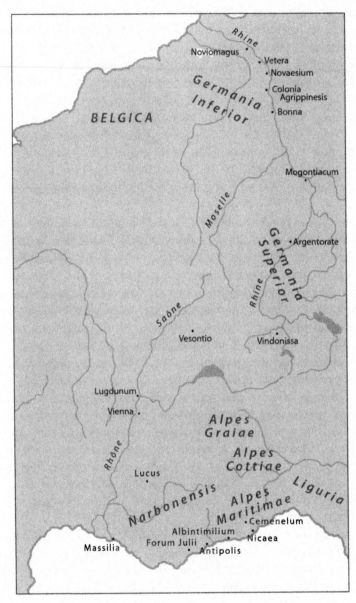

The Germanies and the French Riviera Coast

tactical thinking. Splitting the invasion force would ease supply problems, for the troops as well as for the communities across whose lands they marched. And two relatively small columns could make better speed than one large one on the trek to Italy, this when speed was of the essence.

No matter how old and helpless the Vitellians believed Galba to be, they recognized that he must respond vigorously to any threat of invasion. To keep him off balance and win the war, therefore, they had to achieve two objectives as rapidly as possible. First, they had to cross the Alps as soon as the passes opened. Depending on the weather, this could happen at any time between March and May. Since the winter of 68/69 was mild, the passes were already open in March and Caecina would take advantage of this. But it looks as if he and Valens based their original plan on a crossing in April (this being one reason why Valens prolonged his march through Gaul). Now, the earlier they crossed the Alps, the sooner they could achieve their second objective, seizing control of northern Italy. So long as Galba and any armies he summoned to his aid followed the rule book and began serious preparations around the start of the campaigning season in March (not quite, but near enough to the procedure Otho would adopt), the two Vitellian columns would be able to combine, to defeat the scratch forces Galba could assemble in Italy itself, and to avert a fight with any reinforcements summoned from outside the peninsula by presenting them with a *fait accompli.*

Tacitus does not say that the two columns were supposed to coordinate their arrival in northern Italy, to carry out the second part of this plan for a *blitzkrieg*, but he probably took that for granted. To achieve their aim, Caecina and Valens would have had to finalize their plan before leaving Germany, since communications between them would have been impossible en route. It is not significant that Tacitus talks of Vitellius' following the two columns with "the main weight of the attack." That part of the scheme was a sop to the emperor's vanity. Caecina and Valens disposed of ample troops with which to win the one decisive battle necessary, and they had every incentive to win it before Vitellius arrived. It is no more significant that Caecina had to cover only about a third of the distance Valens' column would march, since he had to traverse more arduous terrain. And if we accept the idea that when the two men laid their plans in Germany, they had no inkling that the weather would prove so mild, it is not surprising that Caecina started his offensive a month or so before Valens arrived. He was given an unexpected chance to secure a foothold in northern Italy. Even had he found military reasons for ignoring his good fortune, his rivalry with Valens and his high opinion of his own skills would never have let him do so.

Valens commanded a force drawn from the legions of Lower Germany. This comprised the bulk of legion V Alaudae, probably 4,000 men, and detachments of between 2,000 and 2,600 men apiece from the three other units in the province, I Germanica, XV Primigenia, and XVI.[3] He was also given auxiliary forces, numbering between 10,000 and 12,000 men and including the eight Batavian cohorts that, previously attached to XIV Gemina Martia Victrix, had prevented that legion from supporting Nero in his last days. (They were to prove just as unruly during this campaign.) The first task assigned to the column was to march south through Gaul, winning over the inhabitants wherever possible and reducing those who resisted—and it seemed likely that there would be some resistance. The governors of Belgica and Lugdunensis had sworn allegiance to Vitellius, but there were also the provinces of Aquitania and Narbonensis in the south, and both declared for Otho until the threat of force brought them to their senses. Then the column was to invade Italy from the west, by way of the Mont Genèvre Pass (1,860 m), and to emerge near Augusta Taurinorum (Turin).

Caecina was entrusted with a column drawn from the units in Upper Germany. It was built around an entire legion that had played no visible part in the uprising, XXI Rapax at Vindonissa (Windisch in Switzerland). This seems to have made the men all the more eager to demonstrate their prowess. In addition he was given detachments, again between 2,000 and 2,600 men strong, from IV Macedonica and XXII Primigenia, and auxiliary units totaling some 9,000 to 10,000 men. Setting out from Vindonissa, he was to march southward through the territory of the Helvetians on the western flank of the province Raetia (more or less equivalent to Switzerland). And since no resistance was anticipated there, he was to cross into Italy by way of the Great St. Bernard Pass (2,428 m), and so emerge not far from Mediolanum (Milan).[4]

On the day Valens' column set out, Tacitus tells us, the commander and his men were vastly encouraged by a good omen. For many miles an eagle flew ahead of the column, as if to guide the troops on their way, and it was neither upset nor frightened away when the men raised cheer after cheer. No doubt the incident happened (Suetonius reports it too), and no doubt the troops were delighted to watch a bird whose representation topped the standard of every legion. For us, however, it might have been more helpful had Tacitus specified when exactly the column left Colonia Agrippinensis. As it is, we can only guess, but a date between 12 and 15 January seems likely. The units in Lower Germany ought to have needed about two weeks to get ready for the march south, and to take care of other business too, for example, dealing with Pompeius Propinquus, the loyalist procurator of Belgica, and the four centurions of XXII Primigenia who had tried to stop their troops overthrowing Galba's statues.

Tacitus gives us a detailed account of Valens' itinerary through much of Gaul. Hence we can plot his progress even on a map of modern France, since the column followed in sequence the lines of the Rivers Rhine, Moselle, Saône, and Rhône. Tacitus depicts the march very much as a descent into anarchy, a chapter of accidents, each demonstrating more clearly than its predecessor Valens' loss of control over his men and over himself. The slide began when the troops reached Divodurum (Metz), the principal town of the Mediomatrici. Here they suddenly set about slaughtering the inhabitants, not from a wish for plunder, but "from a kind of madness difficult to diagnose and so all the more difficult to stop." Some 4,000 natives were supposedly killed before the troops were calmed by their general's entreaties. Yet there was an upside. This incident so terrorized the rest of the country that, from now on, every community would open its gates without delay and all but grovel in the dirt the moment the column appeared.

News of Galba's murder and Otho's accession reached the column as it was marching through the territory of the Leuci, in the neighborhood of Tullum (Toul), apparently toward the end of January. The news made no difference. The troops were neither alarmed that Otho had seized power in Rome nor gratified that Galba was dead. They wanted war, and when they moved into the territory of the Lingones, the joy with which these allies received them turned quickly to consternation. Here Valens picked up the eight Batavian cohorts that had been assigned to his column (they had wintered in the area), and a fight soon broke out between the legionaries and the Batavians. The latter never tired of boasting how they had prevented legion XIV Gemina Martia Victrix from aiding Nero and so how they had determined the outcome of that war. Much as the legionaries respected the Batavians' fighting abilities, they found their arrogance hard to swallow. Hence the fight, which imperiled the tribesmen caught in the middle, and would allegedly have evolved into a full-scale battle, had not Valens intervened and restored order by punishing a few of the auxiliaries.

For all the havoc the Vitellians caused in the lands of their allies, they were unable to find a pretext for attacking a tribe that qualified as an enemy, Vindex's erstwhile friends the Aedui, who lay to the west of their line of march. The Aedui not only handed over the money and matériel asked of them, but contributed supplies too. What the tribesmen did from fear, says Tacitus, the population of Lugdunum (Lyon) did from joy. It too was cut short, however, when Valens decided to incorporate into his column the principal forces stationed in the city, legion I Italica and the *ala Tauriana*, its squadron of auxiliary cavalry, and to leave behind only the resident urban cohort (*cohors XVIII urbana*). This move nearly cost him dear. The inhabitants seized this opportunity to even scores with their hated rivals, the people of Vienna (Vienne), spurred on all the more by the fact that in this feud the Viennenses then had the upper hand. When Lugdunum had shut its gates against Vindex in 68, the Viennenses had promptly supported the rebel, and had been richly rewarded by Galba at Lugdunum's expense.

The moment the citizenry learnt of Valens' decision, they began working on the sympathies of his men. Stressing the help the Viennenses had given Vindex, they exaggerated beyond recognition the threat they posed to a Lugdunum stripped of its garrison. So successful was their agitation that the troops were eager to march on Vienne and sack the town. Valens naturally tried to stop this. He may have recognized that the allegations were largely rhetoric, deriving his knowledge from Manlius Valens, as legate of I Italica the man on the spot. But since he disencumbered himself promptly of his namesake, it is just as likely that Valens thought the locals' complaints justified and refused to act anyway. He could argue that legion I Italica made a welcome addition to the strength of his column, whereas leaving the unit behind in Lugdunum risked exposing his rear to attack one day. (Since the legion had been created by Nero and stationed at Lugdunum by Galba, it had no close ties with the Vitellians.) Then too, Vienne was a Roman settlement, however barbarous the citizens of Lugdunum made it out to be. Sacking the town would do irreparable damage to the Vitellian cause, and Valens' soldiers could scarcely make good progress on the march to Italy if laden down with plunder. Yet, says Tacitus, the men were so out of control that the Viennenses saved themselves only by coming out to meet the army and making an abject surrender—in the traditional Roman manner.

Since this had the desired effect on the troops' emotions, their feelings swung to the opposite extreme. It does not matter whether the men were really as fickle and as changeable as our sources declare when they describe scenes like this. What counts is that their leaders thought them so, and had to guard against yet another swing of the pendulum. While Valens disarmed the town and made the citizenry furnish supplies of all kinds, therefore, he also decided to pay the troops 300 sesterces apiece (one-third of their annual pay). Where he found the ten to twelve million sesterces he needed Tacitus does not say, but he probably raised it from the hapless Viennenses. From now on, however, there were to be persistent and disruptive rumors that Valens had enriched himself too. Whether they were true it is difficult to say. That Valens had not wanted the Viennenses to suffer is no proof that his hands were clean or his pockets empty. Conversely, if he made a huge profit in this way, it seems a little strange that, as Tacitus puts it, he trafficked openly in march routes and camp sites in the later stages of the march, and even threatened to burn down Lucus Augusti (Luc-en-Diois), if his demands were not met. Perhaps despoiling the hapless Viennenses whetted his appetite for cash. Or perhaps the poverty of his youth and the strength of these rumors encouraged him to live up to the reputation he had acquired.

At this point, probably around the end of February, Tacitus breaks off his account of the column's progress. Yet Lucus Augusti lay in the territory of the Vocontii, several hundred miles and three weeks short of the Alps. For this there seem to be three reasons. First, since the column would continue on its merry way until it reached Turin, Tacitus thought it unnecessary to mention it again until it had to deal with Otho's maritime expedition. Second, the degeneration in the behavior of men and general alike was now complete, and Tacitus has made his point. And third, as Tacitus tells the story, the nadir in the conduct of Valens' column is juxtaposed with the low point in the behavior of Caecina's force, and that low point occurred at the very start of the march. For he presents Caecina's expedition as the reverse of Valens', with a progression from the indiscipline of legion XXI Rapax to the masterful generalship with which Caecina took his men through enemy territory and Alps alike.

Tacitus says nothing about Caecina's opening moves. Though the meeting at which he and Valens settled their plans must have been held in Vitellius' HQ at Colonia Agrippinensis, there was no point in Caecina's tagging along with Valens' column on the march south. He may have ridden to Mogontiacum, to pick up the detachments from IV Macedonica and XXII Primigenia, and then marched to Vindonissa. Or he may have ordered these detachments to catch up with him by forced marches while he rode straight to Vindonissa. Either way, XXI Rapax had already started a war with the Helvetii. According to Tacitus, the tribesmen were unaware of Galba's death and refused to acknowledge the troops' right to demand campaign contributions from them. So when some legionaries seized the money being sent to a small fort the Helvetii maintained on the northern frontier of the province, the tribesmen retaliated by intercepting a small party under a centurion that was carrying letters from the German legions to those in Pannonia, and threw it in prison. At this point Caecina arrived and, "greedy for war," decided to punish the culprits before they could ask for forgiveness. He sent orders to the auxiliary infantry and cavalry forces stationed on the far side of the Helvetians' territory to attack from the rear, and marched his force down the Aare valley, killing all who opposed him, devastating their lands, and desstroying Aquae

Helveticae (Baden), a picturesque village already known for its healing springs.

The Helvetii were no longer the formidable fighters who had faced Caesar a century before. Though defiant at first, they panicked as soon as they were attacked, and since they could not agree on a coordinated plan of resistance, they were crushingly defeated in one engagement after another. When they fled for refuge to the Mons Vocetius (perhaps the Bötzberg, on the left bank of the Aare about half way between Basel and Zürich), they were promptly dislodged by a cohort of Thracian auxiliaries. And when they scattered in the forests, they were hunted down or winkled out of their hiding places by German and Raetian auxiliaries. For the Vitellians the campaign was so obviously a walk-over that Tacitus may be right to claim that "many thousands were killed, many thousands sold into slavery." Yet all this happened before Caecina even approached their principal settlement, Aventicum (Avenches). Unsurprisingly, its leading citizens surrendered the town unconditionally the moment he appeared at the gates.

Caecina wound up this campaign by putting to death only one man, Julius Alpinus, alleging that he was responsible for the war. All the other dignitaries he rounded up were sent to Vitellius for judgment and, as Tacitus gleefully reports, they escaped with their lives, thanks largely to the emperor's ineptitude. Vitellius thought he had an open-and-shut case on his hands and did not expect even a high-born provincial to be much of an orator. So he let the culprits plead their case before the soldiery, and their spokesman, a certain Claudius Cossus, delivered a first-class speech. This worked so effectively on the feelings of the troops that, overcome by unreasoning sentimentality, they pressured Vitellius into pardoning the offenders.

Caecina probably spent ten more days in Helvetian territory, partly to complete the pacification of the area, partly to rest his men after a campaign that, though short, had been strenuous. Here he received the unexpected news that a squadron of auxiliary cavalry in northern Italy had declared for Vitellius. This was the *ala Siliana*, quartered in the neighborhood of the River Po as a result of all the to-ing and fro-ing that preceded Nero's death. Neither the officers nor the men knew anything of Otho, but they had served in Africa when Vitellius governed the province in the early 60s. Besides, they were far more impressed by the strength and the reputation of the Rhine legions than they were with the scratch forces Otho was assembling. The vital point, however, is that as a pledge of their loyalty they also brought over to Vitellius four key towns in the area north of the river, Eporedia, Vercellae, Novaria, and Mediolanum (Ivrea, Vercelli, Novara, and Milan). Recognizing that a unit of 500 men could hardly hold down four towns unaided, Caecina at once sent on ahead a batch of auxiliary infantry (Gallic, Lusitanian, and British cohorts), detachments of German tribesmen (it is unclear if infantry, cavalry, or both are meant), and a cavalry squadron he knew from Mogontiacum, the *ala Petriana*.

In the meantime, so says Tacitus, Caecina briefly contemplated marching across the width of Raetia and invading the neighboring province of Noricum (Austria). Its procuratorial governor, Petronius Urbicus, had assembled all the auxiliary forces at his disposal and had broken down the bridges leading into his province, and so "was thought to be loyal to Otho." This account Henderson elaborated into an ambitious strategical plan, formulated now by Caecina, to traverse Noricum, to turn south into the Transpadana through the Brenner Pass, to drive a wedge between Otho's forces in Italy and any support he planned drawing from the Balkan provinces, and to catch the Othonians in Italy between his own army and that of Valens, when the latter emerged from the western end of the Alps. No matter how seductive the thesis may appear, it is mistaken, if only because Tacitus reports the episode in a way showing clearly that Caecina gave only passing thought to an incursion into Noricum. What, then, did Caecina have in mind? If Caecina and Valens had agreed that they would enter northern Italy on a specified date, and if Caecina was well ahead of schedule (as he was), he probably viewed an attack on Noricum as a splendid way of keeping the troops busy until it came time to cross the Alps.

On further reflection, Caecina decided not only to abandon his plans for Noricum but also to ignore any idea of timing his arrival in northern Italy to coincide with that of Valens. Even without jealousy to spur him on, he had sound military reasons to press ahead. The Alpine passes were already open or, at least, traversable without undue difficulty. He had four towns in the Transpadana under his control and, though reinforced, they would not be able to withstand a sustained Othonian assault such as could be made if he dallied north of the Alps. If he marched into Italy forthwith, on the other hand, he could use the towns as bases from which to make further conquests. So Caecina decided, before the middle of March as far as we can tell, to lead his legionaries through the Great St. Bernard.

Tacitus devotes a single sentence to this trek: "Caecina led his legionaries, in formation and laden down with baggage, through the Alps while they were still wintry." As a result, he is often criticized for an indifference to terrain and for belittling Caecina's magnificent achievement. This is unjustifiable. Even if the winter of 68/69 had not been mild, there would have been nothing particularly epic about what was in

fact the third crossing of the pass. The trip had already been made from
south to north by the messengers of the *ala Siliana*, and from north to
south by the auxiliaries Caecina sent to reinforce the squadron. By Tacitus'
day too, elaborate descriptions of armies struggling through the Alps
were trite beyond belief. And most important of all, Tacitus recognized
that the telling detail was not the crossing of the mountains, even if it
was made much earlier than expected by friend or foe. It was Caecina's
popping out of the Alps, like a genie out of a bottle, larger than life in his
parti-colored cloak and his Gallic trousers.

5

Otho Prepares for War
(January and February)

When Otho assassinated Galba on 15 January, he may have had no idea how serious the situation in Germany had become. Galba, from 9 January on, tried to restrict the information he was receiving to his immediate entourage, and—despite Plutarch—Otho cannot have been invited to their meetings. In public, before the guard and in the senate, Galba talked only of a mutiny by two legions. Since mutinies had been brought under control fairly easily in the past, Otho had no more reason than anybody else outside the charmed circle to imagine that this outbreak would be different, especially once he began planning to remove the man everybody thought the source of the troops' grievances. No doubt he heard the rumors circulating through the city, but he could discount them. Hence Suetonius can tell a story about his own father: Suetonius Laetus served as a military tribune in the war against Vitellius, and he asserted repeatedly that during the campaign "Otho had stated that he would not have made away with Galba, had he not been confident that he could carry through the business without a war."

Still, there is another way of taking Suetonius Laetus' story. It is possible that Vinius was leaking the information from Germany to Otho as fast as it came in. This would not contradict Tacitus' statement that the messages became common knowledge only after Galba's death. But even if we assume that Otho knew of Vitellius' activities, it would not follow that his seizure of power was "an act of consummate and suicidal folly."[1] Vitellius was notoriously a glutton and a sluggard, and the correspondence between the two men suggests that Otho started from the assumption that Vitellius would back down when presented with a *fait accompli*, perhaps pleading as a face-saving measure that his quarrel had been only with Galba. What apparently occurred neither to Otho nor to anybody else for that matter is that gluttons and sluggards do not start revolts, and can hardly be expected to halt them once they get under way. Otho, that is, assessed his rival correctly, but failed to allow for—and without more information could not have allowed for—the influence of Caecina and Valens.

Then too, Otho could not have anticipated that these two would throw away the rule book. Since the assassination of Galba fell in mid-January, and Romans began campaigns normally only in March or April, Otho probably fancied that he had two months or so to rally support. And the same assumption was probably made by the legions he summoned to his aid from the Balkans: Tacitus states explicitly that they arrived late because they did not bestir themselves as they should have done. Again, when Romans believed that what happened in Rome was more important than what occurred elsewhere, and Otho was the emperor in Rome, he could appeal to governors and army commanders throughout the empire and expect them to obey. As many did. He was recognized by the men in charge of a whole string of distant provinces (Dalmatia, Pannonia, Moesia, Syria, Judaea, Egypt, and Africa). And initially he received assurances of support even from the governors of provinces practically under the eyes of the Rhine legions, Narbonese Gaul, Aquitania, and Hispania Tarraconensis. For some of these men possession was nine-tenths of the law. Others, Tacitus says, accepted Otho because they heard of his elevation before they learnt of Vitellius'. But since they accepted him, Otho had reason to believe that if Vitellius challenged him, he would have the time and the troops to meet that challenge. To hold that Otho responded too late to the threat from Caecina and Valens misstates the case.

Otho would not give up easily. At 36 years old, he was not an imposing figure. Suetonius reports that he was of medium height, not a desirable quality in an emperor, whatever the average height of the population.[2] He was also splay footed and bandy legged, and as his hair was thin, he wore "a wig so carefully fashioned and fitted to his head than no one suspected it." The feature on which the sources dwell, however, is his "almost womanish" concern for his appearance. Not only was his body depilated. For fear of looking as if he had not shaved (shaving had been the fashion for some two centuries, and would continue so until Hadrian's time), he smeared his face with bread poultices every day, a practice used by Roman women to whiten and tighten the skin. Otho's soldiers never took his behavior amiss, but what we should make of this is another question. The praetorians, after all, had been schooled by Nero to expect such conduct from young men of fashion, and they were themselves open to similar charges. Before long Vitellius' legionaries would dismiss them too as effeminate idlers. On the other hand, neither Otho nor his followers were to fight like fops and dandies, and to that extent there is reason to doubt the assessments of those with a more austere cast of mind, men like Galba as well as Plutarch.

However much or little Otho knew of Vitellius' activities on 15 January, as emperor he had to deal first with problems closer to home, the soldiers and the civilians in the city. Once Galba, Vinius, and Piso had been murdered—so says Tacitus, reveling in the ludicrous picture his words summon up—senators, knights, and people emerged from their hiding places and raced one another to the praetorian camp, every one of them fearful of being the last to congratulate the new emperor. They maligned Galba, they praised the soldiers' "judgment," and they kissed Otho's hand. Neither Otho nor his troops were deceived by this onset of loyalty, and the latter supposedly wanted to kill these civilians out of hand. But though Tacitus concedes that Otho was able "by his voice and his expression" to hold the men in check, he plays up the difficulty the new emperor faced in trying to save Marius Celsus from the wrath of praetorians angry that he had been one of Galba's most faithful supporters. He did so only by pretending to reserve the man for direr punishment in the future. "Otho had the standing to order a crime, but not the standing to prevent one."

This assessment sets the tone for Tacitus' presentation of Otho as a ruler whose freedom of action was limited constantly by his links with the guard. This did not make him putty in their hands. It was a symbiotic relationship. Otho needed the praetorians, and needed always to consider their preferences and prejudices, because they were his most devoted and valuable supporters, and loyalty was not to be disregarded in a civil war. And the guardsmen pinned their hopes on Otho, and refused resolutely to trust their officers or the senatorial generals Otho would place over them. Time and again they would decide that these officers and generals were dragging their feet, if not actively obstructing or conspiring against the emperor. Sometimes these suspicions were baseless, sometimes they were not. But they invariably made it difficult for Otho to win over other elements in the population as fully as he would have liked.

The relationship between Otho and the guard is illustrated by the events in the praetorian camp after the murders. Putting the worst interpretation on the situation, Tacitus asserts that "the soldiers now had the last word on everything that was done." Yet when we look at the steps taken, we see neither a soldiery out of control nor an emperor forced to yield to their whims. True, the guard seized the chance to pick new commanders for themselves, choosing Plotius Firmus and Licinius Proculus to be their prefects, and Flavius Sabinus as prefect of the city and commander of the urban cohorts.[3] The one objection that could be raised to this lay in the fact that all three men were elected from below rather than designated from above. The choices were reasonable. Plotius Firmus had risen from a ranker or a junior officer to the prefectship of the watch, but this rapid advancement was due to Otho's predecessors. And since Firmus had supported Otho when Galba was still alive, it was by no means extraordinary for him to move up to prefect of the guard. (Tigellinus had done the same in Nero's reign.) Of Licinius Proculus we know only that he was a close associate of Otho, elected because *presumed* to have been an accomplice in the coup. It would emerge later that he was an energetic soldier only on the parade ground, but prefects of the guard were seldom chosen for their military skills. As for Flavius Sabinus, he had served two terms as commander of the urban cohorts under Nero. Galba had replaced him with Ducenius Geminus. Whether or not Geminus survived the bloodletting of 15 January, he could scarcely keep his post. So Sabinus was an obvious choice and, as he was a mediocrity, a safe one too.

Similar reservations can be made apropos of the other issue raised at this time. In all Rome's armed forces many centurions were supplementing their already considerable income by granting the men time off and exemption from fatigues only in return for the payment of sizable sums. The more money a ranker had, the more determined the centurions were to relieve him of it, until—says Tacitus—every soldier was reduced to a penury he could alleviate only by taking up banditry or menial work. The guard seized their opportunity to clamor for an end to this abuse, and Otho could not ignore their wishes. But since he could not afford to alienate the centurions either, he offered a compromise. From now on the imperial purse would pay the centurions enough to make up for the sums they had been extorting, and the men would be granted their rights free of charge. Even Tacitus concedes that this was "undoubtedly an excellent scheme, later established as a permanent rule of the service by good emperors."

The interesting aspect of Tacitus' narrative, nonetheless, is what he fails to say. It is a minor point that nothing indicates that Vitellius had already taken the same steps in Lower Germany, proving that this complaint was not raised only by allegedly venal praetorians. That detail turns up later. What is significant is that Tacitus mentions neither promises nor payment of a donative, though the money was probably available. According to Suetonius, the first document Otho signed as emperor was a grant for 50 million sesterces to help complete Nero's opulent palace, the Golden House. Whether or not this sum was raised by confiscating Vinius' ill-gotten gains, it could readily have been diverted to the guard. For all the praetorians' resentment over Galba's refusing them the donative Nymphidius had promised, they demanded no money now. Perhaps they believed Galba's murder reward enough. Perhaps they thought that his death canceled the promises made by Nymphidius—though this would not have absolved Otho from paying a donative to mark his own accession. Or perhaps they regarded the ending of the abuses to which they had been subjected by their centurions as adequate recompense. No matter how we explain their conduct, the lack of demands for a donative proves that the troops were by no means out of control, the emperor by no means their helpless victim.

Once Otho had reassured the soldiery, he made his way from the camp to a senate meeting, to dispel the apprehensions of his peers. We need not credit the story of Dio's epitomator Zonaras, that the soldiery paraded the heads of Otho's victims through the house. It was bad enough that the corpses lay in the Forum when the meeting was called. But Otho may have claimed that the praetorians had made him emperor against his wishes (this story appears in Suetonius and in Dio's other epitomator, Xiphilinus), and so prompted Tacitus' statement that "the soldiers had the last word on everything that was done." But since a reluctance to take power or even a refusal of power (*recusatio imperii*) was a standard feature of the rhetoric employed on such occasions, it is possible that Tacitus was offended, not by what took place in the camp, but by Otho's spending so much time there instead of going at once to the senate. Like Galba, Otho made the senators wait while he took care of other business. But then, again like Galba, he may have recognized that the senators needed time to assemble. Whatever the truth, Tacitus focuses on the behavior of the audience. Magistrates and senators, he declares, fell over themselves to ensure that Otho was granted the powers of an emperor, and each speaker attempted to paper over any insults or reproaches he had voiced against Otho in the past.

In one sense their servility was predictable. When Romans harbored grudges as a matter of course, Otho's former critics were very awkwardly placed. Plutarch, surprisingly, states flatly that nobody was given the impression that Otho bore a grudge against him, but he loses this senate meeting in the switch from the *Galba* to the *Otho*. Tacitus places the question firmly in the context of this meeting, and promptly undercuts its effect by adding that, since Otho's reign was so brief, senators never discovered whether he had put aside his enmities, or was waiting for a more suitable occasion to gratify them. The issue is important, because the innuendo reflects a way of thinking to which senators were perhaps especially prone. It was not just that people at every level of Roman society were horrified by the fact as well as the manner of Galba's assassination, and accepted Otho out of fear more than conviction, let alone affection. No matter what Otho claimed, many were convinced that individuals could no more change their behavior patterns than leopards can their spots. It followed that Otho would not try "to run on honorable lines a principate he had gained by evil means." He had killed before and he could kill again. Until time proved otherwise, it was safest and easiest to conclude that he was only playing the role of a good emperor.

As best we can tell, nonetheless, Otho had planned a coup that would remove only Galba, his heir, and the three pedagogues—hence the roundabout manner of Laco's execution later. So when the predictable demands began for a more general settling of accounts, as one group or another clamored for the execution of this alleged criminal or that, Otho's first and showiest move was to summon Marius Celsus to a ceremony held on the Capitol on the morning of 16 January. In this Otho spared Celsus' life and praised his loyalty to Galba explicitly. In fact, he made Celsus one of his own intimates and, before too long, one of his principal generals. Even the soldiery, says Tacitus, were impressed by Celsus' unswerving fidelity to Galba, although that was what had aroused their hostility to him in the first place. The pardoning of Celsus, in other words, was supposed to be a programmatic act that set the character for Otho's reign.

This done, Otho could yield to widespread demands for the execution of Tigellinus. The ex-prefect may have dropped out of sight in Nero's last days, but he had not dropped out of mind. He had survived the clamor for his execution in Galba's reign not only by making a deal with Vinius, but also by withdrawing to Sinuessa, a spa where he was taking the waters. Tacitus minimizes Otho's role in the affair (it is not clear why), but it was a letter from the emperor that ordered Tigellinus to commit suicide. After an unsuccessful attempt to bribe his way out of his predicament, Tigellinus "delayed shamefully amid the embraces and kisses of his concubines, and at last cut his throat with a razor, disgracing an infamous life with a tardy and dishonorable death." Apparently emboldened by Otho's giving up Tigellinus, the people shouted for the execution of Calvia Crispinilla too, Nero's "mistress of orgies" and the woman who had stirred up Clodius Macer, the errant legionary legate of III Augusta in Africa. This demand Otho refused, in part no doubt because, unlike Galba, he was reluctant to kill women, in part because it ran counter to his claims that he wanted no more deaths among persons of consequence. But as Tacitus observes, there was also the fact that Calvia Crispinilla had connections, wealth, and character. She might not be somebody whom "respectable" aristocrats welcomed into their homes, but nor would they celebrate her execution. So she survived the reigns of Galba, Otho, and Vitellius, witnessed the accession of Vespasian, and lived to a ripe old age.

For much the same reasons Otho played the strict constitutionalist when it came to the running of the state. He appointed himself and his brother, Salvius Titianus, consuls for January and February, to replace Galba and Vinius. But otherwise he tried to respect the arrangements for consulships long since made for the rest of the year by Nero and Galba. He inserted Verginius Rufus and Pompeius Vopiscus into the list for March and April 69, but this merely shortened the terms of the other consuls-to-be. Besides, the elevation of Verginius may have been prompted by the idea that it would pacify the Rhine legions, while that of Vopiscus was perhaps a gesture to Galba's few partisans: Vopiscus was linked closely with Vienna, the town that had supported Vindex enthusiastically. Again, as we know from the evidence of inscriptions, Otho did not rush the meetings where his assumption of various powers and positions was ratified formally. The session to confirm his grant of a tribune's powers was held on 28 February, that for the position of chief priest (Pontifex Maximus) on 9 March. Finally, Otho distributed other priesthoods to senior members of the senate, or to young sprigs of the nobility whom Galba had recalled from exile. And he too brought back prominent senators exiled by Claudius or Nero, presumably with the idea of implanting in the upper reaches of the senate more men who, while they might not care for him, were at least under obligation to him.

The same urge to reassure everybody shows up in the coinage Otho struck in Rome during his first month as emperor. Before the second week in March the mint issued four main types in gold and silver, and each of them seems to have been intended to proclaim not only that Otho was excellently suited to rule, but also that all was well with the empire. One issue advertised "Peace throughout the World" (PAX ORBIS TERRARVM), a second the people's ability to be free from anxiety (SECVRITAS P. R.). The other two issues are less straightforward. The silver denarii emblazoned CERES AVG(VSTA) are usually taken as Otho's assertion that there would be no interruption in the supply of grain from Egypt and Africa on which the common people depended for survival. He could make this assertion with confidence: he was recognized by Tiberius Alexander, the prefect of Egypt, as readily as had been his predecessor, while a Neronian freedman named Crescens swung first Carthage and then the rest of the province Africa over to his side, without even waiting for a lead from its new governor, Gaius Vipstanus Apronianus (a Neronian appointee). The question is for whom the message on the denarii was meant. Silver coinage was hardly seen by the common people. Mostly it ended up in the hands of the soldiery and of the upper classes. Since neither troops nor senators had reason to worry about their food supplies, it may be better to take these types as a statement aimed at the upper classes, to tell them that they need not fear the unrest food shortages tended to generate in the city. Finally, there was an issue carrying the legend "The victory of Otho" (VICTORIA OTHONIS).

What victory Otho and his mint-master had in mind is arguable. We could see it as an announcement of the one Otho intended winning over Vitellius. But the issue is better connected with the celebrations, led by Otho personally on 1 March, for a victory gained in the province Moesia (Bulgaria, more or less), since Tacitus asserts that these were out of all proportion to the success gained.[4] The Rhoxolani or "Red Alans," one of the seminomadic Sarmatian tribes from the Caucasus area, had begun appearing along the northern banks of the Danube in Nero's reign, and had gotten into the habit of raiding Roman territory on the southern bank during the winter, when stretches of the river froze and Roman forces stayed snug in their camps. In the winter of 67/68 they had cut to pieces two cohorts of auxiliaries. And in January or February 69 about 9,000 of their horsemen tried to repeat this success. This time, however, they were taken unawares by the weather and the Romans.

As Tacitus tells the story, and he is our only source, the Rhoxolani were roaming the Moesian countryside, some laden with spoil, others still questing for loot, and all "keener on booty than battle." Legion III Gallica and its auxiliaries responded faster to this raid than was expected, perhaps because the unit, newly transferred from Syria, had been toughened up by years of campaigning against the Parthians. As there was also an early, if temporary thaw, the Romans had the advantage. The Rhoxolani fought superbly on horseback, with spears and two-handed swords, but poorly on foot. As their leaders wore leather-backed sheet- or scale-armor reaching from the neck to the knees, they were practically invulnerable and unstoppable in a charge. But once they were unhorsed, the weight of the armor made it impossible for them to get up again. And none of the tribesmen carried shields to defend themselves in close combat. In this encounter, therefore, their horses were unable to keep their footing because the ground was slushy; the tribesmen had to fight on foot in deep, soft snow; and the more agile Romans were able to annihilate most of the raiding party with their javelins and short swords.

When the news reached Rome, so Tacitus claims, Otho was ecstatic. He saw to it that "consular ornaments," the distinctions normally borne by men who had held the consulship, were granted not only to the commander of III Gallica, Titus Aurelius Fulvus (the paternal grandfather of the emperor Antoninus Pius), but also to the legates of the two other legions in the province, Tettius Julianus (VII Claudia) and Numisius Lupus (VIII Augusta). And though the ultimate credit rested with the emperor, as commander in chief, Otho wisely allowed for any claims to have coordinated the affair that might be made by Moesia's governor, Marcus Aponius Saturninus. He was rewarded with a statue depicting him in the garb of a man who had celebrated a triumph through the streets of Rome. The rewards were excessive, but this resulted, partly, from Otho's wish to guarantee the loyalty of these legions. (They were among the forces on whose aid he had by now called.) But Tacitus' criticism is also excessive. He may be correct that Otho behaved as if his generals had added to the territory of the empire, when all they had done was drive raiders from Roman territory, but he is ax-grinding. He sets this incident immediately before his account of a mutiny by the praetorian guard, and to intensify the contrast, he exaggerates the celebrations of this victory on the frontiers and the uproar in the city, asserting that it very nearly destroyed Rome.

In any event, Otho's main problem in the area of public relations was to define his attitude toward Nero and Poppaea. Since the latter had been his wife and everybody agreed that he had truly loved her, it raised few eyebrows when he restored the statues to her that had been overthrown in the initial rejoicing over Nero's suicide. Yet he acted not in virtue of his powers as emperor, but—seemingly to allay doubts about the implications of his action—through a decree of the senate. The situation with Nero was more complicated. Since Galba's rule had proved such an unpleasant contrast, many outside the senate now lamented Nero's passing, and there was no more harm in letting such people re-erect statues of Nero than there was advantage in stopping them. The problem lay in Otho's being a one-time intimate of the emperor and, in a real sense, a throwback to his reign. On this basis, the people and the soldiery at first hailed him as "Nero Otho." The sources report that Otho did nothing to stop this, but the real question is whether he encouraged the demonstrations. The chances are that he did not. As Plutarch and Suetonius are careful to say, it was merely an allegation that early on he signed documents as "Nero Otho," and desisted only after influential senators expressed disapproval. There is even less reason to credit the rumor that he considered holding a memorial service for his erstwhile friend. In fact, that story may have been spread to embarrass him, and to inhibit him from giving way to further Neronian proclivities after he earmarked 50 million sesterces for the completion of the Golden House.

The main order of business being to decide how to deal with Vitellius, Otho seems at first to have hoped to achieve a peaceful solution. He sent a letter to his rival, in which he tried to persuade him to step down by offering him money, influence at court, and a luxurious retreat in the country. The response was a letter making him the same offer. The two men continued the correspondence through the rest of January

and February even so, but each exchange proved more acrimonious, and
more farcical, than the last. Both ended up hurling insults at the other,
and both—as Tacitus and Plutarch snidely remark—were accurate. Otho
was no more successful when, in the name of the senate, he sent envoys
to the Rhine legions and to I Italica at Lugdunum. The envoys, as Tacitus
puts it, stayed with the enemy too readily for anyone to believe that they
were being held against their will. But the praetorians who accompanied
them, ostensibly as their escort, were turned back before they could mingle
with the Vitellian troops. And when they returned to Rome, they brought
a letter from Fabius Valens, penned in the name of the armies of Germany and addressed to the praetorian and urban cohorts. It reproached
them for making Otho emperor "so long after" the title had been conferred on Vitellius by the Rhine legions, talked menacingly of the strength
of Vitellius' armies, but offered to let bygones be bygones if the address-
ees abandoned Otho. As the guard was not impressed by this mixture of
threats and promises, the two rivals attempted finally to assassinate one
another. Neither achieved his aim. Otho's men were quickly spotted as
strangers in the closed world of a legionary camp and were executed on
the spot. Vitellius' men merged easily into the cosmopolitan crowds that
thronged Rome, but were never able to get close to their target.

To this Tacitus adds another detail, meant on its face to indicate
how bitter the struggle finally became. Vitellius, he says, wrote a letter
to Otho's brother Titianus, threatening him and his son with death, if
harm befell Vitellius' mother and children in Rome. The story may not
be quite as straightforward as it looks, however. For one thing, it was not
standard practice to take reprisals against a man's family, least of all against
the womenfolk, even though Galba had broken the rules. Again, Otho
took Vitellius' brother Lucius with him when he marched north, treating him no differently than he did all other members of his entourage,
while Vitellius' wife Galeria seems to have been protected by the fact
that one of Otho's principal associates was Publius Galerius Trachalus.
Third, the letter was addressed to Titianus, suggesting that it was written after Otho's departure from Rome, when his brother had charge of
the city. So Tacitus may be sneering at Titianus, for whom he had un-
mitigated contempt. Two more details may confirm this. Plutarch states
that before Otho marched north, he took strong measures to ensure the
safety of Vitellius' wife and mother, something he need not have done
unless he was aware of a vindictive streak in his brother. And Tacitus
uses odd wording to end his acount: both houses survived, "*under* Otho
perhaps from fear, while Vitellius in victory took credit for clemency."

Whatever hopes Otho pinned on a peaceful solution, he was neither
so shortsighted nor so complacent as to shun preparations for war. Be-

fore we can discuss them, however, it is important to recognize that three different problems are raised by Tacitus' narrative of the two months that Otho spent as emperor in Rome (mid-January to mid-March). First, his account deals with Otho's actions, not with Otho's plans, especially if those plans—like his initial ideas on how to counter the Vitellians—failed to bear fruit. Second, his narrative may look as if it follows a chronological order, but it does not. Although Tacitus provides a blow-by-blow description of the first two days of the reign, thereafter he lays out much of the material by categories. In episodes like Otho's exchange of letters with Vitellius this makes little difference. It does when Tacitus groups together Otho's attempts to win over specific groups in provinces like Africa and Cappadocia.[5] Third, Tacitus revels in juxtaposing episodes that create the strongest possible contrast. So the Rhoxolani's raid into Moesia is set against the mutiny by the praetorian guard in Rome, and the only indication of their interrelationship in time is a "meanwhile." And this bears on our immediate subject, because it can be maintained that Otho began preparing for war before the close of January, even if he took few substantive measures before the start of March.

In Rome Otho had no battle-hardened troops to oppose Vitellius' forces. There was the newly formed legion of ex-marines, I Adiutrix, but nobody can have expected it to fight as well as it did. Otherwise, Otho had at his disposal only parade and paramilitary units, the 12 cohorts of the praetorian guard and 4 or 5 of the urban cohorts. To make a fight of it, he needed the seven legions stationed in the Balkan provinces, Dalmatia, Pannonia, and Moesia. If Otho heard by 25 January that these units had sworn allegiance to him, we can assume that he soon gave them, if not their marching orders, at least a sign of what he expected from them.[6] What he had in mind we do not know, but it is a reasonable guess—if only a guess—that he meant from the first to march north with the forces he had in Rome, to rendezvous in northern Italy with at least the four legions from Pannonia and Dalmatia (VII Galbiana, XI Claudia, XIII Gemina, and XIV Gemina Martia Victrix), and then—weather permitting—to cross the Alps into Gaul and do battle with the Vitellians wherever they might be found.

If so, Otho had to jettison this plan when he learnt that the Vitellians were approaching Italy in two columns, and we can date that around the middle of February. That is when he could have gained the information either from the diplomatic exchanges with Fabius Valens or from the complaints surely made by the Helvetii against Caecina. This development still left Otho with the possibility of holding the Alpine passes against the invaders, and this might help to explain why he chose no less than three senators to serve as his commanders: Suetonius Paulinus, "thought to be the best general of his day," the faithful Marius Celsus, and Appius Annius Gallus, a man who had held the consulship in the latter part of Nero's reign. Yet this plan had to be abandoned too, probably before the start of March. Once the *ala Siliana* seized control of the four cities in the area north of the Po, Otho was forced to realize that the river would have to become his first line of defense. Not that he could afford to settle for its southern bank. As the Balkan legions had to enter Italy by way of Aquileia to join up with him, he had to hold the northern bank too, at least at the eastern end of the peninsula.

These changes made no difference to the essence of Otho's plan. So far as we can tell, he still meant to concentrate his main forces in northern Italy and to fight the decisive battle there. But the speed at which the Vitellians were moving caused him to introduce three modifications. First, he must by now have ordered the Balkan legions to begin their march to Italy, whether or not he also instructed them to send detachments of 2,000 men apiece ahead of the main body.[7] Then, to ensure his hold on the line of the Po, he sent off an advance force of some 10,000 men, comprised of five praetorian cohorts, legion I Adiutrix, a large (but unspecified) number of cavalry detachments, and 2,000 gladiators, all of them under the command of Annius Gallus. And finally, he dispatched a maritime expedition to the southern coast of Gaul (Gallia Narbonensis).

Of all these measures the maritime expedition is the most controversial by far. Tacitus' account is our only source, and he is as vague about the strength of Otho's force as he is about its goals, apparently because he followed a source that was well informed only about the Vitellians' countermeasures. He asserts, for example, that Otho decided to attack Narbonensis "with a strong fleet." Yet this fleet cannot have been large. Though Otho won the marines' loyalty by restoring to I Adiutrix the handful of trouble-makers Galba had imprisoned in October, and so by inspiring the rest with the hope that they too would see promotion to legionary status one day, he held back—or at any rate had available—a sizable number of marines for his own march to the north. Again, the number of troops embarked on the ships was relatively small. The landing force, Tacitus declares, was made up of the urban cohorts and "many praetorians." His wording implies that Otho mobilized the urban cohorts stationed in Rome, and probably others too (at least those quartered in Ostia and Puteoli), but these units seem to have been included to make up the numbers, while the "many" praetorians were to do the fighting. And these praetorians could have totaled as few as 1,000 to 1,500 men, drafts taken from each cohort rather than entire units. Then there are the ranks of the men Otho put in charge: Aemilius Pacensis had been the tribune of an urban cohort until he was cashiered by Galba, while his colleagues Antonius Novellus and Titus Suedius Clemens were senior centurions (*primipilares*). Tribunes and senior centurions were not given charge of major expeditions.

As for what the expedition was supposed to achieve, it is just as well that it is unsafe to deduce intentions from results. Whatever Otho had in mind, it was not the failure the expedition proved to be. This, however, does not justify our dismissing as baseless the contemptuous manner in which Tacitus reports the campaign, nor our going to the opposite extreme, as do theories that credit Otho and his advisers with specific, far-reaching plans. To claim that the objective was to assert Othonian naval supremacy in the western Mediterranean is meaningless as well as anachronistic: the Vitellians had no ships and needed none. Difficulties crop up too, if we adopt the more limited view that the Othonians meant to seize control of the Aurelian Way, the road running along the southern coast of Gaul, by way of Arelate (Arles), Aquae Sextiae (Aix), Forum Julii (Fréjus), Antipolis (Antibes), and Albintimilium (Ventimiglia), from there to Genoa, and so down to Rome. Valens had no reason to follow this route, Otho and his advisers no reason to imagine that he would. The road was easy and free from snow, but the Apennine range lay to the east of Genoa and effectively blocked Valens' column from joining up with Caecina's.

The suggestion that the expedition was supposed to make an attempt on Forum Julii itself looks more attractive, especially as the town was an outstation of the Misene fleet. It might even be argued that the Othonians hoped to use the facilities as a means of extending their own time on station and radius of action.[8] But even this is probably too ambitious. It is wiser to adopt Henderson's explanation. Though he overstated his case, he held that the Othonians wanted simply to raid the southern coast of Gaul. This would create an uproar that would delay the advance of Valens' column, and perhaps divert it from its primary mission, the invasion of Italy. By the third week of February, the date when the expedition apparently set sail, Otho must have known not only that the Vitellians were advancing in two columns, but also that Valens' was the stronger. Whether he knew too that Caecina was making faster progress (he may have done), he could reasonably hope to defeat him with the forces at his disposal, while vigorous action by the maritime expedition delayed Valens long enough to allow the Balkan legions to reach northern Italy first. With these reinforcements, Otho would then be able to dispose of Valens' column too, when it appeared.

Although this expedition must have followed the mutiny of the praetorians, it will be best to finish the story here, since it was only a sideshow. According to Tacitus, then, the force set sail from Ostia and made its way up the western coast of Italy. Problems arose at once. There was strife between the commanders: Aemilius Pacensis was thrown in chains, and Antonius Novellus was ignored. So effective command devolved on Suedius Clemens, "a popularity seeker more interested in winning victories than in enforcing discipline." Worse still, the fleet created havoc wherever it put in, even before it had passed the confines of Italy. Like invaders in enemy territory, the men pillaged, murdered, and burned their way up the coast (how often Tacitus is careful not to say, but it would have taken the fleet something like four days to sail to Gaul). This "was all the more terrible, because nowhere had precautions been taken against such horrifying actions. The fields were full of people and livestock, the houses open and unguarded. The landowners who came to meet them, along with their wives and children, were overwhelmed by the evils of a war they never expected." It might in any case have been difficult for Tacitus to report the expedition's activities objectively, since the mother of Agricola, his own father-in-law, was one of the victims. But as this idyllic scene deliberately recalls the picture of Italy painted by Sallust on the eve of Spartacus' revolt, Tacitus is obviously trying to bring these Othonians down to the level of gladiators and runaway slaves.

When the expedition reached the tiny province of the Maritime Alps, a strip of territory between Italy and Narbonese Gaul, it encountered determined opposition from Marius Maturus, the procurator. Though he had at his disposal the *cohors I Ligurum*, for some time past the garrison of Cemenelum (Cimiez), his administrative headquarters a few miles inland from Nicaea (Nice, of which it is now a suburb), he decided not to use this unit. When his main duty was to police the inland tribes, there was no point in leaving them unguarded while trying to deal with a threat off the coast. Instead, he called out the local militia, young men who acted as a kind of defense force in emergencies. Being untrained and inexperienced in war, they took to flight the moment they were attacked. The Othonians, however, were so provoked by their inability to kill and plunder their opponents, let alone to catch and enslave them (Ligurians were proverbially fast on their feet), that they turned their anger on the citizens of Albintimilium. "What made their conduct more odious still was the exemplary courage of a Ligurian woman. She had hidden her son from the raiders, and they had come to the conclusion that she had concealed her money with him. So they tortured her to make her reveal the hiding place, but she pointed at her womb and declared 'he's in here.' And neither their terrible threats nor even death itself could induce her to modify this brave and noble answer."

Instead of pressing on westward along the coast, the Othonians settled down in Albintimilium. Perhaps they wanted to enjoy the fruits of conquest, perhaps they thought they had achieved their aim. In either case, the town's fate terrified the other inhabitants of Narbonensis and they sent envoys posthaste to Fabius Valens. At this point, as far as we can tell, he was making his way south from Lugdunum to Lucus Augusti, and he could not ignore their demands for protection. As the province had originally taken the oath of allegiance to Otho, its inhabitants could not be left to repent of their switching sides to Vitellius at this juncture. So he detached from his column a force of perhaps 2,600 auxiliaries. On these Tacitus gives us a wealth of detail: there were 2 cohorts of Tungrian auxiliaries, 4 squadrons of cavalry, and the entire *ala Trevirorum*, 16 more squadrons of horse. Command of the cavalry, and perhaps of the entire force, was entrusted to Julius Classicus, a romanized chieftain of the Treveri.

Eight squadrons of horse and probably three-quarters of the foot were sent to protect Forum Julii. The rest, their numbers augmented by the cohort of Ligurians and "500 Pannonians not yet under the standards" (raw recruits), were ordered to deal with the Othonians. The two sides made contact in a relatively small plain on the coast, probably near Menton (some six miles west of Albintimilium). The Othonian line faced west: on the foothills on their right wing they positioned a mix of marines and local inhabitants (perhaps pressed, perhaps volunteers). The praetorians occupied the center, on the flat ground between hills and sea. And for their left wing they used their ships, with the prows turned toward the shore (the opposite of normal practice). Since there is no mention of the urban cohorts, they may have been held in reserve, but they were more probably embarked on the ships. That would have made real the threat to the Vitellians' flank. For their part, the Vitellians positioned the cohort of Ligurians on the foothills, to make up their left wing, drew up the Tungrian cohorts they had with them in close order on the flat ground. But since their strength lay in their cavalry, they made the Treveran horsemen their front line (the Treveri were considered among the best cavalry in the Roman army). Apparently overconfident, the horsemen led off the attack incautiously, and paid heavily for their mistake. With trained soldiers in their front, a rain of missiles (slingbolts and lances) coming in from their left flank, and the fleet making threatening moves on their right, the Treveri lost their nerve and turned tail. It sounds suspiciously like a formula, but since Tacitus asserts that the entire force could have been destroyed, had not darkness fallen, the cavalry's retreat may have thrown their own infantry into disorder too.

Refusing to admit defeat, the Vitellians sent for reinforcements from Forum Julii. Then they renewed the offensive some days later, and this time they caught the Othonians off guard. Victory had made the latter careless, and the Vitellians overran their outposts easily, penetrated their camp, and even caused a panic among the men on the ships. The praetorians managed to rally on a nearby hill, however, and eventually to go over to the attack. The prefects of the Tungrian cohorts made a valiant attempt to hold their ground but, like the Treveri in the first engagement, they were overwhelmed by a rain of missiles and forced to retreat. This time, however, their cavalry saved the day, encircling and wiping out the most enthusiastic of the Othonians who came up in pursuit. Tacitus gives the impression that the two sides counted this a stalemate and so withdrew, the Vitellians to Antipolis (Antibes) in Narbonensis, the Othonians to Albingaunum (Albenga) in Liguria (northwestern Italy). As he puts it, there was no formal agreement, but each force acted as if the territory in the 70 or so miles in between had been declared a demilitarized zone, the Othonians holding their fleet in check, the Vitellians their cavalry. And so the maritime expedition died aborning. Though the Othonians managed to delay Valens' march briefly, they did nothing to alter the outcome of the war. As Tacitus goes on to say, the only effect of their raids on events elsewhere was to inspire the procurator of Corsica, Picarius Decumus, to make a pointless attempt to swing the island over to the Vitellians. He was murdered for his pains by the local inhabitants. They had no wish to be drilled for, let alone to be caught up in, a civil war.[9]

Now we come to the episode that, despite the controversy still swirling around its origins, must have occurred just before the departure of the maritime expedition in February, the mutiny by the praetorian guard in Rome.[10] Otho triggered the outbreak, unwittingly, when he summoned to Rome the urban cohort stationed in Ostia (*cohors XVII urbana*). At Ostia the unit's principal task had been to act as a fire service, and for that it had not needed all its weapons. Whether Otho thought his purpose self-evident, or saw no reason to announce it, he probably intended to make the cohort part of the maritime expedition, and for that it had to be issued with the matériel kept in the armory in the praetorian camp. So Varius Crispinus, a praetorian tribune, was ordered to open the armory and load the cohort's weapons and equipment on wagons. As the sources fail to state why wagons should have been needed to move this matériel when the cohort was coming to Rome, or where the wagons were to take it, various reconstructions are possible. But idiotic as it may look to those who have not served in the armed forces, the simplest solution may be that the cohort was brought to Rome to participate in a parade or review with the other units selected for the expedition. After that the force would march to its embarkation point, Ostia. Meanwhile, the wagons would convey the heavy equipment—the items not needed for the parade—from Rome to Ostia, to load it on the ships taking the force to its destination.[11]

Whatever the truth, Crispinus unwisely opted to carry out his assignment at or around nightfall, hoping to finish the job without fuss or distraction. He failed to take into account the fact that any number of praetorians would be wandering about off-duty. Since they had nothing else to do, many of them were drunk (or so Tacitus declares), and since it was evening, they found his activity extremely suspicious. Unaware of any plans that required the issuance of weapons and seeing no grounds for it, they interpreted the scene as evidence of treachery on their officers' part. From this they leapt to the conclusion that the weapons were to be distributed to the household slaves of senators for an attack on Otho. So they halted the loading, killed Crispinus and two centurions who tried to stop them, and then, grabbing weapons, they jumped on horses and rushed to the palace a mile and a half away, determined to make sure that Otho was safe and, if he was not, to massacre every senator they could find.

At the palace Otho was presiding over a banquet he had thrown for some 80 leading senators, many of them accompanied by their wives. His guests were thunderstruck when they heard the uproar outside, and Tacitus dwells lovingly on their perplexity. Was this a trick by the emperor to test their loyalty, or was it an accident? Should they stand their ground and risk being taken captive, or split up and make a run for it? One minute they tried to put the best face on things, the next their fear showed through. All the while they kept an eye on Otho, but this was no comfort, since his expression was positively frightening when he was frightened himself. Having dramatized the scene, Tacitus admits that Otho had no more idea what was happening and was terrified as much for his guests as for himself. So his first moves were to summon the two prefects of the guard, and to get his guests away, through another part of the palace, long before the mutineers could break into the room. Yet Tacitus refuses to tone down his rhetoric: prominent men threw aside their every badge of rank, avoided one another's company, and slunk away down backstreets. And to be on the safe side, few of them returned to their own homes; the majority went into hiding in the houses of friends or dependants.

The mutineers were so worried about Otho's safety that they were in an ugly mood by the time they reached the palace. Breaking into the banqueting room, they voiced threats one minute against their officers, the next against the senate. Small wonder that they wounded the officers who tried to slow them down, one victim being Julius Martialis, the

unfortunate tribune who had had guard duty at the praetorian camp on
15 January. But only anticlimax and frustration resulted. Though reassured to find Otho unharmed, the men had no way of venting their rage
and no excuse for doing so. Otho lacked the presence to calm the men at
the head of the mob, and he was too short to be seen by those pressing in
behind. So he climbed on a couch (a most undignified action for an emperor, says Tacitus), and only then did he bring the men under control.
They still left reluctantly, convinced that they had done no wrong in
showing such devotion to their emperor, and they may have gone on a
rampage as they returned to the camp, taking out their anger on any
person or object that caught their attention along the way.

This is probably why Rome is said to have resembled a city captured
by an enemy the next morning: shops and houses were shut up tight, the
streets deserted, and the people despondent. The situation in the camp
was hardly better, as the guardsmen were sullen rather than repentant.
Their two prefects made their way from company to company, talking
to the men, one in tough terms, the other with more leniency. When
this too failed to remedy the situation, it was decided to promise the
guardsmen 5,000 sesterces apiece. Tacitus fails to say if this was to be a
down payment on the donative the men had so often been denied by
Galba, or a donative meant to mark Otho's accession, or just a bribe to
calm them down. He implies—probably rightly—that it was only a bribe,
and he asserts, unwarrantably, that it was only after this promise had
been made that Otho had the courage to enter the camp. Once inside, he
was immediately surrounded by the officers, indignantly demanding their
own discharge because they refused to go in constant peril of their lives
as a result of the troops' distrust and refusal to carry out orders. And this,
not the promise of money, supposedly brought about a change of heart
in the soldiery. Of their own accord they now demanded the punishment of the men primarily responsible for the mutiny. Once again, it
seems, they were more sensitive to reflections on their honor—and less
venal—than is sometimes imagined.

Tacitus turns next to the dilemma facing Otho, but perhaps to avoid
the obvious, perhaps because he credits Otho with knowing his men better than we do, he does not present it in terms of the tension between
officers and rankers, with the former demanding stern measures if they
were to remain at their posts and the latter refusing to submit. Though
that aspect of the situation is implied by his narrative, he focuses on the
men, separating them into two categories. Some were ready to obey their
officers and eager for an end to the anarchy, but for that reason less
enthused about civil war. And there were the troublemakers, only too
happy to fight a civil war, but so insubordinate in the meantime that they

were a constant threat to everybody else, from the common people up to the emperor. To this audience Tacitus has Otho give a speech that is widely considered one of the historian's most brilliant creations.

Otho dwells on three themes. First there is an interpretation of the mutiny as proof only of the soldiery's bravery and devotion to their emperor. These virtues they must curb, however, because they are too fierce and dangerous when misdirected, as had happened the previous night at the instigation of a handful of drunken agitators. Next comes a disquisition on the needs of military discipline. On the eve of war, the troops must recognize that they cannot expect to be told about, let alone to discuss, each move beforehand. The reasons for some orders are not divulged even to tribunes and centurions (perhaps a passing reference to Varius Crispinus' tribulations). There can be no repetition of the previous night's behavior on the battlefield, unless the men want to create the chaos that will enable the Vitellians to crush them. It is the men's duty to obey, Otho's to plan, to lead, and—for that matter—to punish. But he will execute only two men, since a mere handful had started the trouble. The rest of them must draw a line and put the whole business behind them. (Moralists incline to interpret this as weakness on Otho's part, but decimating the marines had done Galba no good.) Finally, there must be no more threats against senators. The senate is not only an institution bound up inextricably with the glorious history of Rome. It is the agency that has conferred legality on Otho and made theirs a just cause. Vitellius is a rebel, calling on barbarous German tribesmen to destroy the very flower of the youth of Italy, the praetorians. And just as praetorians can hope one day to become senators, so it is from senators that emperors are made.

Tacitus undoubtedly placed his account of the praetorian mutiny as late in his narrative as he could, partly, at least, to persuade his readers that Otho's final weeks in Rome were shrouded in gloom and fear. This accords with his assertion that the guardsmen were mollified rather than pacified by the emperor's speech. Peace and quiet did not return to the city. There was still the clash of weaponry and the outward appearance of war. Although the soldiers no longer ganged up to cause trouble, individual rankers in plain clothes supposedly roamed the streets and entered houses, looking askance at anybody whose aristocratic birth or conspicuous wealth had made him the subject of gossip. Since many believed widespread rumors that Vitellian spies had arrived to scout out the situation, suspicions ran so deep that people felt unsafe even in the privacy of their own homes. Nonetheless, so Tacitus maintains in order to prolong this dire atmosphere, the apprehension was greatest in public. Everybody waited eagerly for each fresh bit of news, but when it arrived, they had to be careful not to look too downcast if it was bad, nor less than delighted if it was good.

It is not surprising that the senators were not reassured by Otho's speech to the guard. The mutiny probably undermined whatever trust they had developed in their emperor, and they surely regarded its suppression as a close-run thing. Besides, the news from the north must have made them wonder if Otho could hang onto power. Hence the way Tacitus talks about the next senate meeting he called. Whenever it met, and whatever the planned agenda, the senators were impaled on the horns of a dilemma again. As Tacitus unsympathetically puts it, they could not decide how to act. To remain silent might be considered dumb insolence, to speak out would incur suspicion. They could not flatter Otho blatantly, since he was wise in the ways of sycophants. But nor could they abuse his rival explicitly, for fear that he might one day take reprisals. So they twisted their speeches this way and that, abusing Vitellius as a matter of course, although prudent senators limited themselves to generic themes. A few voiced abuse that was all too true, but only when other voices drowned out theirs, or else they buried their accusations in a torrent of verbiage.

To accentuate the gloom, Tacitus reports prodigies that, he asserts, people might have ignored in other circumstances, but to which they paid attention now that the situation looked dire. But he gives more space to a natural phenomenon. Thanks to the mild winter, the Tiber flooded, rising much higher than usual and bringing down the Pons Sublicius, the oldest bridge in the city, in such a way as to dam the river. So the flood waters overran even higher ground normally spared from inundation. Many were swept away, others drowned in their shops and apartments. More serious still was the loss of livelihood: people were put out of work and could not earn the money to buy food. Not that there was much grain to be had, since the granaries and the grain market appear to have been damaged too. Also, Otho was unable to alleviate the shortage by purchasing grain elsewhere, since every penny was going to the troops. So prices rose steadily, and people in Rome began to experience the evils of war as they had not done since Augustus seized power a century before. To add to their woes, the foundations of the apartment houses were rotted out by the standing water, and collapsed when the river receded. And since the northwestern part of the city bore the brunt of the flood, the Campus Martius and the road to the north, the Flaminian Way, were blocked by debris at various points, something else people could take as an omen now that Otho was about to leave.

Whenever the flood occurred, it was around the same time that Otho made his arrangements for the rest of the aristocracy. He placed under house arrest in Aquinum (Aquino), some 65 miles southeast of Rome, the man once thought his main rival as Galba's successor, Cornelius Dolabella. He ordered many of the magistrates and most of the senior senators, among them Vitellius' brother Lucius, to accompany him to the north. He had no intention of using them as advisers or ministers. They were hostages in the guise of companions, says Tacitus, to stress what an ill-assorted crew made up the entourage. Otho's companions fell supposedly into three types. Some were old and inexperienced in war, fearful and unable to hide their fear. Some tried to win Otho's favor and to cut a fine figure by purchasing expensive armor, fine horses, and everything needed for banquets and orgies, as if these too were essential components of a campaign (whereas men of sense, motivated by love of country, wanted only peace). And, in what may be an accurate statement, or another echo of Caesar's description of the Pompeians on the eve of Pharsalus in 48 B.C., some took part because they were up to their ears in debt, and saw war as the best means of evading their creditors and their creditors' attentions.

As his final official act in the city, Otho summoned a meeting of the people and delivered a speech so fluent and sonorous that many in his audience thought it written for him by Publius Galerius Trachalus, consul in 68 and somehow a relative of Vitellius' wife. Otho stressed his role as the representative of a unified senate and people, but showed great restraint in talking of his adversaries. He refused to name Vitellius, and he accused the Rhine legions of gullibility rather than troublemaking. The people's applause was "overdone and unreal," says Tacitus, since they had long since been broken to servility. But whatever we make of that, Otho entrusted the running of the city and the empire to his elder brother Titianus and, on 14 March, set out for the north.[12]

Otho took with him the seven remaining praetorian cohorts, an unknown number of time-expired praetorians called up for the emergency, a large force of marines, and a bodyguard of *speculatores*. It has been estimated that the force totaled 9,000 men, but this may be too high. Certainly none of the praetorian cohorts can have been at full strength, when Otho had skimmed off detachments for his maritime expedition. Their destination was Brixellum (Brescello), some 350 miles from Rome and about 15 miles short of the position his advance guard took up at Bedriacum. And since Suetonius Paulinus and Marius Celsus had been sent on ahead a few days earlier, Otho headed the column, on foot, in an ordinary soldier's breastplate, and (in Tacitus' words) "ill-shaven, unkempt and quite at variance with his usual image."

6

The War between Otho and Vitellius
(March and April)

Once Caecina emerged from the Alps toward the end of March, he swiftly overran much of the western half of the Transpadana, that part of Italy north of the River Po. He already had four good bases in the region, Eporedia, Vercellae, Novaria, and Mediolanum. Tacitus adds that the local inhabitants felt no loyalty to Otho or Vitellius and did not care who won the war, because a century of peace had schooled them to bow to superior force, no matter who applied it. The comment loses much of its sting as soon as we ask what else they could have done. Besides, Caecina took care not to alienate them. He kept his column on a tight rein as he moved south. And surprise appears to have been the tactic used by his advance forces, the auxiliaries sent on ahead, as they neutralized Othonian units in the area. Tacitus reports that a cohort of Pannonians was taken prisoner near Cremona, while 100 cavalry and 1,000 marines (drawn perhaps from the Ravenna fleet, perhaps from the squadron stationed earlier at Forum Julii) were captured as they made their way from Placentia on the southern bank to Ticinum (Pavia) on the northern. Tacitus does not say that Caecina's advance guard occupied Cremona when they rounded up the Pannonians there. But if they did not, their activity was probably enough to persuade the inhabitants to open the gates as soon as Caecina himself appeared. Either way, Tacitus seems to have taken it for granted that his readers would know that Cremona and Placentia were the keys to north Italy. They had been founded in 219 B.C., the former on the northern bank of the Po and the latter on the southern, as bulwarks against invasions out of the Alps, and the Romans still viewed them as such in 69.

Tacitus' refusal to labor the obvious enables him to dwell on what was for him a more congenial and significant topic, the petty-mindedness with which the leading townsfolk throughout the area insisted on being treated with a deference they had not earned. As Caecina marched south, Tacitus says, the magistrates of the various towns came out to meet him in full official dress. They were put out by what they regarded as the arrogance of a man who received them wearing a parti-colored cloak and Gallic trousers. As Marc Antony had once discovered, Roman commanders were expected to reciprocate by appearing in formal, not fancy, dress. Then there was Caecina's wife, Salonina. Summoned from their home in Vicetia to join him and accompanied by a cavalry escort, Salonina either rode a fine horse with purple trappings or was so bedecked herself. Tacitus never mentions wife or horse again, but as he says, people felt insulted. It was "human nature to look with a jaundiced eye on those who had just risen to high position, and to demand moderation especially from those who had been until recently on the same social level as their critics." There is another side to this story, however. Placentia lay some 190 miles from the Great Saint Bernard Pass, and Cremona another 20-odd miles beyond that. Caecina's army could complete the trek in ten days or so, if not delayed unduly by welcoming committees en route. To ignore these self-important dignitaries would be impolitic. Greeting them in military garb, outlandish or not, proclaimed his determination to press on.

So Caecina took up position at Cremona, the town that became the Vitellian headquarters in the north during this war as well as in that against the Flavians later in the year. Here he could have waited for the arrival of Valens' forces, but he decided to launch an assault on Placentia. He may have been egged on by the citizens of Cremona: the two cities had been rivals ever since they were founded, even if they were not ready to carry their feud to the extremes favored by the inhabitants of Lugdunum and Vienna. He may also have believed that his men needed—and deserved—to be let off the leash. But his primary motivation was clearly a wish to pull off another striking success. Occupying one of the two key cities in the area gave the Vitellians control of much of the northern bank of the river. To hold both would give them a bridgehead nullifying any Othonian plans to make a stand on the southern bank. The enemy would have to pull back south and east of the Po, for fear of being taken in flank. No matter where they took up position, of course, they would be able in turn to prevent Caecina from exploiting the fact that Placentia lay at the head of the Aemilian Way, the road leading to Rome. But that probably worried Caecina not at all. He would have been more than happy to sit in Placentia and rehearse the jibes he could make at the expense of Valens, his johnny-come-lately rival.

It was by no means absurd for Caecina to expect Placentia to fall into his hands like a ripe plum. His scouts must have informed him that the Othonian troops garrisoning it would be unlikely to offer effective resistance. At this stage Otho's advance force had reached the line of the Po, but its commander, Annius Gallus, was preoccupied with holding territory further east. Gallus had to keep open the road to Aquileia, to ensure that the leading elements of the Balkan legions could join up with him, and so he set off for Verona with two of the five praetorian cohorts and the bulk of the cavalry. The defense of Placentia he entrusted to the 45-year-old Titus Vestricius Spurinna, giving him some 3,000 men, 3 praetorian cohorts, 1,000 *vexillarii* (a detachment probably from I Adiutrix), and a handful of cavalry for reconnaissance duties.

This force was as unruly as it was small. Tacitus considered this important enough to illustrate at length, and Plutarch provides us with another version of the episode, though he misses its paradigmatic nature. Throughout the campaign there was to be constant tension between the Othonian soldiery, who wanted only to have at their enemy, and their generals, who were more conscious of the troops' lack of training than of their fighting spirit. The heterogeneity of Otho's forces compounded the problem. Just as the men knew neither one another nor their officers, so the officers respected neither the men nor their capabilities. The result was endless distrust. So when Spurinna tried to keep his untested forces safe inside Placentia, they accused him of planning to surrender without a fight. Determined to do battle with the enemy, the troops threatened their officers—and Spurinna himself—with violence when they tried to restrain them. As the first, but far from the last Othonian general to be denounced for treachery by his own men, Spurinna was forced to bow to their folly.

Spurinna was able to persuade the troops to march to the west rather than the north, perhaps by passing it off as an armed reconnaissance to Ad Padum (Pievetta), the next river-crossing some 20 miles upstream. But as the Po looped away to the north here, the men found themselves tramping across open ground, terrain where they could easily have been caught and overwhelmed by Caecina's superior forces. Nightfall brought another alarming discovery, that they must build a camp. This being exertion to which few of the praetorians and ex-marines of I Adiutrix were used, it prompted second thoughts. The officers seized their chance to praise "Spurinna's foresight in selecting Placentia as a strongpoint," and this did the trick. Once discipline had been restored, Spurinna addressed the troops, avoiding any reproaches and—not before time—explaining the reasoning behind his plan of action. Then, leaving behind a few scouts, he marched the men back to Placentia. There they set to work strengthening the fortifications enthusiastically. So "it was not only their defenses that were made ready, but also their willingness to obey, which was the one thing lacking in the Othonian soldiery, since nobody could fault their bravery."

Whether or not Caecina was aware of Spurinna's difficulties, he knew that his own forces were larger, tougher, and better disciplined. He may have been overconfident and impetuous too, as Tacitus charges, but it is just as possible that the historian misunderstood his plan. This was not to lay siege to Placentia, but to take it by assault. Naturally, he tried to persuade the Othonians to surrender without a fight, but determined as he was to seize the town before Valens appeared, he could not let the Othonians string out the talks and so give Gallus time to come to their aid. He continued the parleys until the last minute, therefore, and then launched an attack without warning. On the first day he sent in his troops without any standard equipment except scaling ladders, to avoid tipping his hand, and to enable his troops to cross the open ground outside the city walls as quickly as possible. But his men were overconfident and careless. According to Tacitus, they had breakfasted far too well, and were heavy with food and drink when they went into the attack.

Although Plutarch reports that the Vitellians derived vast enjoyment from abusing the praetorian defenders as "actors, dancers, spectators at Pythian and Olympic games, men who had never seen or experienced a campaign or military service, and plumed themselves on having cut off the head of a defenseless old man," neither he nor Tacitus says more about the progress of the assault than that Caecina's troops were driven back with heavy losses. But Tacitus fleshes out his narrative with another instance of local petty-mindedness. Outside the walls there was a wooden amphitheater, the finest and largest edifice of its kind in northern Italy according to the citizens of Placentia. This burnt down during the attack. It may have been caught in the crossfire between the two sides, or the attackers may have used it as a firing-platform from which to bombard the city. Either way, the inhabitants attributed the fire to arson by the Cremonans. Certain persons from other nearby towns, as they told one another meaningfully, were so consumed with jealousy and hatred, that under cover of the Vitellian attack they had reduced the structure to ashes.

Tacitus dwells on the way in which the two sides spent the night preparing for the next day's fighting. The Vitellians readied the equipment they should have brought up earlier, while the Othonians collected lumps of iron and lead, millstones and the like, to drop on the attackers' heads. Each side was inspired by the same feelings, he says, shame that they had not done better the first day, and determination to fight gloriously on the second. His love of antithesis may have led him astray. The Vitellians need not have been downcast by the failure of their first attack. But the Othonians must have been buoyed up enormously by their success in repelling men from the legions considered the finest fighters in the empire. Tacitus uses this interlude of reflection and mutual encouragement also to work in the jibes that Plutarch sets at the start of the first day's fighting. This could be a fit of authorial caprice, but it is the only point in his narrative where he talks of the Othonians inside the walls. The attacks are presented exclusively from a Vitellian perspective.

The next assault began at daybreak on the second day. The city's ramparts were jammed with defenders, says Tacitus, while the open plain glittered as the rising sun caught the attackers' arms and armor. This time Caecina employed his auxiliaries to keep up a suppressing fire while the legionaries tried to undermine the walls and break through the gates. But the avalanche of missiles, rocks, and lumps of metal unleashed by the defenders created heaps of dead and wounded at every point, and since the Othonians redoubled their efforts as soon as they saw the attackers falter, Caecina called off the assault, recrossed the river, and returned to Cremona. According to Tacitus, he was ashamed of his rashness and reluctant to be mocked by the enemy, but there was no point in remaining near Placentia after the assault miscarried. Tacitus adds one last interesting detail. As Caecina withdrew, he was joined by Turullius Cerialis, a senior centurion, with "many marines" (perhaps refugees from the force captured by Caecina's advance guard), and by Julius Briganticus, a Batavian cavalry prefect, with a handful of horsemen. Perhaps they did not regard his failure as a disaster. Or perhaps they were unhappy with the heterogeneity of Otho's forces, allowed that to outweigh their opinion of Caecina's prowess, and deserted a commander they did not know for one they did. According to Tacitus, both men had served in Germany, the former actually with Caecina.

Spurinna at once sent word of Caecina's withdrawal to Annius Gallus, who was rushing back from Verona with his forces. Relieved that Spurinna had withstood the assault and, for that matter, that he would not be required to commit his own untried troops, Gallus halted at Bedriacum. This was a village near the Postumian Way, on the north bank of the Po some 22 Roman miles east of Cremona. Gallus probably picked the spot by accident, but it proved to be an excellent base at which to await the arrival of the reinforcements from the Balkan legions, and from which to check any attempts by Caecina to extend his grip on the Transpadana east of Cremona.[1] His troops saw the matter differently, and there was nearly a mutiny before they could be persuaded to encamp. Apparently under the impression that they could smash Caecina's force while it was still demoralized by its failure outside Placentia, they suspected that their general was holding back because he was not truly committed to Otho.

So fertile was this soil that it needed only one more incident to produce an uproar. This was triggered by Martius Macer and his group of 2,000 gladiators, another part of the advance force Gallus had brought north. Macer and his men had taken up position on the southern bank of the Po more or less opposite Cremona. Now they made a raid across the river, shortly after Caecina's return from Placentia. Since Macer was a man of some experience and perhaps some seniority (Otho planned to make him consul for the last two months of 69), and since Tacitus devotes a disproportionate amount of space to this episode, it has been claimed that this raid was not just important militarily but even part of a larger plan. It was neither. Macer's force was too small to take the offensive in any meaningful sense. Its function was to prevent nuisance raids across the Po such as Caecina's auxiliaries had made earlier, and possibly to safeguard Othonian communications between Placentia and whatever position Annius Gallus might be occupying at any time. Also, the raid (and there was only one) was a hit-and-run affair that caught some Vitellian auxiliaries off guard, killed a few, and sent the rest scurrying in panic to the shelter of Cremona's walls. Finally, it was Macer's enthusiasm that prompted the raid, to spread some alarm and despondency along the northern bank of the river.

For Tacitus the aftermath matters most. When the troops encamped at Bedriacum heard of the raid and the retreat, they began denouncing all their generals, not merely Macer and Gallus. By now Suetonius Paulinus and Marius Celsus had arrived, and they were abused roundly too. It is easy to see why. The troops were tied much more closely to Otho than were their generals. Like the rest of the senators, the generals had taken no part in Galba's murder, and the soldiery naturally suspected that they had less incentive to fight to the bitter end. Spurinna may have relieved their doubts momentarily by his defense of Placentia. But Gallus had halted at Bedriacum instead of pressing on, and now Macer had made a raid, only to withdraw at the moment of success. The men clearly thought that a pattern was beginning to emerge: their generals were pulling their punches, and for that treachery was the only explanation.

This presented Otho with a dilemma. His generals were not as brilliant as has sometimes been maintained, but nor were they incompetents. To dismiss them might calm the troops' suspicions, but it would harm his own standing with the generals and their peers in the senate. But if he did nothing, it would make no difference whether his generals were geniuses or not. The troops would never trust them, let alone obey their orders. So he attempted a compromise. He summoned his brother Titianus from Rome, with the idea of putting him and Licinius Proculus, the prefect of the praetorian guard, in overall command. But he also left Paulinus, Marius Celsus, and Annius Gallus at their posts. As far as we can tell, Titianus had no more military experience than Proculus, and he was not a forceful personality (one reason perhaps why Proculus was associated with him in the command). But Titianus was the emperor's brother and his loyalty was beyond question. That was the crucial consideration. Even if Otho knew that his five generals would be unable to work in harmony all the time, he could hope that they would agree at least on the fundamentals, thus allowing his troops to focus on their primary task, fighting and defeating the enemy.

In fact, this arrangement would give Otho the worst of both worlds. Yet, ironically, as Tacitus points out, Suetonius Paulinus and Marius Celsus managed to thwart another of Caecina's plans, even as Titianus traveled up from Rome. Once again Caecina seized the initiative, from anger that his undertakings had gone badly since the crossing of the Alps and that the fame of his army was fading. Tacitus credits him with four specific reasons. Two were minor, that his auxiliaries had suffered losses in Macer's raid, and that he had come off worse in skirmishes between the scouting patrols both sides sent out. Two were major, his failure to take Placentia, and the likelihood that Valens would soon arrive with his army. Nothing is said to suggest that Caecina was anxious also to bring the Othonians to battle before they could be reinforced by the Balkan legions. This has been thought odd, especially as the advance detachment from XIII Gemina had turned up by now. But despite their misfortunes Caecina's scouts must have discovered that the bulk of the Othonian reinforcements were farther away than Valens. It was the imminent arrival of friends, not foes, that spurred Caecina on.

His plan was simple. Aware that he could not afford to fight a set piece battle after the casualties he had suffered outside Placentia, Caecina decided to stage an ambush on obstructed ground. Much of the Postumian Way lent itself to this, since it ran along a causeway above the surrounding, water-logged plain, and the land was often broken up on both sides into small plots, many of them separated by drainage ditches. Ad Castores, the site of an altar to Castor and Pollux, was especially suitable. It lay about halfway between his base and the Othonian camp at Bedriacum, and here the road was flanked by groves of trees. Caecina left his legionaries behind, partly because they had suffered the heaviest losses at Placentia, partly because an ambush was best entrusted to agile, light-armed troops who could fight in open formation. Taking with him a sizable force of auxiliary infantry and cavalry (neither Tacitus nor Plutarch gives us figures), he positioned the infantrymen in the groves on the sides of the road, under his own command, and ordered the horsemen to move ahead toward Bedriacum. They were to make contact with the Othonians, and by feigning flight to draw them back onto his infantry. If the plan worked, he could inflict heavy casualties on the enemy without taking similar losses himself; he would restore the morale of his troops along with parity, if not superiority, in numbers; and he would regain his reputation for striking successes.

Tacitus and Plutarch report that Caecina's plan was betrayed to the enemy, and it has been asserted that he was a fool not to reckon with this possibility, as it doomed his plan. But when he had to induce the enemy to fight at a time and place of his own choosing, did it really matter whether the enemy learnt of his intentions from their scouts or from deserters? The plan was hardly novel; supposedly Romulus had used it once. And it should have required little intelligence in either sense of the word for the Othonians to tumble to his scheme. Yet the Othonians' response was odd: they assembled every last man they could scrape together, perhaps 13,500 in total. It may look as if they hoped to dispose of Caecina once for all, before Valens could arrive. But the commanding general was Paulinus, and he notoriously refused to run risks. Tacitus terms him "temperamentally a delayer," and this is not praise. Inspired by the generalship of his own father-in-law, Tacitus had no more patience with overly cautious commanders than he had with rash ones. Paulinus probably mustered all his forces to ensure that nothing went wrong.

The command of the Othonian cavalry, some four squadrons or 2,000 men, was entrusted to Marius Celsus, and they made contact with the enemy first. It is difficult to reconcile their reported movements with the dispositions with which, according to Tacitus, they went into battle. But Celsus and two of the squadrons seem to have advanced along the road, some distance ahead of the main column of infantry. When they encountered the Vitellian cavalry, the latter put up hardly any fight before turning tail. Then, since Celsus checked his men, the Vitellian auxiliaries broke from cover, attacked the Othonians, and pursued them along the road as they fell back on their own infantry. Caecina would claim later that the auxiliaries had disobeyed his orders, presumably because they should have retreated as soon as Celsus' reining in his men proved that the ambush was not going to work. But as the Vitellians had been hidden in ambush on obstructed ground, they may have discovered too late that they faced the entire Othonian army. It is hard to fault them for trying to come to grips with the enemy, especially if their own cavalry failed to alert them as it galloped past.

By rights the Vitellians should have fallen into the kind of trap they had set for the Othonians, but it was not to be. Though Celsus' cavalry wheeled around them, to take up position in their rear, the Othonian infantrymen were still in column at this stage, and they had to bustle to take up their assigned places on the front and flanks of the enemy. Tacitus states that the Othonian left was made up of a detachment of 2,000 men from XIII Gemina, the first legionaries to arrive from the Balkans, 4 cohorts of auxiliaries, and 500 cavalry. On the right wing, legion I Adiutrix was supported by 2 auxiliary cohorts and 500 cavalry. In the center, on the Postumian Way, 3 praetorian cohorts were deployed in depth, since the causeway was too narrow to allow of anything else. And 1,000 cavalry, a mixture of praetorian and auxiliary squadrons, were held in reserve.

There were two problems with this. First, Celsus and his two squadrons of cavalry were incapable of shock tactics, and could do little offensively so long as the Vitellian auxiliaries stood their ground. In fact, the Othonian horsemen were unable even to cut the Vitellians off from Cremona. Whenever exactly Caecina began sending for reinforcements, his cohorts had no difficulty in joining him, even though he called them up one at a time. The best Celsus' horsemen could do was to pin the auxiliaries until their own infantry advanced. Second, Paulinus held the infantry back, refusing to give the signal to advance, until the drainage ditches had been filled up, the ground cleared, and the battle line extended. It may seem hard to believe that Paulinus was put off to find the ground so rough. But he had only just taken up his command, and he need have been no more familiar with the terrain than were the Flavian generals who campaigned here in the fall. Again, if he had no idea how large Caecina's force was, it was wise to advance on a broad front so as to frustrate the ambush. And finally, he knew that his troops were untrained and untested. That three praetorian cohorts had managed to beat back the assault on Placentia was no guarantee that their peers, let alone the unblooded legion I Adiutrix, would show the same courage in the field. Paulinus could have let them learn to fight by fighting, as Henderson observed, but he ran no risks if he kept them under tight control, left nothing to their initiative, and mounted an attack by the numbers.

The delay allowed the Vitellian auxiliaries to get off the road and again take refuge on broken ground, presumably to fall back without exposing themselves to Celsus' cavalry. But, says Tacitus, they sallied onto the roadway a second time, cut down the "the most enthusiastic of the praetorian cavalry, and wounded Gaius Julius Antiochus Epiphanes, prince of Commagene." This would be readily understandable, if Celsus took all four squadrons of cavalry with him when he wheeled around the enemy rear. If he took only two and, as Tacitus has it, left two in reserve, one praetorian and one auxiliary, the prince probably commanded the latter. In that case, the Vitellians can have wounded him only if this cavalry reserve skirted their own infantry—with or without orders—and acted as a screen for the foot soldiers carrying out Paulinus' instructions.

Whatever the case, these Othonian losses persuaded Paulinus to commit his infantry at last, and it looks as if the Vitellian force promptly fell apart. But the rest of Tacitus' narrative is sketchy. Though he reports that Caecina summoned reinforcements from Cremona a cohort at a time, he does this mainly to secure a transition to the camp, where a mutiny was taking place. The men there were unhappy that they were not being called out en masse, and they blamed Julius Gratus, the prefect of the camp, suspecting him—wrongly—of conspiring with his brother Julius Fronto, a tribune in the Othonian army.[2] In fact, Fronto had already been thrown in chains by his men on the same charge. In any event, Caecina called up his reinforcements piecemeal, and for this too Henderson criticized him harshly, and perhaps rightly. Yet Caecina's aim was clearly not to prolong the fighting, but to break away, to feed in enough men to rescue those in the trap without allowing the engagement to develop into a full-fledged battle. The arrival of these cohorts added to the confusion, however. The fresh troops were nowhere strong enough to make a stand, and all the men were swept away once panic took hold. Yet the Vitellian losses cannot have been heavy. Though Tacitus gives no figures, he ends his account with the claim that "the setback did not so much frighten the Vitellians as teach them the value of discipline." Then too, Paulinus sounded the retreat as soon as the enemy line broke.

Paulinus' decision gave rise at once to bitter arguments whether "Caecina and his entire army" could have been annihilated. Plutarch holds that it could, Tacitus that it could not. The explanation for Plutarch's view is straightforward. Since he omitted Macer's raid, he used this uproar to account for Paulinus' supersession by Titianus and Proculus. In reality, however, the debate centered on the meaning of the phrase "Caecina and his entire army." Plutarch took this to denote the Vitellian force in the field at Ad Castores, men who could have been wiped out, if Paulinus had acted boldly. Tacitus recasts the question. For him "Caecina and his entire army" covers the troops in the field and the legionaries left behind at Cremona. On this view, Paulinus made the right decision. Though his infantry were still relatively fresh when he sounded the retreat, he could legitimately wonder whether they possessed the stamina for a 12-mile march, let alone for fighting a second battle at the end of it. Neither Paulinus nor his men were aware of the mutiny in the Vitellian camp, of course. But what the general knew was that if anything went wrong in the pursuit or in the attack on the camp, he would lose control of his men, and that was courting disaster.

The more interesting question is why Tacitus chose to defend Paulinus, and for this too there is more than one possible answer. Since

Paulinus had to justify his conduct of the battle repeatedly, for example, he may have been the first to exploit the ambiguity inherent in the phrase "Caecina and his entire army," and Tacitus could have followed his lead unwittingly. But as Tacitus attributes a similar rhetorical trick to the general during the council of war before Bedriacum, it is more likely that he seized on this ambiguity for his own purposes. Tacitus was still preoccupied with the issues of trust and loyalty aired in his account of Macer's raid at this stage in his narrative, and his reading of Paulinus convinced him that the man was loyal. It followed that, however inept his generalship, he must have been doing his best to win the engagement, and so merited the best defense Tacitus could make. As every Roman advocate knew, the best tactic was to sweep the lesser charge under the rug, especially if it was unanswerable (as it was in this case), and to substitute—or to follow Paulinus in substituting—a more serious charge against which a plausible defense could be offered.

Caecina blamed his defeat on his men, "readier to mutiny than to fight." But according to Tacitus, the setback also induced Valens' men to put aside their contempt for the enemy and to show more discipline— as well they might, after a mutiny and a near mutiny during the march from Lucus to Ticinum (Pavia). The mutiny proper was caused ultimately by the eight Batavian cohorts Valens had added to his column. Their boasting about their prowess not only infuriated the legionaries to the point where insults and fist fights were a daily occurrence, but even induced Valens to suspect that the Batavians were trying to sabotage his march. So when, seemingly at Augusta Taurinorum (Turin) around the end of March, Valens was informed of the defeat of the auxiliary forces sent to counter Otho's maritime expedition, he seized what he thought a perfect opportunity to reduce the friction by sending some of these cohorts to deal with the raiders. The plan backfired. With one of those lightning-swift mood changes to which the troops were supposedly liable (in this instance, no doubt, one encouraged by the Batavians), the rest of his men concluded that he was trying to rid himself of the bravest and most experienced units in his force. When Valens attempted to assert his authority, the soldiery stoned him, and chased him off. He escaped by disguising himself as a slave and hiding in the quarters of one of his cavalry commanders. Meanwhile the men beguiled themselves with the idea that he had pocketed huge sums of money from the people of Vienna that should rightfully have been theirs, then plundered his baggage, searched his tent, and even probed the ground beneath with spears and lances in case he had buried the loot.

This mutiny was brought to an end by the ingenuity of Alfenus Varus, the prefect of the camp (Valens' second-in-command on the administrative side). The disturbance naturally lost momentum when the troops found no treasure, and Varus decided to throw them off balance altogether by depriving them of the normal structure of their existence. He ordered the centurions not to make their rounds and the trumpeter not to sound the watches. This disoriented the men so much, says Tacitus, that eventually they stopped whatever they were doing and stared at one another in stupefaction. Lacking a leader, they finally begged for pardon, and Valens made his reappearance, dirty, disheveled, and still in slave's clothing, but also unharmed. Hoisting him onto their shoulders, the men carried him to the tribunal in delight, and conscious of the realities, Valens reprimanded a few but demanded the punishment of none.

The column was making camp at Ticinum (Pavia), some 95 miles further on, when the news of Ad Castores arrived, probably around the end of the first week in April. This provoked the near mutiny. Claiming that Valens' trickery and foot-dragging had robbed them of any chance to participate in the battle, the men refused to wait for orders, set off on a forced march of between 50 and 55 miles, and joined up with Caecina probably in less than 48 hours. It was not a joyous reunion. Caecina's men took care not to find fault with Valens' troops, but they shifted the blame their general had laid on them onto Valens' shoulders, and complained bitterly that he had left them in the lurch. Because Valens' troops were also attempting to shift the blame away from their conduct, they sided with the younger commander as well. Valens neither relished nor forgave this. With about twice as many troops as Caecina, he thought that he merited proportionately more respect. But the men still preferred Caecina, and there was a slanging match in which Caecina abused Valens as "a dirty old man" and Valens called Caecina "a pompous idiot."

Yet once the two men had relieved their pent-up feelings, they put aside their enmity for the time being, and began preparing for the one decisive battle that would win the war. Tacitus puts it a little differently: Caecina and Valens sat back and waited for the Othonians to make the next mistake. This is inaccurate, in that Caecina would set his men to constructing a pontoon bridge. But as this was to be a feint, Tacitus is basically right. And he expresses himself this way because it enables him to make a smooth transition to the Othonians. They were about to make a fatal mistake, as a result of Otho's decision to come up from Brixellum to Bedriacum and to preside over a council of war.

At this meeting the Othonians reached two decisions, that they would give battle immediately, and that Otho personally would not take part. Since this led to their defeat and to Otho's suicide, it is essential to form a clear picture of the purpose of this meeting, the reasoning behind the views expressed, and the effects produced. This is not easy. Plutarch and Tacitus give us accounts of what happened but, as usual, they disagree on some points, and they embed those on which they agree in different interpretations. It would be simple to blame Tacitus for the confusion. He identifies and focuses on the key issues, but he handles them in elliptical fashion. Plutarch's version is more straightforward, and has often been thought more plausible. But he compresses the material, to keep the focus on his vision of Otho, and he ignores or misunderstands key points.

To begin with a fact that tends to get lost in all the discussion, everyone present took it for granted that they had to fight. The Othonians had marched north to do battle with the Vitellians, and all assumed that this one engagement would end the war. The question was timing, whether to fight now or later. Between the meeting and the Othonians' defeat, however, there would be incidents suggesting that more devious motives were involved, and after the defeat the arguments for delay became inextricably entangled with suspicions that their advocates had been trying to reach an accommodation with the enemy. Plutarch retrojected all this into the meeting, to support one of his explanations for Otho's decision to fight at once. In so doing, he not only misrepresented the emperor's character, but also based his account on a misinterpretation of the military situation. As Tacitus saw, the foundations for these conspiratorial views were laid only after the meeting ended.

According to Plutarch, Salvius Titianus led off the discussion, as the nominal commander in chief. He offered two arguments for giving battle forthwith. The praetorians were elated by their recent success at Ad Castores, and it would be folly not to take advantage of their high morale. And the Othonian troops would lose their enthusiasm and their edge if made to wait "until Vitellius arrived in person from Gaul." Tacitus, on the other hand, characterizes Titianus and Proculus later as "the men responsible for the worse plan," but he puts no specific arguments into their mouths. Instead, he launches into the counterarguments for delay, and he has been denounced for abdicating his responsibilities as an historian. This is absurd. When the obvious course was to fight at once, what needed comment and elaboration was the less orthodox plan, to delay.

This case was presented by Suetonius Paulinus. Plutarch credits him with three arguments, but of these the second (that the Othonians were outnumbered) is simply wrong.[3] And since the first and third appear also in Tacitus' account, he is probably a better guide to what the general said. His Paulinus delivered a full-dress speech, "a comprehensive review of the entire military situation," in which he expatiated—under four

headings—on the disadvantages from which the Vitellians were suffering and the advantages that would accrue to Otho from delay. The first,
identical with the first of Plutarch's arguments, was that the Vitellians
had brought up all the troops they could, whereas Otho had many more
men on the way. So to give battle now was to play into the enemy's
hands. Second, Paulinus asserted that the Vitellians had devastated the
areas through which they had marched, and so were suffering from lack
of supplies, whereas Otho had ample provisions, was backed by the senate and people, and occupied a strong defensive position (this is Plutarch's
third argument, made more immediate and more graphic). Third, he
contended that if the battle was delayed "into the summer," the Germans in the Vitellian force would be disabled by the heat, whereas Otho's
troops were used to the climate. Finally, in what may be a fourth argument or an indication of Paulinus' awareness that he had failed to persuade important members of his audience, he suggested that Otho wait
at least the few days needed for the main body of XIV Gemina Martia
Victrix to come up. Tacitus appends the information that Paulinus' opinion was shared by Marius Celsus and Annius Gallus. (The latter had
been disabled by a fall from his horse a few days before and sent a letter.)
Then he states flatly that Otho "inclined to fight to the finish," and that
Titianus and Proculus, "rushing things as a result of their own inexperience," endorsed his decision, and foreclosed discussion with an abundance of flattery.

It would be easy to conclude that the others present, most of them
civilians, were supposed to heed the advice Paulinus dispensed so liberally. And since Plutarch and Suetonius were convinced that the decision
to fight at once was Otho's crucial mistake, it has been argued that Tacitus
shared their view. This is far from certain. We can make little of his
describing Titianus and Proculus as "the men responsible for the worse
plan." This is a relative judgment, and nowhere does he hint that delay
would have assured victory, the impression created by the other two
writers. Similarly, there is no merit in the theory that because Tacitus
gives only Paulinus a speech, the general has to be echoing his opinion.
This is as implausible as the idea that Tacitus endorsed the views he gave
Galba when he adopted Piso. Finally, Tacitus prefaces this speech with
the remark that Paulinus offered his review of the situation, because he
"thought it appropriate to his reputation, since nobody at that time was
considered to be smarter in military matters than he." This could be
praise, but it is more probably criticism of a mixture of vanity and long-
windedness. Although Tacitus was convinced of Paulinus' loyalty, he
had reason to doubt the man's competence. Prior to Ad Castores, which
he had bungled, Paulinus had fought only against tribesmen, in

Mauretania and Britain, and the methods he had used to suppress Boudicca's rebellion had cost the Romans heavy losses.[4]

That Tacitus entertained such doubts emerges as soon as we examine the substance of the speech. Tacitus undoubtedly gave Paulinus the best arguments he could make, but they are not convincing. It may be that of the seven legions Otho had summoned from the Balkans, XIII Gemina alone had arrived in full force (the vanguard before Ad Castores, the rest after). As far as we can tell, the only other units to have come up were the van of XIV Gemina Martia Victrix, and two cavalry squadrons.[5] But against this we must set the facts, first, that even when Paulinus had mustered every Othonian soldier for Ad Castores, he had mismanaged the engagement; and second, that despite Plutarch's claims to the contrary, the two sides were more or less evenly matched at the time of the meeting. Otho need not have been alone in concluding that to let Paulinus go on accumulating troops would endanger rather than improve the prospects for the decisive victory the general yearned to win without running any risks.

Next, there is no evidence that the Vitellians had ravaged any territory they had seized. Caecina had kept his men on a tight leash, and Valens had not had time to go plundering since he arrived. We have independent evidence that the Transpadana produced no large surplus of grain, but it would have taken much longer than Paulinus pretended for the Vitellians to starve, and the longer they waited, the closer the harvest came. (It fell in June and July or, in other words, in summer.) Even if we ignore the resulting contradiction between Paulinus' second argument and his third, there is an unspoken and wholly disingenuous transition here. It is by picturing the Vitellian columns as barbarian hordes that Paulinus can claim out of the blue that the Germans were "the most formidable type of soldier in the enemy army." So his third argument is also unpersuasive. We cannot legitimately narrow the timespan Paulinus had in mind to a week or so when he urged waiting "into the summer." Roman summer began in mid-May, a month after the meeting. Moreover, German tribesmen were not the core of the enemy force. So even if the argument from climate was not absurd (it is one Tacitus employs frequently), it ignored the possibility that Caecina and Valens would find ways to acclimate their men. Paulinus' final suggestion, that Otho wait at least a few days until the bulk of XIV Gemina Martia Victrix arrived, was suspect too. It demonstrated the general's ongoing lack of confidence in the other Othonian units and the combat experience they had gained in spite of his efforts. It also suggested that his primary concern was to create a comfort zone for himself: XIV Gemina had been the one full legion he had commanded when he at last crushed Boudicca's revolt in Britain.

If Paulinus' was the better plan, in short, it was not much better. Small wonder that Otho "inclined to fight to the finish." The decision to offer battle, however, raised another question, whether or not Otho should be present. In republican times this issue would never have come up: generals then had almost invariably led from the front. Under the principate it was seldom possible for an emperor to do so, and it was inadvisable for Otho to break this pattern, when an Othonian victory that cost Otho his life would be worthless. The point was not that his principal adversary was safe and sound miles away in Germany. Had Vitellius lost Caecina and Valens, he would almost certainly have been forced to throw in his hand anyway. The important fact was that Otho had not designated a successor, and perhaps had had neither the time nor the inclination to consider the matter during the three short months of his reign.

Tacitus alone reports this second part of the debate.

> Once the decision to fight had been taken, they discussed whether it would be better for Otho to take part in the battle or to be kept out of it. As Paulinus and Celsus no longer offered any opposition, for fear of seeming eager to put the emperor in harm's way, the two men responsible for the worse plan [Titianus and Proculus] prevailed: Otho would withdraw to Brixellum and there, free from the uncertainties of battle, he could retain overall control of the situation and of the empire too. This was the first day to damage the Othonian cause. For not only did a powerful force of praetorian cohorts, speculatores and cavalry leave with the emperor. The spirit of those who remained at Bedriacum was also broken: they were suspicious of their generals, and since the troops had faith only in Otho, while he for his part put his trust only in the troops, he had left the commanders' responsibilities undefined.

Recognizing that the two armies were about equal in numbers at this stage, Tacitus rightly emphasizes that Otho's first critical error was to take a large force back to Brixellum. Presumably the emperor was under the impression that the troops who remained would fight with the same determination they had shown at Ad Castores, and that even if they were outnumbered by the Vitellians, they would show the élan to compensate for this (an argument Plutarch attributes to Titianus). But he may have had no choice. There was nothing to fear from the senators gathered at Brixellum, even though they included Vitellius' brother Lucius. No more did Otho need a large *corps d'élite* to impress the reinforcements from the Balkan provinces. But Brixellum lay only some 15 miles behind the front. So perhaps Otho himself or those who insisted on accompanying him, "the most enthusiastic of his supporters," imagined that he needed a sizable guard because Brixellum lay within reach of a small but daring Vitellian raiding party.

If we leave aside for the moment Tacitus' statement that Otho's departure "broke" the spirit of the troops who remained at Bedriacum (its importance lies in the damage it does to Plutarch's assessment of the situation), he makes two problematic remarks here. First, he comments that "the troops were suspicious of their generals." That the men still distrusted Paulinus, Celsus, and Gallus is unsurprising: the plan these three supported in the council of war must have became common knowledge as soon as the meeting ended, and it reopened the question of the generals' commitment to Otho's cause. But if we take Tacitus' words literally, the troops were no more impressed with Titianus and Proculus. One possibility is that they recognized their lack of experience. Another is that they saw them as poor substitutes for Otho. But there is a third possibility, if we take into account Tacitus' other problematic remark, that Otho "left the commanders' responsibilities undefined." This is misleading, perhaps even wrong. In his narrative of the battle's aftermath Tacitus pairs Paulinus with Licinius Proculus and Celsus with Titianus. If it is legitimate to see this as the result of the emperor's attempt to combine expertise and enthusiasm, by pairing his two fit senatorial generals with his two strongest supporters beforehand, the troops may have feared that Paulinus and Celsus would be able to influence Proculus and Titianus too much.

Whatever the case, it is time to ask why Otho was so determined to offer battle immediately. On this Tacitus says almost nothing except that the emperor "inclined to fight to the finish." Since this was the orthodox course, and since it is entirely consistent with Tacitus' portrait of a tough-minded emperor, there is no reason to expect more. But Plutarch was so fascinated by this that brevity was the last thing on his mind. Because he needed an explanation that accorded with his vision of a helpless emperor, he provided three different views aired by "various writers." Plutarch himself favored the idea that Otho succumbed to pressure from the praetorians. Now that they had experienced the discomforts of military service, they were eager to end the war and to return to the pleasures of duty in Rome, confident that even though outnumbered, they could overwhelm the enemy. As his second possibility Plutarch declared that the emperor "seems" to have been unable to bear uncertainty or, "as a result of his inexperience and his effeminacy," to face up to evaluating the dangers that beset him. So, choosing to put his trust in luck, he shut his eyes "like somebody leaping off a cliff. This at any rate was what Secundus used to say, the rhetorician who was Otho's secretary." Against this Plutarch balanced a third possibility, developed at greater length. "Others," he claimed, held that the two armies were strongly inclined to confer, to jettison Otho and Vitellius, and either to pick the best of their commanders as emperor or else to leave the choice to the senate. This created the suspicion that Celsus championed delay, so as to allow for a peaceful settlement, and Otho decided to hurry on the battle to preclude this outcome.[6]

As regards the first interpretation, there is nothing against the idea that the praetorians wanted to fight because they were keen to get back to Rome. But this is a red herring. The point at issue was not why the praetorians were eager to give battle immediately, only that they were eager to do so, and this was something of which any commander would have taken account. All this tells us, therefore, is that Plutarch used the praetorians' high morale to generate a theory "proving" that Otho was at the mercy of his troops.

Secundus' claims, on the other hand, have been embraced enthusiastically by those who accept Plutarch's portrait of Otho—actually, it is the only one of the three they can adopt. Undeterred by Plutarch's lack of enthusiasm for Secundus' theory (he says only that it "seems" to have been the case), they have tried to reinforce their argument by claiming, first, that Secundus must be Julius Secundus, a senator and a speaker in Tacitus' *Dialogue on Oratory*, as if this guaranteed the veracity of the tale; and second, that comments later in Tacitus' narrative confirm its truth. On the eve of the battle, when everything had supposedly been settled, Tacitus reports that the emperor lost his temper with his generals, and describes Otho as "impatient of delay and unable to bear the suspense." This is no evidence that the emperor had lost his nerve, only that he was exasperated. Having ordered his generals to get on with it, he could reasonably fire off letters two days running in which he told Titianus and Proculus to stop dragging their feet. As for Secundus, the name is so common that the man is much more likely to have been a slave or freedman than a senator, and it is entirely possible that, after drafting these letters, he turned a molehill into a mountain, to build up his own status as a source of information.[7]

This leaves us with the story that Otho insisted on fighting immediately because he feared that the two opposing armies wanted to confer, to dump both claimants to the throne, and either to pick the best of their commanders as emperor or to leave the choice to the senate. This idea undoubtedly goes back to the common source, since Tacitus devotes considerable space to it too. But he sets it after the meeting and he rejects it as nonsense—rightly. There was no reason to fear fraternization between the opposing armies. In civil wars such behavior is the norm, not the exception. What Tacitus recognized, as Plutarch did not, was that the Othonian troops would never have dreamt of jettisoning their emperor before the council of war. Only the decisions taken at the meeting had the potential to generate the kind of discontent presupposed by such a scenario. First, there had to be Otho's decision to withdraw to Brixellum, which "broke their spirit." And on this there had to follow the bungling and procrastination of his generals, which revived the men's suspicions that their cause was being betrayed.

These are not the reasons Tacitus gave for rejecting this interpretation. Like Plutarch, he roundly declared the troops too corrupt to have contemplated adopting an honorable course of action. But in his analysis of the situation he argued too—at some length—that Paulinus had more sense than to imagine that the troops would consider another candidate for the throne. Just as he had defended Paulinus' trustworthiness at Ad Castores, so now he insisted that Otho's generals, competent or not, were too honorable to contemplate betraying their emperor. It was a point worth making again. When, in due course, Paulinus and Proculus were brought before Vitellius, they claimed in their own defense that they had done their utmost to sabotage the Othonian war effort.

There is one last question to ask. If Otho was so hellbent on fighting at once, why did he call this council of war? Neither Tacitus nor Plutarch raises the issue, but nor do moderns. Yet Roman military commanders were as convinced as their counterparts in more recent centuries that a council of war should not be allowed to become a debate. When Caesar summoned such meetings, indeed, it was only to inform his officers what *they* were going to do. So there is something to be said for the idea that Otho called this council because he had made up his mind to give battle at once, and wanted to discover only if his generals were on board and, if they were not, to exert the pressure that would bring them into line. This fits Tacitus' flat statement that the emperor "inclined to fight to the finish." It gives us another possible reason for the historian's not crediting Titianus and Proculus with explicit arguments for fighting straightaway. It provides another explanation for Otho's pairing his generals, as he apparently did afterwards. And since Paulinus and Celsus may have continued to slow the progress Titianus and Proculus made, it helps account for Otho's writing the two angry letters he fired off in the last two days before the battle. Loyal as his senatorial generals might have been, nothing could persuade them to carry out their orders with enthusiasm.

How Valens occupied his time while the Othonians deliberated we are not told. Caecina, however, ordered his men to build a pontoon bridge across the Po, more or less opposite the position occupied by Macer and his gladiators. Tacitus, our main source, does not say where the Vitellians found the boats, probably because the answer was obvious. Since bridges over the river were few and far between, the local inhabitants must have relied heavily on waterborne transport, from rowing boats to barges. But Tacitus does provide a detailed description of the bridge's construction. The ships were aligned with their prows pointing upstream, and were fastened together at bow and stern with heavy beams that carried the roadbed. They were anchored too, but the hawsers had enough play in them for the line not to break if the level of the river rose suddenly, as it could in spring. And at the far end of the bridge, out in the river, Caecina positioned an artillery tower, to bombard the gladiators on the far bank and to repel any counterattacks they launched.

Tacitus' explicit statement that this was a feint failed to convince Henderson or Wellesley, and the latter maintained steadfastly that only a genuine attempt to cross the river would have justified the lengthy description Tacitus provides. But pontoon bridges were in the news when Tacitus was composing the *Histories*. Trajan built them to cross the Danube in both his Dacian Wars, and a scene near the base of his Column depicts two being put to use at the start of the first war in 101. Again, a technical description of an engineering feat required great literary artistry, and authors from Caesar onward could not resist the temptation to insert at least one such set piece into their narrative. Finally, as Caecina saw, only a realistic feint would have the desired effect on the Othonians and, in the meantime, keep his own men occupied with the kind of busywork Roman generals rarely hesitated to inflict on their troops.

Whatever the Othonians imagined the purpose of the bridge to be, they began their counterattacks immediately. First, says Tacitus, they built a tower of their own on the southern bank of the Po, and tried to destroy the bridge with fusillades of rocks and firebrands. When that failed, says Plutarch (supplying an episode Tacitus omits), they launched fire ships against it from the south bank. These ignited prematurely because of a sudden change in the wind, and the crews had to jump overboard and swim for their lives, to the amusement of the watching Vitellians. So, finally (here Tacitus resumes the tale), Macer and his gladiators decided to seize an island out in the middle of the river upstream from the bridge, and to launch attacks from there. But Caecina's German auxiliaries swam to the island faster than the Othonians could row to it. By the time Macer and his gladiators tried to land, therefore, they were exposed to an intense and accurate shower of missiles. Their confusion was increased by the rocking of the boats as they tried to return

fire, and by the rising number of casualties they were taking. And then
the Vitellian auxiliaries jumped into the water, climbed aboard the boats,
and cut down the Othonians at close quarters. Gladiators lacking the
skills and the stomach for such warfare, Macer and the survivors fled,
amid the jeers of the Vitellian troops who had lined up once again to
watch the struggle.

The Othonian troops, who had lined the south bank of the river for
the same reason, were so angry that they would have killed Macer when
he landed, had not other officers rushed him from the scene. This time
the troops had cause to be angry. The casualties must have been high,
since Otho ordered Spurinna to bring up two of the three praetorian
cohorts in Placentia as replacements. He also made a senior man commander of this force, Flavius Sabinus, the son of the city prefect and
nephew of Vespasian (Sabinus was due to take up a consulship on 30
April). But while the troops were delighted by the change of command,
Tacitus says, it was the generals' turn to be angry, at being assigned the
leadership of soldiers in a constant state of mutiny. How seriously we
should take this remark it is hard to decide. It may be true. But it is the
hook on which Tacitus hangs his commentary on the stories of fraternization between the armies, the suspicions that Otho's generals were trying to exploit the situation for their own ends, and his own conclusion
that these tales were rubbish.

That digression serves also as the *entr'acte* enabling Tacitus to switch
the scene from the south bank of the Po opposite Cremona to Bedriacum
on the northern bank. Since he is about to embark on his account of the
Othonian army's last days, he begins with the divisions that continued to
plague it after Otho left for Brixellum. Starting at the top and working
downward, he draws attention to serious weaknesses at every level. The
overall command was vested nominally in Titianus, but real power lay in
the hands of Licinius Proculus, the prefect of the guard and parade-
ground soldier. Neither listened to Paulinus and Marius Celsus, who
tagged along as advisers in name, in fact as scapegoats for any mishaps
that occurred. There were similar splits among the junior officers, tribunes, and centurions. The "better element" were angry that the "worst"
had greater influence, the "better element" in this context referring probably to the more competent and experienced officers. And the rankers
were still full of spirit, but as inclined as ever to criticize their orders
rather than to obey them.

How the Othonians planned to force a battle is a subject on which
more ink has been spilt than blood was shed on the field—and Plutarch
reports that when he walked the ground years later with his friend
Mestrius Florus, the latter pointed out to him a temple against which,

just after the battle, Florus had seen corpses piled so high that they touched the gable. It is a truism, of course, that no battle is the neat and tidy affair to which historians reduce it, but over Bedriacum the "fog of war" has never lifted. The one clear, basic point is that to bring on a battle, the Othonians had to carry the fight to the Vitellians. So they needed to move westward from Bedriacum along the river's northern bank, and approach close enough to Cremona to draw the enemy out of his camp. But this time they could not take all their forces with them, whether or not this was as ill advised as it appears. Some men had to remain at Bedriacum, since it was the staging post for the reinforcements expected from the Balkan provinces. But as the command was entrusted to the injured Annius Gallus, the men left with him were probably those less fit for active duty. This *was* risky. But the other generals presumably concluded that the Vitellians would not attack the village, so long as their own main force was operating in the area and, for that matter, so long as Otho's troops at Brixellum remained on the alert.

Whatever distance the main Othonian force marched on the first day (14 April), it covered enough ground to bring it up onto the Postumian Way, the road leading to Cremona.[8] But progress was much slower than it should have been, and Otho was not alone in taking this as a mixture of faintheartedness and incompetence. Even as he sent the generals an angry letter, telling them to carry out his orders, they were beset by complaints from the rankers too. Some demanded that the emperor come up to lead the army; many others urged that the force of gladiators and praetorians under Flavius Sabinus on the southern bank of the Po be summoned to join them. This latter move, incidentally, seems to have been carried out on the next day, but exactly how and when it was done remains obscure. As if this were not enough, Tacitus and Plutarch comment on the lack of expertise with which the generals pitched camp late in the day, asserting that though the landscape was dotted with springs, all of them full at this time of year, the generals picked a site where water was short. Tacitus sums up the situation with the sardonic observation that, in retrospect, it was harder to decide what it would have been best for the Othonians to do than it was to conclude that what they did was the worst thing possible.

The Vitellians naturally refused to respond on the first day. They would have had to undertake a significantly longer march than the few miles the Othonians managed, and there was no point when Caecina and Valens were resolved to let the enemy make the errors. So the Othonian generals held another conference, on how, when, and where they would fight the battle, and it was probably at the meeting that Otho's letter was read out and steps taken to ensure that Sabinus brought his force of praetorians and gladiators across the Po to join them. But it also looks as if the lack of a Vitellian response encouraged the Othonian generals in the delusion that the enemy would remain inactive on the next day too. The upshot, according to Tacitus, was a decision that the army would advance to the confluence of the Po and the Adua (or Adda), some five to seven miles *beyond* Cremona. To make better progress, they would keep to the Postumian Way as long as possible, but arc around Cremona, perhaps as little as four or five miles from the enemy camp. Having reached their destination safely, they would pitch camp, since Tacitus stresses that when they set out on the next morning, they took their baggage train with them, "as if marching off on a campaign rather than to a battle." Then, after a night resting and recovering their strength, they would offer battle on the following (third) day.

That this was the absurd plan put into effect on the second morning (15 April) may be confirmed by the nonstop critique to which Paulinus and Celsus subjected it en route. They pointed out repeatedly that when Cremona lay so close to their line of march, not only was an attack inevitable, but the Vitellians would be able also to choose when and where to launch it: they could make their move while the Othonians were in column, encumbered by their baggage train and weary from marching, or after they halted, when the men dispersed to build a camp. Though their advice was prescient for once, it was dismissed with the assertion that they were no longer in command. Titianus and Proculus refused to modify the plan, and they were spurred on by another peremptory dispatch from Otho, rebuking them for their lackadaisical progress. And so, it seems, they blundered into a Vitellian army drawn up and ready to fight.[9]

It remains unclear how accurate a reflection of the situation this is for two reasons. First, Tacitus and Plutarch open their accounts in an unusual way. They switch away from the Othonian column, focus on Caecina's absorption with his pontoon bridge, and then return with him to the battle at a point when the first contacts have been made (however they were made), and Valens has begun forming up the Vitellian battle line. Plutarch has no excuse for this, since he makes nothing of it. Tacitus does, bringing up another mystery. As Caecina was working on his bridge, he was approached by two praetorian tribunes. Where they came from is unknown.[10] So too is what they had in mind, whether to befuddle Caecina, to betray their own leaders, or to offer yet another plan. Before they could start their talks, Vitellian scouts rushed up to report that the main Othonian force was about to make contact, and Caecina sent the two tribunes packing while he raced back to Cremona.

The second reason why it is hard to unravel the situation lies in the stress Tacitus puts on the confusion prevailing amongst the Othonians as they tried to deploy. Supposedly, their column was in total disarray, strung out along the road, and the troop formations were tangled up with baggage carts and sutlers' wagons. This confusion worsened when they realized that the Vitellians were going to confront them. The deep ditches on both sides of the causeway, not to mention the terrain north of the road which—like that at Ad Castores—was broken up by irrigation and drainage ditches, and impeded by vines trained from tree to tree, made it difficult for the men to fan out. And since the generals were jumpy and the soldiery fed up, clear orders either were not given or were not heard in the uproar. Some troops gathered round their standards, others went looking for theirs. Some shouted as they ran to join their units, others called to comrades who had not joined them. So, says Tacitus, while the braver men pressed forward to take their places in the front ranks, the cowardly lost themselves in the rear. All this may be true, but dwelling on such details tends to obscure two important facts, that the Othonians deployed despite the obstacles they encountered, and that since they were able to deploy, there must have been a time lag between the moment when the two sides became aware of each other's presence and the moment when they actually joined combat.

Neither Tacitus nor Plutarch provides the order of battle for the two sides. But so far as we can tell, Caecina and Valens positioned V Alaudae on their left wing (north of the road), I Italica in the center, straddling the causeway, and XXI Rapax on their right wing, south of the road, where the relatively open ground allowed a legion to fight a standard pitched battle. On the extreme right, next to the river, they added a force of Batavian auxiliaries, infantry and cavalry, under Alfenus Varus, since it was here—to all appearances—that the mixture of Othonian gladiators and praetorians from the southern bank took up its position. The rest of their troops Caecina and Valens must have held in reserve, as Tacitus talks of their feeding reinforcements into the battle as and when necessary. Now, there is one interesting point about these dispositions. Valens' two legions, V Alaudae and I Italica, were given the more difficult assignments, whereas XXI Rapax, the core unit from Caecina's column, was posted on the open ground south of the road. This may be happenstance, but if Caecina's men had had to rush back from the pontoon bridge, keeping them on the open ground enabled them to come up and deploy quicker. This may even underlie Plutarch's rather odd remark that, in the battle, the men of XXI Rapax fought bravely but "were old and past their prime." Perhaps they were winded.

Because of the varying nature of the ground, Tacitus and Plutarch (in less detail) describe the battle in a series of vignettes, as if each set-to was a separate encounter. This may be how the battle played out. The first encounter, in any case, was a cavalry skirmish while the Vitellian legions were still forming up. The Vitellian horse sallied forth to do battle with two squadrons of Pannonian and Moesian cavalry at the head of the Othonian column.[11] The latter routed them and would have driven them back onto their own lines, had it not been for the steadiness of I Italica. By now up on the causeway, the legionaries drew their swords and forced their own horsemen to rejoin the fray, and this gave the rest of their infantry time to form up without interruption.

The next contact was also made on the causeway. Here the men of I Italica were faced, apparently, by Otho's five praetorian cohorts, in all some 2,500 men. According to Tacitus, a disconcerting rumor began to spread through the ranks of the Othonian van that Vitellius' army had deserted him. As he also says, it is unclear if this report was planted by Vitellian agents to throw the Othonians off guard (this is Suetonius' view, derived probably from his father, Suetonius Laetus, who fought in the battle), or if it arose within the Othonian lines, by accident or design (this is closer to Plutarch's opinion). Either way, the praetorians in the front line were so elated that they offered friendly greetings to the Vitellians facing them. This proved doubly unfortunate. It elicited angry murmurs from the enemy, and it created suspicions of treachery among their own comrades in the ranks behind, as yet unaware of the rumor. But once they had recovered from this surprise, the two sides got down to business. Both dispensed with the customary hurling of javelins, because they were so close to one another, and were hemmed in anyway by the precipitous edges to the road. Instead, they fought shield-to-shield, hacking away with swords and axes.[12]

Tacitus alone talks of the fighting on the Othonian right wing, on the broken ground north of the road, and he provides only two snippets: that XIII Gemina, the one Balkan legion to have arrived in full force, was driven back by the attack of V Alaudae; and that the advance detachment from XIV Gemina Martia Victrix was surrounded by superior numbers and overwhelmed, though some men managed to fight their way out of the encirclement. By now, Otho's generals seem to have fled, but Caecina and Valens continued feeding in the reinforcements to guarantee victory. The situation was no better on the Othonian left wing. Here, on the more open ground, the newly recruited I Adiutrix faced the veterans of XXI Rapax. The ex-marines, he declares, were so eager to win renown that they cut down the front ranks of their opponents and captured their eagle. The loss of this emblem being the greatest humiliation a legion could suffer, the Vitellians were infuriated. So once they had rallied, they drove back the Othonians, killed their commander Orfidius Benignus, and took many of their standards—but not their eagle. Even

under this onslaught I Adiutrix seems to have attempted a fighting retreat. But they collapsed when taken in flank by the Batavian infantry
and cavalry under Alfenus Varus. These latter, having made short work
of the band of gladiators and praetorians brought across the river, attacked the legion's left flank and rolled up its line.

Although the Othonian center fought long and hard, it gave way
once it was stripped of protection on both flanks. A rout followed, but
on this neither Tacitus nor Plutarch has much to say, largely because
ancient authors cut away from, not to the chase. All over the field Othonians began rushing back to Bedriacum, and for men worsted in battle
this was an enormous distance away, between 12 and 20 miles. Some of
the fugitives had to cut their way through the enemy (this may be a reference to XIV Gemina), and all were impeded by the piles of corpses. It
would be unwise to accept Dio's assertion that the casualty figures for
both sides totaled 40,000, but the slaughter must have run into the thousands. The victors had no incentive to spare their defeated opponents,
because Romans taken prisoner in a civil war could not be ransomed or
sold into slavery, and Othonian corpses still littered the ground some 40
days later, when Vitellius arrived to view the site of his victory.

Paulinus and Proculus avoided returning to the camp at Bedriacum,
for fear—rightly—that the troops in their rage and frustration would kill
them out of hand. This fate nearly befell the blameless commander of XIII
Gemina, Vedius Aquila. The moment he entered the camp late in the day,
he was surrounded by rankers denouncing him as a deserter and a traitor.
That he survived (he was still commander of the legion in the autumn) was
due probably to the intervention of Annius Gallus. Left in charge of the
camp at Bedriacum, Annius did everything he could to calm the men.
Urging them not to give way to despair, he begged them not to make
matters worse by turning on one other. Whether they wanted to surrender or to continue the fight, he said, they must come together first.

Order had been restored by nightfall, when Titianus and Celsus returned. Of Celsus Tacitus says no more, but Plutarch has him call a meeting of officers, in which he urged surrender. If they took the larger view
and considered the public good, he supposedly declared, they would recognize that the war was over. As they had suffered such enormous losses,
even Otho, "if he was a good man," would not squander more lives. Recognizing that his cause was lost, he would follow precedent, take the honorable way out, and commit suicide. That Celsus said something seems
undeniable. That it bore any resemblance to Plutarch's speech is improbable. Devoted to Otho's cause, Celsus would not have made suicide the
emperor's only choice. This is Plutarch's work, an attempt to limit Otho's
options, and to devalue the decision he took by representing him as a

helpless prisoner of convention. To the same end, Plutarch papers over the divisions within the soldiery to whom the officers conveyed Celsus' words. He claims that the men followed their officers' advice, whereas Tacitus emphasizes that there was a major split within the soldiery. The praetorians remained violently opposed to surrender and insisted that Otho's cause was not lost. With this conclusion the Vitellians obviously agreed. Caecina and Valens led their troops to a point some five miles from Bedriacum and halted there. In part, no doubt, this reflected their inability to storm the camp at once, in part their hope that the enemy would surrender if given time to think. Yet their caution also demonstrated their respect for adversaries who were beaten but not yet broken.

The Vitellians' tactics paid off. By the following morning (16 April) even the most bellicose Othonians had decided that they must surrender. While Titianus remained at Bedriacum, Celsus and Gallus set off to negotiate with their opposite numbers. Plutarch paints a vivid picture of the dangers they encountered. They were intercepted by a detachment of Vitellian cavalrymen, who recognized Celsus as the man responsible for their defeat at Ad Castores, and were all for killing him. He was saved only by the intervention of Caecina, who came up and personally escorted the envoys into the camp. Once terms had been agreed, Caecina returned with the Othonians to Bedriacum. Here there had been a change of heart, misgivings prompted perhaps by the length of time the envoys had been gone, perhaps by doubts that an agreement was possible. But Caecina's taste for theater saved the day. He stretched out his hand in friendship to the camp's defenders and they laid down their arms and opened the gates.

Tacitus omits all reference to the envoys' misadventures and Caecina's gesture. He dwells on the way the rankers from the two armies fraternized after agreement had been reached. They bewailed the evils of civil war, mourned for their dead kinfolk, and gave honorable burial to Orfidius Benignus, the valiant commander of I Adiutrix. His account is as melodramatic as Plutarch's, but it makes a serious point. Plutarch is captivated by the picturesque, but Tacitus stresses the fact that this was the first major battle between Roman troops in the first unquestionably civil war since Nero's death—and a bloody affair it was. True, this enables him to draw attention to the horrors that continuing the fight would have inflicted on both sides, and so to the boon Otho conferred on the survivors by ending his life. But this was reasonable. Whatever the Othonians at Bedriacum felt, those at Brixellum were not ready to surrender. There would have been more slaughter and suffering, had Otho not committed suicide at dawn that same morning, so ending the campaign and, with it, the war.

7

The Reign of Vitellius
(April to September 69)

Otho's suicide ought to be treated—so some might think—as the last event in his reign. It was his final act as emperor and, since he ended his life before he heard the news of the surrender at Bedriacum, it also marked the high point of that reign, setting up the paradox over which both contemporaries and posterity would puzzle, that "nothing in his life became him like the leaving it." Tacitus certainly reports it in this manner, but not only in this manner. He has already set a passage immediately after his obituary for Galba, in which he describes the reactions of Rome's inhabitants—senators, knights, and common people—to the prospect of choosing between Otho and Vitellius. Nobody, he asserts, could see themselves going to the temples to pray for the safety of either man. They were the vilest of mortals, seemingly picked by the fates to destroy the empire. In fact, "the one thing you could expect to learn from a war between them was that the victor would be the worse." This makes Otho's suicide as much a beginning as an end, and Tacitus builds it up programmatically, to overshadow the reign of his successor, a man who, in Tacitus' opinion, ought never to have become emperor.

As Tacitus tells the story, Otho must have committed suicide at dawn on 16 April, after he heard the news of the defeat of his troops at Bedriacum, but before he learnt or could learn that the survivors were going to surrender.[1] In one sense this detail is not as significant as it may appear. The soldiers who straggled in from the battle, after all, cannot have held out much hope. And Otho could not expect Vitellius to spare his life, even if clemency was extended—as it was—to each and every one of his generals. The senators who could claim to have been following orders, like Suetonius Paulinus, Marius Celsus, Annius Gallus, and Flavius Sabinus, were not the only ones to benefit. So too did close associates like the two prefects of the praetorian guard, Licinius Proculus and Plotius Firmus, and even Otho's brother Salvius Titianus. Yet aside from Plotius Firmus, who was already with the emperor, none of these men made their way to Brixellum after the battle. Three of them, Celsus, Gallus, and Titianus, found it necessary (or convenient) to oversee the surrender at Bedriacum. Sabinus returned to Placentia to wait on events, since one praetorian cohort was still there. And Paulinus and Proculus made themselves scarce, reappearing in the record only to grovel before Vitellius a month or so later. In effect, Otho was deserted by his generals.

Since Tacitus insists that when the first stragglers from the battle reached Brixellum late on 15 April, Otho had already made up his mind to commit suicide if his troops lost the battle, and had done so fearlessly and calmly, there is clearly no direct link between Otho's decision and his being abandoned by his generals. But if we see their action, accidental or deliberate, as another stage in the conflict of opinions the council of war had not resolved, it is easier to understand why Otho refused to fall back on Aquileia, and to use the Balkan troops to fight again. This was the course the praetorians at Brixellum urged on him, while the cavalry squadron that had arrived from Moesia claimed (falsely, as they could not know it) that their legions had already reached Aquileia, with the result—says Tacitus—that "nobody can doubt that the fighting could have been resumed, cruel, grim and perilous to victors and vanquished alike."[2] Otho clearly disagreed with this conclusion, and his reasons are easy to see: he had run through the generals at his disposal; he did not expect to find competent or devoted replacements among the Balkan troops still on their way to Italy; and he recognized that he lacked the ability to take command personally.

This in no way devalues the stories that Otho had not wanted to fight in the first place. Whether or not we believe Suetonius' story that during the campaign Otho shuddered whenever the names of Brutus and Cassius were brought up in conversation, he had tried to negotiate with Vitellius before the march north. Nor had he ever been so much the prisoner of his troops that he could not have backed down. But there was a major difference between the situation before the campaign of Bedriacum began and the situation after it was launched. Earlier, as emerges from the speeches Tacitus gives him, Otho refused to accept "a secret of empire, that an emperor could be made elsewhere than in Rome." In Otho's eyes, Vitellius had started the civil war, and the fact that his uprising had begun two full weeks before Galba's assassination made no odds. Vitellius was a rebel, because he had not been proclaimed emperor in Rome, nor had his elevation to the principate been ratified by the senate. Otho, as the legitimate emperor, had every reason to campaign against him at first. But once the war got under way, Otho faced two choices if the battle went against him: he could continue to defend his legitimate right to the throne or he could bow to reality, renounce his powers, and by proclaiming that he was doing so in hopes of ending the bloodshed, prove the nobler as well as the braver of the two contenders.

Viewed in this light, Otho's suicide becomes an exercise in public relations, and that is why it is misguided to reject Tacitus' statement that Otho made his decision not only before the battle but fearlessly and calmly too or, failing that, to dismiss his account as too melodramatic. If we adopt Plutarch's picture of Otho as a hysterical coward, we destroy the paradox that entranced the Romans. Nor is much gained by accepting Suetonius' portrait of Otho as an impetuous gambler, willing to stake all and, if luck turned against him, to lose all. For one thing, he undercuts Otho's action by asserting that the suicide of a straggler from Bedriacum inspired the emperor to take his own life. For another, Otho had not staked all, so long as there were troops he could call on. Third, on Suetonius' scenario too, Otho's suicide would never have fascinated later generations of Romans as comprehensively as it did. Like Nero's, it would have been dismissed as a matter of little consequence. The fascination, in short, rested on the conviction to which Tacitus gives voice, that Otho's suicide was the result of a calculated and cold-blooded decision, and so the action of a truly brave man.[3] It may look melodramatic, but that does not make it unhistorical. It was Otho who staged the drama, not the ancient sources. Schooled in role-playing by his years as a courtier, Otho knew that he had to give the performance of his life.

Obviously, he would not have publicized his decision before the battle was fought. But once the bad news arrived from Bedriacum, first as rumor and then as hard evidence provided by stragglers, the troops at Brixellum had the wit to recognize that there was now a distinct likelihood that Otho would end his life. So they urged him not to lose heart. Not only were reinforcements on the way, but they themselves were willing to fight to the last. Tacitus emphasizes that these protestations were entirely sincere, and Plutarch too concedes that "the feelings of his soldiers toward him passed all belief." Supposedly, Plotius Firmus, the prefect of the guard, went further still, arguing—according to Tacitus— that Otho should not desert so loyal an army. Since it was braver to bear adversity than to yield to it, cowards alone were driven by panic to despair. But this may be only a hook on which to hang the speech Tacitus has Otho make to calm the soldiery. We have three versions of it, one each from Plutarch, Tacitus, and Dio, and all of them credit Otho with much the same sentiments, though the wording (for once) shows few resemblances. Of the three Tacitus' is by far the most illuminating. It is built around a rival definition of bravery, that refusing to continue the fight is no less glorious and brave.

> To expose men of your spirit and courage to further danger I think too
> high a price to pay for my life. The more hope you hold out to me, the

more glorious my death becomes. We have gotten to know each other, Fortune and I, and you should not discount the shortness of my reign. For when you know that you will not enjoy your good fortune for long, it is more difficult to show restraint. Vitellius began this civil war by forcing us to fight for the throne. I will end it, by ensuring that we fight no more than once. Let this be how posterity judges me. Let Vitellius take delight in his kinfolk: I seek neither revenge nor consolation for my defeat [i.e., by taking reprisals against his family]. Others may have reigned longer, but none will relinquish his power so bravely. You cannot expect me to allow the flower of Rome's youth, so many splendid army units, to shed their blood a second time. Let me carry away with me the thought that you were ready to die for me, but survive you must. No more delay! I must not endanger your safety, nor you impede my decision. To dwell on one's last moments is a coward's way. The ultimate proof of my determination is that I make no complaints. To find fault with gods or men is the behavior of one who would prefer to go on living.

Whether this was or was not the speech Otho gave, two points are worth noting. First, there is the remark that "when you know that you will not enjoy your good fortune for any length of time, it is more difficult to show restraint." This has been turned into a statement that at some stage Otho must have realized that he would not remain emperor long, and so has become the basis for claims that Otho had recognized the folly of his bid for power much earlier. The comment cannot carry this kind of weight. Otho is talking about the present, not the past. He is setting up the thesis that showing self-control when there is nothing to gain is the acid test of character, self-control he is showing by refusing even to take reprisals against the members of Vitellius' family. Far from asserting that he has long felt this way, he is putting the best face on the brevity of his reign, and that reign he will end now without dragging anybody else, friend or foe, down to destruction.

Second, when Otho tells his troops that he wants posterity to judge him by this renunciation, it is not in the hope that this will somehow obscure or cancel out the murder of Galba. Neither he nor the Greco-Roman sources who report his actions believed in redemption. Zonaras' summary of Dio may assert that "the manner of Otho's death eclipsed the impiousness and wickedness of his life," but Zonaras was a Christian monk who imported an alien idea into Dio's account. In fact, it had been Otho's view all along that murdering his predecessor was justifiable, and he never changed his mind about that. But just as he had recognized in the past that he had to conciliate and reassure those who held different views, so now he acknowledged that he must shoulder the responsibility for his own actions—and the most effective way to do that was to set up a balance between the assassination of Galba and his own suicide. Then, as Tacitus puts it, he would "win as much praise among succeeding generations as he had gained opprobrium among his contemporaries for the murder." By showing that he was capable of the best as well as the worst of acts, he could guarantee that he would be judged favorably—if only for one action—by later generations, the aim of every Roman aristocrat, and that by setting this against the murder of his predecessor he would create a paradox that would never cease to fascinate those later generations.

Whatever Otho actually said in his speech, he next summoned his friends individually, treating all alike in kindly fashion but urging them to leave rather than bring down the victors' anger on their heads. Firmly but placidly resisting their entreaties to change his mind, he ordered boats and carriages found for them. He destroyed incriminating correspondence (this was traditional behavior also). And he distributed what money he had left to his slaves and freedmen sparingly, here too showing the restraint expected of a man who had made a rational decision. Later, supposedly, he reassured his nephew Salvius Cocceianus, Titianus' son whom—so Plutarch says—he had planned to adopt as his heir once the war was over. Telling the boy that he should neither fear for his own life nor grieve over his uncle's decision, Otho pointed out that Vitellius would not kill Cocceianus when he himself had spared Vitellius' kin, and that the boy should be grateful to Otho for setting the family in the forefront of the aristocracy. The boy should go on with his life, neither forgetting Otho nor yet remembering him too well—a piece of advice Tacitus may have added to the story, because he knew that Cocceianus would be killed by Domitian in the early 90s, as Suetonius alleges, for celebrating Otho's birthday too enthusiastically.

After dismissing everybody Otho took a rest. Tacitus states that he wanted to compose himself for death, but Suetonius has him writing letters, one to console his sister, and one exhorting Statilia Messallina to cherish his memory. Statilia had been Nero's third wife and Suetonius asserts that Otho had contemplated marrying her, but what he would have gained by this if he was going to adopt Cocceianus is unclear. A sudden uproar in the camp interrupted his meditations. The troops were making threats against the dignitaries trying to leave, and they even blockaded Verginius Rufus in his billet. Rebuking the men, Otho returned to his quarters and spent time in conversations with those who were leaving, until he was assured that all could get away safely. Yet Verginius stayed, possibly by choice. As Otho had designated him suffect consul for March and April, he may have imagined that he had some kind of official standing and so should remain, but Plutarch claims that the troops refused to let him depart.

By now it was evening. Yet Otho continued to exercise rigorous self-control. Instead of wining and dining too well, as a Nero or a Vitellius might have, he took only a drink of ice-cold water, and then, after being brought two daggers, chose one and put it under his pillow. When he had been reassured again that his friends had left, he went to bed, sleeping peacefully and dreamlessly.[4] He awoke at first light and with a single, firm stroke drove the dagger unhesitatingly into his heart. His freedmen and slaves, posted outside the bedroom, rushed in as soon as they heard the one groan he made, and along with the prefect Plotius Firmus immediately began preparations for his funeral. Although it was customary for a body to lie in state for several days, Otho had insisted that he be cremated without delay, so that there would be no corpse for the enemy to seize and mutilate. The praetorian cohorts carried his body to the funeral pyre, some loud in their praises, some in tears, and some kissing his hands, his feet, and even the wound. Once the corpse had been placed on the pyre, so Tacitus says, some of the soldiers committed suicide alongside it, both because they wanted to emulate his glorious act and from love for him. Nor did this happen only at Brixellum, he goes on. There were suicides at Bedriacum, at Placentia, and in every other camp where Othonians were to be found.

Tacitus is content to observe that Otho's grave was modest and so destined to survive. Suetonius, by contrast, uses that detail to report Vitellius' reaction to the sight of it, and to illustrate how petty-minded the victor was. For Vitellius declared it a little tomb, fit for a little man, and sent the dagger his rival had used to kill himself to Colonia Agrippinensis (Cologne, his former HQ) to be dedicated in the temple to Mars. The story is probably true. Vitellius was given to blunt and tactless remarks, but since Tacitus omits comments he thinks in bad taste, he uses mention of the grave to introduce Otho's necrology. Then, after some coughing and spluttering, seemingly designed to emphasize an episode that scarcely deserves it, he tells the story of a bird, of a type never seen before, that took up its perch in a crowded grove at Regium Lepidum (Reggio), 17 miles southeast of Brixellum on the day of the battle. The bird, he declares, was entirely unperturbed by the people and the other birds that flocked around it, and kept its position until the moment Otho killed himself. Then it disappeared from sight for ever more. This was taken as an omen, though an omen of what Tacitus does not say. Why, then, does he report it? The likeliest explanation is literary and symbolic: the bird was supposed to mark the end of the fighting between Otho and Vitellius, just as the eagle that had accompanied Valens' column on the first day of its march had marked its start. Suetonius too finds a bird omen to balance Valens' eagle, but his tale concerns Vitellius.

The funeral was followed by another uproar. According to Plutarch, in his last surviving contribution to our story, this one was triggered by the prefect Plotius Firmus. When emotions were running so high, he might have done better to wait, but he tried to administer to the troops the oath of allegiance to Vitellius. Unlike the men at Bedriacum, the Othonians at Brixellum balked. They turned to Verginius since he had still not left, or had not been allowed to leave, the camp. While some urged him to bid for the throne again, others asked only that he serve as their emissary to the Vitellians. He ducked both assignments, slipping away through the back door of his quarters, presumably in disguise. To save the man's dignity, Plutarch declares that Verginius thought it "insane" to accept from a defeated army a throne he had refused from a victorious one, and feared to negotiate with legions "he had often forced to act contrary to their wishes." So Rubrius Gallus, a much more flexible personality, pleaded the troops' case, and pardon was granted forthwith. In the same way, the men at Placentia were pardoned through the intercession of their commander, Flavius Sabinus.

For much of what follows Tacitus is our sole source, and as usual he does the unexpected. A modern historian would probably turn next either to the dispositions made of the defeated troops, or else to Vitellius' activities now that he was the uncontested emperor of Rome. After all, one would not expect the Vitellians to have left large numbers of Othonians milling around unsupervised in northern Italy, while an immediate transition to a description of how Vitellius took the news of his victory would point up his inadequacies as Otho's successor. But the way Tacitus tells the story suggests that Caecina and Valens thought the Othonians' taking the oath of allegiance to Vitellius sufficient to keep them quiet until their new emperor issued appropriate orders. This detail is worth stressing, since it gives us another indication that oaths of allegiance were taken more seriously than we might imagine, for all that there was nobody else to whom the Othonians could appeal once Verginius refused to intervene. And since Tacitus delays all talk of Vitellius too, in order to introduce a string of other events in different parts of the empire, it looks as if his aim is not just to work in material for which he could find no other place. He wants also to illustrate the proposition that, as bad an emperor as Vitellius was, there was nobody else out there—as yet—with greater gifts of leadership. The long pause between Otho's death in mid-April and Vitellius' arrival in Rome around the end of June created a power vacuum like the one that had followed Nero's suicide, but this time nobody in the city took control. Without a strong hand at the helm of the ship of state, the crew spent their time quarreling amongst themselves.

The senators, for example, who were marooned at Mutina (Modena), some 30 miles southeast of Brixellum, had no idea what to do. True, they were handicapped by having an escort of Othonian soldiers who dismissed the news of their emperor's defeat and death as rumor. But these were leading senators and they included Vitellius' brother Lucius. Attempting desperately to avoid taking any official action until they were sure that Otho was dead, they quarreled with one another and, in the interim, fell back to Bononia (Bologna), another 24 miles further to the southeast. In fact, they would probably have continued this desultory progress in the general direction of Rome indefinitely, had not Valens sent them an official communiqué confirming the reports of Otho's sucide and so putting them out of their misery.

In Rome, on the other hand, the announcement of Otho's death produced only indifference. The games in honor of Ceres (*ludi Ceriales*) were being held at the time (19 April), and when the audience heard that Otho was dead and that Flavius Sabinus, the prefect of the city, had administered the oath of allegiance to Vitellius to such armed forces as were based there, they only applauded politely. After the games, however, they went to the site where Galba had fallen, to heap flowers on the spot. Perhaps they felt genuine regret now that Galba was dead. Perhaps they were just performing a courtesy it would have been un-safe as well as unwise to carry out sooner. But they too received no official guidance. In a rump meeting of the senate it was decided that Vitellius should be granted all the titles due to an emperor without debate or dispute, a vote of thanks was passed in honor of the Rhine legions, and envoys were chosen to convey it to the troops. At the same time a dispatch from Fabius Valens was read to the senators, but this put their backs up. Miffed that the letter came from an underling, not from Vitellius, they stood on their dignity, and praised Caecina's re-straint in not having written to them.

Meanwhile, so says Tacitus, the Vitellian troops showed no restraint. Since there was no plan to march the victorious troops to Rome until Vitellius could arrive and assume command, they were billeted in the towns of northern Italy, and spent their time looting and raping without regard for right and wrong. Tacitus concedes that there was a certain amount of score settling by civilians who pretended to be part of the army. But he insists that the soldiers who knew the area went around noting down the wealthy farms and the rich town houses, determined to strip them bare and, if necessary, to murder their owners. All this Caecina and Valens countenanced, the former more from popularity seeking than greed, the latter because he connived at the depredations of others to cover up his own. But the two generals could not have controlled the men anyway, so Tacitus asserts, to validate his thesis that Italy north of Rome was reduced to penury by this gigantic force of infantry and cavalry. This being a stock depiction of the brutal soldiery at play, it may or may not be true. Tacitus neglects to mention until later that Caecina and Valens would be summoned to a victory celebration in Lugdunum (Lyon), and so deprived of any chance personally to keep their troops in Italy under control, whether they wanted to or not.

In this same period there was an uproar in the two procuratorial districts of Mauretania on the northwest coast of Africa: Tingitana, the more westerly, less settled region (Morocco and Fez); and Caesariensis, the relatively more civilized area (western Algeria), next to the Roman province Africa. Galba had entrusted both to Lucceius Albinus. When Galba was murdered, Lucceius inclined to join Otho, but he was determined to aggrandize himself too. So he raised additional troops, and began planning an incursion into Baetica, the richest province in Spain on the other side of the Straits of Gibraltar. He could justify this on the ground that the most important official in the peninsula, the unwarlike Cluvius Rufus in Tarraconensis, had deserted Otho for Vitellius. In the event, Cluvius thwarted Lucceius' plans by sending several centurions across to Africa, to act as *agents provocateurs* and—if necessary—assassins. These men alienated Lucceius' Roman supporters by spreading rumors that he planned making himself king, with all the trappings the native dynasts of Mauretania had once worn. But, interestingly, it was auxiliaries who murdered Lucceius, and his wife too, when she tried to shield him. But Tacitus makes little of this, since he sees the episode as another stick with which to belabor Vitellius for not enquiring into the details.

This criticism provides Tacitus with the transition that enables him at long last to make Vitellius the main subject of his narrative. Yet his account still shows marked peculiarities. For a start, he says far more about Vitellius' march to Rome than he does about his actions as emperor in Rome. Then too, the trek is fleshed out with more side stories. There was Mariccus, a Boian tribesman who caused an uproar in central Gaul by declaring himself a god and raising a band of 8,000 believers. With them he raided the territory of the neighboring tribe of the Aedui until he was caught and killed. There was a runaway slave named Geta, who caused alarm in northeastern Italy (Histria) by claiming to be a scion of the Sulpicii Camerini, an aristocratic family Nero had wiped out in 67. Finally, Tacitus cuts Vitellius' trek in half, so that in between the two segments he can insert his description of Vespasian's proclamation as emperor by the legions of Judaea, Syria, and Egypt. After all this, he telescopes Vitellius' actions as emperor in Rome into about half the space he has devoted to the trek.

Whatever other reasons are offered for Tacitus' tactics, three are worth spelling out. First, setting Vespasian's acclamation as emperor within his rival's trek to Rome substantiated Tacitus' view that the Flavian bid for the throne before Vitellius reached Rome (as Josephus tells us, Vespasian asserted the opposite). Second, the behavior of the Vitellian troops during the trek gave Vespasian's henchman, Licinius Mucianus, the material for the arguments he used in a speech that supposedly helped precipitate the revolt. And third, the idea behind telescoping Vitellius' actions in Rome, and perhaps backdating some of them to the period before he reached the city (a possibility suggested by Suetonius' setting some of these incidents after Vitellius' arrival in Rome), may have been to justify sidelining Vitellius as a sluggard once the fighting began. Tacitus will certainly focus on the campaigns conducted by Caecina, Valens, and their opponents from September onward, and reintroduce Vitellius himself only in his last days, when he played the role "not of an emperor but only of a cause for the fighting."

The net result is that it is even more difficult to reconstruct the "reign" of Vitellius than it is those of Galba and Otho. The main lines he pursued, during his trek south and after his arrival in Rome, are clear enough. In his early days (and from this perspective there were no later days), Vitellius was preoccupied with the need to reward his allies, to neutralize his enemies, and to placate everybody else. So though he showed some restraint in punishing the Othonian soldiery, he took steps to disarm and disperse them, and meanwhile tried to gratify his own troops. Yet he did all this in a fashion that would work effectively only if his own position were not challenged by a new contender for the throne. And he was too ready to believe the news that, initially, the legions stationed in the eastern provinces were content to take the oath of allegiance to him. According to Tacitus, indeed, the arrival of such a report from Syria induced Vitellius and his troops to "break out into the cruelty, debauchery and rapine expected of an oriental despot." This is a deliberate overstatement, designed to rest Tacitus' transition from Vitellius to Vespasian on the paradoxical contrast between a quasi-Persian king in Rome and a simple Roman in the east. But Caecina and Valens too must have been relieved to hear this news. In the civil sphere Vitellius attempted to appease and reassure senators and populace, although this created as many problems as it solved. And fiscally, he found interesting methods for raising money to satisfy immediate needs. But all his actions smack of shortsighted opportunism, whether or not we attribute this—as Tacitus does—to the emperor's indolence, his inability to focus on serious issues when his pleasures beckoned, and his tendency to change his mind whenever he was presented with a different viewpoint.

This hand-to-mouth behavior is illustrated by the snippets of information we have about Vitellius' dynastic plans. That he intended founding a dynasty is obvious. To this end he exploited both his children by Galeria Fundana. One of his first moves, taken at Lugdunum, was to proclaim the six-year-old boy his heir. Around the same time he betrothed his daughter to Decimus Valerius Asiaticus, a power in the land not only because his family came from Vienna (Vienne), but also because Asiaticus himself was governor of Gallia Belgica, an appointment—along with a consulship for 70—he owed seemingly to Galba. Both children were advertised from the first on Vitellius' gold and silver coinage (he also honored his father on his gold coins). And Vitellius himself accepted from his troops the title "Germanicus," aptly when he was the candidate of the Rhine legions, and this is his commonest title on the coinage.

There has been some dispute over the interpetation of a comment that Tacitus and Suetonius report in almost exactly the same words. When the senate voted on 19 April to invest Vitellius with his assorted powers, "he sent an edict to Rome in which he put off the title 'Augustus' and refused that of 'Caesar.'" That he rejected "Caesar" is understandable. By then the title was becoming the mark of the heir apparent (as in Piso's case). But his "putting off" the title "Augustus" has been taken in opposite ways. Some see it as a statement of fact, in which case Vitellius was thinking of founding a new dynasty forthwith. Others regard it as a retrospective view of the situation, conditioned by the emperor's giving in to popular pressure once he reached Rome and accepting the title anyway. The former possibility looks more straightforward and more likely too, and yet we are told that Vitellius hailed his mother "Augusta" as soon as he arrived in the city. This is not the only complication. Vitellius shared Otho's fascination with Nero, and it was not long after his arrival in Rome that he carried out official sacrifices to Nero's memory. The simplest solution may be to maintain that Vitellius wanted to satisfy everybody's hopes for a return to normal conditions. So he fell in with whatever sentiments were expressed, no matter how contradictory. Playing things by ear, he presented himself as heir to Augustus, or Nero, or Galba, as the situation demanded.

In any event, Vitellius was still in Gaul when the battle of Bedriacum was fought, and Suetonius trots out more omens of doom. Not only does he assert that "equestrian statues that were being erected to Vitellius all over the place suddenly fell down all at once with broken legs." He also tells a story designed specifically to balance that of Fabius Valens' eagle: "later, as he was dispensing justice on the tribunal at Vienna, a rooster perched first on his shoulder and then on his head." Since the rooster indicated that he would be brought down by a man from Gaul, Antonius Primus as it turned out, "the outcome corresponded with these portents." Tacitus ignores such twaddle, commenting merely that Vitellius was bustling about raising additional troops. These new recruits were sent north to join—and presumably to be trained by—the handful of veterans left on the Rhine frontier, and this entire area was entrusted to Hordeonius Flaccus. The balance of the German legionaries, constituted around XXII Primigenia, together with detachments totaling 8,000 men from the three legions in Britain (II Augusta, IX Hispana, and XX Valeria Victrix), Vitellius marched south through Gaul. The moment he heard of the victory, of course, he halted and heaped praises on his armies. But he did not cut too fine a figure, being still as poverty stricken as when he first arrived in Lower Germany. As a result, the governor of Lugdunensis, Junius Blaesus, generously provided him with all the splendors appropriate to his new rank, and it may have been in return for this that Vitellius decided to hold a victory celebration in Lugdunum.[5]

For this ceremony Vitellius was joined not only by Caecina and Valens, but by four of Otho's defeated generals, Suetonius Paulinus and Licinius Proculus, Marius Celsus and Salvius Titianus. Whether or not these four were part of the parade, Caecina and Valens figured prominently. They were praised loud and long, and then set one on each side of Vitellius' own chair of office. After this he ordered his entire army to salute his young son, dressed him in the accouterments of an emperor, in effect proclaiming him officially his heir, and so—as Tacitus points out—condemned the boy to death once he himself fell from power. Against the boy's future death Tacitus sets Vitellius' ordering the execution of the most energetic of Otho's centurions. How many suffered we do not know, but since Otho had built his conspiracy against Galba on noncommissioned officers, it made sense for Caecina and Valens to round up these loyalists, and bring them north for exemplary punishment. No steps were taken against the rest of the Othonian soldiery, but this restraint failed to offset the executions. They alienated the Balkan troops especially, and disquieted "all the other legions."

For Otho's generals Vitellius showed open contempt. Paulinus and Proculus undoubtedly deserved it. Alleging that they had done everything possible to sabotage Otho's campaign, they "were acquitted of loyalty" to their late emperor. Titianus was pardoned because of his devotion to Otho and his own incompetence. Only Marius Celsus came out of the episode well. Vitellius too, it seems, was willing to think him an honorable man, and allowed him to keep the consulship Otho had assigned to him. Celsus was supposed to hold office for July through September 69, and did so in fact for July and August, losing only a month, so that Caecina and Valens could be fitted into the schedule for September and October. Finally, there was Galerius Trachalus, Otho's adviser and purported speechwriter. He was saved by Galeria, who apparently traveled north with her children to attend the celebration.

In one area Vitellius showed no restraint: "if only Vitellius had been able to control his love of luxurious living, nobody would have had reason to fear his greed." To support this observation, Tacitus gives us a synoptic description of Vitellius' progress from Lugdunum to Rome. For lavish banquets, he declares, the emperor's lust was as insatiable as it was disgraceful. Delicacies to tickle his palate had to be brought from every direction, so much so that the roads echoed with the creaking of the wagons conveying them. When he stayed with local dignitaries along the way, he beggared his hosts and devastated their towns. Exaggerated as this may be, it is not fiction. For Suetonius tells similar stories of the emperor's behavior after he reached Rome. None of his banquets, he asserts, cost less than 400,000 sesterces, and Vitellius got through four a day. He goes into detail on the two most lavish affairs. The first was a *cena adventicia*, the kind of banquet put on for a friend or relative who had just returned from a journey or, in this case, from a term as governor of a province. This one was thrown for Vitellius by his brother Lucius, to honor the emperor's arrival in the city. The second banquet was occasioned by Vitellius' own wish to show off a brand new silver serving dish (Dio claims that it cost a million sesterces), in which he mixed delicacies brought from the ends of the earth. Suetonius rounds out his account with the comment that Vitellius was unable even so to resist eating between meals, devouring snacks whenever and wherever he found them. Still, the best anecdote is preserved by Dio. One of Vitellius' courtiers, Vibius Crispus, had to absent himself from these eating marathons for several days because of illness. After recovering, he observed that if he had not fallen ill, the banquets would surely have killed him.

To his version of Vitellius' excesses Tacitus adds another, much weightier charge, that his troops—as Wellesley renders it—"became flabby and work-shy as they acquired a taste for indulgence and a contempt for their leader." This is clearly another overstatement. Although the troops' discipline suffered on the march to Rome and after their arrival, the rankers never grew contemptuous of their emperor. But the officers—Caecina and Valens above all—most certainly did. This being the first opportunity they had to observe Vitellius in his new guise as emperor, Caecina and Valens need not have been upset by the torpor he was now showing, since that gave them free rein to pursue their own plans. But it must have come as a nasty shock to find that they had been misled by the activism he had shown in his first month as commander of Lower Germany.

To document the moderation Vitellius showed in all but his taste for luxury, Tacitus provides three examples. There was, first, his sending ahead to Rome the annnouncement that he was putting off the title "Augustus" and refusing that of "Caesar," an announcement—Tacitus adds—that made no difference to his actual powers. Second, he ordered all astrologers expelled from Italy. On this Tacitus says no more, but Suetonius reports that the emperor ordered them to quit Italy by 1 October, and that the astrologers responded by publishing the wish that he would be dead by then. (Dio sharpens up the story by having the astrologers predict the correct date of his death, 20 December.) To explain this measure we need not hark back to Vitellius' horoscope. Astrologers were a threat to public order whenever they forecast that somebody or other was destined to take the throne. Though Vespasian maintained a personal astrologer, he too expelled all other practitioners of the art from Rome once he had become emperor. As for the third example of Vitellius' moderation, he forbade Roman knights to enroll in the gladiatorial schools or appear in the arena, practices that earlier emperors had condoned in Rome and so had spread through the municipalities of Italy, ever eager to ape the latest fashions in the capital.

Having paid Vitellius this tripartite, if backhanded, compliment, Tacitus once more sets the emperor on a downward path, but he subdivides his subject matter by categories in the Suetonian manner, making it virtually impossible to reconstruct the chronology of Vitellius' movements. We know only where he was when Bedriacum was fought on 15 April (somewhere in Gaul), what point he had reached about 40 days later, in late May (he visited Bedriacum), and by what date he must have reached Rome (18 July). In any event, the first action reported under these several headings is Vitellius' disposing once for all of what appeared to be the sole surviving claimant to the throne, the Cornelius Dolabella who had once been considered a possible successor to Galba. Put under house arrest in Aquinum by Otho, Dolabella returned to Rome as soon as he heard of the emperor's suicide. One of his so-called friends thereupon informed the prefect of the city, Flavius Sabinus, that Dolabella was trying to win over the troops in Rome. Sabinus was reluctant to act on this wild charge, but his hand was forced by Triaria, Lucius Vitellius' wife, who was "far more ferocious than women usually are." So the details were forwarded to Vitellius and he reacted out of a mixture of fear and jealousy. Supposedly he hated Dolabella because the latter had married Vitellius' first wife Petronia, and presumably had made her much happier than Vitellius had been able to. So the new emperor ordered Dolabella to take up residence in the town of Interamna (Terni) in Umbria. But he also ordered that he be accompanied by a man who would kill him on arrival. As it happened, the assassin was averse to a long, dull journey and killed his victim out of hand in a tavern on the main road north. The news spread quickly, of course, and people took it as a sign of the way Vitellius would behave in future—or so Tacitus says, illustrating not only the idea of the programmatic act that makes or breaks an emperor's reputation, but also the presupposition that this act must take place in or very close to Italy before it registers.

Triaria's role in this affair gives Tacitus his pretext for talking of the imperial womenfolk—and to strike another gloom-filled note. Triaria's excesses, he asserts, were thrown into high relief by the moderation of Vitellius' wife Galeria and his mother Sextilia. According to Dio, Galeria shared her husband's taste for luxurious living, finding the interior decor of Nero's "Golden House" laughably inadequate, but Tacitus observes merely that she was never involved in Vitellius' grimmer acts. The only specific evidence is her intervention on behalf of her kinsman Trachalus. As for Sextilia, she is praised as a woman of the old school and a positive paragon of virtue, in other words, as a very depressing old lady. This is where Tacitus sets his version of the story that she gave her son up for lost when he became emperor. As he tells the tale, "the moment she heard that her son had been proclaimed emperor with the title 'Germanicus,' she responded that she had borne no Germanicus, only a Vitellius. Nor was she ever moved to joy by the enticements of fortune or the flattering attentions of the populace after that, but registered only the ills that had befallen her family." As Tacitus will add later, she died a few days before Vitellius fell from power, and "by a timely death forestalled the destruction of her house."

Next Tacitus takes up the fates of two provincial governors. The first was Cluvius Rufus in Tarraconensis. He left his province now, and hurried to join the emperor. On the surface he was all joy and congratulations, but underneath he was deeply fearful. An imperial freedman named Hilarus was alleging that Cluvius had tried to create a power base for himself in Spain, after the manner of Galba. The supposed evidence for this was his issuing official documents with neither Otho's nor Vitellius' name at the head (the implication being that Cluvius planned to set his own name there, not that he was sitting on the fence until he knew who would win), and that he had made speeches in which he had insulted Vitellius and sought popularity for himself. Cluvius was fluent enough not only to save himself, but also to induce Vitellius to punish Hilarus (Vitellius—like

Claudius earlier—is said usually to have been the dupe of his freedmen). Yet Cluvius was not allowed to return to his province. He was attached to the emperor's entourage and exercised his governorship in absentia. The other governor, Trebellius Maximus, was accorded less consideration. His feuding with the legates commanding Britain's three legions had not only delayed the dispatch of the detachments summoned by Vitellius to aid the war effort, but by now had induced Trebellius to flee his province and take refuge with the emperor. Unimpressed, Vitellius sent out Marcus Vettius Bolanus, a man described as one of his intimates, but an intimate who would show him no loyalty when the time came, and by way of reward would be kept *en poste* by Vespasian until 71.

Although these stories help illustrate the different ways in which Vitellius dealt with possible threats to his own position, they are the kinds of details that might fascinate a Roman senator but tend to irritate modern readers, eager to learn more about Vitellius himself. It is worth noting, however, that Tacitus turns next to the final dispositions made in regard to Otho's troops, leaving it to the reader to make the necessary connection. For the two most troublesome legions, XIV Gemina Martia Victrix and I Adiutrix, were sent to Britain and Spain respectively. The former was to exhaust its pugnacity fighting the unruly natives, while the latter was "to sober down in peace and quiet" in a province without a governor to take advantage of any residual discontent among the men.

There are two significant aspects to Tacitus' account of these movements. First, he makes Vitellius' fear of the soldiery the guiding motif, and so records a progression from the unit causing the emperor the greatest alarm (XIV Gemina Martia Victrix) to that arousing the least (XIII Gemina, kept in north Italy to build amphitheaters). Otho's praetorians he sandwiches in between. Second, it may look as if he contradicts himself, by reversing the feelings he has attributed to the men in the past. After Bedriacum, supposedly, the fighting spirit of the other troops was broken, but the praetorians' morale was undiminished. Now the praetorians are said to be relatively quiescent, whereas the legionaries of XIV Gemina Martia Victrix are especially defiant. But the legionaries claimed that they had not been defeated, because only their advance detachment had participated in the battle In other words, the bulk of the men, having failed to appear in time for the battle, overcompensated now for their failure with defiant talk. For their part, the praetorians may have been cowed to an extent, but they may merely have been leaderless. Vitellius had executed "the most enthusiastic Othonian centurions" at Lugdunum, and while some of his victims must have come from the Othonian legions, to cause the alienation of the Balkan troops, others were surely taken from the praetorian cohorts.

In any case, Tacitus spreads himself on the misadventures of legion XIV Gemina Martia Victrix. Vitellius decided to return the legion to Britain, where it had been stationed before Nero summoned it to Italy. But he also made what would prove a less fortunate decision. Planning initially to attach to his own column the eight Batavian cohorts who had thwarted the legion's attempts to support Nero in 68, he changed his mind almost at once, probably at Valens' urging, and disencumbered himself of these unruly allies by ordering them back to the Rhine frontier. Under the new plan, legion and cohorts would march to central Gaul, keeping each other in check until they came to a parting of the ways. Then the legion would continue on to Britain, the cohorts to the German frontier. Vitellius, however, underestimated the hatred the two forces felt for each other. So, when they reached Augusta Taurinorum (Turin), there was a set-to when a Batavian picked on a local inhabitant in whose house one of the legionaries was quartered. This grew into a mêlée, and says Tacitus, an outright battle would have flared up, had not two praetorian cohorts in the town backed the legionaries and induced the Batavians to think again. Then, on the night the legion quitted Turin, the men neglected to extinguish their camp fires, from carelessness or malice, and part of the town was burned down. As for the Batavian cohorts, they made their way peaceably back to the Rhine frontier, perhaps subdued by the "battle of Augusta Taurinorum." But once there, they would use the pretext of supporting Vespasian to cover a rebellion against Roman rule in Germany and Gaul.

The presence of the two praetorian cohorts in Turin shows that Caecina and Valens had taken some steps to disperse the Othonian units through the towns of North Italy. To this Vitellius gave his approval, but it was not enough for him. So he offered the men honorable discharge and the pension that went with it, and according to Dio, the sum normally disbursed in Augustus' day was 20,000 sesterces a head. Whether or not Otho's praetorians received this much, it was risky to give them large sums of money, but it was riskier still to give them none at all. Mollified for the time being, the guardsmen turned in their weapons, and there was peace until they heard of the plans to make Vespasian emperor. As for the remaining legions, I Adiutrix was sent off to Spain; XI Claudia and VII Galbiana were merely ordered back to their winter quarters in Dalmatia and Pannonia respectively; and XIII Gemina was retained in northern Italy for a month or so, to exploit the men's engineering skills in the construction of two amphitheaters. Caecina was planning a gladiatorial show in Vitellius' honor at Cremona, and Valens one at Bononia (Bologna). This was as good a way as any of disposing of the suvivors from the 2,000 gladiators whom Martius Macer had commanded.

Besides, as Tacitus puts it, Vitellius never paid so much attention to serious business that he forgot or forwent his pleasures.

This sneer gives Tacitus his transition from defeated Othonians to victorious Vitellians. So he deals next with disturbances that he can blame squarely on the emperor's love of pleasure. Vitellius, we are told, held an early and lavish dinner at Ticinum (Pavia) and invited Verginius to join him. Since officers and men aped the habits of their commander in chief, there was disorder and drunkenness everywhere, the scene closer to an all-night orgy than to a camp under military discipline.[6] Trouble started when two of the soldiers decided to have a friendly wrestling match. One was a legionary from V Alaudae, the other a Gaul from an auxiliary cohort. When the Gaul threw the legionary, he started taunting him, and that provoked a fight among the spectators. Supposedly, two cohorts of auxiliaries were wiped out by the legionaries before a fresh alarm brought the fighting to a halt. A cloud of dust and the glinting of armor was seen in the distance, and the troops panicked, under the impression that it was legion XIV Gemina Martia Victrix, returned to renew the war. Eventually they realized that it was their own rearguard (the men sent to ensure that the Othonian legion left no stragglers behind), but in the panic one of Verginius' slaves seems to have been caught acting suspiciously. He was accused of trying to murder Vitellius, and as it was taken for granted that his master had put him up to it, the troops rushed to the emperor's quarters and demanded that Verginius be put to death. Even Vitellius refused to believe this, but he found it hard to restrain the men who had served under Verginius. They still admired him, says Tacitus, but they hated him too, because he had spurned their offer of the throne.

The embassy the senate sent to congratulate Vitellius was given a hearing in Ticinum on the day following the uproar. Then he made his way to the camp and delivered a speech in which he praised the legionaries' devotion to him. This upset the auxiliaries, their victims, and it was now that Vitellius decided to rid himself not only of the Batavian cohorts, but of a large number of Gallic auxiliaries too, the latter being sent back to their various communities. As an economy measure Vitellius also ordered that legionary and auxiliary units be allowed to fall below their nominal strength, that there be no fresh recruiting, and that those legionaries who requested honorable discharge be let go. This, says Tacitus, wrecked the state's finances, as it may well have done, coming on top of the money paid out to Otho's praetorians, and it went unappreciated by those who remained. They complained that there were now fewer men to carry out the unpleasant and difficult assignments. And they were probably not consoled by being billeted on civilians in the towns of northern Italy, even if this gave them the chance to indulge in luxurious living during their off-duty hours.

Meanwhile Vitellius attended Caecina's gladiatorial show at Cremona and then, being in the neighborhood, took it into his head to view the battlefield of Bedriacum as well. Tacitus provides an elaborate description. He dwells on the horror of the site, littered with the unburied Othonian dead, and the reactions of the various elements in the victorious army. Caecina and Valens gave Vitellius a guided tour, the junior officers' exaggerated their exploits in the battle, and the rankers felt a range of emotion from joy at having survived the struggle to compassion for those who had not. Then comes the contrast with their bloodthirsty, civilian commander in chief, fascinated by the gruesome scene. But Tacitus leaves out, as inappropriate to the dignity of his work, the most striking detail—the smell of the corpses of men and animals left to rot for 40-odd days. Suetonius is less reticent. He reports that Vitellius declared the smell of a dead enemy sweet and that of a dead fellow citizen sweeter still, and that he drained large jolts of strong wine to combat the stench and distributed it to others who needed medication. In the same way, Tacitus omits to report here that Vitellius must have gone next to view Otho's grave and make his petty-minded remarks about the tomb.

After viewing Valens' gladiatorial games at Bononia, Vitellius at last began the march to Rome, a locustlike advance by some 60,000 soldiers and an even larger number of soldiers' slaves and camp followers. It was a horde almost impossible to control—says Tacitus—even if the emperor had wanted to enforce discipline.[7] The nearer he approached the city, the "more corrupt" his journey became. Valens had brought up all sorts of equipment from Rome to ensure that his was the more impressive show given the emperor. Next to join the column were "actors, flocks of eunuchs and all the other characteristic features of Nero's court." They were followed in turn by senators and knights, eager to ingratiate themselves with the emperor, and a trickle soon became a flood, as none wanted to be left behind. But the theme on which Tacitus dwells is conflict. There was still tension between legionaries and auxiliaries, he says, but the soldiery were able to put aside their differences when there were civilians to fight. And civilians there were. When the column was some seven miles out and Vitellius was preparing the men for a triumphal entry into Rome, the common people poured out of the city and made their way to the camp. Some stood and gawped. Others exercised their taste for practical jokes by stealing the soldiers' sword belts, and then asking their victims whether they had all their equipment. Since to be caught without one's sword belt was a punishable offense, the troops found this singularly unfunny. They turned on the crowd, cutting down many until—by accident—they killed the father of one of their own men who had come to greet his son. Only that halted the slaughter.

Apparently while this was going on, other troops rushed on ahead, eager above all to see the site where Galba had been murdered. This has been taken as evidence that they considered themselves Galba's avengers. It makes better sense to interpret it as the ultimate gratification of the hatred for the emperor that had led them to rebel against him originally. In any case, so says Tacitus to play up their outlandish appearance, the men were more of a spectacle than the site they came to view. Clothed in the hides of wild beasts and brandishing gigantic spears, they lacked the skill to negotiate Rome's narrow and crowded streets. Sometimes they were forced off the sidewalks, sometimes they tripped and fell, and every accident led to abuse and brawls with the locals. To add to the confusion, there were tribunes and prefects, who "charged about, spreading terror with their armed bands," but Tacitus does not specify their purpose. Perhaps they were supposed to keep order, but they may have been sent ahead to pick sites where the troops could be billeted after the parade. As in Galba's day, the praetorian camp was the only barracks in Rome, and the men would have to be quartered in open spaces and public buildings all over the city.

When Vitellius began preparing his entry into Rome at the Milvian Bridge, just outside the city limits, he envisaged a military parade in which he himself—like Galba nearly a year earlier—would wear his imperial cloak, carry a sword, ride a horse, and drive senators and people before him like sheep. Friends and advisers quickly pointed out that to celebrate a victory gained in civil war would be a gigantic blunder. So he changed into a toga and entered Rome on foot. His troops followed, and a brave show they made. At the head of the column were the eagles of the four legions present in full strength (I Italica, V Alaudae, XXI Rapax, and XXII Primigenia). Next came the standards or banners of the seven legions represented by detachments, four from the Rhine frontier (I Germanica, IV Macedonica, XV Primigenia, and XVI), and three from Britain (II Augusta, IX Hispana, and XX Valeria Victrix), and the emblems of 12 squadrons of cavalry. Then came the main body of the legionary troops and cavalry, along with 34 cohorts of auxiliary infantry, these last separated into their units by the tribal titles of the regiments or the type of weapons they carried. The senior officers, that is, the prefects of the camp, the tribunes and the leading centurions marched ahead of the eagles, all of them conspicuous in the white togas that indicated equestrian rank. The rest of the officers marched with their men, wearing all their decorations. It was a magnificent display, says Tacitus, and an army worthy of any emperor but Vitellius.

At the end of the parade Vitellius climbed the Capitol to sacrifice to Jupiter Best and Greatest, and there too he hailed his mother "Augusta." That evening he attended the lavish *cena adventicia* thrown for him by his brother, and on the next morning he set about winning over the senate and people. He had prepared a grandiloquent speech full of self-praise, says Tacitus, but it did not go down well with the assembled senators, aware as they were of the failings the emperor and his army had displayed so far. The common people, on the other hand, greeted Vitellius with shouts of approval. Tacitus, predictably, attributes this to their disregard for important issues, their inability to distinguish between truth and lies, and their being thoroughly versed in the flattery expected on such occasions. But they had other reasons too. Caring more about the present than the past, they wanted some sign of a return to normal conditions, and that is no doubt why they pressured the emperor now to assume the title "Augustus."

On what remained of the peaceful segment of Vitellius' reign, the period between his arrival in Rome and the departure of his army for the north in mid- to late September, Suetonius has little of value to say; Dio records evil omens, including a comet, the moon's undergoing two eclipses, and the people's seeing two suns in the sky at the same time; and Tacitus reports a string of incidents, only two of which can be dated, one at the start of the period and one at its end. The former involved another blunder. As the newly installed Pontifex Maximus, head of the official state religion, the emperor was supposed to know which days in the official calendar were appropriate for public business and which were not. On 18 July, nonetheless, the anniversary of two massive Roman defeats in the dim and distant past, and so one of the darkest days in the entire year, he published an edict. The sources do not point out that even a century earlier few aristocrats knew their calendar well. Instead, Tacitus and Suetonius use this as yet another stick with which to belabor Vitellius. So, says Tacitus, in a community inclined to put interpretations on every event, this was taken as a dire sign, but the historian himself declares it proof that Vitellius was ignorant of all law, human and divine, and since his freedmen and his friends showed much the same indifference, the emperor "conducted himself as if in the midst of a world of drunkards."

The only hard information we have on why Vitellius published the edict now is Tacitus' unhelpful comment that it concerned "the conduct of religious ceremonies." What it may have announced, however, was his plan to honor Nero's memory. Tacitus, admittedly, reports this incident much later in his narrative, in a catalogue of Vitellius' grossest excesses, but it may be wiser to follow Suetonius and Dio, both of whom make it an early, programmatic step, in the former's words, "to leave no doubt about what model Vitellius intended following in governing the state." In any event, Vitellius gave orders that an altar be built in the middle of the Campus Martius, and sacrifices made to Nero's shades by the Augustales, a priesthood founded by Romulus and reformed by Tiberius to honor the imperial family. Thus—it is implied—was an antique priesthood with a noble purpose reduced to honoring the worst of the Julio-Claudians at the behest of the worst of his successors. According to Tacitus, this "delighted the basest elements in the population and disgusted all right-thinking citizens."

Vitellius had some success in appeasing the "right-minded" in the electoral ceremonies (they can hardly be called elections), which ratified arrangements made during the trek south in the matter of men to be designated consuls for the remainder of the year. Under the new dispensation, Marius Celsus and Arrius Antoninus would hold office for July and August (that is, for a term a month shorter than Otho had allotted to them), Caecina and Valens would be rewarded with a term occupying September and October, and Gnaeus Caecilius Simplex would be partnered with Gaius Quinctius Atticus, one of Otho's choices, for November and December.[8] Suetonius regards this as more proof of Vitellius' disregard for the laws, partly because he runs it together with Vitellius' designating consuls for the next ten years, an act Tacitus rightly sets in the emperor's last, desperate days, partly because he asserts that Vitellius "made himself consul in perpetuity," an action Tacitus does not mention.[9] In reality, these arrangements created a compromise between the claims of men supported by previous rulers and those of the men Vitellius had to reward.

Also to humor the senators, the emperor attended meetings and acted as one of them, even when trivial matters were discussed. But one result was a confrontation with that prickly champion of "free speech," Helvidius Priscus. Helvidius seems to have proposed a motion contrary to Vitellius' wishes. It is unclear how the situation played out. Dio reports the exchange in neutral terms, but Tacitus insists that Vitellius was angered at first and then calmed down, passed off the incident as a dispute between two senators, and commented that he had had disagreements with Helvidius' father-in-law Thrasea too. The realists in the audience, says Tacitus, were staggered by the effrontery with which Nero's minion set himself on the same level as Thrasea. But the optimists were taken in, imagining that Vitellius had picked on Thrasea rather than one of the powerbrokers in the senate, because he favored the free expression of opinion over the backroom arm twisting of the influential.

With the people Vitellius followed a different tack. They had played no real part in the elections since Caligula's time. (If there was a choice, senators made it.) At best the people might be summoned to the Campus Martius to hear a formal announcement of the results, and so they had shown little interest in the doings of senators for years. In fact, the evidence suggests that they perked up only when a senator fell from grace, this delighting them as much as did the downfall of an imperial favorite. To gratify them, Vitellius made sure to attend the shows and, more important still, to take a keen interest in everything that went on in the theater, the amphitheater, or—his favorite—the circus where the chariot races were held. (Julius Caesar had angered the people by doing his paperwork during the shows.) But since Vitellius in his younger days had been so enthusiastic a supporter of the Blues, one of the four racing stables, that he had even gone to the circus wearing their uniform and had helped rub down the horses, there were those—senators no doubt—who looked askance. While Tacitus concedes that these were "actions that would have won him favor and popularity, if prompted by honorable motives," he adds that those who remembered the emperor's youthful indiscretions found his conduct "inappropriate and cheap." This is not criticism for its own sake, incidentally. Suetonius declares that Vespasian's son Titus excelled at blending chumminess with dignity.

Where the armed forces in Rome were concerned, Vitellius had less input than his two henchmen. He countenanced the appointment of Publilius Sabinus and Julius Priscus as the new prefects of the praetorian guard, even though both were low-ranking officers. (Sabinus had commanded only a cavalry squadron, while Priscus was a legionary centurion.) The selection was made by Caecina and Valens, each of whom wanted one of his own adherents in charge. Sabinus being Caecina's creature and Priscus Valens', these two transmitted their masters' feuding down the chain of command. More importantly, their appointment dashed the hopes of Sextus Lucilius Bassus. The emperor had made him commander of the two main fleets, that at Misenum and that at Ravenna, an extraordinary measure and—perhaps—a tribute to his efficiency. But Bassus had wanted to be prefect of the guard So, out of vanity and anger, he supposedly began plotting to betray Vitellius as soon as he had the chance.

This is Tacitus' first salvo in a sustained onslaught designed to demonstrate that Vitellius and his lieutenants between them managed in every conceivable way to destroy the victorious army they had brought to Rome, and so helped cause their own destruction. Hence he turns next to the billeting of the troops from one end of Rome to the other. Though he fails to admit that this was more or less unavoidable in the circumstances, he points out rightly that it broke down not only the troops' organization and unit cohesion, since the men could not be assembled and drilled, but their discipline and morale too, since they spent their time slacking and fornicating. Then there was negligence. A large number of Gallic and German auxiliaries (or perhaps tribal contingents) were quartered in the circus located in the Vatican area, one of the least healthy in Rome. Whether they were given the worst billet because they were judged the least important elements in the army or the ones least likely to complain, the tribesmen's inability to stand the heat and their resulting eagerness to take to the waters of the nearby Tiber led reportedly to serious illnesses and many deaths.

With the men thus demoralized, Tacitus brings up Vitellius' plan—or it may have been the work of Caecina and Valens—to recruit 16 new cohorts of praetorian guard and four of urban cohorts, each to be 1,000 men strong. The decision was not as capricious as Tacitus' account implies. The Othonian cohorts of the guard had been disbanded, and we have no clue to what happened to the members of the urban cohorts assigned to Otho's maritime expedition. Some may have made their way back to Rome, by land or by sea, as individuals or in groups, but it is also possible that many of the men were still marooned in and around Albingaunum (Albenga) in Liguria, the site they had occupied when the expedition petered out. Whatever the case, the Vitellians' reason for making the change was manifestly to create units unswervingly loyal to their emperor. But to achieve this end, they had to draw recruits from the forces already under their command, and there lay the rub.

First, the praetorian and the urban cohorts were élite units: a praetorian ranker was paid 750 denarii (3,000 sesterces) a year before stoppages and served for 16 years, and an urban ranker received 375 denarii (*HS* 1,500) a year and served for 20 years. By contrast, an ordinary legionary was paid only 225 denarii (*HS* 900) a year and served for a minimum of 20 years, while an auxiliary who already possessed Roman citizenship seems to have been entitled to a similar sum, though he had to serve for 25 years.[10] Hence much more cash had to be found to pay these new cohorts. Second, and perhaps more important, we know that while legionaries or even auxiliaries could be promoted into praetorian or urban cohorts for meritorious service, the bulk of the men were drawn exclusively from citizens resident in Italy, a restriction that was not applied to legionaries and auxiliaries. So the Vitellian plan struck down one of the main distinctions between élite units and the regular armed forces, and was greeted by traditionalists with shock and horror. In Tacitus' words, "the distinction of serving in the units stationed in Rome was shattered."[11]

Obviously, any legionary or auxiliary ought to have been delighted to secure promotion into the city units, but now another problem surfaced. At first, so Tacitus seems to say, Vitellius left his two lieutenants to take care of the details, and Valens' followers benefited much more than did Caecina's. Valens had managed to recover his standing with the troops, by claiming not only to have rescued Caecina from the jaws of defeat after Ad Castores, but also to have played the leading role at Bedriacum. And since he was much better at intrigue, his men or—more likely—his officers secured the plum assignments. Then, perhaps to limit the bickering, Vitellius himself announced that any ranker who wanted to apply for service in the city units could do so, no matter what his record. Tacitus allows that some good men opted to remain in the legions and the auxiliaries, by choice or because they were fed up with the diseases they were catching and the changeability of Rome's climate. But he insists that "the legions and cavalry lost the pick of their men," and he seems to have believed (wrongly) that this affected the fighting quality of the troops who would shortly face the Flavian incursion into Italy. But he is right to claim that their numbers were reduced. On his calculations, one-third of the 60,000 men Vitellius had brought to Rome were siphoned off into the new cohorts, and they were "not so much selected as drafted at random."

How Vitellius, Caecina, and Valens imagined that they would pay for these steps is unclear, but here too they seemingly followed a hand-to-mouth policy. Tacitus has little to say, and that little is usually attached to something else. So, for instance, he ties one example to his account of the feuding between Caecina and Valens. As he tells the story, these two were feuding openly now that the fighting was done. Encouraged by their friends and adherents, they ran the state in a hothouse atmosphere. "They competed with one another and invited comparison in the numbers who courted their favour, attended them when they went out, and crowded their morning levees." Besides, they seized town houses, suburban estates, and the wealth of the empire, while "a plaintive and poverty-stricken mass of aristocrats," restored from exile by Galba, received no consideration from the emperor. Actually, Vitellius off-loaded the problem. He reimposed on the freedmen of the former exiles the requirement that they help their erstwhile masters out of their difficulties, a measure—says Tacitus—that won plaudits from leading men and common people alike. But the freedmen evaded their duty through "slavish ingenuity." Either they hid their funds with men too obscure to be noticed or too powerful to be challenged. Or they entered the imperial household, and so made themselves not just untouchable by anybody save Vitellius, but more influential than their former masters.

It was presumably to counter this, and to raise funds for himself too, that Vitellius decided to impose an extraordinary property tax on imperial freedmen, both the ex-slaves he had inherited from his predecessors, and those he had acquired willy-nilly when they transferred into the imperial household to avoid the earlier decree. Tacitus does not point out that Vitellius was being consistent, by forcing *his* freedmen to support their patron, or that this measure must have won him immense popularity with everybody else. As he remarks in another passage, it took the emperor's freedman Asiaticus only three months to become as hated for his avarice as had been all Nero's freedmen put together. But what complicates the situation is, first, that Tacitus reports this later decree as if it were the result of Vitellius' awareness that he lacked the cash to pay his troops a donative; and second, that he seems to imply that Vitellius imagined just passing the decree would solve the problem. He asserts that the emperor meanwhile thought only of extravagance, building stables for the horses used in the chariot races, filling the circus with gladiatorial bouts and animal shows, and "playing the fool with his money as if it would never run out."

This reference to a donative is usually taken at face value, but it is more likely a misunderstanding. By Tacitus' day donatives were a part of the system, handed out to the soldiery as a matter of course by each emperor in turn. There is simply not enough evidence to support the assumption that this was the rule in Vitellius' day too. Otho, after all, had paid no donative until the praetorian mutiny forced his hand two months after his accession. And not even Tacitus asserts that the Vitellian soldiery actually pressured their emperor to cough up the money. In fact, if they had looted their way down Italy, as Tacitus has claimed, they should have had ample supplies of cash already, and have been satisfied with their future pay prospects as a result of the measures taken to let all comers enroll in the praetorian and urban cohorts. It may be best to hold that Vitellius never even considered paying a donative.

For the rest, Vitellius had always been a spendthrift, and he did not change now. Hence Tacitus' comment that "in Vitellius' court nobody got ahead by showing honesty or application. There was but one route to power, satisfying Vitellius' limitless appetites with monstrous banquets and extravagant gastronomy. The emperor thought it quite enough if he could enjoy what he had already, taking no thought for the longer term, and in just a few months—so it is believed—he consumed some 900 million sesterces. Truly, it shows Rome's greatness, and her misfortune, that she survived an Otho and a Vitellius within a single year, and suffered humiliation of various kinds at the hands of a Vinius and a Fabius, an Icelus and an Asiaticus."

Although Tacitus is careful to declare the charge that Vitellius frittered away 900 million sesterces a rumor, some scholars positively gobble with indignation that he even mentions it. Yet they can offer no valid reason why the historian should have omitted a widespread perception of the emperor. Nor can they claim that Vitellius would have been unable—in theory or practice—to squander so much money in a few months. According to Suetonius, Caligula got through three times this amount in less than a year, while Vespasian declared early in his reign that he needed a staggering 40,000 million sesterces to put the empire back on its feet.[12] So if a sum like 900 million sesterces was available, Vitellius could have run through it without difficulty. If we must cavil, the question to ask is whether this sum was actually available, especially when Tacitus has said so little about the emperor's fund-raising efforts. The simplest solution may be to contend that Vitellius was able as emperor to run up bills on a scale even grander than Otho had managed when he was heir presumptive, whether or not he incurred these debts for purposes as frivolous as Tacitus would have us believe.

As for Tacitus' statement that under Vitellius nobody could get ahead on the basis of honesty and effort, this is designed to help explain the speed with which he fell from power. It was not by military prowess alone that his opponents overthrew him within four months. The first sign of the trouble to come reached Rome in September, perhaps around the same time as the one other incident Tacitus gives us enough information to date securely, his report that Caecina and Valens celebrated the emperor's birthday with gladiatorial shows, held on a scale without precedent or parallel in every single ward into which Rome was divided.[13] What arrived was a dispatch from Marcus Aponius Saturninus, the governor of Moesia, reporting that legion III Gallica had defected to Vespasian. As Saturninus followed the legion's example almost at once, and so provided no more details, the emperor's courtiers—like Galba's in January—were able to put an optimistic spin on the report. Only one legion had mutinied, they asserted, and there was nothing to worry about when all the other troops were loyal. Whether or not additional information came in later from other sources, Vitellius took the same line in an address to his troops. He put the blame on Otho's praetorians. Criticizing them for spreading baseless rumors, and suppressing any reference to Vespasian, he asserted repeatedly that there was no threat of civil war. But as he stationed troops around the city to break up groups of gossipers, says Tacitus, he caused more rumor mongering.

This does not mean that Vitellius believed his own claims, though Tacitus seems intent on creating that impression. He summoned aid from Germany, Britain, Spain, and Africa, albeit in a casual manner that veiled the urgency of the situation. Unfortunately for him, the governors and legionary legates in these provinces were just as dilatory about responding. For this Hordeonius Flaccus on the Rhine frontier and Vettius Bolanus in Britain had valid excuses. Both were beset by serious disturbances among the native tribes they were supposed to control. In Hispania Tarraconensis the absence of the governor, Cluvius Rufus, left matters in the hands of the legionary legates of the three units stationed there (VI Victrix, X Gemina, and I Adiutrix), and they procrastinated. Ready to obey so long as Vitellius was successful, says Tacitus, they had no wish to be dragged down with him in adversity. In Africa the situation was different again. The commander of III Augusta was Valerius Festus, somehow a kinsman of the emperor, and he was able to raise additional troops without difficulty. The men who had been formed into military units by Clodius Macer (all disbanded by Galba) took up arms again happily, and the local youth volunteered for service enthusiastically, as they had good memories of Vitellius' governorship and bad ones of Vespasian's. The problem was Festus. Initially enthusiastic, he began to waver and wrote secretly to Vespasian.

Vitellius was able to capture some of the envoys Vespasian sent to Raetia and Gaul, but more got through, thanks to their own craftiness or because they were hidden away by friends. The upshot was that Vitellius' preparations were much better known to his rival than were the latter's to him. For a start, Vitellius did not tackle the matter as energetically as he should have done. Then too, the messengers he sent eastward were seized by the pickets the Balkan legions had stationed in the three main passes through the Julian Alps (that is, the passes east of Aquileia). And since, finally, the seasonal Etesian winds were favorable at this stage to sea voyages from west to east, but not vice versa, Vitellius was able to receive no more intelligence by sea than he did by land. Hence it was only after the Balkan legions actually invaded northern Italy before the end of September that dire news coming in from every quarter galvanized him into action. Then he gave orders that Caecina and Valens set out for the north, but since Valens was still recovering from a serious illness, only Caecina could undertake the march.

Caecina, however, was not happy with his emperor, and the army of which he took command was very different from the one that had been brought to Rome—or so says Tacitus, to introduce a set piece description that contrasts as strongly as possible with his account of their triumphant entry into Rome three months earlier: "The men showed neither physical energy nor mental ardor. The column moved along lethargically and full of gaps. Their horses were spiritless, their arms neglected. The men could not bear the heat, the dust or the weather, and they were as prone to disobey orders as they were reluctant to endure hardship." Caecina was no better. "There was Caecina's long-standing tendency to seek popularity, and of late his lethargy. Owing to the excessive indulgence of good fortune he had given way to pleasure-seeking." So Caecina took no steps to enforce discipline on the column or to get the army into shape.

> Or perhaps he was already contemplating treachery, and destroying the strength of his troops was one of the tricks he was using to achieve his objective. Many believed that by now Caecina's loyalty had been undermined by advice from Flavius Sabinus, passed to him in secret conversations with Rubrius Gallus. If Caecina were to change sides, so Gallus asserted, Vespasian would meet any terms he set. At the same time Gallus reminded Caecina of his hatred for and jealousy of Valens, and pointed out that since Valens held first place in the Vitellian court, Caecina would do better to seek influence and position with a new emperor.

This passage raises two sets of problems. The first set involves the expeditionary force itself. It may have been in terrible condition when it left Rome, and even if it was not, any moralist would have claimed that it should have been, because wrecked by its time in the city (hence the contrast Tacitus draws). But it was never Caecina's intention to wreck it, nor did he. As he would have known from his trek to Rome earlier in the year, and as Tacitus too seems to have recognized, a route march would whip the men back into shape. But Dio and Josephus assert that it was because Caecina's troops were still in terrible shape when he reached his destination that the sight of the better disciplined and more combat ready Flavian troops persuaded him to open negotiations, with a view to switching sides. If it is legitimate to suggest that Dio and Josephus are repeating claims made by Caecina after the event, claims similar to those he had voiced after Ad Castores, when he blamed his failure on the inadequacies of his troops, we can conclude that the poor condition of his army was a mere pretext.

The advantage of this view is that it allows us to see Caecina's aim as being to face the enemy with an army that was combat ready, a valuable bargaining chip if he could negotiate with them, and a fail-safe if he could not. This accords well with another aspect of the situation. Caecina was entrusted with every last legionary and auxiliary soldier the Vitellians could muster (less those siphoned off into the praetorian and urban cohorts). So he controlled the men he had led south from Vindonissa (XXI Rapax, plus the detachments from IV Macedonica and XXII Primigenia), the troops Valens had marched through Gaul (the bulk of V Alaudae, along with detachments from I Germanica, XV Primigenia, and XVI), the legion picked up at Lugdunum (I Italica), and the men Vitellius had brought with him to Italy (the balance of XXII Primigenia, together with the detachments from the three British legions, II Augusta, IX Hispana, and XX Valeria Victrix). Now, at some point after Caecina left Rome, Valens wrote a letter to the troops he had commanded, and urged them to wait for him en route, claiming (truly or falsely we cannot tell) that this was the arrangement he had made with Caecina. But the latter "pretended" that the plan had been changed, that they must face the enemy with all their forces, and that they should keep marching north as fast as possible. And "as he was there in person, it was his lead that the troops followed." If Caecina's aim was to betray Vitellius, in other words, he meant to do so comprehensively, and to hand over to the enemy every soldier he could. And if he had to give battle, he had an army that could win the victory and the glory that went with it.

Now the second set of problems, the matter of Caecina's loyalty and the stories told about that. He had reason to be unhappy. When the praetorian and urban cohorts had been reformed, Tacitus reports, Caecina had been humiliated by his inability to get his way, and this blow to his vanity "is believed to have been the first thing that caused Caecina's loyalty to Vitellius to waver." Still, to judge by Caecina's behavior, he seems only to have played with the idea of changing sides until late in his trek north. He split his expeditionary force in two. The smaller group, composed of the full legions I Italica and XXI Rapax with "part of the cavalry," he sent to Cremona. Command of this group was vested presumably in the two legionary legates (whoever they may have been), but as little was expected of them, it cannot have mattered much. While Cremona had been the Vitellians' HQ in their campaign against Otho, and was an excellent base from which to block any enemy advance southward into Italy, it was best suited to deal with a force emerging from the western end of the Alps. What needed countering now was an offensive launched from their eastern end. So Caecina took personal command of the larger, more heterogeneous group and led that to Hostilia (Ostiglia), 50 or more miles further east. Although a mere village attached for administrative purposes to Verona, Hostilia commanded the road that ran south from there to Mutina; it lay on a road running westward to Bedriacum and Cremona; and it shielded Ravenna, the port for the squadron of the imperial fleet second only to that based at Misenum. An enemy advancing through the gap between Cremona and the east coast had to confront troops positioned there.

In the final stage of the march, however, Caecina decided to let the troops go on ahead while he turned aside and made for Ravenna, "under the pretext" of addressing the members of the fleet. If we look at this positively, we can say that Caecina had to ensure that the fleet in his rear was not disloyal or hostile. The marines at Ravenna could have taken the field, just as the marines from Misenum had during the war with Otho. As Tacitus says (though he phrases it differently), the members of this fleet made up the only organized force in northern Italy that had ever sworn allegiance to Otho, and as he reports later, many had been recruited from Dalmatia and Pannonia, provinces that by now had declared for Vespasian. Again, Caecina may well have suspected not just that their commander, Lucilius Bassus, resented Vitellius' failing to make him prefect of the praetorians, but also that he "was intent now on taking revenge for his unjustifiable anger." But all these were reasons also for Caecina to ponder treachery. As Tacitus observes, "it became clear later that Caecina's aim was a secret meeting with Bassus to fix the details of a plan to switch sides." Either way, Caecina can have made his decision to defect only after he had met with Bassus.

Tacitus refuses to say who corrupted whom: "it is impossible to determine whether Bassus persuaded Caecina to change sides, or if the same evil impulse inspired both of them. When you put villains together, they try to top each other's villainy." Tacitus probably lacked hard evidence on the point, and he may not have cared. For this is also a maneuver to lump the two men together, so that they can be denounced with equal vigor. In Vespasian's reign, so Tacitus asserts, writers credited these two with acting out of "concern for peace and love of the state," but their motives were the exact opposite. "They were both by nature fickle and, having betrayed Galba without a qualm, they seem clearly to have acted out of rivalry and jealousy in betraying Vitellius because he favored others over them. Hence Caecina hurried after his army and began undermining by various methods the loyalty of his centurions and soldiers, Bassus that of the fleet." So ends Tacitus' account of the Vitellians' preparations to meet the incursion by the Balkan legions that would set Vespasian on the throne before the end of the year.

8

The Beginning of the End:
Vespasian through August 69

To understand the campaign by the Balkan legions that unseated Vitellius in late December 69, we must deal first with the man in whose name—if not always with whose blessing—they undertook their offensive. Discontented as these legions were, apparently from the moment Otho committed suicide in mid-April, they had no cause to embrace until Vespasian was proclaimed emperor and invited them to take up arms in his behalf. It was as well that they did so. For of the four men who became emperors in 68/69, Vespasian must have seemed to contemporaries as well as to posterity the one whose bid for power was the least likely to succeed, by reason of his birth, his age, and his career to date. Hence Tacitus' frequent references to "the luck of the Flavians," the many stories Suetonius retails of signs portending Vespasian's elevation to the throne, and—for that matter—his insistence that Vespasian and his two sons, Titus and Domitian, believed or came to believe firmly in the workings of Fate.

To reconstruct Vespasian's activities we must rely on a relatively brief life by Suetonius, a comprehensive if eulogistic account of his campaigns in Judaea by Josephus, stray details from what remains of Dio's history, and above all, the information Tacitus chooses to provide. As usual, Tacitus is the most important of our sources, but—also as usual—he provides the information in ways that suit his purposes much better than they do ours. The bulk of the material he serves up in three segments, each set at more or less the appropriate chronological point in his overall account, the first in the survey of the empire's situation in January 69; the second where Otho and Vitellius have been brought on stage and the possibility of Vespasian's taking a hand in the game is raised; and the third where Vitellius has not yet reached Rome, but has already given what Tacitus presents as clear evidence that he is unfit to rule. In none of these segments, however, does Tacitus favor the emperor who gave him his own start in public life. Though he declares Vespasian the first man to be improved by becoming emperor, a relative judgment anyway, one of his aims throughout is to debunk the idea that Vespasian had undertaken his revolt to save the empire from Vitellius. Though the new emperor fostered this claim assiduously, chronology alone—as Tacitus recognized—proved that it was never more than a pretext.

The most notable feature of Vespasian's early career, and of his family as a whole, was its lack of distinction. Suetonius apologizes for this in his very first paragraph, maintaining that this obscurity was nothing of which Rome needed to be ashamed when Vespasian's own achievements compensated so fully for it. Yet the need to apologize shows how reluctant Romans still were to embrace the idea that ability could be found in a man without a pedigree. The first member of the family to make anything of himself, says Suetonius, was Titus Flavius Petro, Vespasian's paternal grandfather. He came from Reate (Rieti), a small village in Sabine territory (central Italy). Petro fought as a centurion or an *evocatus* (a time-expired veteran recalled to the standards) at Pharsalus in 48 B.C. Though he had backed Pompey and the republicans, he managed to win honorable discharge and a pardon from Caesar, and this convinced him that profiting by civil wars was safer than participating in them. So Petro became a debt collector, and since indebtedness remained a major problem until Augustus ended the civil wars, Petro must have amassed a tidy fortune. But in aristocratic eyes this was nothing to be proud of: gentlemen might need ready money constantly, but they would not stoop to handling "filthy lucre."

Petro married a woman named Tertulla, who in later days at least owned a suburban estate near Cosa on the coast of Etruria. The pair had one son, the first member of the family to bear the name Titus Flavius Sabinus, and he followed in his father's footsteps. There were stories that he held the rank of centurion in the military (Suetonius denies them), and he certainly became a money lender or banker. Early on he collected the duties levied on goods entering or leaving the province Asia, so scrupulously—says Suetonius—that cities there erected statues to him with the oxymoronic inscription "to an honest tax-farmer." Later, Sabinus plied his trade among the Helvetii in Switzerland, taking advantage probably of the growing wealth of the Gallic provinces, and there he died in Claudius' reign, perhaps at Aventicum (Avenches), the town forced to surrender unconditionally to Caecina early in 69.

Sabinus married up. His wife Vespasia Polla came from an "honorable family" from Nursia (Norcia). Her father had risen to prefect of the camp, while her brother became a senator of middling rank. The couple had three children, a daughter who died in her first year, and two boys. For them the prospects were bright, as the family now possessed the wealth and standing to underwrite senatorial careers for both. Vespasian (Titus Flavius Vespasianus), the younger son, was born on 7 November 9 A.D. The elder boy was Titus Flavius Sabinus, born sometime between

3 and 8. He has already figured in our story as the man who was installed as prefect of the city by Otho after Galba's murder, and who put up only weak resistance when Vitellius' sister-in-law Triaria forced the execution of Galba's kinsman Cornelius Dolabella. But this was the key to Sabinus' success, assiduous and unquestioning loyalty to one emperor after another. Some called him passive, says Tacitus, but others preferred to think him a moderate. Sabinus must have started his career under Tiberius, since Tacitus states that he spent 35 years in public service, but all we know for certain is that he held a consulship around 45, was governor of Moesia for 7 years (perhaps between 49 and 56), and for 12 served as prefect of the city. This last post he occupied for two terms under Nero, the first between 56 and 60 so far as we can tell, and the second from 62 to 68. Galba then replaced him with Ducenius Geminus, but his reinstatement was accepted by Otho in January 69 and confirmed by Vitellius in June. The identity of Sabinus' wife is unknown, but his like-named son was designated consul for May and June 69 and took command of the Othonian forces previously led by the unfortunate Martius Macer, and his daughter married into an established consular family.

Tacitus gives Sabinus only faint praise, declaring him a man of integrity and justice, though he talked too much. But he concedes that "what everybody would agree is that until Vespasian became emperor, the dignity of the house depended on Sabinus."[1] He also credits the stories that Sabinus was not on good terms with his younger brother. Although some prefer to sweep these tales under the rug, Vespasian was not a younger brother of whom a Sabinus could be proud. His career prior to 69 resembled a country cousin's progress, an impression heightened by the rustic accent and the delight in coarse jokes he retained to the end of his life. Initially, we are told, he was not even sure that he wanted to become a senator, and it took his mother's taunting to drive him to follow his brother's example. Then, as he made his way up the ladder of offices, he became aedile under Caligula, but—Suetonius and Dio tell us—failed so badly in his duty to ensure that the streets of Rome were kept clean that the emperor stuffed handfuls of muck down his toga. He fared better under Claudius, at first anyway, as the legate of legion II Augusta in the conquest of southwestern Britain between 43 and 47. This won him not only triumphal ornaments and a consulship for the last two months of 51, but also a reputation that would stand him in good stead with the legion 20 years later. Yet after his consulship, Vespasian withdrew from public life, probably as a result of Claudius' deciding to marry his niece Agrippina in 49. Like Galba, Vespasian had incurred her enmity, originally by supporting Caligula's charges that she had been involved in the conspiracy of Lentulus Gaetulicus. Agrippina was ever ready to take revenge on those who had crossed her, justifiably or not.

It was during this same period that Vespasian married—down, as Suetonius points out, by taking as his wife Flavia Domitilla, a woman of highly suspect origins. Whatever her exact status, she gave him three children. There were two sons, Titus, born in December 39, and Domitian, born in October 51. There was a daughter too, Domitilla, born perhaps in 45, but she and her mother died before Vespasian became emperor. Vespasian made no attempt to remarry after his wife's death. Instead, he took up once again with Antonia Caenis, his mistress prior to the marriage, and he treated her "almost as if she were his lawful wife" until she died around 75. It is another question whether this affair began by choice or of necessity. Vespasian seems never to have had much money, one reason no doubt why tight-fistedness became a dominant trait in his character, to the embarrassment of Suetonius and Tacitus' amusement. Not only was Titus born in one of the least select areas of Rome; he also had his future foretold by a *metoposcopus*, a character with all the social standing of a palmist today.[2] And though Titus was educated at court with Claudius' son Britannicus until 55, Domitian would claim that as a boy he had not had even one piece of silver plate at his disposal (making a point for which Americans have a more homely expression).

Vespasian emerged from obscurity only in the early 60s, just like Galba, and perhaps for the same reasons. He was appointed governor of Africa for 62/63. Although he returned from his province no richer than when he entered it, this failed to endear him to the provincials. It would be unwise to generalize from Suetonius' story that on one occasion Vespasian was pelted with turnips by the enraged citizens of Hadrumetum (Sousse), but it is significant that in 69 the province's inhabitants were still so ill disposed toward him that they preferred Vitellius. It was also over Vespasian's financial situation at this stage that he and Sabinus had their most serious falling-out. According to the story, Vespasian was so hard up that he had to ask for an unsecured loan from Sabinus, but was given financial assistance only in return for mortgaging his estates to his brother. This much is reported by Tacitus and Suetonius alike, but Suetonius goes on to say that, to recoup his fortunes, Vespasian was forced to take up selling mules (Reate was famous for them). In all likelihood he engaged in operations on a scale large enough to avoid being dismissed as a mere tradesman, but he was still saddled with the nickname of "the Muleteer."

For all that, Vespasian became a member of Nero's court and accompanied him on his pilgrimage to the home of all the arts in 66. A more ill-matched pair it is hard to imagine, and there is good reason to wonder about Nero's reasons for taking him along, especially as Vespasian supposedly made a habit of either disappearing or falling asleep whenever the emperor sang. Still, it is probably an exaggeration to hold that he was saved from disgrace or even death only by the outbreak of the Jewish revolt in 66. This assumes both that Nero was infuriated by Vespasian's conduct, and that he thought the revolt the major crisis the ax-grinding Josephus depicts. It is true that Gessius Florus, the procurator of Judaea, had proved unable to handle the uprising he had so largely provoked, and that the governor of Syria, Gaius Cestius Gallus, had bungled his attempt to nip the movement in the bud. Yet if Nero decided that he needed a competent commander who could be sent to the area at once, and so had to pick somebody from his own entourage, Vespasian no doubt looked like the best choice. He was unlikely to threaten the emperor's position, no matter how many legions he was given to carry out his task—and Nero gave him three, V Macedonica, X Fretensis, and XV Apollinaris. What we can say, however, is that for Vespasian this command was a godsend. Nearly 60 years of age, he should have had little hope of receiving another chance to make his name as a soldier. Instead, he was packed off to Judaea.

This was not Nero's only step. He had to find a governor for Syria too, as a result of Cestius Gallus' incompetence. His choice fell on Gaius Licinius Mucianus, the first person to whom Tacitus grants a character sketch in the *Histories*. In his youth, Mucianus had cultivated the friendship of the powerbrokers in Rome, but something had gone wrong, and he was thought even to have offended the emperor Claudius. So he had withdrawn into seclusion in the wilds of the province Asia, "as close to exile then as he was later to an emperor." He returned to Rome presumably when Nero succeeded Claudius in 54, but his career under the new emperor is another almost complete blank. All we know is that he held the consulship, probably in the mid-60s, and was appointed governor of Syria in 67. For Tacitus these details are much less important than his character, a mix of virtues and vices: Mucianus could be lazy or industrious, arrogant or cordial, too given to his pleasures when off duty, but capable of great energy when he undertook campaigns. (This is a reference to his military exploits in and after 69, not before.) "You might praise his public activities, but his private life was much criticized" is Tacitus' elliptical way of indicating that Mucianus was gay. Then comes the key point, and the reason for his being given so much space so early: an influential man in 68/69, he was more inclined to play kingmaker than king.

Still, Mucianus had no chance to try out for either role so long as Nero lived. At first, indeed, he failed to display even the principal gift expected of him in his new post, diplomacy. Though Mucianus commanded three legions (IV Scythica, VI Ferrata, and XII Fulminata), his main function was to deal with the Parthians on the far side of the Euphrates, and to prevent their intervening in Rome's eastern possessions, especially at times when there were disturbances they could exploit. Instead, Mucianus spent his first months in squabbles with Vespasian, partly jurisdictional and partly logistical. The word "province," in Latin *provincia*, meant originally an assignment, "the war against the Jews" or *bellum Iudaicum*, for example, and it never lost this sense, even when it became common to use it to denote a specific area like Judaea, a province in the modern acceptation.[3] Now Vespasian's task was to suppress the Jewish rebellion, and when he began operations in February 67, much of Judaea was in revolt. As he had no choice but to move from north to south, he began his campaign from bases in the lower reaches of Syria, and no doubt drew supplies from there too. When Mucianus arrived, in September or October (traveling from Rome rather than Greece, he arrived much later), he took exception to this. Since he would demonstrate a marked yearning for military glory in 69, he may have hoped to take part in suppressing the revolt, and so win the distinction he coveted. He certainly objected to Vespasian's making free with *his* province, so much so that the latter had to negotiate with Mucianus, using his elder son, the 28-year-old Titus, as intermediary. Titus, the legate of XV Apollinaris under his father's overall command, was sent off to Antioch, the administrative capital of Syria. It still took until the end of 67 to iron out the differences between the two governors, and even then the negotiations were concluded successfully, so it is said, only because Mucianus took such a shine to the youthful Titus.

There matters rested until news arrived that Nero had committed suicide and Galba had been recognized as emperor by the senate. Besides Vespasian and Mucianus, there was one more commander in the East with legions at his disposal (two as it happened, XXII Deiotariana and III Cyrenaica). This was Tiberius Julius Alexander, the prefect of Egypt, and we know that he recognized the usurper at once, publishing the appropriate edict on 6 July 68. It has been suggested that Alexander had reached some kind of agreement with Galba beforehand, but it is far more likely that he found a compelling reason to avow his loyalty to the new emperor as rapidly as possible in the fact that Nero had contemplated taking refuge in Alexandria. Some two or three years younger than Vespasian, Alexander had made his way up through the civil and military posts open to a member of the equestrian order. He had been procurator of Judaea between 46 and 48; he had gained some military experience under Nero's best general, Domitius Corbulo, in 63; and he had held the prefecture of Egypt, the highest position he could realistically hope to achieve, since the middle of 66. There was one more rung on the ladder he had climbed, that occupied by the prefect of the praetorian guard, but Alexander was an apostate Jew, the son of a prominent member of the Jewish community in Alexandria. Though the Roman governing class grew more cosmopolitan as the years went by, Alexander's unusual ancestry made it improbable that he would ever be put in charge of a guard drawn exclusively from men born in Italy. Even to keep his current post he had to allay any suspicions that he sympathized with Galba's predecessor.

There is nothing to indicate whether Alexander's prompt acceptance of Galba gave the lead to Mucianus and Vespasian too, but since they also were Neronian appointees, it seems likely enough. The only specific evidence we have, however, is Josephus' comment that once Vespasian heard of Galba's accession, he halted his campaign against the rebels "until he received further instructions from the emperor about the war." From this some have concluded not only that Vespasian sat back and waited for Galba to contact him, but also that he feared that the new emperor would replace him. The first of these views goes far beyond the evidence. For a start, the obvious way for Vespasian to have solicited those instructions was to send Galba a letter in which he professed his allegiance and asked for the emperor's guidance on the campaign. Then too, halting operations against the rebels around July 68 and seeking advice was a sensible course to take, no matter what was happening in Rome. By now Vespasian had completed his slow but systematic conquest of rebel strongholds. Discounting the three small fortresses of Herodium, Machaerus, and Masada, he was under the impression that Jerusalem alone remained to be subdued, and he had long since recognized that investing the city would be a massive undertaking. In the winter of 67/68 his officers had urged him to begin an assault on Jerusalem at once, because the rival factions in the city were at each other's throats. He had rejected their advice, preferring to let the factions destroy one another first. So Vespasian had good military reasons not to embark on a long and difficult task until he had been reassured about the views of his new emperor, a man who was supposed also to possess a good deal of military experience.

Whether Vespasian had grounds to fear that Galba planned to replace him as commander of the war is harder to answer. If we suppose that he sent Galba a letter in July, the emperor clearly failed to respond to his overtures. Yet that may have been simply because Galba did not reach Rome until October 68, and by then the matter was scarcely urgent, when the campaigning season for the year was over. But this failure

to reply could well have disquieted Vespasian. Suetonius not only reports that Vespasian thought later that Galba had sent assassins from
Spain to murder him, but also implies that Vespasian said as much officially in the winter of 69/70, when he annulled a senatorial decree to set
up a memorial to Galba in Rome. This story is usually dismissed as propaganda, and so it could be. A usurper customarily justified his rule by
claiming that his predecessor had tried to assassinate him. But this particular example may not be as far-fetched as it looks. If true, it could
even have generated a major misunderstanding, and much greater fear
on Vespasian's part than was warranted by the facts.

It is entirely conceivable that early in 68 Galba resorted to the methods he used later to dispose of Clodius Macer in Africa, and sent a centurion from Spain in an abortive attempt to remove Vespasian. But if so, it
was not because Galba viewed the Flavian as a rival. That idea invests
Vespasian with far too much importance. Rather, in April or May 68,
Vespasian was in much the same boat as Tiberius Alexander, that is, an
official who could be considered loyal to Nero. He had been attached to
Nero's entourage during the pilgrimage to Greece, and Nero had put
him in charge of the Jewish War. Until Nero committed suicide in June,
therefore, Galba had to consider the possibility that Vespasian and his
battle-tested legions might choose to support the legal emperor against
him. Once Nero was dead, Galba could drop such plans, confident now
that Vespasian would find nobody else to back against his new ruler, and
no incentive to bid for the throne himself. This is perhaps confirmed by
Plutarch. As Galba made his way through Gaul in July and August, so
the biographer tells us, Nymphidius Sabinus plied him with alarmist letters that included allegations not only against Clodius Macer in Africa
but also about trouble brewing in Syria and Judaea. If Galba had still
regarded Vespasian as a threat, he should have acted on these charges.
Instead, he ignored Vespasian even as he eliminated Clodius Macer.

For his part, Vespasian need have had no idea what the emperor's
silence betokened. Even if he had thwarted the assassin or assassins sent
by Galba from Spain, he may well have concluded that the emperor would
send more from Gaul and Germany, no matter how vigorously he expressed his loyalty to the new dispensation. Nor will the nonappearance
of hit men have reassured him, as he heard about Galba's "long and bloody
march" to Rome. Besides, he now knew something that should have given
him still more reason to worry. Though Tacitus ignores most of the
stories about signs portending Vespasian's elevation to the throne, one
of the two incidents he records is the first visit Vespasian made, in May
or June 68, to Basilides, priest of an ancient shrine on Mount Carmel.
Although it has sometimes been held that the purpose of this trip was to

confer with Mucianus, that happened only a year later, during a second visit in May or June 69. In 68, as Tacitus states explicitly, Vespasian wanted to test "his secret hopes," and these were confirmed in full. When Basilides turned to the intricacies of his craft, he found to his astonishment that "whatever it is, Vespasian, that you have in mind, be it to raise a house, or to extend your estate, or to add to your slaves, to you is given a mighty house, enormous boundaries, and a mass of men."

For our purposes, it does not matter what generated Vespasian's secret hopes, since he was a superstitious man anyway. But it is tempting to connect them with an incident that had occurred a year earlier. As Josephus tells the story, mainly to excuse his own conduct and, more specifically, his capture by the Romans at Jotapata in July 67, he was brought before Vespasian soon after, and was so impressed that he informed his new master that, according to "the word of God," Vespasian was destined to become emperor. Josephus adds that it took Vespasian time to swallow this prophecy, but even so obviously self-serving a prediction would have prompted Vespasian to start entertaining secret hopes, and to decide in due course to check them out by consulting a more antique, and so more reputable source.[4]

Vespasian himself grasped the meaning of Basilides' prediction at once, but he did not act on it straight away. On the contrary, as Tacitus also points out, he was still mulling it over when he made his second visit to Mount Carmel a year later, in May or June 69. But all this proves is something to which Suetonius also draws attention, that Vespasian's beliefs were always tempered by his native caution. What counts is that, having been given two predictions of future greatness by the time Galba was recognized as emperor, Vespasian had reason to worry about Galba's failure to indicate what he thought. Vespasian, in other words, regarded neither Josephus' prophecy nor Basilides' prediction as a cast-iron guarantee that he would accede to the throne, and so had to allow for other outcomes, one of them being that Galba might not only try to remove him from his command but also put him to death before they came to pass.

This is the background that makes some sense out of Vespasian's decision to send his son Titus to Rome late in 68. To explain this trip, Tacitus states only that Vespasian felt neither public nor personal hostility to Galba, clearly under the impression that otherwise he would never have risked letting Titus become Galba's hostage for his father's good behavior (yet Vespasian's younger son, Domitian, was apparently in Rome at this time). What Tacitus' comment fails to explain is why Vespasian had not sent Titus to Rome sooner, as he could have done, since there was no serious campaigning in Judaea during the second half of the year; why he insisted that Titus take ship for Rome in the winter of 68/69, when winter travel—especially by sea—tended to be undertaken only in emergencies; and why he sent Titus in particular, when the ostensible reason for the trip was to offer allegiance and pay his respects to the emperor, actions that could probably have been carried out by almost any of his officers.

Tacitus is unconcerned with these questions, because for him it is not the fact of Titus' journey to Rome that matters, but its effect on public opinion, first in Rome, and then on people in the eastern provinces. In the city it sparked gossip about Titus as another potential candidate for adoption by Galba. As he was young, good-looking, and able, "the populace could not be restrained from identifying successors in bulk until one was actually chosen." Tacitus adds that Titus was of an age to seek the next office in the sequence laid down for senators, namely, the praetorship he should have held before he took command of XV Apollinaris. In reality this too could have waited, or have been dropped altogether.[5] So it looks very much as if Galba's continued failure to give Vespasian guidance made the latter truly fearful for his own future, and led him to send Titus posthaste to Rome for two reasons: first, his willingness to entrust his elder son to Galba was supposed to prove his own loyalty to and respect for the emperor; and second, if that failed to do the trick, he could always hope that the young man would charm Galba as he had Mucianus, and so secure or regain the emperor's goodwill toward his father.

Vespasian, of course, was always too crafty to put all his eggs in one basket. Hence it seems reasonable to assume that even as he sent Titus off to Rome, he was also setting up a coalition that could help guard him against the failure of his son's mission. But though we know that Vespasian had made his peace with Mucianus by now, and to this can add the distinct possibility that he had already won over Tiberius Alexander as well, there is little point in speculating. Any such plans were overtaken by events. Titus had reached only Corinth in Greece when he received the news that Galba had been assassinated, and that Otho and Vitellius were fighting for the throne. He is said to have summoned a few friends and debated the options open to him. This led him to the conclusion that it was more prudent to turn back than to become a hostage of one or the other rival, and "that any offence given by his own non-appearance in Rome would be overlooked when Vespasian declared for the victor."[6]

With this out of the way, Tacitus turns to the effects of Titus' return on those in the eastern provinces. As he made his way back, Titus decided to visit the temple of Paphian Venus on Cyprus, and Tacitus includes a lengthy disquisition on the temple and the goddess to lend weight to the glad tidings of great joy that Titus received there. Supposedly, the priest in charge, one Sostratus, declared publicly that every single omen favored great undertakings, and then took Titus aside for a private consultation. What else Sostratus imparted we are not told, nor does Tacitus pretend to know. As he recognized, what needed to be said was, first, that Titus was greatly encouraged by the priest's words, and second, that when he rejoined his father at Caesarea Maritima, the administrative capital on the coast of Palestine, "he allayed the great anxiety of the provinces and their armies by bringing them enormous confidence of success."

The fact of the matter, nonetheless, was that Vespasian and Mucianus had agreed on a plan of action already. When they received the news of Otho's accession, during Titus' absence, they decided to acknowledge him as their emperor, and administered the oath of allegiance to their troops forthwith. Neither of them was particularly enthused about Otho's cause. Rather, they were playing a waiting game, planning—according to Tacitus—to sit on the sidelines while Otho and Vitellius slugged it out. In their view, it did not matter which contender won the war, because both were so horribly flawed that the one would be brought down by the war, the other by his victory. This is a classic example of a motif as popular with Greco-Roman historians as are conspiratorial theories of history today, that of the *tertius gaudens*, the third party who waits till a struggle between two other rivals has been fought, and the victor has been so weakened by his success that he can be defeated. Yet there is no reason to doubt its veracity in this instance. This was the plan Vespasian had adopted in the winter of 67/68, when he had rejected his officers' advice to attack Jerusalem while the rival factions within the city were so busily killing each other off.

There can be little doubt that Vespasian forced the adoption of this plan. Supposedly, his officers were already pushing for more vigorous action. Few were motivated by love of country, Tacitus tells us, most by thoughts of gain; some were deeply in debt, and others found the prospect of loot too attractive to resist. It is an interesting assertion, given that one of those officers was Marcus Ulpius Traianus, the legionary legate of X Fretensis and father of the emperor in whose reign Tacitus wrote and published the *Histories*. Perhaps he was supposed to be one of the handful motivated by love of country. As for Mucianus, he too was more enthusiastic than Vespasian. Since he lacked military experience, he was already hankering after a command in which he could win some glory. And he seems to have been keeping his troops in shape by constant drilling, while the men themselves were fired up by their envy of the successes Vespasian's legions had gained in Judaea.

Vespasian's three legions had been hardened by campaigning against the Jewish rebels, and they had been impressed too by their commander's old-style generalship: he led from the front, never shirked battle, ate the same food as the men, and could scarcely be distinguished from them in dress and bearing. Yet, says Tacitus, either Vespasian recognized that it might be too much to ask them to embark on a civil war, or else he projected onto them his own doubts about the wisdom of bidding for the throne. To an extent, this presentation of the situation may owe something to Flavian propaganda. The more reluctant to undertake a civil war Vespasian's troops were made to appear, after all, the easier it became to maintain that they were forced into it by the need to save the state from the excesses of an Otho or a Vitellius. On the other hand, none of the Flavian legionaries—as yet—felt grievances like those that had animated Otho's praetorians or Vitellius' legions in Germany. Nor had troops in the eastern provinces been involved in a civil war since Augustus' victory at Actium a century earlier. So it was only as Otho and Vitellius fought out their civil war that the troops grew more and more restive about the idea of submitting to the victor in that war.

Even so, it is not surprising that when it came time to act (this opens the third segment Tacitus devotes to the uprising), Vespasian, Mucianus, and Tiberius Alexander all began by administering to their troops the oath of allegiance to Vitellius—and the moment Vitellius heard this news, supposedly, he concluded that the fighting was over, and so he and his followers became ever more grasping and cruel. In recognizing Vitellius, of course, the three men were again playing for time. For one thing, they were almost certainly caught off guard both by the speed with which Vitellius disposed of Otho, and by Otho's refusal to continue the war after Bedriacum. Then there was the fact that since Otho had not asked expressly for their help, the three governors had had to sit on the sidelines literally as well as figuratively. They could no more have afforded to make overt preparations for a war than they could have to be caught by their emperor corresponding or meeting with one another. The winner of the struggle could declare all such conduct treasonous. So until the war between Otho and Vitellius was over and a victor had emerged, they could formulate plans to their hearts' content, but they could not afford to come out into the open and begin the down-to-earth preparations for a campaign to overthrow the winner. And there was a third point. Now that the moment of decision was upon him, Vespasian hesitated.

This temporizing—another example, perhaps, of the "luck of the Flavians" at work—lent credibility to a flattering portrayal of Vespasian's motives for going ahead with his revolt. So Josephus depicts the uprising as in every respect a last-minute, spontaneous affair. There was no prior discussion or planning, only disgust with Vitellius' excesses as the news of them arrived. Yet Vespasian, for all his deep concern about the state's best interests, was reluctant to put himself forward, and offered "many reasons" for not acting. Hence his officers had to draw their swords and threaten him before he accepted the title of emperor. Once this step was taken, he entrusted to Mucianus what he is said explicitly to have considered the most important task, leading an expeditionary force to Italy. As Tacitus recognized, there are three difficulties in this version of events. First, Vespasian was hailed emperor on 1 July, when Vitellius had probably not even reached Rome. So there were few excesses to report, let alone to arouse disgust. Second, Vespasian's hesitation sprang neither from love of the state nor from a feeling that he was unfit to be emperor. And third, when Vespasian believed so firmly in leading from the front, it made little sense for him to give the most important military task to another, least of all to Mucianus, whom Tacitus aptly describes as a man who loved ostentation, was a great talker, and a past master of civil administration.

To resolve these difficulties, Tacitus constructed a much more elaborate account of the situation. In this Vespasian's doubts ran so wide and deep that he had to seek reassurances of every kind, in reflections on his overall situation, in a rousing speech by Mucianus, and in pondering on omens he had received in the past. Much of this material has been declared pure fiction, and so it could be. That does not make it an implausible reconstruction. If Vespasian was truly determined to take on the winner in a war between Otho and Vitellius, after all, he should not have hesitated, when such a plan demanded that the offensive be launched immediately, before the victor could recover from his losses in the struggle. And since Tacitus found it hard to credit Vespasian with any marked love of country, it was logical to conclude that the Flavian suffered a sudden, if momentary, attack of cold feet. Vespasian was notoriously cautious and canny.

When the first overt meeting between Vespasian, Mucianus, and their followers was held on Mount Carmel in May or June 69, therefore, Vespasian is said to have reflected on the advantages and disadvantages of rebellion. There is not one word about the excesses of Vitellius. Instead, Vespasian concludes that the advantages are few. He can count—up to a point—on the spirit of his own men; on the support of Mucianus and Tiberius Alexander; on legion III Gallica in Moesia, because it had been based in Syria until nearly the end of Nero's reign; and on its being able perhaps to win over other legions in the Balkans, because the arrogance of Vitellius' emissaries was alienating every unit to which they were sent. But against this he had to balance, first, the fact that failure would destroy him and his two sons, both old enough to be considered threats in their own right. Then too, he refused to underrate the strength of Vitellius' legions. The surviving Othonian troops would be no use to him, since in defeat they were more inclined to air complaints than to show courage. And his own legions, finally, were untested in civil war. He could rely on most of his men, legionaries and auxiliaries alike, but there was always the risk that one or two might sell him out to the enemy, for cash or to secure a promotion. This being how Camillus Scribonianus had been brought down in 42, it was clearly going to be difficult to avoid an individual assassin.

In the face of this hesitation Vespasian's friends and commanders did all they could to reassure him. The lead was taken by Mucianus, to whom Tacitus gives a lengthy speech. In this Mucianus cannot respond directly to the fears dogging Vespasian, since they have been expressed in an "interior monologue." But as Tacitus constructs his account, the main problem is solved by Mucianus' own eagerness to gratify his ambitions. Consumed by his yearnings for military glory, Mucianus volunteers to lead the expeditionary force that must march to Italy, and once he has made this offer, it cannot be rejected without damaging the friendship between the two men. The offer itself makes excellent sense in a context where Vespasian is suffering from a momentary failure of nerve. And, more importantly, Vespasian's accepting the offer frees him from his fears of assassination by one of his own men. For now neither he nor (for the most part) his men will have to contend with the stresses and strains of making war on their fellow citizens. All in all, it is a very artful piece of work.

If this explains—in an appropriately unflattering manner—how Mucianus came to be given the command of the expeditionary force, it fails to address the other major problem Vespasian had noted in his musings, the strength of the German legions. But Mucianus resolved this too in his speech. In fact he must have presented arguments not too unlike those Tacitus puts in his mouth, be it in a speech or in a more informal conversation. In essence, the Tacitean Mucianus makes two points, that the overthrow of Vitellius is both possible and necessary, and that the speaker is trustworthy and ready to undergo the dangers that adopting this course of action will bring down on the person he is advising. Overthrowing Vitellius, he observes, is necessary because Vespasian has already won too much renown to avoid the risk of being removed as a potential rival by a worthless ruler: distinction leads only to extinction. And it is possible, because Vitellius' elevation proves that an emperor can be made by an army, and the army that has put him on the throne because it hated Galba is now being ruined in victory by Vitellius' own laxness.

To establish the purity of his own motives, Mucianus accepts unreservedly not only Vespasian's fitness to found a new dynasty but also his right to reward his coadjutors as he sees fit. In fact, to demonstrate his loyalty to Vespasian come what may (and to gratify his own ambitions, of course), Mucianus will undertake the more perilous task of leading the expeditionary force to Italy. Recognizing that neither he nor his legions are the obvious candidates for this task, he skirts this difficulty by claiming that all Vespasian's forces are in great shape. Then he minimizes the dangers they will face, by claiming that the Vitellians are wrapped in lethargy as a result of their victory, riddled with indiscipline, and too arrogant to imagine that they will be called upon to beat back a fresh challenge. Even the defeated Othonian legions in the Balkans, he asserts, are in better shape. Their discipline is still intact and their desire for revenge strong. In short, a campaign will bring into the open the weaknesses with which Vitellius and his troops are beset, but—Mucianus concludes—the campaign must begin at once, since "those who contemplate rebellion have already rebelled."

It would be foolish to imagine either that Vespasian failed to see the self-serving motives behind Mucianus' protestations of loyalty, or that he was convinced by Mucianus' thesis that Vitellius' troops were in such bad shape. So this is where Tacitus sets the story of Basilides' prophecy, and this serves two purposes. First, pondering anew on its significance at last reassures Vespasian. Since he is clearly fated to become emperor, he—and presumably his allies—are not likely to encounter disaster along the way. And second, the gossip among the others present, the gossip that prompts this pondering, is what leads these people (according to Tacitus) to work out what Vespasian had grasped long since, that Basilides had promised him the throne. And since Tacitus chooses to regard the two governors' followers as more orientalized than perhaps they were, the impact of a prediction from an ancient and important shrine in the East works its magic on them too. It should have been more than enough to overcome any lingering scruples about breaking the oath they had sworn to Vitellius.

Yet the first proclamation was made in Egypt. Tiberius Alexander jumped the gun, administering the oath of allegiance to Vespasian to his two legions on 1 July. Perhaps he was trying to create the impression that Vespasian was answering a draft, another staple in the role-playing of usurpers. Or perhaps this was his way of precluding more foot-dragging—as there might otherwise have been. As Tacitus tells the story, the troops in Judaea followed suit on 3 July in an entirely impromptu manner. Supposedly, they were casting about for a way to hail Vespasian emperor, when their commander emerged from his quarters that morning, and a handful of men outside simply greeted him as emperor. This broke the ice, and everybody else rushed up to join in a chorus that heaped one imperial title after another upon him. For his part, Vespasian now abandoned his fears and thought only of his new position. But "in his behavior there was no vanity, no arrogance, no change despite his changed circumstances. Once he had dispelled the giddiness that his elevation had spread over his eyes, he addressed those who had gathered in simple, soldierly terms, and responded in the same way to the congratulations flooding in from every side."

As for Syria, a much larger area to cover, Mucianus administered the oath to all the legions *and* all the civilians there before 15 July, and while he was at it, he found a way to galvanize his own men still more. He went to the theater in Antioch, since it was the Greek habit to hold public meetings in their theaters. (It was a habit of which Romans thoroughly disapproved, convinced as they were that politics and entertainment were poles apart.) There he gave a speech in fluent Greek, for "thanks to his feeling for style he set off to best advantage everything he said and did." And in this speech, fully aware that the allegation would spread like wildfire through the province, he insisted repeatedly that Vitellius had decided to reward the legions from the German frontier with a transfer to Syria, a cushy and peaceful billet, while the three legions currently stationed there were to be reassigned to the German frontier, where nothing awaited them but discipline and work as harsh as the climate. It was an outright lie, but it was well calculated to upset the civilian population as much as it did the soldiery. Not only did the civilians take pleasure in the company of the soldiery billeted on them (with many they had ties of friendship or kinship). The legionaries themselves had served in the area so long that they regarded their quarters as their homes. In fact, VI Ferrata and XII Fulminata had been stationed in Syria since at least Tiberius' reign, while IV Scythica had been there since 58, a full decade earlier.

How to proceed was the subject of a council of war held in July in Beirut, mid-way between Antioch and Caesarea. To this Mucianus and Vespasian brought the pick of their men, while the three most important client kings in the area turned up too, with all the appropriate pomp and circumstance. This created "the appearance of an imperial court," and Vespasian gave it substance by putting in hand measures taken normally by the emperor alone. The first order of business was to determine what else was needed in the way of resources. So Vespasian set in motion a program to raise fresh troops and recall veterans to the standards, to designate cities to manufacture arms, and to arrange for gold and silver to be coined in Antioch. Suitable subordinates would be put in charge of each operation, to ensure that they were carried out efficiently and speedily. But Vespasian's readiness to take in money was not matched by a willingness to disburse it. To encourage his officers, Vespasian gave many prefectships and procuratorships (that is, he raised them to or confirmed them in equestrian rank), and on some he conferred senatorial status. These were outstanding men, says Tacitus, who later reached the highest posts, even if "there were a few cases where wealth substituted for qualities." As for the troops, they had only been promised a tiny donative by Mucianus, and that is all they received. Vespasian set his face against handing out large sums, and, says Tacitus in his one favorable comment on the emperor's tight-fistedness, "his army was all the better for it."

Next, there was the plan of campaign to discuss. Presumably to make the point that Vespasian hesitated—as Vitellius had not—to strip his provinces of troops for a civil war, Tacitus reports first that envoys were sent to Vologaeses I of Parthia and Tiridates of Armenia, to try to ensure that the two kings made no incursions into Roman territory while the legions were otherwise occupied. It was probably hard to determine how serious a threat these rulers represented. Corbulo, Nero's general, had fought a long, hard war with Vologaeses, and there was no telling whether the king had learnt his lesson or was thirsting for revenge. Tiridates, on the other hand, was technically a client-king of Rome, having sworn allegiance to Nero in 66. But Nero was dead and Tiridates was Vologaeses' brother. Besides, both would no doubt have assured Vespasian of their peaceful intentions, whatever they planned to do in fact. So it may well be that one reason for Vespasian's deciding to remain close to the eastern frontier of the empire—now that he could—was to guard against the possibility that these two would make trouble. In the event, Parthian ambassadors would turn up in Alexandria toward the end of the year, and offer Vespasian the help of 40,000 mounted archers. This offer he declined, not merely because the civil war was almost over, but also because it would have been ill-advised to accept foreign aid when it suited his ends as much as it did Tacitus' to play up the Germanic character of Vitellius' troops.

For the rest, Titus was to keep the pressure on in Judaea, that is, to police the rebels who had already been conquered and prevent any new outbreaks. But he was not to begin the siege of Jerusalem (that was launched only in April 70). Vespasian would move south to Egypt, "in order to secure Alexandria." Since Vespasian had no reason to doubt the loyalty of Tiberius Alexander or, for that matter, to fear a Vitellian counterattack on Egypt, this suggests two things. First, Vespasian must have meant to stay in Syria until winter approached, this being the best vantage point from which to keep an eye on the Parthians and to receive messages from Mucianus in the early stages of his march. Second, he would spend the winter in Alexandria, a natural center of communications, so that in the following spring he could move east or west as circumstances demanded. As for Mucianus, he was given a relatively small force, one entire legion from Syria (VI Ferrata) and detachments of 2,600 men apiece from the other five legions operating there and in Judaea, for a total of approximately 18,000 legionaries. But as he advanced through the Balkans, he was supposed to pick up more troops, first from the legions stationed in Moesia, Pannonia, and Dalmatia (the armies to which letters were certainly sent), and then from the dissident, ex-Othonian praetorians who had been dispersed about northern Italy by Vitellius. It seems to have been taken for granted that all these men would wait until Mucianus appeared to answer the call of "the name of Vespasian."

This was Vespasian's idea of how the business should be conducted, and he has often been credited with "a bloodless strategy" or, in more modern terms, a plan of winning by intimidation. On the one hand, he would blockade the city of Rome by cutting off the grain supplies from Egypt. On the other, he would use the threat embodied by Mucianus' expeditionary force to destroy the Vitellians' will to resist. Clearly there was much to be said for such an approach in political terms, since Vespasian stood to lose far more than he gained by shedding or allowing others to shed the blood of fellow citizens. And from a military point of view, such a plan not only matched his own cautious mode of campaigning in Judaea, but was well calculated to allay such doubts as he had about the ability of Mucianus and his troops to win any battle they might have to fight.

Yet there are problems in this interpretation. It is a fact that Vespasian—or Tiberius Alexander—cut off the grain supplies from Egypt, but it may be unwise to view this as an essential part of the overall plan, rather than as an action that might as well be taken since it could be taken. Unless Vespasian failed to realize it (which is possible), depriving Rome of its Egyptian grain would create a food shortage in the city, but hardly starvation, and it would hurt the common people far more than the Vitellians. The latter could simply appropriate all the available grain for their own uses, and grain there was in plenty, as Africa had become perhaps the most important source of supply since Augustus' day. This may be why there have been attempts to backdate Tacitus' report that Vespasian later contemplated invading Africa too. But while this plan would have created real shortages in Rome, had it been carried out, it was prompted—as Tacitus says—by Vespasian's learning of the Vitellians' defeat at Cremona in October, and by his recognition that this setback had bottled them up once for all in the Italian peninsula.

This is not the only obstacle to ideas of a "bloodless strategy." Even if Vespasian hoped that Mucianus' expeditionary force could overawe the enemy into surrender, Mucianus did not. Tacitus underlines this difference of opinion by including in his account of Mucianus' departure from Antioch a plan of action that would have entailed considerable bloodshed. Some time before Mucianus set off, so Tacitus reports, he ordered the fleet of about 40 ships stationed in Pontus to gather at Byzantium. This was part of a plan to lead his expeditionary force by a different route from the one he took. In this scenario the troops would march the 907 Roman miles of the Egnatian Way from Byzantium to Dyrrachium (Durres) on the Adriatic coast, cross by sea to southern Italy, and fight their way up the peninsula to Rome, much as had Lucius Cornelius Sulla when he had invaded Italy in 83 B.C. There was a risk that the landing would be opposed by Vitellius' much larger fleets at Misenum and Ravenna, but Mucianus argued seemingly that his adversary would be unable to concentrate either fleet because uncertain where exactly the Flavians would try to land, and so would be forced to distribute his warships in penny packets round the southern coast of Italy. There is no reason to think Vespasian was enamored of this plan, but Mucianus was, and since he behaved—as Tacitus puts it—more like Vespasian's associate than his subordinate, he would no doubt have put it into effect, had he had the chance. As it was, the time of year ruled it out. Since Mucianus left Antioch near the start of August, there was little chance of reaching Dyrrachium before the first week in November, and even if Vitellian countermeasures took the form Mucianus anticipated, the Adriatic Sea was notoriously stormy in winter.

This was not Tacitus' only reason to criticize Mucianus, or Vespasian for that matter. There was more moneygrubbing too. Mucianus had claimed that his alternative plan of action, by carrying the war to Italy, would protect Greece and Asia against the depredations of Vitellius. There was no plan to protect them from Flavian plundering. So when Mucianus left Antioch, he took with him only a small, lightly loaded advance guard, and with this he adopted a pace that was neither too slow, because that would depress the morale of his troops, "nor yet too fast, since he wanted the news of his advance to grow by exaggeration." The people to be intimidated were not the Vitellians far away in Italy, however, but the inhabitants of the territory between Antioch and Byzantium. They were now soaked for monetary contributions to the war effort, collected by the advance guard and compelled by the main force that followed, the 18,000-odd legionaries organized around VI

Ferrata. So the provinces through which he passed "rang with the preparation of ships, troops and weaponry, but nothing plagued them as much as the quest for cash." To all complaints Mucianus replied that money provided the sinews of civil war, undeterred by the fact that this was a cliché. "He held hearings where he ignored law and equity and focused exclusively on the wealth of his potential targets, so that informers sprang up at every turn and all men of substance were plundered without mercy."

Conceding that this heavy burden was excused by the demands of civil war, Tacitus involves Vespasian too, by going on to say that these practices continued after the war. "Though Vespasian himself at the start of his reign was not keen to enforce unjust decisions, he learnt to do so, and he got up the nerve to do so, thanks to the indulgence of fortune and his having bad teachers." The best of these teachers being Mucianus, we are told next that he contributed out of his own pocket to the costs of the war, "being open-handed because he knew that he would be able to draw more greedily from the state's resources. The rest of the officers followed his lead and made contributions too, but very, very few of them enjoyed the same license in recovering their investments."

Here Tacitus ends the third segment of his narrative, leaving Mucianus somewhere between Antioch and Byzantium, happily extracting funds from others who will never see their money again, but secure in the knowledge that he will reap the benefits of his own generosity many times over. It looks like an odd place to change the subject, especially when Mucianus turns up next in Moesia, but quite apart from Tacitus' aversion to reporting pedestrian details about crossing the Dardanelles or advancing into Europe, two interlocking reasons seem to be at work. There is a point he has made before, that while an amalgam of Vespasian and Mucianus would have produced an excellent emperor, they were neither of them estimable characters on their own. And there is the likelihood that this stress on money is designed ironically to draw attention to the one substantive gain the two Flavian leaders made. For Tacitus turns next to the campaign led by Marcus Antonius Primus, a campaign in which the Balkan legions preempted every Flavian plan, Vespasian's hopes for a relatively bloodless victory, and Mucianus' desire for military glory.

9

The Opening of the Flavian Offensive
(August to October)

The campaign conducted by the legions under Antonius Primus' control falls naturally into two parts. Their initial moves, the subject of this chapter, established them firmly in northern Italy with the sack of Cremona, still the enemy's main base in the area. Then came their more dilatory advance south toward Rome, culminating in the killing of Vitellius in late December. For the first stage Dio provides material on a few episodes; Suetonius skips over almost every event between September and November, referring explicitly to the sack of Cremona only in his *Life* of Vespasian; and Josephus contributes an interesting snippet or two. So Tacitus is our most detailed and our most reliable source. Not that all agree. A discrepancy has been discerned in Tacitus' portrait of Antonius, a more heroic figure allegedly in the first stage of the campaign and in the second more of a villain. This supposed discrepancy in turn has been held to prove that Tacitus failed to combine two sources, one favorable to Antonius (no doubt the memoir by Vipstanus Messalla), and one to Vespasian whose plans Antonius wrecked so comprehensively. If we were to accept this thesis, we could impugn any detail we judged unsatisfactory on any ground and declare Tacitus wholly unreliable. But the thesis itself is misconceived. Tacitus may gloss over some of Antonius' mistakes, but at base he presents us with a man who might show scruples when circumstances permitted, but showed none when they did not.

The uprising against Vitellius started in August among the legions stationed in Moesia, and as Vespasian had hoped, III Gallica took the lead. But VII Claudia and VIII Augusta followed readily, as a result of events in April. As all three units had been gratified by the lavish rewards Otho heaped on them for the defeat of the Rhoxolani, they had obeyed his summons to join him in Italy. But none had advanced beyond Aquileia when they heard of his suicide. Suetonius and Tacitus disagree on what happened next. According to Suetonius' overly condensed and so misleading account, only the advance detachments had reached the town. They took the news badly, "giving way to every form of plundering." But since they recognized that Vitellius would punish them eventually, they proclaimed

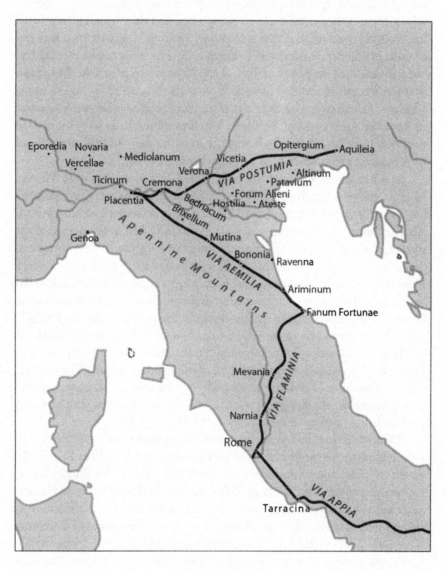

Northern Italy

Vespasian emperor. Tacitus, however, states that the legions reached Aquileia in their entirety, refused at first to accept Vitellius as their ruler, but took advantage of the prevailing disorder to plunder only their military chest, their operating funds, sharing out the proceeds among themselves. He too states that the men recognized that they would be punished for their misconduct, but that the idea of backing Vespasian as a way out of their predicament occurred to them only after they heard that he had been proclaimed emperor in July. This is far more plausible. His claim that the legions plundered only their own funds is unlikely, but so too is Vitellius' failure to punish the men, if they had truly proclaimed Vespasian in April. In April or May, however, Vitellius would have found it easy to overlook their plundering, whatever it was that they had plundered, and their rejecting him briefly out of their devotion to Otho.

It is harder to work out the role played by the governor of Moesia, Marcus Aponius Saturninus. He sent Vitellius the dispatch that informed the emperor of the defection of III Gallica. But no sooner had he sent it off than he followed the legion's example. Perhaps he had underestimated the chances for success, not expecting the other two legions in the province to make common cause with the rebels so enthusiastically. Rivalry between legions in a province was common, even when they staged a mutiny, as the events of 14 had shown. Or he may have seen joining the revolt as a way to cover settling a personal score. He certainly claimed that he was acting in the state's interests when he sent a centurion to kill Tettius Julianus, the legate of VII Claudia. Tettius evaded the assassin and eventually took refuge with Vespasian, but the feud had one important result. The military tribune Vipstanus Messalla, commander of one cohort, became the legion's acting legate for the next two months, and he, says Tacitus, was "the only man to bring good qualities to this campaign."

Once the Moesian legions had decided on their course of action, they sent letters to the units stationed in Pannonia, urging them to join the revolt or suffer the consequences of remaining loyal to Vitellius. The response was immediate. Legion XIII Gemina, stationed at Poetovio, still resented the defeat inflicted on it at Bedriacum and the humiliation of being forced afterwards to build amphitheaters at Placentia and Cremona. The men of VII Galbiana at Carnuntum seem to have been just as hostile to Vitellius, even if what counted in their eyes was that they had been recruited by Galba. But it was Marcus Antonius Primus, their commander, not they who made the decision. Not unlike Caecina earlier in the year, he saw revolt as an opportunity to make a name for himself.

Though nearly twice Caecina's age, Antonius had an equally spotty record. Born at Tolosa (Toulouse) in Gallia Narbonensis early in Tiberius' reign, he had been convicted of knowingly witnessing a forged

will in 61 and had been sent into exile. Yet Galba had restored his senatorial rank and made him legate of VII Galbiana. When the war between
Otho and Vitellius broke out, as Tacitus is careful to phrase it, Antonius
"was believed to have written repeatedly to Otho, offering the emperor
his services as a general, but since Otho ignored him, he played no useful
role in that campaign."[1] Whatever this means, Antonius climbed on the
Flavian bandwagon without hesitation. As Tacitus observes, he was a
man of great physical bravery and oratorical ability, but to these essential qualifications for generalship he added less desirable traits. He was a
master at making mischief for others, at his best amid riots and mutinies.
He was always ready to plunder the property of others and to squander it
in bribes for his own followers. In short, he was the worst kind of man to
have around in peacetime but not one to underrate when there was a
war. And he demonstrated these attributes in a meeting, held apparently
at Poetovio (Ptuj) in Pannonia in late August. A letter from Vespasian
was read to a gathering of delegates, officers and men, from all the
Pannonian legions, calling on them to support his revolt. The men favored the idea, but the generals temporized—with one exception.
Antonius came out openly for Vespasian, and so won the soldiers' respect. They thought him "one as ready to accept the consequences of
failure as he was to share the glory if they succeeded."

Perhaps at this same meeting, the delegates also discussed plans of
action. They had two choices. The bolder move was to launch an offensive into Italy at once, the alternative to wait for Mucianus and his army.
To wait was the course Vespasian had recommended in his letters to the
various legions, or at least the one that his letters assumed they would
follow. He cannot have insisted on it, however, since his wishes were not
an issue in this debate. Unsurprisingly, most speakers favored delay. They
had already posted guards at the three main Alpine passes through which
a Vitellian force in Italy could counterattack them, and all they needed
to do now, so they claimed, was to reinforce these pickets until they had
assembled all the troops stationed in the Balkans. Only then would they
be able to match the strength and prowess of the Rhine legions. Their
own men were not only inferior in numbers but defeated as well. No
matter how boldly they talked, their morale was questionable. This would
not be a problem, if they limited themselves to occupying the passes in
force. They would lose none of the advantages they possessed already,
and they could only benefit by waiting for Mucianus and his army. And
since Vespasian controlled the sea with his fleets, and had the enthusiatic
backing of the eastern provinces, they would be able to fight as part of an
overwhelming force in a brand new war.

Antonius was not alone in urging an immediate offensive, even though
it was likely to run into the winter months. But he was the most forceful

speaker. Responding point by point to the procrastinators' arguments, he held that to attack immediately would work to the Flavians' advantage and complete the ruin of the enemy. Victory had made the Vitellians lazy and complacent. Instead of being kept combat ready in camp, they were billeted in municipalities around Rome, intimidating only their unwilling hosts. "They had drunk deep of these unaccustomed pleasures with a greed all the greater because of the rough life they had lived before." But though softened up by the pleasures of city living, or worn down by sickness, even they could be whipped back into shape, if given time to recover their energy under the threat of war. Vitellius could draw more troops from the two Germanies. Britain, Gaul, and Spain would furnish him with men, matériel, and money. And at his back he had Italy and its resources. This was not all. If the Vitellians seized the initiative while the Flavians held the Alpine passes, they themselves would end up in a trap. The Vitellians controlled two large fleets, and since the Adriatic was unguarded, they could land troops in Dalmatia and take their enemy in the rear. In the meantime the Flavians would be unable to secure pay or supplies from the area they occupied.

If these were Antonius' arguments, it is easy to see why Tacitus typed him as a demagogue. They were more frightening than convincing. The idea that the Vitellians could conduct combined operations in the Adriatic is especially far-fetched. Otho's maritime expedition may have shown that such operations were feasible, but its failure hardly suggested that the Flavians faced serious danger. Yet these arguments were less specious than those he made for immediate action. They must take advantage of the fact that the Pannonian legions were thirsting for revenge, since they had been deceived rather than defeated at Bedriacum. The infantry from Moesia had taken no part in the battle and so had suffered no losses. And if one counted men rather than companies, the Flavian forces were superior, while the shame of defeat had strengthened their discipline and their resolve. Besides, the Flavian cavalry had not been defeated at all. Though the battle had gone against the Othonians, a mere two squadrons—one each from Pannonia and Moesia—had broken through the enemy line. Now they had 16 squadrons and with these they could overwhelm the enemy. Conceding—or, more accurately, exploiting the fact—that his plan involved high risk, Antonius announced that he was ready to take personal command of the force and put his scheme into effect at once. Those unwilling to join him could stay with the legions. They would hear soon enough that the power of Vitellius had been shaken to its foundations, and then "follow in the footsteps of his victory."

This speech was so effective that Antonius won over at least some of the doubters, while the bulk of his audience hailed him as "the only man and only general" among their leaders. The caution of the rest they dismissed as inertia, and this confirmed his standing with the troops. But he was aided and abetted by Cornelius Fuscus, who stood second only to him in the troops' regard. This was because Fuscus had criticized Vitellius so often and so harshly that, if things went wrong, there was no way out for him.[2] But now Fuscus gave them a name to hide behind. The governor of Pannonia, nominally Antonius' as well as Fuscus' superior, was Tampius Flavianus, a procrastinator by nature and by age. His initial inactivity had aroused the troops' suspicions that he was foot-dragging on Vitellius' behalf, since he was related to the emperor. He had also decamped to Italy when the first overt stirrings of revolt occurred, and then had returned, less of his own accord than because he yielded to Fuscus' powers of persuasion. This encouraged the troops to overlook his earlier conduct and to believe that he was as eager now to take part in a civil war as they were. But Fuscus had not worked so hard because he wanted a display of energy from Flavianus, only a consular figurehead, to lend an air of respectability to the proceedings.

Immediately after the meeting, therefore, a message was sent to Aponius Saturninus, telling him to bring up all the Moesian troops as fast as possible. In the meantime, to avoid leaving the Danube frontier uncovered while the tribes were still restless (it was less than a year since the Rhoxolani had been defeated), arrangements were made with two of the stronger tribes on the far side of the river, the Sarmatian Iazyges to the east of Pannonia, and the Suebi along its northern frontier. This left only one obvious threat, the procurator of Raetia, Porcius Septiminus, who was unshakably loyal to Vitellius. To hold him in check, the governor of Noricum, Publius Sextilius Felix, was given a cavalry squadron (the *ala Auriana*), eight cohorts of auxiliary infantry, and the militia of his province, with orders to take up position on the banks of the Inn, the river that separated Raetia from Noricum. There may have been some fighting, since the archaeological record is said to show traces of devastation in this general period, but there were no battles. Like Otho's maritime expedition in the spring, this campaign faded out in a stalemate.[3]

Although this secured Antonius' right flank, he rushed forward only some of the troops available to him, detachments from the cohorts and "part" of the cavalry. Command of the cavalry was entrusted to Arrius Varus (Cornelius Fuscus was required for another, more important task). Varus had made his name in Corbulo's campaigns in Armenia, but though always ready to fight, he also had a reputation for being devious, allegedly having traduced Corbulo behind his back, in order to win his own promotion to higher rank. Their first step was to seize Aquileia, the gateway to northern Italy, and from there they pressed on, unopposed, westward along the Adriatic coast to the two villages of Opitergium (Oderzo) and Altinum (Altino). At Altinum they left a garrison, of unspecified size, in case the marines of the Ravenna fleet tried to make a raid from the sea. They had not yet heard, says Tacitus, that the fleet was intent on defecting thanks to the ministrations of Lucilius Bassus. From here they struck inland and took two much more important towns, Patavium (Padua, birthplace of the historian Livy) and Ateste (Este). And at Ateste they learnt that they must fight.

Apparently on Caecina's orders a Vitellian force of three cohorts and one cavalry squadron (the *ala Sebosiana*) had taken up position near Forum Alieni, a town usually identified with Legnano or Ferrara on the south bank of the Adige. They had built a pontoon bridge across the river and encamped on the northern bank. But as they were not expecting the enemy to advance so fast, they failed to keep watch. So the Flavians mounted a surprise attack at dawn, under the no less mistaken impression that if they killed a few defenders, the rest would change sides. Some surrendered, but the majority put up a stalwart resistance, managed to retreat across their bridge and, by breaking it down behind them, to prevent pursuit. A modern writer would probably draw attention to the determination shown by the Vitellians in this encounter, and to the Flavians' underestimation of their opponents' caliber. Tacitus is more result oriented. He stresses the Flavians' winning the fight, because this gave them a programmatic victory, and the news spread fast, through Italy and through the Balkan provinces as well.

This may have been the stimulus for two of the Balkan legions to join the advance guard now and take up position at Patavium (VII Galbiana and XIII Gemina, both under the command of the latter's legate Vedius Aquila). Although Vedius' troops had nearly killed him at Bedriacum for alleged treachery, he had since been restored to their good graces. Then, says Tacitus, came "an act long desired, because of the construction put on it and the boasting with which it was done." Antonius ordered that the statues of Galba overthrown after his murder be set up again. Presumably this gratified the men of VII Galbiana, but who else it was supposed to please it is hard to say. Perhaps Antonius imagined that, as appalling an emperor as Galba had been, it would not hurt to claim to be avenging his murder when Vespasian was almost certainly unknown to the inhabitants of northern Italy. It is odd, nonetheless, that Antonius seems not to have worried about the reaction of those of Otho's praetorians who were scattered about the area. Perhaps he expected them to let their hatred of Vitellius overshadow this slur on Otho's name.

What did cause discussion among the Flavians at this stage was picking a headquarters for their campaign. Their choice fell on Verona, an important town not only because it was rich in resources, but also because it was set at the head of the Postumian Way. This made it both a good roadblock against any Vitellian offensive out of the north, and a first-rate base from which to march down the road that would become the main axis of the army's advance. Still, says Tacitus, all this was either unknown to Vespasian or had actually been forbidden by him. Urging that the force hold its position at Aquileia, he made his instructions more palatable by setting out his reasoning, according to Tacitus, the unrealistic claim that, as the situation now stood, the Vitellians could be forced by lack of resources and food to surrender without a fight. Mucianus said the same in frequent letters, but for different motives. He wanted to fight a regular battle that would win the glory of victory for him. But because both men were so far away, their recommendations arrived too late.

As a result, Antonius decided to press on, and a small, indecisive skirmish followed, apparently with the outposts of Caecina's force. For shortly after this Caecina himself took up position in the area between Hostilia and the river Tartarus, fortifying a camp where his rear was covered by the river, his flanks by marshes. "Had he still been loyal to Vitellius," says Tacitus, "it would have been possible for him either to overwhelm with all his troops the two Flavian legions that made up the core of the enemy force or to drive them out of Italy in panic flight." And so perhaps he could have done, but he temporized—and this may be why Josephus and Dio assert that the sight of the Flavians was enough to persuade him that the Vitellian cause was lost, and that he must come to terms with the enemy. But whatever we make of the allegations that Caecina had been contemplating treachery for some time, Tacitus provides the details to show that the situation was not so straightforward.

As he tells the story, Antonius and his forces must have been at Verona, a town they had not yet fortified. Caecina refused nonetheless to move out of the strong position he occupied, and spent his time writing letters to the enemy in which he upbraided them for turning on their legal emperor, and at the same time dickered over the terms on which he was to change sides. This handed the initiative to the enemy, and gave Aponius Saturninus time to bring up another legion, VII Claudia. Though three legions were still no match in numbers for the Vitellian force, Caecina sent them another batch of letters in which he upbraided them as beaten men, dwelt on their folly in taking up arms again, and extolled the prowess of the German legions. Yet he made only casual references to Vitellius and no insulting remarks about Vespasian. The overall effect, says Tacitus, "was nothing to undermine the enemy's confidence or to frighten them into surrender." The Flavian generals did not even defend their actions: "they spoke grandly of Vespasian, confidently of their cause, showed no anxiety about their own troops, and showered Vitellius with personal insults. Also, they held out to the Vitellian tribunes and centurions the prospect of retaining the posts their emperor had given them, and openly urged Caecina to change sides. Finally, they read the correspondence to their own troops, and that did wonders for the men's morale, because it looked as if Caecina had written submissively, fearing to offend Vespasian, whereas their generals had written back contemptuously to insult Vitellius."

The oddity in all this lies in the fact that if Caecina dickered over the terms of his betrayal in his first letters, as Tacitus states explicitly, why was this information withheld from the Flavian troops? They knew only that Caecina spoke "submissively." The likeliest answer is surely that Caecina's plan involved carrying his army with him. For that to work, he needed both secrecy and time, secrecy to ensure that no information leaked to his own men before he made his move, and time to set up the blow to their morale that would induce them to follow his lead, namely, the news that his collaborator, Lucilius Bassus, had taken the Ravenna fleet over to the enemy. And Caecina achieved two more aims by remaining at Hostilia. He occupied a strong position where, if his plan failed, he could fight on ground of his own choosing, and compel the Flavians to make a costly frontal attack on him. And refusing to advance on Verona reduced the chances that his men would discover how much weaker the enemy forces were.

While this was going on, the Flavians were reinforced by the two remaining legions from Moesia, III Gallica and VIII Augusta. The former was led by Gaius Dillius Aponianus, somehow a relative of the governor Aponius Saturninus; the latter's commander was Numisius Lupus, the man in charge when the Rhoxolani had raided Moesia the previous winter. Their arrival touched off a series of incidents that led to major changes in the leadership. It began with a decision "to surround Verona with a military rampart." This seems to mean only that the Flavians had to expand their camp to accommodate the new arrivals, but there was a sudden panic. Working on a part of the rampart that faced the enemy, the men of VII Galbiana mistook as an enemy force a body of their own cavalrymen returning from patrol. Snatching up their weapons from fear that they had been betrayed, they turned their anger on the hapless Tampius Flavianus. Calling loudly for his execution, they asserted that he was a kinsman of Vitellius, that he had betrayed Otho, and that he had pocketed a (probably imaginary) donative due to them. Scared out of his wits, Tampius broke down in tears and threw himself on their mercy. In the troops' eyes this only confirmed his guilt.

Saturninus tried to talk the men around, presumably in his capacity as the most senior officer present. But the troops would not even listen to Antonius, though his skills—says Tacitus—included an ability to calm troops down as well as to stir them up. They were set on killing their victim out of hand. So Antonius resorted to trickery, and ordered Tampius thrown in chains. Then, as the troops realized that he was trying to fool them and became more unruly still, he fell back on the last resort of desperate generals, bared his chest, and swore that he would die either by their hands or by his own before he would allow them to commit murder. Let them turn their madness on the enemy, not on one another. Whether this worked or not, the demonstrators finally ran out of steam toward the end of the day, and Antonius sent Tampius off to Vespasian that same night.

Yet there was another flareup around noon the next day, the victim this time being Aponius Saturninus, the aggressors his own troops in the Moesian legions. As they had neither forgotten nor forgiven his equivocal conduct at the start of the revolt, somebody circulated what was allegedly another letter from Saturninus to Vitellius. "As if they had caught the disease from the Pannonian troops," the Moesian legions demanded his execution, and the Pannonian troops backed them up, "delighted to repeat their wrong-doing, as if their previous conduct was excused by the mutiny of others." Although Antonius, Dillius Aponianus, and Vipstanus Messalla tried desperately to calm the men, it was "the obscurity of his hiding-place" that saved Saturninus' life. He had taken up residence in a luxurious villa on Verona's outskirts, and since the baths attached to it were not in use, he concealed himself in the hypocaust beneath. Unable to lay hands on their victim, the mutineers finally calmed down, and Saturninus too was rushed unobtrusively from the camp. He was relegated to Patavium and there, so far as we can tell, he played no further part in the campaign.

Tacitus rounds out his account of the two mutinies with a comment that has sparked much discussion about pro- and anti-Antonian strands in his narrative. "With the departure of the two consulars, power and influence over both the Pannonian and Moesian legions fell to Antonius Primus alone. His colleagues [i.e., Vedius Aquila, Dillius Aponianus, Numisius Lupus, and Vipstanus Messalla] yielded place to him and the troops had no time for their other officers. And there were some (soldiers) who believed that both mutinies had been set up by Antonius' trickery, in order to leave him in sole command of the campaign." In fact, there is no reason to credit Antonius with such motives, or to think that Tacitus did. For one thing, Tacitus has said already that there were two key figures in the revolt, Antonius and Cornelius Fuscus, and there had to be one more development before Fuscus quit the scene. For another, Tacitus is using one of his favorite literary devices, linking events by contrast. Here the contrast is between the alleged trickery of Antonius and—in the next segment of his narrative—the real treachery of Lucilius Bassus and Caecina.

Bassus must have rated his chances of success fairly high, aware as he was that many of the marines under his command had been recruited from Dalmatia and Pannonia, provinces whose governors had declared for Vespasian. Yet he acted in an oddly craven manner. He called a meeting to which he invited only the ships' captains he had taken into his plot, and then failed to show up himself. Those at the gathering agreed to transfer their allegiance to Vespasian, but they were unimpressed when Bassus reappeared and claimed credit for the plot. In fact, they promptly made contact with Antonius, and he sent Cornelius Fuscus to take over the command. This he did without resistance from members of the fleet, and Bassus' only reward—for now—was to be shipped off to Vespasian.

Caecina showed more daring once it came to the point, but he achieved no success. Still, his actions attracted the attentions of Josephus and Dio as well as of Tacitus, and all three dramatize the episode, even if Tacitus gives us the fullest and most coherent account. According to him, Caecina no sooner heard that the Ravenna fleet had deserted Vitellius than he summoned the leading centurions in his force as well as some of the soldiers to a meeting in his HQ, choosing a time of day when the rest of the men had left the camp to take care of their duties. He heaped praise on Vespasian and the strength of his forces and emphasized their own isolation: "the Ravenna fleet had deserted; their own supplies were running low; Gaul and Spain were hostile; and no help could be expected from Rome. On top of this, everything he said about Vitellius was derogatory." There can be no doubt that Caecina overstated his case to make his point. Neither Gaul nor Spain was hostile yet, and he himself may have been the only person unable to count on help from Rome, thanks to his feud with Valens. But the supply situation may have looked tight, especially if the Ravenna fleet had been used to bring up food, and Caecina could reasonably suggest that the marines might be called upon to mount an attack on their rear overland.

His listeners were persuaded, took the oath of allegiance to Vespasian, tore down all the Vitellian emblems, and sent men off to tell Antonius what they had done. But when the rest of the troops returned late in the day, the news of the betrayal spread through the camp like wildfire.

> At first, there was a massive silence, and then all hell broke loose. Had the glory of the German legions fallen so low, they asked one another, that they should hand themselves and their weapons over to the foe without a fight, without even taking a wound. What were the legions that faced them now, if not ones they had defeated? They did not even include legions

XIV Gemina Martia Victrix and I Adiutrix, the backbone of the Othonian army, and they themselves had routed and laid low those same troops on these same plains. To think that Caecina should make a present of so many thousands of men, as if they were a bunch of slaves for sale, to the exile Antonius. That would mean eight legions following in the wake of a single fleet. Such was the decision Caecina and Bassus had reached. Having robbed the emperor of town houses, country estates and cash money, they meant now to steal his troops too. Even fresh and unbloodied, they themselves were held cheap by the Flavians, and what answer could they give later to those who asked them what they had done in the war.

The first to give concrete expression to their anger, says Tacitus, were the men of V Alaudae, the core of the force, and they restored the Vitellian emblems and put Caecina under close arrest. (It is interesting that though the legion had formed part of Valens' column, the men apparently respected Caecina enough not to kill him outright.) Then the troops picked new generals, Fabius Fabullus, the legionary legate of V Alaudae, and the prefect of the camp, Cassius Longus (nothing else of significance is known about these two). While this was going on, three galleys from the Ravenna fleet put in. Their crews neither knew of nor were party to Bassus' treachery, but they were butchered anyway. Then the Vitellians decided to abandon their position, to fall back behind the Tartarus and the Po after breaking down the bridges, and to make their way as quickly as possible to Cremona and join up with legions I Italica and XXI Rapax.

Though Josephus condenses this episode to the point where it is almost unrecognizable, he adds one important detail taken for granted by Tacitus, the fact that the uproar in the camp continued into the night. And Dio makes a meal of this, claiming that the confusion was increased by an eclipse of the moon. Not that the moon's disappearance troubled the men, "but that it looked blood-red and black and other frightening colors too." Yet not even this persuaded the men to change their minds or to give up. So why mention an omen without an impact in an account of questionable reliability? If we allow that there was an eclipse, we can date the episode exactly, to 9:50 P.M. (local time) on 18 October. So few are the fixed points we have for the chronology of this campaign that we must seize on any usable snippet, so long as it looks halfway plausible.

Antonius discovered that the Vitellians had slipped away only after the deed was done, perhaps on the following morning. Faced with the prospect of chasing around the countryside a Vitellian force with which he had lost contact, or of taking on enemy units whose location he knew, he settled on the latter course. A council of war must have been held in Verona, to discuss the risks as well as the rewards of his plan, but Antonius won the day with two arguments: that it was better to attack the Vitellians at Cremona while their forces were divided; and that it must be done promptly, because there was the risk that Valens would arrive from Rome and restore the enemy's morale and unity of purpose. So it was decided that he should lead the troops, five legions (III Gallica, VII Claudia, VII Galbiana, VIII Augusta, and XIII Gemina), an unknown number of auxiliary cohorts, and at least 4,000 cavalry, on a two-day forced march from Verona to Bedriacum, and take up position some 20 miles east of his target.

On the morning after his arrival at Bedriacum, however, Antonius made the first of several mistakes. His plan underestimated the spirit and energy of both Vitellian forces. Not only did he imagine that the troops from Hostilia could not arrive as soon as they did (they appeared only 24 hours later than Antonius, having made a forced march of 30 miles on that last day). He also assumed that the two Vitellian units encamped outside Cremona would not respond at once to his own arrival. Thinking that he had two days to play with, he decided on the first to leave his legionaries behind, to fortify a camp; he sent auxiliary cohorts into Cremonan territory, with orders to forage but (so Tacitus asserts) also to accustom them to the plunder of Roman civilians, and to give the auxiliaries scope to pursue their activities unmolested; he himself advanced with 4,000 cavalry eight miles down the Postumian Way toward Cremona, and told his scouts to range yet further ahead. As he saw it, he could ready the camp, bring in the supplies he had sacrificed during the march from Verona, and spy out the land all on the first day, and then draw I Italica and XXI Rapax from their camp by offering battle on the second, before their comrades from Hostilia could reinforce them.

Around 11:00 A.M., however, one of Antonius' scouts rode in with the news that the enemy were approaching. The vanguard of the Vitellian cavalry was close at hand, while "the movement and noise of the main body could be heard over a considerable distance." While Antonius hesitated, thrown off by this unexpected development, his second-in-command, the impetuous Arrius Varus, rounded up the boldest of their cavalrymen and charged off to engage the enemy. Initial success turned into defeat, as more and more Vitellian horses came up, and though the Flavians managed a fighting retreat, Varus himself lost his head. By now Antonius had recognized that the situation was out of hand, and had summoned the legions from Bedriacum and called in his foragers from the fields. But he also took the very risky step of trying to leave a gap in the center of his battle line, so that his cavalry could pass through to safety. Instead, Varus' panic threw everything into chaos, and the Flavians were driven back along the road, probably for a considerable distance.

Tacitus lauds Antonius' prowess as a general in this crisis, but even if he ignores the fact that Antonius caused the crisis, the praise is two-edged. The description he provides owes much to Sallust's account of Catiline's last stand at Pistoria in January 62 B.C., and this literary debt proves that the historian has not forgotten his original assessment of Antonius as the worst kind of man to have around in peacetime but not one to underrate in war. In any event, he states that Antonius displayed the best qualities of a general, even killing with his own hand a fleeing standard bearer, picking up the standard and turning it toward the foe. Though less effective than it might have been, this persuaded about 100 cavalrymen to join him, and since the ground too was favorable, that turned out to be enough. Antonius had come upon a wooden bridge over a rivulet or stream. This being a structure his men could break up temporarily, Antonius made his stand here, and the Vitellian cavalry were checked. This heartened the rest of his troops to rejoin the fray, and the pursuers became the pursued.

Though all the Flavian troops must have covered ten or more miles in this race for Cremona, and some of them between 16 and 18 miles (men rushed up from the camp at Bedriacum), Tacitus cuts away from the chase, as usual, to focus on the scene four miles from Cremona. This was as far as the Vitellian legions I Italica and XXI Rapax had advanced. Although their aim was probably to back up their own cavalry, but not to fight a pitched battle unless the circumstances looked favorable, Tacitus pictures these units as poor specimens.

> Now that fortune had turned against them, they did not open up their ranks and receive back their defeated cavalry. Nor did they move forward and attack the enemy, even though the latter were weary from the distance they had covered and the fighting in which they had engaged. Immobilized by their own cavalry's setback, the two legions stood rooted to the spot, missing in adversity, as they had not done in success, a general to give them orders. As they wavered indecisively, the victorious Flavian cavalry along with Vipstanus Messalla and a force of Moesian auxiliaries charged them. And since a goodly number of light-armed Flavian legionaries had managed to catch up and stay with them, this mix of infantry and cavalry broke the Vitellian line. And because the nearness of Cremona's walls encouraged thoughts of refuge rather than resistance, Antonius called off the attack, mindful now of the exhaustion of and casualties among his own men and reluctant to tempt fate once more.

Most of the criticism in this passage seems to have been designed more to excuse Antonius than to belittle his adversaries. The Vitellians' being chided for not opening up their ranks and receiving their cavalry helps to palliate Antonius' attempting such foolishness earlier, and the stress on the Vitellians' lack of leadership highlights the Flavians' being well served in this regard. The one true oddity in the two legions' conduct was their failure to advance to the attack, and this is explicable too. If it never even occurred to the Vitellians that Antonius had advanced without his own legionaries, they would have imagined that becoming entangled in a battle would lead eventually to their being overwhelmed by sheer numbers. So they just held their ground. They also left the field in better order than one might think. The nearness of Cremona induced thoughts of refuge rather than resistance, not thoughts of refuge instead of resistance. And this best explains Antonius' not pressing on. He had made a string of errors, but he had prevailed. Now he showed sense enough to halt the attack while he was ahead.

Not that the main body of Flavian troops shared his view when it reached the scene around 5:00 P.M. Impressed by the evidence of the victory, the men concluded that the war was all but over, and demanded to be led to Cremona forthwith. Publicly they supposedly claimed that they could either accept the enemy's surrender or take the place by storm. But privately, says Tacitus, they thought that if they waited till daybreak, there would be a negotiated surrender, and that all they would get for their efforts would be a reputation for mercy and empty talk of glory, while the wealth of Cremona ended up in their officers' pockets. When a city yielded, the loot went to the higher-ups. When a city was stormed, it went to the troops. Tacitus must have drawn this material from Vipstanus Messalla, and it is an interpretation that is not only plausible, but also consistent with assessments made in similar circumstances by other generals, Julius Caesar included. But it is also a first step in an attempt to explain the sack of Cremona rationally and accurately.

The second step follows immediately. The troops were so determined to march on Cremona, says Tacitus, that they refused to obey their officers, and made so much noise that they could claim colorably not even to have heard the orders they issued. So, taking the bull by the horns, Antonius made his way from company to company, and delivered a speech that opened with the same theme as Otho had stressed in his address to the praetorians the day after their mutiny. Reassuring the men that he had neither the wish nor the intention to rob them of their plunder, he emphasized that it was the troops' task to fight, their generals' to take care of the planning. To enter an enemy city with which they were unfamiliar in the dark was folly. They could be ambushed at every turn. Even if the gates stood wide open, he was not prepared to enter except in daylight, and he would still check everything out first. Then he shifted to the problems they would face if the city resisted. Unless they reconnoitered the ground, there was no telling whether they would need only the weapons for an assault or all the impedimenta for a siege. Turning to individual soldiers, he asked them whether they had the tools for the job, or if they intended standing like dummies outside the city, gaping at the towers and the fortifications on the walls. If they were willing to wait just one night, they could bring up the artillery and the force to win outright. This said, he sent the sutlers and the freshest of the cavalry back to Bedriacum to fetch the supplies and equipment they had left behind. Yet his words had no effect. What brought the men round was a report by their own scouts that the Vitellians in Cremona had been reinforced meanwhile by the troops who had trekked all the way from Hostilia.

So why does Tacitus credit Antonius with a long and futile speech? Once the question is framed in these terms, it does not matter whether Antonius made a speech, or whether he made *this* speech. Tacitus is after something else. First, he is drawing attention to one of the predicaments faced by generals in a situation like this, that the worse conditions grew, the more the general had to speechify. And second, he is emphasizing that on this occasion the situation was so bad that even the best of mob-orators could not win over the men. Tacitus is not endorsing the overarching theme so prominent in Plutarch, that in these civil wars the troops led and the generals followed. His scope is narrower, to lay more groundwork for the sack of Cremona. And he does not acquit Antonius of culpability. The disagreement between the general and his men was not whether to storm Cremona, but when to do it. But the more deter-mined the troops were made to appear, the heavier the onus that could be placed on their shoulders.

The Vitellians were no less determined, as was proved by the fact that the troops from Hostilia had covered 30 miles in a day. What is more, the Flavian scouts reported that these units had no sooner reached Cremona and learnt of the setback suffered by their comrades than they began preparing to march out again, and "would arrive at any minute." This brought Antonius' troops to heel, enabling him to draw up his forces for an engagement on the Postumian Way. He placed XIII Gemina on the actual causeway; VII Galbiana occupied the open ground on its left (i.e., south of the road), while VII Claudia held the extreme left, on ground fronted by a drainage ditch. To the right (north) of the causeway he positioned VIII Augusta along an open side road, and beyond it III Gallica, though its ranks were split into small groups by close-planted vine trel-lises. This was their order of battle, Tacitus then adds, but in the dark-ness the troops took up position more randomly. Though this is an oblique way of reminding the reader that a night battle is about to take place, the rarest of encounters in Greek and Roman times, the comment also en-ables Tacitus to avoid explaining oddities like the way in which a batch of Otho's former praetorians suddenly appears out of nowhere, to be set next to III Gallica.[4]

For the Vitellians, as Tacitus observes, the best plan would have been to take a break in Cremona, eat some food and catch up on their sleep, and then attack the following morning, when the Flavians had spent a night in the open, worn down by the cold and by lack of food. But "because the Vitellians lacked a leader and a plan," they advanced and made contact with Antonius' forces at about the third hour of the night (approximately 8:30 P.M.). Numerically, they were more or less a match for their opponents. Besides I Italica and XXI Rapax, they could muster two more full legions (V Alaudae and XXII Primigenia), the bulk of another four (I Germanica, IV Macedonica, XV Primigenia, and XVI), and detachments (*vexillationes* probably of 2,600 men apiece) from the three units out of Britain (II Augusta, IX Hispana, and XX Valeria Victrix). They had their auxiliaries and cavalry too. Tacitus, however, hesitates to specify the Vitellian order of battle, and limits himself to repeating what "others" had reported. According to these "others," the center of the line was held by V Alaudae, XV Primigenia, and the detachments from the British legions; XVI, XXII Primigenia, and I Germanica took up position on the left wing, on the broken ground north of the road, while IV Macedonica held the right wing, the more open area to the south. The men from I Italica and XII Rapax, Tacitus adds, joined companies along the line on a catch-as-catch-can basis. As he gives no reason for this, it has been suggested that these men had been demoralized by the earlier battle. But it is just as likely that the column from Hostilia never even broke formation when it reached Cremona, and that the town's original defenders had to scurry after them, if they wanted to take part in the action.

The battle itself was to last a staggering ten hours, until sunrise the next morning around 6:45 A.M., a tribute to the endurance of the troops on both sides, even if—just as in more recent battles—the fighting took place in short bursts interspersed with long lulls. Neither Tacitus nor Dio attempts a comprehensive description. If it is safe to judge by Xiphilinus' abridgement, in fact, Dio devoted more attention to the lulls than the fighting, emphasizing how the the troops fraternized with the other side. He even talks of women from Cremona bringing out food and drink for the Vitellians, and adds that the latter shared it with their Flavian counterparts.[5] Dio seems to have done this to stress the ferocity with which the two sides fought in between times: "they battled as if against foreigners and not their own countrymen, and as if all must die at once or become slaves ever after." Tacitus too comments on this savagery, but he presents only vignettes, putting more emphasis on the fact that "courage and strength were of little use, and the men could not even see clearly what was in front of them. Neither side had an edge in weaponry; each soon learnt the other's password because demands for it were constant; and the unit emblems got all mixed up, as a band of troops on one side captured the others' and carted them off this way or that."

Specifically, Tacitus reports that the Flavian legion VII Galbiana (Antonius' own unit) was especially hard pressed. Positioned on the open ground south of the road, and confronted by IV Macedonica, it took heavy casualties, in part because most of the men were still raw recruits. They lost six of their senior centurions and some of their standards, and though they hung onto the legion's eagle, it cost them the life of Atilius Verus, the centurion of the first rank whose duty it was to guard it. To stop the rot, Antonius pulled a body of praetorians from the extreme right of his line (north of the road). But though they drove back the Vitellians, the latter rallied and drove them back in their turn. This reversal, says Tacitus, was aided by the Vitellians' artillery fire. At the start of the battle they had positioned their ballistas and catapults north of the road, with the result that much of the fire was deflected by trees and vine trellises. Now they hauled a gigantic rock-throwing ballista onto the causeway, and it began leveling the Flavian line. The results would have been catastrophic, had not two Flavian soldiers picked up Vitellian shields, slipped in unnoticed among the enemy artillerymen, and managed somehow to put the ballista out of action. These two stalwarts were cut down immediately, of course, "and so their names have been lost, but about their brave deed there can be no dispute."[6]

If Tacitus is reporting events in any kind of chronological sequence (he may not be, since Dio sets the disabling of the ballista near daybreak), all this must have happened in the first hour or so. For the next event of which he tells us is the rising of the moon, and that occurred—it has been calculated—around 9:40 P.M. Since it rose behind the Flavians, says Tacitus, it made their men and horses look larger and therefore closer, with the result that the weapons the Vitellians hurled at them tended to fall short. Conversely, the Vitellians faced into the moonlight, and so were caught as if out in the open by an enemy firing at them from concealment. This may be a trope, inasmuch as Pompey had exploited the setting moon similarly in a battle with Mithridates of Pontus in 66 B.C. Besides, Dio has nothing of this, stating instead that the moon was hidden periodically by "many clouds of all sorts of different shapes." But as there were only a limited number of ways in which a night battle could be fought, let alone described, it may not hurt to accept Tacitus' account.

In any event, Tacitus conveys the impression that Antonius capitalized on this advantage at once, by making his way from unit to unit along his line and encouraging or reproaching them. The Moesian legions, for example, he is said to have egged on by pointing out that they had started

this war and it was high time they transformed words into deeds. The
Pannonian legions he reproved, observing that this was the ground on
which they had been defeated earlier in the year, and now it was time to
recover their lost glory. For the praetorians he reserved the rough edge
of his tongue: for them this would be the end of the line unless they
made up for the inadequacies they had shown at Bedriacum. There is no
knowing how long all this took, or even if Antonius expressed himself in
this manner. One could almost be forgiven for thinking that he spent
nearly all night on it, since Tacitus mentions sunrise next. But this is
probably his alternative to the fraternization between the individual soldiers that turns up in Dio. Both authors had somehow to create the impression of time passing.

When the sun rose, the men of III Gallica hailed it in accordance
with a custom they had picked up in Syria. This act of worship, to whatever god the sun represented, was widely misunderstood. The Vitellians
(according to Dio) or the other Flavian troops (so says Tacitus) fell for a
sudden rumor that Mucianus' troops had arrived, and that the two forces
were greeting one another. This spurred the Flavians to one final effort,
while the dispirited Vitellians began to wilt. Antonius immediately massed
his men and broke through the enemy battle line. There was still some
resistance, but the Vitellians were effectively routed, and the Flavians
pursued them westward along the Postumian Way. There was considerable slaughter, but one incident in particular was recorded by Vipstanus
Messalla, and used by Tacitus to highlight the savagery of the battle.
Julius Mansuetus had been recruited into legion XXI Rapax some years
earlier. He had left a young son behind in Spain, and the boy was drafted
into VII Galbiana in 68, having by then grown to manhood. These two
now came face to face without recognizing each other, and the son cut
down his father. He discovered the identity of his victim only when he
began plundering the body. Tacitus dwells on the pathos of the scene as
the son tried to give his father the last rites. But, he continues, when
those nearby noticed what was happening, and talk spread the news
through the ranks, "there was astonishment, lamentation and much curs-
ing of this most savage war, but there was no slackening in the killing
and plundering of friends, relatives and brothers. They said a crime had
been committed and they went on committing it."

Once the Flavians reached Cremona, they found themselves confronted
with another formidable task, not an attack on the town itself, but an assault on the Vitellian camp on its eastern side, outside the walls and just
north of the Postumian Way. For this Tacitus is our only source, and he
states that the Flavian generals hesitated, unsure what to do next. They
realized that their troops were exhausted, and that launching an impromptu

assault on the camp could prove disastrous. But their other options were less appealing. Withdrawal to Bedriacum would mean abandoning the field, and constructing a camp when the enemy was so close left them open to attack. Still, what terrified them most was their assessment of the soldiery's temper. As they saw it, the troops were readier to endure danger than delay, hostile to what was safe but willing to take any risk, while their greed for plunder outweighed any concern about casualties.

Making a virtue of necessity, therefore, Antonius ordered the men to form a storming line around the enemy rampart. In the first exchanges of artillery fire, unsurprisingly, the Flavians suffered the heavier losses. But the situation did not improve when Antonius assigned specific sections of the ramparts and gates to specific units, probably as much to stop the troops' getting in each other's way as—in Tacitus' words—to fire his legions with a spirit of competition. The troops took up positions in a concave arc facing westward. This time III Gallica and VII Galbiana were set on the left wing and attacked in the south; legions VII Claudia and VIII Augusta occupied the center, opposite the western side of the camp's rampart; and "their own élan carried the men of XIII Gemina toward the gate to Brixia," that is, on the Flavian right and the northern side of the rampart. There was a brief delay while the troops fossicked about in the fields for mattocks, picks, scythes, and ladders. Then they launched their assault in much the same way as the Vitellians had in their attack on Placentia, and with equally disastrous results. In fact, a fatal "hesitation would have set in, had not the generals at this juncture pointed out Cremona to troops by now exhausted and heedless of exhortations they believed idle."

Whatever the generals meant by this gesture, the troops took it as a sign that one final assault on the camp would give them the right to sack Cremona too. This induced the attackers to redouble their efforts, and the bitterest fighting took place on the southern side of the camp. Here III Gallica and VII Galbiana, along with Antonius and the pick of the auxiliaries attacked simultaneously. Unable to beat them back, the Vitellians finally toppled a ballista on them. This caused widespread carnage, but it also brought down the battlements and the top of the rampart in its fall. Meanwhile, one of the wooden towers nearby collapsed under a shower of Flavian missiles, "and here, while the seventh struggled forward in wedge formation, the third broke through the camp-gate with their axes and swords." This gave the attackers the breaches they needed, and all the sources agree—says Tacitus—that Gaius Volusius, a ranker from III Gallica, was the first to mount the rampart. As he hurled down those who resisted, he attracted everybody's attention with his shouts that the camp was taken, and the other attackers poured in. The terrified

Vitellians leapt from the rampart, attempting to find shelter in the city, but few made it. The open ground between the camp and Cremona was turned into a shambles.

Still, the Flavians found themselves confronted now with a truly formidable task. Cremona's walls were tall and vertical (the rampart had sloped), the towers were of stone, and the gates were sheathed with iron. Besides, the enemy troops within gave no sign of yielding, the inhabitants were numerous and devoted to Vitellius, and the city was also filled with traders. An annual fair was in progress that had attracted people from all over northern Italy, and while they represented a source of plunder for the attackers, they could help defend the city too. As a first step, therefore, Antonius tried persuasion through property loss. He ordered his men to fire the most luxurious of the townhouses outside the walls, in the hope that members of the city council would be induced to change sides. And he ordered the boldest of his men to occupy any buildings close to and taller than the city walls. From there they were to dislodge the defenders with salvoes of roof tiles, rafters, and firebrands.

When the Flavian legions began to mass for an assault and the suppressing fire started up, the Vitellians' morale began to crack. The rot set in among the officers, according to Tacitus. The higher their rank, the more they inclined to surrender, for fear that if Cremona too were destroyed, they would be the ones singled out for killing and plundering. The common soldiers, by contrast, gave no thought to the future and, safer because of their lowly status, kept holding out, roaming the streets, and hiding in private houses. Tacitus' assessment may be too cynical. The Vitellian soldiery were obviously determined to fight on no matter what, but this too should have terrified their officers, since it made a sack of the town inevitable. The officers could reasonably wonder whether it was worth the pain and suffering, when Caecina had already tried to betray them, and there was no sign that Valens would be arriving any time soon.

Whatever the case, desperation induced the leading officers to tear down the emblems of their allegiance to Vitellius, to set Caecina free, and to beg him to intercede with the Flavians. Puffed up with resentment, he refused. This, says Tacitus, was the ultimate evil: all these brave men were reduced to imploring in tears the assistance of a traitor. How long they spent in this futile endeavor he does not say, but there was some delay before they settled on an alternative and—like the people of Vienne when faced with Valens and his army—hung the tokens of surrender from the walls. Antonius at once ordered a cease-fire, but here Tacitus telescopes events significantly. There must in fact have been two sets of talks, the first with the Vitellian commanders, since their surrender was not unconditional, and the second with representatives of Cremona's governing council, since the people emerged from the town as soon as terms were agreed. And as Cremona surrendered, there should have been no sack, no matter what the Flavian generals had meant by pointing to the town earlier, and no matter what their troops had taken this gesture to mean. But Tacitus leaves all this aside, to stress the pathos of the scene, and by paying tribute to the defenders' courage to highlight Caecina's shortcomings once again.

According to his account, the Vitellians now brought out their eagles and standards. A dejected column of unarmed soldiers followed, their eyes fixed on the ground. The victors had lined both sides of the road, and at first they hurled insults and shook their fists at their enemies. But when the vanquished suffered every indignity without defiance, the Flavians remembered that these were the men who had shown restraint in their victory at Bedriacum. So there was a revulsion of feeling—until Caecina appeared, in full official dress as consul and with the escort of lictors appropriate to his office. The Flavians' anger flared up again, and they taunted him with his arrogance, his savagery (that is, his lack of consideration for the troops from whom he now marked himself off so conspicuously), and even his treachery, since they thought it no more laudable than did the Vitellians. Moving in quickly to prevent violence, Antonius gave Caecina a guard, and sent him off to Vespasian. Since this is the Vitellian commander's final appearance in what remains of the *Histories*, it is to Josephus that we owe the information that Caecina "was well received by the emperor and covered up the shame of his perfidy with unanticipated honors."

Meanwhile the common people of Cremona had emerged from the city, possibly to take the air after being cooped up for so long, possibly to check on the fate of missing Vitellian soldiers who had been their friends, and possibly because—like the inhabitants of Rome when Vitellius' troops first approached the city—they never could resist a soldier. Initially their appearance provoked only some rough handling, and Antonius attempted to calm things down with a speech. In this he is said to have praised his troops extravagantly, to have spoken mercifully of the defeated Vitellians, and—to avoid inflaming his audience—to have tiptoed around the subject of Cremona. It was not enough, as Tacitus indicates in a dissection of the troops' grievances. The men were determined to destroy the city because of their deep-seated greed for plunder, but over this they laid various pretexts. First, they nursed deep hostility toward the people of Cremona because, so they believed, the latter had assisted the Vitellians enthusiastically throughout the war between Otho and Vitellius. Second, the men of XIII Gemina had been taunted by the locals when they had been made to construct the amphitheater for Caecina's gladiatorial show. Third, there was the behavior of the Cremonan womenfolk, who had taken food to the Vitellians during the night battle. This convicted the women—and perhaps their menfolk too, since they let them do it—of political partisanship. And then there was the last straw. The troops caught sight of some of the wealthy visitors who had come to Cremona for the fair, presumably among the local inhabitants who had ventured out of the city.

At this point Tacitus introduces an episode involving Antonius Primus that remains controversial to this day. Remarking that nobody paid any attention to the other Flavian generals, so that the spotlight fell on Antonius alone, he reports that the latter decided to betake himself to the baths in one of the villas outside the city. Though other explanations have been offered, it looks as if his primary concern was with appearances, to clean off the blood and gore, to change into civilian clothes, and then to return, so that the hostilities could be seen to be over. When he reached the baths, however, he found that they were not ready, and the only response he received to his complaint that the water was cold was an impudent "they'd be hot in just a minute." An eavesdropper heard this remark, made almost certainly by a slave attached to the house, attributed it to Antonius, and so spread the story that he had given the signal to burn down Cremona (fires regularly accompanied a sack). And this, as Tacitus is careful to phrase it, brought down on Antonius the opprobium for the sack, even though Cremona was already in flames when the remark was made. During his absence, 40,000 armed men and a yet larger number of soldiers' slaves and camp followers had poured into the city.

The sacking of Cremona was undoubtedly a horrific business, and there is no telling how many civilians were killed. But as it was hardly the first time Romans had inflicted such suffering on a city, Tacitus' account is made up largely of conventional scenes in conventional phrasing. He was not trying to diminish the intensity of the suffering of young and old, male and female, rich and poor. This was how a Roman audience expected such events to be described, as is shown by Pliny the Younger's use of similar tropes of the chaos in Pompeii when Mount Vesuvius erupted in 79. Besides, Tacitus does indivualize this sack, once again by putting the onus on the soldiery. "As was to be expected of an army with different languages and different customs, since it was made up of Romans, provincials, and foreign tribesmen, their lusts were diverse and there was always somebody to think that what they were doing was acceptable. So for four days Cremona kept them occupied, and at the last, when all else lay in flames, only the temple of Mephitis still stood, outside the walls, protected perhaps by its position, perhaps by its deity."

This final step in Tacitus' attempt to explain the sack of the city has often been misunderstood. Of the various options open to him, it would have been easiest to blame on the Vitellians, as does Dio: "most of the wrongs were committed by the Vitellians, for they knew where the richest citizens lived and how to move around the city quickly. They showed no hesitation about killing those on whose behalf they had fought and they beat up and murdered their victims as if they themselves had been wronged." But this interpretation was hardly plausible, if the bulk of these troops marched out of Cremona before the sack, as Tacitus reports and Dio does not. The other obvious option, adopted by Vespasian and his associates, was to make Antonius the scapegoat. (Vespasian certainly, and justifiably, refused to accept responsibility.) Yet even Josephus, the supposed mouthpiece for the new regime, did not follow this officially approved line. His account is highly compressed, and he may have run together the attacks on the camp and the city. But though he states that "Antonius turned his troops loose to plunder the town," he also asserts that they forced their way into Cremona. In his view, therefore, they took the city by assault and so had every right to sack it, no matter how imprudent it may have been to do so.

In these circumstances, it is not surprising that Tacitus offered a different picture again, taken probably from the eyewitness account of Vipstanus Messalla. On this view, the Flavian soldiery were animated above all by greed for plunder, even though they fabricated grievances to justify their conduct. To that extent they may have fueled the kind of vapid generalizations about brutal and licentious soldiery that Plutarch so adored. But as Tacitus' narrative has also shown, the troops had made a two-day forced march from Verona; they had gone into battle the day they reached Bedriacum; they had fought through that night; and they had stormed the Vitellians' camp the next day. If we judge by the evidence from other, better-documented sacks, the mixture of exhaustion and exhilaration the men felt when Cremona surrendered must have made them absolutely ungovernable. Yet none of this exculpated Antonius. For one thing, Romans believed that the character of an army mirrored that of its general. And for another, the commander in chief could not shrug off the ultimate responsibility if his troops went out of control. It remained a failure of leadership, and even his admirers could not view it in any other light.

10

End Game
(November and December)

The second half of the campaign that led to the overthrow of Vitellius was marked by three disasters, two major and one minor. The halfhearted attempt by Vespasian's brother, Flavius Sabinus, to carry out a coup in Rome when Vitellius attempted his half-baked abdication led to the destruction of the temple of Jupiter Best and Greatest on the Capitol, the most sacred shrine in the city. Then Vitellius' brother Lucius sacked Tarracina, a small town to the south, when he wiped out a group of renegades acting allegedly on Vespasian's behalf. Finally there was an assault on Rome, which culminated in the storming of the praetorian camp amid another welter of blood and gore. For what happened at Tarracina Lucius Vitellius had to bear the blame. For the two major mishaps Antonius Primus was apparently made the principal scapegoat, on the ground that if he had advanced more speedily, he could have saved Sabinus and averted the need for battles in Rome. Tacitus rejects this interpretation, but once again he does not defend Antonius' conduct. He holds that nobody emerged—or could emerge—from these events creditably.

Whatever faults we find in Tacitus, he remains our best guide to the last two months of Vitellius' reign. By now, Suetonius is so committed to his thesis that Vitellius is doomed that for him the only issue is when and how, not whether Vitellius will fall. And since he focuses so closely on the person of the emperor, he talks almost exclusively of Vitellius' last days. Dio's account need not have taken this line, but it was abridged so brutally by his epitomators that the effect is similar. Their summaries give the impression that Vitellius was doomed, not only because of assorted omens, but also because of his inability to follow a consistent course of action. So Dio's account too presses on to the attempts to abdicate. Tacitus, conversely, recognizes that the sack of Cremona marked a, not *the* turning point in the campaign. But because he is writing a comprehensive narrative, he treats it as a natural break in the action, and weaves into his account other more or less contemporaneous developments. As it happens, he does not say that much more about Vitellius personally, but he deals in turn with the emperor, Fabius Valens, and events in a string of provinces running from west to east.

So, of Vitellius, Tacitus reports that he sent Valens off to the north a few days after Caecina's departure (probably near the end of September), and then relapsed into his usual inertia. "He did not make ready weapons, he did not firm up the troops' morale with addresses and drills, and he did not appear before the people." As Tacitus fails to say why he should have undertaken any of these actions, it is easy to charge the historian with carping. So far as Vitellius knew, after all, the war was under control, now that he had sent his two best generals to the front. It was for the prefects of the guard to keep the praetorians in shape, provided always that they were as disorganized and undisciplined as had been the force with which Caecina left Rome. There were no reports of evil omens to depress popular morale, and the people remained firmly committed to Vitellius anyway. And war or no war, September and October were among the slackest months in the senatorial calendar. Yet, as events were to prove, it might have been better had Vitellius remained in Rome.

Not unlike many of the senators, however, Vitellius withdrew to his villa at Aricia, some 16 miles south of Rome, and "hid away in the shady arbor of his suburban estate, as if he were one of those slothful animals that lie around in a torpor, so long as you keep on feeding them." In the second half of October, however, news arrived that Lucilius Bassus had masterminded the defection of the Ravenna fleet and then, a week or so later, that Caecina too had tried to desert. Vitellius was grieved by this, of course, but he managed to look on the bright side. Gladdened that Caecina had been thrown in chains, he returned to the city, and delivered a speech to an assembly, of the people or the praetorian guard, in which he heaped praise on the loyalty of his troops. But one precaution he did take. The prefect of the guard Publilius Sabinus was removed from his post because of his friendship with Caecina, and the vacancy was filled by Alfenus Varus, Valens' second-in-command during his march to Rome.

Next, probably on 30 October, Vitellius addressed the senate in a speech of studied grandiloquence, its subject the state of the state. Once this had been greeted with the appropriate adulation by his audience, his brother Lucius, from now on a prominent figure in Tacitus' narrative, introduced a vote of censure on Caecina. His lead was followed promptly. With a great show of indignation the others present condemned a consul who had deserted the state, a general who had betrayed his commander in chief, and a man who had abandoned the friend from whom he had received so many marks of distinction. In so doing, says Tacitus not unreasonably, "they professed to complain of the wrongs done to

Vitellius, but it was their own resentment they were airing." Without abusing the Flavian generals or mentioning Vespasian, they put the blame on armies that had gone astray out of thoughtlessness. And one senator, Rosius Regulus, even capitalized on Caecina's disgrace and wheedled out of the emperor the last day of the traitor's consulship. So Rosius entered on and laid down his office on one and the same day, 31 October. Self-appointed experts on constitutional law were outraged by the impropriety. Others just ridiculed beneficiary and benefactor.

Here Tacitus launches into a highly dramatic account of an incident that occurred, he says, "during these same days," a vague expression meant—as best we can tell—to denote the end of October or the start of November, before the news of Cremona reached Rome. This was Vitellius' decision to rid himself of Junius Blaesus, the governor of Lugdunensis who had treated him so generously and courteously during his progress south to Rome six months earlier. For this Vitellius earned immediate notoriety, but Tacitus' account is the only version to have survived. Vitellius, now back in Rome, was lying ill in the imperial villa in the Servilian Gardens, a park on the southern side of the city and once one of Nero's haunts. As he tossed and turned, he noticed that a nearby villa was ablaze with torches. When he asked why, he was told that a huge banquet was being thrown that night by Caecina Tuscus in Blaesus' honor.[1] Every aspect of the affair was exaggerated by his attendants, including the enjoyment of all the guests. When Vitellius reacted badly to this, some of his courtiers began to denounce Caecina Tuscus and, still more, Blaesus for making merry "the livelong day" while their emperor suffered so grievously on his bed of pain. And once they saw that the incident could be used to bring down Blaesus, they turned over the leading role in their drama to the emperor's brother Lucius.

The question that seems not to have been asked is why the dinner was held now. The most economical answer is surely that it was a *cena adventicia* just like the affair Lucius Vitellius had thrown for Aulus when he arrived from Germany some two months earlier. If Blaesus had just returned from the governorship of Lugdunensis (since Galba had appointed him, this seems reasonable), Caecina Tuscus would naturally have thrown him a banquet, and Vitellius' hangers-on would just as naturally have seized on this heaven-sent opportunity to bring down the guest of honor, probably out of jealousy. Although Tacitus keeps till last the details of Blaesus' pedigree, in order to accentuate the enormity of the crime, he was a man of high birth. As such, he could exert considerable influence in the senate and, perhaps, with the emperor too, thanks to the generosity he had once shown him. The courtiers were not to know that, according to Tacitus at least, Vitellius had resented that generosity even as he accepted it.

Lucius Vitellius was supposedly eager to play chief prosecutor because he hated Blaesus: the latter was an honorable man and much respected, whereas Lucius' reputation was far from spotless. As far as it goes, this is probably true. Still, we can discern an additional motive, fear, if we raise another question, why Lucius had never joined his brother before Bedriacum. His failure to do so after made good sense, since he could serve then as Aulus' representative among the senators Otho had corralled. Before the battle, on the other hand, Otho could have kept Lucius under close guard and he would still not have found it hard to slip away, had he had the mind to do so. Lucius, it seems, preferred to let events play out however they might, until Aulus became emperor. Then, driven on no doubt by Triaria, Lucius began energetically removing every potential threat to Aulus' position, and Blaesus could be represented as one such. Tacitus admits presently that Blaesus "had been approached by Caecina and others high in Vitellius' favor while things were still going well, because they were already contemptuous of the emperor, but he had rejected their overtures." He says nothing to indicate when or where this had happened, or who else was involved, but it could have occurred during the victory celebrations in Lugdunum, when Caecina first saw Vitellius in his guise as emperor. It is also uncertain whether the emperor or his brother knew about it, but Lucius needed no excuse anyway.

Lucius chose his moment carefully. He burst into the emperor's bedroom, carrying the latter's six-year-old son in his arms and falling to his knees. Asked by the emperor why he was so perturbed, Lucius announced that it was not for himself that he feared, but for his brother and his brother's children. There was no reason to fear Vespasian when so many armies and provinces were keeping him so far away (a ludicrous thing to say, as his addressee would know, unless the news of Cremona had not reached the city). What should worry the emperor was the enemy close to home, a man who boasted of descent from the families of the Junii and the Antonii (as no doubt Blaesus did); a man who was parading his imperial ancestry before the troops (another absurdity, unless Blaesus was newly returned to Rome and Vitellius, ill for a few days, had no information on the point); and a man on whom all eyes were fixed, as indeed they were (the banquet was crowded). Since Vitellius could not be bothered to distinguish between friends and enemies, he was fostering a rival for his own position. And this rival was sitting back, watching his suffering from a banquet nearby. Blaesus must be made to realize that Vitellius still lived, was emperor, and if anything untoward occurred, had a son ready to succeed him.

Vitellius' response to this speech is easy to understand. Clearly shaken by Caecina's defection, he must have been heartened by his brother's confident belief—real or feigned—that military victory would still be his. Then too, his brother's words forced him to take into account the effect of the defection on the senate as a whole. Made to think about it, he could not be nearly as sure of the continuing support of leading senators as he was of the loyalty of his troops. Again, the emperor undoubtedly loved his son, and anybody who could be represented plausibly as a threat to the boy's future would rouse him to action. Finally, he was probably impressed not just by his brother's oratory (Tacitus works hard to give Lucius a compelling speech), but also by his brother's display of concern. As Tacitus remarks in his obituary of Vitellius, he was open and generous. It may never have crossed his mind that Lucius was up to something.

As a result, Vitellius accepted his brother's contention that Blaesus must die. Though driven on by the fear that if he delayed, the other would strike first, he hesitated to order Blaesus' death at once. And since to order the execution openly would bring down fearful unpopularity on his own head, he decided to employ poison. When, where, and how this was administered Tacitus does not say. Instead, he observes that Vitellius "reinforced people's belief in his crime by the remarkable joy he showed when visiting Blaesus. Why, he was even heard to make an inhuman comment (I give his very words), in which he boasted of having feasted his eyes on the death of a personal enemy."[2] In fact, says Tacitus to round out his tale, Blaesus was a man of distinguished ancestry, impeccable breeding, and unshakeable loyalty. Admitting that he had been approached by Caecina, he insists that Blaesus had rejected his overtures. "He was so far from seeking the principate that he scarcely escaped being thought worthy of it." The epigram is typical of Tacitus' liking for giving a story a sting in the tail, but it goes too far. Blaesus had been appointed governor of Lugdunensis by Galba, after all, and Galba disliked administrators with strong personalities. From that it could follow that Blaesus might entertain another offer. Too much depended on who made it, in what circumstances, and under what pretexts. Not that this takes away from the moral Tacitus draws, that Blaesus was a virtuous man and virtue could be as dangerous to its possessors in Vitellius' reign as it had been in that of his role model, Nero.

With this Tacitus switches to Fabius Valens. His conduct is harder to fathom, the chronology of his movements harder to pin down. We know that Valens did not accompany Caecina on the march north because he was seriously ill; that the emperor put strong pressure on him to leave not too much later (around the end of September); and that when he set out on his journey to the north, he took no troops with him, since there was no perceived need for them. Yet he headed a column, says Tacitus, "a large and luxurious column of concubines and eunuchs." No doubt Tacitus wants to remind his readers of the proclivities Valens had displayed earlier and, according to gossip, would exhibit during this march also. But he is making an important point too, that so long as Valens refused to forsake this company, his progress was bound to be slow. Whether or not we assume that Valens' advanced age also impeded a full recovery from his illness, his progress was so incredibly snail-like that he failed to complete even the first stage of his journey before he heard that the Ravenna fleet had deserted.

For clarity's sake it may be best to outline the route Valens would have had to follow to reach Cremona or Hostilia—especially since this turned out to be the route followed, in reverse, by Antonius Primus' troops. The first stage involved taking the Flaminian Way (Via Flaminia) out of Rome. This ran north-northeast, passing through towns like Ocriculum, Narnia, and Mevania (of which we shall hear more later), then made its way through the Apennine mountains to reach the Adriatic coast at Fanum Fortunae (Fano) some 180 Roman miles away. There it ran along the coast for another 32 Roman miles and terminated at Ariminum (Rimini). From there the Aemilian Way (Via Aemilia) took a northwesterly direction, running for a considerable distance alongside the northern slopes of the Apennines, before striking out across the flat land to Placentia, nearly another 180 Roman miles from Ariminum. From Placentia it would have been easy for Valens to make the remaining 20-odd miles to Cremona along the Postumian Way. To get to Hostilia, on the other hand, he should probably have turned off the Aemilian Way a little earlier, perhaps at Bononia (Bologna) or Mutina (Modena). But whichever destination he chose, he had to pass Ravenna on his right, and that is why Tacitus stresses the effect on Valens of the news that Lucilius Bassus had taken the fleet over to the enemy. As Ravenna lay only some 35 miles north of Ariminum, there was a real danger that marines from the fleet would block the Aemilian Way ahead of his advance, or—an eventuality closer to what happened in fact—that the fleet would intercept any force advancing up the last stretch of the Flaminian Way, where it bordered the coast.

So, then, Tacitus asserts that when Valens learnt of the Ravenna fleet's defection, he could have saved the day if only he had hurried on. Supposedly he could have reached Caecina at Hostilia before the latter made up his mind to switch sides or, at least, have assumed command of the legions at Cremona. But even if we were to allow some two weeks for the time-lag between his hearing of the fleet's action and the sack of

Cremona, there is no realistic way of testing this assertion, and it may reflect the later criticisms of armchair strategists or unreconstructed Vitellians. For Valens decided to call a council of war, only to find that the members of his entourage disagreed fundamentally. Some urged the utmost audacity: he should press on, slip past Ravenna on side roads, and make his way to Hostilia or Cremona with a handful of trusted associates. Others argued for extreme caution: he ought to call up the cohorts of the guard from Rome, and fight his way through at the head of this powerful force. Valens, says Tacitus, wasted time listening to this advice and then rejected both plans. Doing "the worst thing possible in a crisis," he settled on a compromise. He sent a letter to Vitellius asking only for some auxiliary troops, presumably with the idea that they could march faster than guardsmen and handle by-roads more easily. How much time this consumed we cannot tell. Vitellius, after all, was still "lazing about" in his villa at Aricia, and unless some subordinate handled Valens' request without checking with the emperor, anything up to a week could have been spent deciding what forces should go and dispatching them. All we know is that Valens ended up with three auxiliary cohorts and one cavalry squadron, a force of some 4,000 men, too many to slip past the enemy unnoticed and too few to fight their way through against determined resistance.

While Valens waited for the arrival of these troops, he showed himself "so indifferent to disrepute that he was believed to be snatching illicit pleasures and polluting the houses of those with whom he stayed by seducing their wives and children; for he had at his disposal power, money and the last-minute lust of a collapsing fortune." Then, when his reinforcements arrived, he found that their loyalty was extremely shaky: "only their sense of shame and their respect for the general prevented them from deserting immediately, restraints that could not hold for long men fearful of danger and indifferent to disgrace." And supposedly it was this that induced Valens to change his plans. He sent the cohorts ahead to Ariminum, apparently to block the road south to Rome. He ordered the cavalry squadron to shield their rear against attacks from the Ravenna fleet, no doubt by taking up position between Ariminum and Fanum Fortunae. And he turned aside with a few companions and cut westward across country to Etruria, with the idea of finding a ship there, sailing to the coast of Narbonensis, and launching a new campaign by raising the Gauls, the armed forces still on the Rhine, and the German tribes on the far side of the river.

There are several difficulties in this narrative. How, for example, did Valens know that his fortunes were collapsing? More seriously, it is questionable if the loyalty of the reinforcements was as uncertain as Tacitus claims. We could hold that even if the subordinate who actually picked the troops was one of the praetorian prefects and notionally Valens' adherent, he would not necessarily have decided to send his best men north. But as this force would put up at least some resistance, Tacitus may have used their supposed low morale to explain the change in plan when it was something else that precipitated it. There are two possibilities. One is that Tacitus is wrong to say that Valens heard of the sack of Cremona when he was already in Etruria, in which case the sack led to the change. The other is to accept Tacitus' chronology and assume that Valens came to two conclusions, that Caecina had already ruined the entire army entrusted to him, and that there was no point in trying to pull his rival's chestnuts out of the fire.

In either case, Valens' departure for Etruria around the end of October unnerved the cohorts he had sent ahead to Ariminum, but not so much that they gave up without a fight. Later, to accentuate the difficulties Antonius' forces encountered when they reached the area, Tacitus describes the neighborhood of Fanum Fortunae as "devastated by war." So there must have been some serious fighting before the cohorts surrendered. Cornelius Fuscus certainly surrounded them, bringing up a force of marines and patrolling the coast with galleys from the Ravenna fleet. And this split control of Italy between Vespasian and Vitellius along the line of the Apennines. As for Valens, he took ship from Pisa, but he was able only to reach Portus Herculis Monoeci (Monaco), because the winds and currents were against him. Luckily, the headquarters of Marius Maturus, the procurator of the Maritime Alps, lay less than 15 miles away, and Maturus was still staunchly loyal to Vitellius, even though all around him had sworn allegiance to Vespasian. Yet while Maturus received Valens warmly, he bent every effort to dissuading him from going ahead with his plan to enter Narbonensis, and that did nothing for the morale of either man's supporters.

By this stage Narbonensis had fallen under the control of Valerius Paulinus. Whatever his title and status, he was an active soldier and had long been a friend of Vespasian. Apparently he saw no point in trying to winkle Maturus out of his mountain redoubt, but as it turned out, he had no need to. First, he rallied to his cause "all who had been discharged by Vitellius and wanted to fight again," that is, Otho's praetorians dismissed from service by Vitellius. And they answered the call because they respected Paulinus for having been once a military tribune in the guard. With this force Paulinus seized and garrisoned Forum Julii (Fréjus), the main harbor on the southern coast. Paulinus was not contemplating maritime adventures of his own. Forum Julii was his home, and the citizenry did all they could to help, partly out of fellow-feeling, partly in hopes that he would use his influence with Vespasian to secure them tangible rewards later. When these successes demoralized the Vitellians so completely that even Maturus decided to take the oath of allegiance to Vespasian, Valens returned to his ships with a mere ten men. He may still have planned to make for the mouth of the Rhône and from there to travel north to the German frontier, but Tacitus implies that his primary motivation was the belief that he would be safer at sea than on land. This too turned out to be wrong. Carried by a storm to the Stoechades islands (the Îles d'Hyères off Toulon), he was captured by warships Paulinus had sent in pursuit, as far as we can tell, in mid- to late November, and not long after that Paulinus sent him on, under guard, to Antonius Primus.

With Valens' capture, support for Vitellius evaporated outside Italy. In Spain the lead was taken by legion I Adiutrix. Still devoted to Otho's memory, the men won over the other two units in the peninsula, VI Victrix and X Gemina. There was no more hesitation in Gaul. In Britain the situation was more complicated. Of the four legions there (II Augusta, IX Hispana, XIV Gemina Martia Victrix, and XX Valeria Victrix) one, II Augusta, strongly favored Vespasian, because he had won distinction as their legate during the Claudian invasion of the island. We could assume that similar feelings animated XIV Gemina Martia Victrix, since it had sided with Otho, but Tacitus may have lost sight of this unit. He states that "in the other legions" many officers and men owed promotion and benefits to Vitellius, and were reluctant to abandon him. And this lack of unanimity, along with all the talk of a civil war raging in Italy, prompted a cross between a civil war and an uprising among the Brigantes, a powerful tribe in Yorkshire that had been allied previously with Rome.

The tribe's queen, Cartimandua, having tired of her husband Venutius at an earlier point Tacitus fails to specify, decided to share her bed and her throne with his squire Vellocatus. Since this outraged her subjects, Venutius seized his chance to overthrow her and to disavow the alliance with Rome. He reduced her to such straits that she had to call in the Romans, but whichever official responded to her appeals, he refused— or was unable—to commit the legions. He just sent in some auxiliary cohorts and cavalry squadrons to rescue the queen. What happened to her is unknown, but "the kingdom was left to Venutius, the war to the Romans." Much is made of this by students of Roman Britain, largely because the Brigantes had acted as a buffer between Roman territory in the island and the warlike tribes to the north. Now they became the leaders of the ongoing opposition to Rome, and there would be many years of fighting by much larger numbers of troops than might otherwise have been necessary. Tacitus took a different view. As is clear from the sarcastic conclusion he attaches to his narrative, and from the equally cursory but rather different account he provides in the *Annals*, Romans saw the business as a squalid affair, the kind of senseless behavior one had to expect from barbarian chieftains, and no real threat to their control of the island. If their forces had to fight larger numbers of recalcitrant Britons in the future, that was the price of empire—and a way for good generals to make their names.

On the German frontier, by contrast, there was genuine danger, thanks to a mixture of "indolence on the part of the governor, mutinies among the legions, incursions from the far side of the Rhine, and treachery among Rome's allies." In detail it is a long and complicated story, but the prime mover was Julius Civilis, commander of one of the Batavian cohorts that had troubled Valens so much earlier in the year. Once back on the Rhine frontier, says Tacitus, Civilis proposed securing independence for his own people, and the Batavians were by no means averse to his scheme. Although they paid Rome no tribute, they were bound by treaty to supply troops, and in 69 the Vitellians pressed them hard for recruits to replace the drafts sent to Italy. Civilis did not publicize his aims in the last months of the year. Instead, he claimed to be fighting on Vespasian's behalf by tying down Vitellian troops on the Rhine. And their commander, Hordeonius Flaccus, took no forceful measures against him, partly because he was old and inert, partly because he too inclined to support the Flavian.

Further east again, in Moesia, there was another outbreak of trouble. When the three legions stationed in the province marched off to join Antonius Primus, the Dacian tribes on the far side of the Danube remained quiet at first, perhaps because a little intimidated by the defeat of the Rhoxolani the previous winter. But when they heard, in November, that these legions were heavily engaged in the fighting in Italy, they swept across the Danube, overwhelmed the winter camps of the auxiliary units left to guard the frontier, and seized control of the southern bank. As their next move, says Tacitus, the tribesmen were planning an all-out attack on one or more of the legionary bases in the province, but luck turned against them. As it happened, Mucianus was marching his expeditionary force through the area, and since he too had heard of the victory at Cremona, he was able to detach the core unit in his force, VI Ferrata, to counter this threat, to reinforce it with two units from the Vitellian armies that Antonius had dispersed through the Balkans after his victory (I Italica and V Alaudae), and to summon Gaius Fonteius Agrippa, governor of the province Asia, to take over command. In what remains of the *Histories* Tacitus does not tell us that these measures proved inadequate. The immediate threat was averted, but Josephus reports that

Fonteius fell in battle against the Sarmatians in January 70, and that only when Rubrius Gallus took over Moesia in the late spring was peace at last restored.

From the fact that Mucianus would enter Rome perhaps no more than two weeks later than Antonius Primus' forces we can probably deduce details Tacitus neglects to mention, among them that Mucianus did not linger in the province to ensure that the situation was under control; that he never considered waiting for Fonteius Agrippa; and that he ordered VI Ferrata to stay put, rather than to try to follow in his footsteps. With a smaller force composed solely of detachments from the other units he could make better speed, and he had to overtake Antonius Primus as soon as possible if he was to win the military victory for which he hankered. This helps to explain the string of letters to Antonius and his fellow generals in some of which, as Tacitus puts it, Mucianus set out at length why they should press on with the campaign, while in others he dwelt on the advantages of delay, "careful always to phrase his advice in such a way that he could take the credit for any successes and avoid the blame for any setbacks." This was his contribution to the stop-start nature of the offensive's final stages, and one reason for Tacitus to think Mucianus as blameworthy as Antonius and his colleagues.

Tacitus has one more uprising of sorts to report, in Pontus (today the northeastern littoral of Turkey bordering on the Black Sea). Earlier, this area had been a client-kingdom, but in 63/64 Nero had dethroned its ruler, Polemo II, and had attached the new province (Pontus Polemoniacus) to Galatia. The royal guard had been given Roman citizenship and turned into a cohort, while the royal fleet had been made into one more imperial squadron to police the seas. Not only did the latter step sit ill with the freedman Anicetus, previously its lord high admiral, but insult was added to injury when Mucianus commandeered the best ships and crews for his own march to Rome. So Anicetus started an uprising, allegedly in Vitellius' behalf. Rousing the indigenous, non-Greek population, he attacked the city of Trapezus (Trabzond), wiped out the cohort there (though taught to fight in the Roman manner, says Tacitus, they had not lost their Greek taste for indolence and indiscipline), fired the warships Mucianus had left behind, and escaped out to sea. This he was able to do because his supporters were seafarers, and they—says Tacitus, adding picturesque details to raise Roman eyebrows over a trivial affair—used "camarae" to get around. These were ships with low sides and a broad beam, fastened together without spikes of bronze or iron. The sides could be built up with planks as high as the waves, to the point where the crew was roofed in completely, and they could be rowed in either direction.

When Vespasian heard of this, he gave some legionary detachments to Virdius Geminus, seemingly a centurion of proved worth, and sent him off to deal with the uproar. Geminus caught up with the pirates as they roved along the coast looking for plunder, and then, "having hastily constructed some warships," presumably by modifying merchantmen, he pursued Anicetus to the mouth of the River Chobus (Khopi) in the Caucasus. Here the (unnamed) king of the Sedochezi, a local tribe, gave Anicetus refuge and, initially, defied Roman demands for the man's surrender. He thought better of this idea, when he was offered either a monetary reward or an all-out war. The king seems to have arranged the killing of Anictus. All the other fugitives he handed over to the Romans, "and so this slave war was brought to a successful conclusion."

Vespasian, says Tacitus, was delighted by this turn of events. This is hardly likely (the emperor would have given the matter little thought), but the claim enables Tacitus to make his transition to Vespasian. And now that everything was going his way—Vespasian learnt of the victory at Cremona either as he marched south to Alexandria for the winter or after he had reached the city—he decided to refine the war plans formulated at Beirut. Although some prefer to ignore Tacitus' evidence and set this change earlier, it was now that Vespasian considered invading the province Africa and cutting off its shipments of grain to Rome. The plan was never carried out, possibly because the legionary legate in Africa and commander of III Augusta, Valerius Festus, was already hedging his bets by making secret overtures to the Flavian. But it was a good idea. Since the defeat at Cremona had bottled up the Vitellian forces in Italy, they were heavily dependent on the grain Rome received from Egypt and Africa. If both lifelines were cut, the troops would commandeer what supplies could be found without regard for the civilian population, but that would create enormous unrest in the city. Besides, seizing Africa would prevent the Vitellians from using the province as a bolthole, a plan adopted more than once in the civil wars of the republic.

With his survey of developments elsewhere completed, Tacitus reverts to Antonius Primus' campaign. But here we encounter what looks like another difficulty. Tacitus does not conclude his narrative of the attack on Cremona, as I have mine, with the town's sack. He adds a few more steps before his survey. Some items reflect well on Antonius and lay some groundwork for the survey. Then, after the survey, he reports further steps that belong in this same timeframe, but now many are charges that reflect badly on Antonius. As a result, some see in this change of perspective an indication that Tacitus has changed the source he is

following. There could be a grain of truth in this, if—that is—we allow
that Vipstanus Messalla's memoir ended with the sack of Cremona. Yet
this is neither helpful nor necessary. Tacitus gives us clues enough to
explain the relative change in tone.

In the earlier segment we are told first that the victorious army was
unable to encamp in the ruins of the Vitellian camp outside Cremona
because of the blood and gore that polluted the site, and so pulled back
three miles along the Postumian Way. This was no ringing endorsement of a victory gained in civil war. And then there was the fact that
some soldiers had seized individual Cremonans with the idea of selling
them later as slaves. Antonius forbade this as soon as he heard of it, but
the troops responded by killing their captives, until the latters' relatives
agreed to ransom them in secret. Still, the Flavians took some positive
actions. They set about the reorganization of the defeated Vitellian legions in order to disperse them through the Balkan provinces, not only
to ensure that they not rejoin the fray, but also to reinforce the frontiers
the Flavians had stripped of men for their own campaign. As usual, Tacitus
is disinclined to group the details, but this was how I Italica and V Alaudae
came to be assigned to Moesia. For the rest, XXII Primigenia was sent to
Carnuntum in Pannonia, to replace VII Galbiana, and XXI Rapax was
returned to Vindonissa, under a new commander, Lucius Flavius Silva,
the man who would reduce Masada in 73 or 74. At the same time, Antonius
dispatched news of the victory to Britain and Spain and, as living proofs,
he sent off two captured Vitellian officers, Julius Calenus, a military tribune from Aeduan territory, to spread the word in Gaul, and Alpinius
Montanus, the Treviran commander of an auxiliary cohort, to pass it
along the German frontier. And in case these measures failed to convince their intended audiences, the Flavians reinforced the patrols block-
ing the Alpine passes.

The later segment Tacitus opens with the explicit statement that
"Antonius acted much less blamelessly than he had before Cremona's
sack, either because he thought that the war was pretty much over, and
that the rest of the campaign would be easy, or else because this success
brought to the surface the greed, the arrogance, and all the other vices in
his nature that had been concealed hitherto." To this we cannot attach
great importance, since it is only another of his relative judgments. Far
from asserting that Antonius had been blameless previously, he repre-
sents the change in behavior as one of degree, not kind. And the charges
Tacitus levels at Antonius amount to a statement that he acted in a far
more demagogic fashion than he had previously. Now, as Tacitus puts
it, he "stamped around" northern Italy, he treated the legions as if they
belonged to him alone, and he tried to create a power base for himself.

To give the troops "greater license," he let them pick the replacements for the centurions killed in the battle, with the result that the "most turbulent" were elected. "No longer were the generals able to control the troops, but they were dragged along willy-nilly by the violent whims of the men." And Antonius "turned this to his advantage," and so acted "without the least regard for Mucianus' attempts to catch up with him, behavior that was to prove far more hazardous to him than was his having ignored Vespasian's wishes."

This passage is often taken as another illustration of how the troops were able to impose their wishes on their commanders. But if this were so, Tacitus would not have brought up the difference of opinion between Antonius and Mucianus. And since he states explicitly that this difference arose from Antonius' exploiting the "violent whims of the men," it follows that Antonius was leading the men. In other words, he did not give the men "greater license" so that they could escape his control, nor does Tacitus say so. The victims were "generals" in the plural, the commanders of the Balkan legions who began opposing Antonius' plans more and more. Initially, Antonius tried to retain control by insisting on his contributions to their successes to date. But most of his colleagues balked. They were led by Lucius Plotius Grypus, a man whom Vespasian had recently made a senator and ordered put in charge of a legion, probably VII Claudia, the unit hitherto under Vipstanus Messalla. Tacitus accuses Grypus and his allies of currying favor with Mucianus. But the situation had changed radically. Before Cremona, the Balkan legions had to act, if they were to prevent Vitellius from accumulating larger forces. After Cremona, it could be argued that the remnants of Vitellius' forces were shut up to Italy, and since winter was approaching, that the Balkan legions should take a breather and wait for Mucianus. So Antonius found another way of getting what he wanted. By engineering the election of the noisiest agitators as centurions, he ensured that the posts went to rankers who would defy the other generals' wishes, and so "turned the situation to his advantage."

Since winter was approaching and the flat land around the Po was waterlogged by rain and flooding, the decision taken by the generals— apparently still outside Cremona—was to press on only with a lightly armed, swift-moving column. The bulk of the legions, the wounded and those whose age had at last caught up with them, and even many who were suffering from neither affliction, all these were "left behind at" or, more accurately, sent back to Verona. Tacitus does not state in so many words that this represented a compromise, forced on Antonius by the procrastinators. But a compromise it was. No matter what else they disagreed upon, "Antonius and the other leaders" were in accord that "the back of the war had already been broken." This enabled the procrastinators to hold back—and rest—the bulk of the troops at Verona. And it enabled Antonius to press on with his personal campaign, albeit only with auxiliary cohorts and squadrons, backed up by a picked force of legionaries—or so it seemed at first.

In fact, events played into Antonius' hands. By now legion XI Claudia had come up from Burnum in Dalmatia, and it brought with it a levy of 6,000 Dalmatian tribesmen. The legion had supported Otho in the spring, but had returned peaceably to its base the moment it heard of his suicide (wherever it was at the time). The men—says Tacitus—were worried because it looked as though they had held back until success was assured, and for this they had no excuse. Though their commander was the lackadaisical governor, the "rich old man" Pompeius Silvanus, real power rested with the legionary legate Annius Bassus, and he got his way—later rather than sooner—by humoring his superior and taking care of important questions. (He would receive a prompt reward, a suffect consulship, in 70.) And a use was found for the Dalmatians. Since at least some marines in the Ravenna fleet were clamoring for promotion to legionary status, Antonius incorporated the best of them into his column and filled the vacancies in the fleet with the Dalmatians. Tacitus leaves his readers to work out the implications, that though the other generals wanted to limit the size of Antonius' force, he acquired extra troops from two groups of men eager to display their prowess, legionaries of XI Claudia who felt ashamed of not joining in sooner, and ex-marines set on proving that they deserved promotion to legionary status.

This may be why, when Antonius set off for the south, he was accompanied by the other generals. They made their first major halt at Fanum Fortunae, the town at the point where the Flaminian Way turned toward the Apennines. This gave everybody pause. Perhaps they were uncertain what to do next. They were no more familiar with this terrain than they had been with that of the Po Valley. Perhaps too the generals failed once again to agree on a course of action. According to Tacitus, they had heard a rumor that the praetorian cohorts were being brought up from Rome, and they fancied that the main pass through the mountains was already blocked by enemy pickets. He never states specifically that they reconnoitered the pass, but the ascent on the northern side was steep, the pass itself was a narrow gorge some 2,400 feet (730 m) above sea level and nearly a mile long, and it was now the second half of November.

This was not the only difficulty they faced. The neighborhood of Fanum Fortunae had been "devastated by war," probably when the cohorts Valens summoned from Rome had encountered the marines led by Cornelius Fuscus. Supplies were short since winter was coming. And on top of this, the troops "terrified their generals" by demanding "nail money," an allowance with which to buy new boots. Tacitus regards this as a pretext for greediness, but the men had marched some 210 miles at speed—and they did not get the money in any case. The generals had made no plans to procure cash or food during their advance, seemingly on the assumption that they would be able to live off the land. So out of a mixture of "haste and greediness," everybody thought only of himself, and "what could have been had for the army as a whole was carried off as plunder by individuals." This too looks like a valid example of an army out of control. But Tacitus is exaggerating. Why, after all, should we blame the men for fending for themselves when their generals had failed to consider their needs? And can we truly say that the men endangered the long-term prospects for success when, as usual, it was only their immediate needs they wanted satisfied? Besides, Tacitus is setting the scene for a story his audience would consider damning evidence of the column's indifference to right and wrong. Many accounts, he asserts, report that an ordinary cavalryman came to the generals and demanded a reward for having killed his own brother in the last battle. The generals had no idea how to respond: ordinary morality forbade their granting his petition, but the needs of civil war ruled out punishment. So they put him off, claiming that he deserved more than they could possibly give him straightaway.

Although this is the end of the story as such, Tacitus goes on to remark, with an appropriate show of indignation, that this was not the first example of fratricide in a Roman civil war. Sisenna had reported that in the battle fought at the Janiculum in 87 B.C. a common soldier had killed his brother and then, out of remorse, committed suicide. Whether or not Tacitus believed his story does not matter, any more than does the question whether the cavalryman waited till now to make his request because he only plucked up his courage after others had demanded "nail money." Two other aspects are more important. There is the obvious point that a Roman soldier asked to be rewarded for a shameful deed. And behind this lurks the point that the story reflected as badly on all the Flavian generals as it did on the cavalryman. Antonius was not alone in placing expediency above morality on this occasion. When Romans believed that the behavior of an army reflected the character of its generals, Antonius' opponents could hardly claim—now or later—that they had seized the moral high ground.

Soon after this, the Flavian generals must have held another council of war, at which they came to two decisions. They would send their cavalry on ahead to scout the area south of Fanum Fortunae, in hopes of finding another, easier way through the Apennines (none existed). At the same time they would summon all their legions from Verona and arrange for the Ravenna fleet to bring convoys of supplies from the north. Once again, it should be clear, the procrastinators prevailed, offering a plan that presented only a show of action. The cavalry was to be limited to scouting passes through the mountains, and the rest of the force would sit on its hands and wait, not just for the supplies but also for the troops summoned from Verona. And the procrastinators prevailed because they could invoke Mucianus' wishes too, this being where Tacitus sets his equivocal letters. And these letters must have made things more difficult for Antonius in another way too, if they showed that Mucianus was steadily overhauling the column. Besides this, Plotius Grypus and his cronies wrote to Vespasian, putting the worst construction on Antonius' actions and praising Mucianus to the skies. This did Antonius no more good.

Antonius did not help his own case. As good a rabble-rouser as he was, opposition made him headstrong and pompous. He not only openly faulted Mucianus for devaluing the dangers he had undergone. More incautiously still, he sent Vespasian a dispatch that was "both too boastful to be addressed to an emperor and too critical of his main associate." Tacitus gives us its purported gist, a thoroughly egocentric overview of the campaign. It was Antonius' efforts that had galvanized the Pannonian legions and the commanders in Moesia; it was his determination that had led them to cross the Alps, to seize control of northern Italy, and to cut off Vitellius' chances of drawing reinforcements from Germany and Raetia. That the Vitellian troops had been attacked while at odds with one another and dispersed, had been overwhelmed by a whirlwind of cavalry, and then routed by the main force of the legions in a battle lasting an entire day and night, these achievements were all his work. The misfortune Cremona had suffered was an accident of war, and much worse had happened in previous civil conflicts. Antonius was not waging war by letter; he was in the thick of things. He had no wish to belittle the glory won by those who had guaranteed the security of Moesia and beaten off the Dacians. His concern was the safety and security of Italy. And his efforts would be in vain if the glory went to those who had taken no part in the campaign. Mucianus soon heard of the contents of this letter, and the result, Tacitus adds, was a feud that Antonius cultivated openly, Mucianus more craftily and more implacably.

At this point Tacitus leaves Antonius twisting in the wind and turns to Vitellius' countermeasures or lack thereof, partly no doubt to tease his readers into wondering how exactly the feud would play out. But it serves his narrative purposes too. From now on, his account alternates between the adversaries, to bring out the contemporaneity of the events occurring in the different theaters. So, of Vitellius, Tacitus declares that he refused to admit that his troops had been crushingly defeated at Cremona, and put off the remedies for his ills rather than the ills themselves. Had he listened to others, he would have realized that he had the forces to make a fight of it. As he pretended that all was well, his condition grew steadily worse. In his own presence nobody spoke out, and gossip was forbidden elsewhere in the city. So "there was even more talk, and those who might have told the truth if allowed, spread much more appalling rumors because it was forbidden." The Flavian generals aggravated the situation. Vitellian scouts sent to check on the enemy's progress were captured by the Flavians, but instead of killing them, the Flavians gave them a guided tour of the victorious army and then sent them back to Rome.

Vitellius, says Tacitus, interrogated these scouts in private and then ordered them executed. Some doubt the veracity of this statement, but unless something of the sort was happening, there would be little point in the story of a centurion named Julius Agrestis. No mere ranker, he tried to goad Vitellius into action in numerous conversations (a comment perhaps indicating that the luckless scouts had been numerous too). Then he induced the emperor to send him out to look things over. With remarkable bravery, or effrontery, he went straight to Antonius and informed him why he had come. So the general let him see for himself what had happened at Cremona and what had been done with the defeated legions. When Agrestis returned to Vitellius and the latter refused to believe him, the centurion won his place in history. "Since you need compelling proof," he declared, "and I am no more use to you alive or dead, I will force you to believe me." Quitting the imperial presence, he killed himself, and this finally broke through the wall of Vitellius' resistance.[3]

As if roused from sleep, Vitellius ordered his praetorian prefects, Julius Priscus and Alfenus Varus, to take 14 cohorts of the guard and all the cavalry squadrons up the Flaminian Way, and to block the passes through the Apennines. They were accompanied, Tacitus adds, by "a legion of marines" from the Misene fleet. As Vitellius could not have produced this legion out of thin air, it has been held that he must have been making more preparations than Tacitus allows. But Tacitus terms them specifically "all picked men," and that should count for something, even if he does so only to add that "had they been entrusted to any other general, they would have been fully capable of taking the offensive." In numbers at any rate it was a powerful force; 19,000 or so strong. The rest of his troops Vitellius held back to guard the city, entrusting them to his brother Lucius. So Lucius took command of the two remaining praetorian cohorts and all the auxiliary cohorts still in the city (of which there could have been up to 30). But he would not have taken over the four urban cohorts, since they belonged to Flavius Sabinus, the prefect of the city, and there was no point in angering him. No account appears to have been taken of the seven cohorts of the watch. And an imperial troupe of several hundred gladiators was entrusted to a disreputable specimen named Claudius Julianus. Even so, Lucius' force may have been nearly as large as the one Aulus sent to the north.

Having parceled out responsibilities like this, Vitellius made no adjustments to his own lifestyle. But since he was still unsure whether everything was under control, he decided to court the favor of other elements in the population. To win over members of the governing class, he hurried on the elections at which consuls were designated for perhaps ten years to come.[4] And like Otho in a similar predicament, he issued edicts raising the political status of cities and communities inside and outside Italy, remitting tribute in some cases and in others granting autonomy. "In short, he inflicted severe wounds on the body politic with no regard for the future." The common people gawked at the magnitude of the favors he conferred, but they were "favors for which the stupid paid cash down, whereas the sensible thought them worthless, since they could be neither granted nor accepted without harm to the state."

At length, probably around the end of November, Vitellius yielded to the importunities of his expeditionary force and traveled north to join it. For the moment, Tacitus makes nothing of the fact that this army had marched only some 72 miles up the Flaminian Way and had halted at Mevania (Bevagna), on open ground about 5 miles short of the point where the road emerged from the foothills of the Apennines. But he dwells on Vitellius' being accompanied by a long train of senators, many eager to win his favor, but more motivated by fear. Uncertain in purpose and an easy prey to unreliable advice, Vitellius was also assailed by a burst of prodigies, the first Tacitus has mentioned in this entire campaign and—more surprisingly perhaps—a batch Suetonius omits. For a start, Vitellius was addressing the troops one day, when so huge a flock of "ill-omened birds" flew over that they shut out the daylight like a black cloud. Dio, more dramatically, declares them a flock of vultures that nearly knocked him off the rostrum. Then a bull selected for sacrifice, to assure success in the campaign, escaped from the altar and was struck down some distance away and not in the proper manner. But, says Tacitus, resorting to one of his rhetorical tricks, the most striking portent was Vitellius. With no idea of what active service entailed and no plan to offer, he kept asking about orders of march, how to scout, and whether they should speed up or slow down operations.

As Vitellius was unable to focus on any one matter for any length of time, each new piece of intelligence caused him "to show his anxiety in both his looks and his gait." So he took to drinking. This did not insulate him either. For next news arrived that the fleet at Misenum had defected to Vespasian, and so he returned to Rome, "unnerved by each new setback and blind to where the real danger lay." It is now that Tacitus comments on the lack of progress made by the army and the indecisiveness of its leader. While Vitellius could have crossed the Apennines with a strong force of fresh troops and have attacked an enemy suffering severely from cold and want of supplies, he decided instead to split his forces (one group to check Antonius' offensive and one to deal with the revolt in Misenum), and to abandon his best troops, men determined to fight to the last, to be killed or captured by the enemy. The most experienced centurions would have told him this, had they been asked, so Tacitus declares. "But the courtiers kept them at arm's length, having trained their ruler to find the truth unpalatable and only what would hurt him pleasant."

Yet the defection of the Misene fleet was not something that could have been foreseen, whether or not it was triggered by Vitellius' departure for the north, or by his skimming off the most enthusiastic marines for his "legion." The uproar began with Claudius Faventinus, a centurion dishonorably discharged by Galba. He showed up in Misenum with a forged letter from Vespasian, offering the marines a donative if they deserted. Faventinus was apparently a freelance, interested only in finding his way back into the service, but no steps were taken against him by the fleet's commander, Claudius Apollinaris, "neither firm in loyalty nor energetic in treachery." So the ongoing uproar attracted another opportunist, the ex-praetor Apinius Tiro who happened to be in the nearby town of Minturnae. Apollinaris and Tiro now elbowed Faventinus aside (we hear no more of him) and made common cause against Vitellius. They also encouraged neighboring towns to join in, and this spread the unrest further, because local rivalries surfaced immediately. When Puteoli (Pozzuoli) declared for Vespasian, says Tacitus, Capua promptly announced for Vitellius.

The emperor's initial response, made at Mevania, was to dispatch a third Claudius, Julianus, to deal with the situation. He had preceded Apollinaris in command of the fleet, and was known to the marines as a lax disciplinarian, the kind of unthreatening figure who might just win them back. Still, he was given the imperial troupe of gladiators under his command and one of the four urban cohorts to back him up, these forces being sent—like himself—from Rome, no doubt because it was nearer to the source of the trouble. But Julianus showed no greater eagerness to take a hard line now than he had earlier. So, after a show of offering battle, he too switched sides, and the three men occupied Tarracina, a town on the Appian Way some 65 miles south of Rome and about the same distance north of Misenum. This lay on the coast in what Roman aristocrats had long viewed as a resort area. As Suetonius tells us, Galba had been born in a villa on a hill overlooking the town, "on the left-hand side as you make your way (south) to Formiae."

Since Tacitus asserts that Tarracina was "better protected by its walls and its natural position than by its new garrison," Vitellius took the town's seizure more seriously than he need have done. Perhaps he was worried by the prospect of a rogue fleet interfering with the grain ships bringing supplies of food to Rome. Or, like Nero, he could have been taking precautions against the day when he might have to flee Italy by sea (the legionary legate in Africa, Valerius Festus, was his kinsman, after all). Whatever the case, once Vitellius was back in Rome, he decided to split his forces three ways. Again Tacitus alludes only elliptically to this redistribution, but it came to this. When Vitellius quitted Mevania for Rome, he took 7 of the 14 praetorian cohorts with him, compensating for this by allowing the forces under the prefects to fall back 35 miles to Narnia (Narni), a much stronger position. Perched on a hilltop, the town commanded the imposing bridge on which the Flaminian Way crossed the River Nar (Neri), and the Flavians would have taken enormous casualties trying to force it. Of the 7 cohorts Vitellius took with him, he kept 1 to serve—along with the 2 still in Rome—as his personal guard. The other 6, with 500 cavalry, he assigned to his brother Lucius, and ordered him to quell the unrest in the south.

This three-way split was a bad idea, but not perhaps in quite the way it is usually said to have been. Tacitus himself clearly thought that the emperor left inadequate forces in the north, and his verdict has been widely endorsed. From a military point of view, however, it is belied by the caution and the respect with which Antonius treated this force. Seven praetorian cohorts held up his advance for a week or more, and when they surrendered because their officers were deserting in droves, it was on honorable terms. There was never a battle, even after the Flavian legions came up. True, it is impossible to tell how much longer the cohorts could have held out, but what Antonius won was a political victory. This is not all. It can be argued that Vitellius' decision to send Lucius south was far more significant. This deprived the emperor of the services of the one man who might have given him some backbone, and so have averted his attempts to abdicate and the bloodshed they occasioned. As Tacitus remarks later, Lucius was the one Vitellian general left who could have defended Rome effectively. And if he had held the city with 9 praetorian cohorts, he would have made the final battle into a much bloodier affair.

Vitellius was not so foolish as to think his dispositions an ideal solution to his problems, but his spirits were raised at first by the genuine enthusiasm of his praetorians and by "the clamor of the people, demanding that he arm them as well." Though his prominent friends had made themselves scarce (the higher their rank, the more disloyal they were), the emperor's freedmen urged him to take the people up on their offer. When he did, the turnout was enormous. At first the emperor registered the volunteers' names personally, but eventually he had to hand the task over to the consuls, Caecilius Simplex and Quinctius Atticus. Meanwhile he demanded contributions of money and slaves from the senators. The knights spontaneously offered their services and their cash. And this led even the nonimperial freedmen to volunteer their resources, at first from fear, but then with genuine enthusiasm as they caught the mood of the moment. Then Tacitus undercuts the positive effect of all this:

> It was not so much Vitellius for whom many felt compassion as for the level to which the principate had sunk. Not that he failed to elicit sympathy by his expression, his remarks and his tears. He was generous with his promises and—as the fearful tend to be—immoderate in his behavior. Why he even wanted to take the title "Caesar." . . . But just as everything that is started on a thoughtless impulse eventually loses way, so the senators and knights began to slip away, at first hesitantly and when he was not present, but later with open contempt and without concern, until Vitellius grew ashamed of his vain efforts and forgave them what they would not give him.

This is an odd piece of writing, but there is no need to invoke malice or Flavian propaganda. Nor is it helpful to turn the material on its head, so as to produce a favorable picture of Vitellius. Though Tacitus makes nothing of the emperor's being able to rally the people as Nero had not, he will report later that they actually marched out to offer battle. Nor does he undercut the people's enthusiasm, as does Suetonius. The biographer claims that the people enrolled so enthusiastically because Vitellius "promised to release them from service the moment victory was won and to pay them the bounties given to veterans after they had served their full term." Had this been so, Tacitus would never have omitted it.[5] What justifies Tacitus' version of events is practicality. The common people lacked military experience, since there had been no citizen militia for over a century, and an effective force could not be manufactured overnight. And even a trained force needed leaders, and there were none to be had. The emperor's friends had made themselves scarce, and his freedmen urged him on only because they stood to lose most from a change of regime.

Antonius and his forces meanwhile were much heartened by what they considered Vitellius' cowardly withdrawal from Mevania. The peoples south of the Apennines were likewise encouraged to change sides, a development that promised to ease the supply difficulties Antonius' men were having. And the troops must have known too that their own legions were now close enough to permit an advance. So Antonius and the other generals began making their way through the mountains. Though battered by a severe winter storm, they were unmolested by the enemy (as Tacitus sees it, another proof that luck was as important to the Flavians as the leadership of their generals). And in this trek they met up with Quintus Petillius Cerialis, "a kinsman of Vespasian and a distinguished soldier." What actually distinguished Cerialis' soldiering—as Tacitus remarks frequently elsewhere—was its rashness: as legionary legate of IX Hispana in Britain in 61, he had let his troops be routed by Boudicca's rebels. But as Antonius favored risk takers, this as much as his kinship with Vespasian may have led to Cerialis' being made one of the leaders of the column.

Cerialis had escaped from Rome, whatever he had been doing there, by disguising himself as a peasant, and had used his knowledge of the area to get through the Vitellian lines. His escape from Rome may also have been what prompted the generals to communicate with Flavius Sabinus, the prefect of the city, and with Vespasian's 18-year-old son Domitian. Although Tacitus disagrees with the "many authors" who asserted that these two could easily have escaped from Rome, he allows that Antonius' messengers made contact with them. Sabinus, however, kept using as his excuse "ill-health that would not permit exertion or bold action," while "Domitian had the courage, but though the guards set over him by Vitellius promised to accompany him in his flight, it was feared that they were trying to trap him." Neither Sabinus nor Domitian emerges creditably from this episode. The older man is presented as a buffoon, the younger as too suspicious. But given Tacitus' hostility to Domitian, it is noteworthy that the historian refrains from specifying by whom "it was feared" that the young man's guards were trying to trap him.

The Flavian generals made their next halt at Carsulae (Casigliano), so far as we can tell early in the second week of December. Ten miles north of the Vitellians' position at Narnia, Carsulae gave them a panoramic view of the countryside to the south, and this was a useful safeguard against surprise attacks by enemy cavalry. In this arm the Vitellians seem to have been much stronger, and they even sent a force of 400 horse to occupy a town five miles to the west of their position, Interamna (Terni, the site of Cornelius Dolabella's murder). For the Flavians, nonetheless, supplies were easy to procure, since there were now any number of flourishing towns in their rear. Besides, the column needed a few days to rest, and the generals used this break to allow their legions at last to catch up with them. The generals also contemplated parleys with the Vitellian forces, in hopes of inducing them to desert, but their troops were much less keen on this idea. As before Cremona, the men wanted a military victory that would enable them to loot to their hearts' content. They were reluctant even to wait for their own legions, potentially "allies in plunder rather than in peril."

This led Antonius to call an assembly and deliver a speech in which he laid out his plans. In this speech he seems to know more about events south of Rome than he should have done, but perhaps Cerialis brought him up to date. Vitellius, so Antonius supposedly declared, still had troops enough to warrant being taken seriously. If his men were given a chance to reflect on their situation, they would waver in their allegiance, but they would fight desperately if pressed. When people started a civil war, they had to trust to luck. Winning the war demanded planning and calculation. As things stood, now that the Misene fleet and many cities on the Campanian coast had deserted Vitellius, he controlled only a narrow band of territory between Tarracina and Narnia. They themselves had won ample glory by their victory at Cremona, and incurred too much unpopularity by sacking the city. They had to give up any idea of storming Rome. They would win larger rewards and the greatest glory if they did everything they could to preserve the senate and people of Rome without bloodshed.

Whether or not these are the views Antonius claimed to have expressed later, after he was made responsible for the assault on Rome, he was able to calm the men, and they waited for their legions. Once they were reinforced, the loyalty of the Vitellian forces in Narnia began to flag. None of the officers urged them to fight, says Tacitus. On the contrary, many took their units over to the enemy, "as a gift for the victors and insurance for their own futures." From the deserters the Flavians learnt of the Vitellian outpost at Interamna, and sent Arrius Varus to crush it. The majority of the cavalrymen surrendered without a fight, and the handful who escaped only increased the panic in Narnia. So more and more officers deserted, until the prefects, Julius Priscus and Alfenus Varus, gave up and left for Rome, "thus freeing all alike from the shame of treachery." Yet the praetorian rankers remained steadfastly loyal to their emperor, still convinced that Valens had made his way to the Rhine frontier and was raising a new army. This decided Antonius to order Valens' execution. So he was brought up from the nearby town of Urvinum Hortense (Collemancio) and executed, so that his head could be displayed to his former troops. It was in its way a tribute to the prowess and reputation of these praetorians that such ruthlessness was used. For that reason too they were allowed to surrender formally, and to march out of Narnia under their eagles and standards, on or around 15 December.

The prisoners were ordered to encamp, some of them at Narnia, and some at Interamna, both groups under the eyes of Flavian troops whose "task was not to threaten them if they remained quiet, but who were strong enough to quash any defiance." Meanwhile Antonius pressed ahead with attempts to persuade Vitellius to surrender, sending off messages that offered him his life, a substantial sum of money (Suetonius mentions 100 million sesterces), and a retirement villa in Campania, if he laid down his arms and entrusted himself and his children to Vespasian. Since Mucianus wrote letters in the same vein, Vitellius inclined to trust these undertakings, and raised queries only about the number of slaves he would be allowed to keep, and where exactly on the coastline his retirement villa would be situated. "So great a torpor had overtaken him," says Tacitus in one of his best-known epigrams, "that if everybody else had not remembered that he was emperor, he himself would have forgotten it."

This verdict is unfair. Dio's epitomator insists that Vitellius at this time was changing his mind constantly, "driven this way and that like a ship in a storm." Though he substantiates his claim only with vague generalizations, it was now probably that Vitellius had one more distraction to deal with, the death of his mother Sextilia. Tacitus tends to harp on Sextilia's feeling that Vitellius had never come up to her expectations, but he says nothing about the emperor's attitude to her. It may be unwise to assume that he lacked affection for her, even though he had treated her shamefully in the past. Suetonius, however, tells two bizarre stories to suggest the opposite. In one, the emperor's German prophetess predicted that his rule could be set on a lasting foundation only if he outlived Sextilia, and so he starved her to death. In the other, marginally more plausible, Sextilia asked her son for poison, and he gave it to her, because she wanted to end her life "out of distaste for the current situation and fear for the future."

Whatever the circumstances of her death, it must have looked at this stage as if Antonius would win the game, by reaching an agreement with Vitellius and forestalling Mucianus' attempts to appropriate the glory. And so he might have, had not another player decided to take a hand. Aware of the dickering between Vitellius, Antonius, and Mucianus that went on from the first week of December, leading senators in Rome began approaching Sabinus, the prefect of the city, and urging him to seize his share in the victory and the glory. In private talks with him, says Tacitus, they pointed out that he could rely on his own troops, the urban cohorts, he could rally the seven cohorts of the watch, and he could use their slaves too. Fortune was on their side, and he should not let Antonius grab all the glory. Vitellius was backed by only a few cohorts of praetorians, whose morale had been sapped by the bad news coming in from every side. The common people were fickle and, once they were given a strong lead, they would heap on Vespasian the flattery they had paid to Vitellius. And the emperor himself was no obstacle; scarcely up to handling things when they were going well, he was crippled now. The glory of ending the war would go to the man who took control of Rome. It behooved Sabinus to reserve the throne for Vespasian, just as it behooved Vespasian to rank his brother above all others.

Tacitus says nothing to indicate that the rhetoric of these conversations was far superior to the accuracy of the claims they contained. For a start, Sabinus had only three urban cohorts under his command (the fourth was with Apinius Tiro somewhere south of Rome), and these cohorts had supposedly been filled up with Vitellians when the emperor overhauled the praetorian guard.[6] Again, the cohorts of the watch were a paramilitary force, called out only in the direst emergencies and only as backup. And arming slaves, no matter whose they were or for what purpose, was very dangerous, since it excited adverse comment about servile wars. Then too, Vitellius might have only three cohorts of praetorians with him in Rome, but there was no hint that they would accept a change of regime, no matter what had happened at Narnia. And the people's fickleness was irrelevant. Militarily they possessed no more than nuisance value.

Instead of belaboring the obvious, Tacitus focuses on Sabinus' lack of enthusiasm for these calls to action. The prefect was incapacitated by age, being somewhere between 60 and 65 years old. The uncharitable, Tacitus continues, surmised that Sabinus was also jealous of his brother and reluctant to yield first place to him in the family hierarchy, and so that while there was a semblance of harmony between them, the brothers disliked one another at heart. But, he adds, "a better interpretation" would be that Sabinus was a gentle soul, predisposed to negotiate because he shrank from bloodshed. This is no sudden onset of benevolence on Tacitus' part, since he is not praising Sabinus. Aristocrats put in command of troops were not supposed to be gentle souls. Tacitus' thesis is that Sabinus was an aging, indecisive character whose best course would have been to remain neutral, the course to which he had hewed before and after his brother's proclamation as emperor in July.

Yet Sabinus decided to inject himself into the negotiations and held several meetings with Vitellius. In these they discussed the terms on which the emperor would lay down arms. The earlier sessions were held in private, but their last meeting took place in the temple of Apollo next to the palace on the Palatine Hill, presumably because it qualified as both neutral and sacred ground. Nobody ever discovered what agreement they reached or if they reached one. For this Tacitus provides one reason explicitly: there were only two witnesses, the peace-loving ex-governor Cluvius Rufus, and Silius Italicus, an ex-consul and close friend of the emperor, best known today for his turgid epic poem on the Hannibalic War. Everybody else was kept at a distance and—like Kremlin watchers during the Cold War—had to draw conclusions from the gestures and facial expressions of the principals: "Vitellius seemed dejected and humbled, Sabinus not triumphant but closer to compassionate." But there may have been another reason too. Tacitus does not state specifically that this last meeting was meant to be their final get-together, and since he implies later that Sabinus was caught off guard by Vitellius' formal announcement of his wish to abdicate, the two men may have agreed only on terms, not on a timetable.

Whatever happened in this meeting, it must have been obvious that any agreement would require Vitellius to abdicate, and it is on this basis that Tacitus turns to the ways in which the emperor's followers, the praetorians especially, reacted to news of the discussions. Then he provides the details on what, so he says, was the emperor's single attempt to go through with the abdication on 18 December. And he presents this as the result, not of the discussions, but of Vitellius' learning that his forces at Narnia had surrendered. Suetonius, however, attributes the abdication to Sabinus' efforts and has Vitellius make three attempts to go through with it, the second and third of them splitting between them the details reported by Tacitus. Hence it is regularly claimed that Tacitus boiled down three attempts to one for artistic reasons, and that Suetonius would never have inflated one into three, when the hallmark of his account is extreme brevity. Two important points have been overlooked, however. First, it is all but certain, on chronological grounds, that Suetonius carved into two the attempt at abdication recorded by Tacitus. Second, while Suetonius rightly separated off the first attempt, this was only a tentative and unofficial testing of the waters on 17 December. It was tentative because, as Suetonius says, Vitellius made an informal speech to the one cohort of the guard on duty at the palace, and it was unofficial because he made it during the evening. What is more, this timing supports the idea that it was Vitellius' reaction to the news from Narnia, not a response to his meetings with Sabinus. If Tacitus is guilty of anything, it is of omitting a relatively unimportant preliminary, even if that helped spread the news, intensified the hostility with which the praetorians viewed Vitellius' plan to give up power, and caught Sabinus unawares.

In passing immediately to the initial reactions of Vitellius' partisans to this plan, Tacitus is able for a start to award Vitellius his due meed of blame: "if the emperor could have changed the minds of his followers as easily as he changed his own, Vespasian's army would have entered Rome without bloodshed." Then he can launch into the angry, if predictable, rhetoric of Vitellius' supporters. This came down to assertions that abdication would involve danger and disgrace, since everything would depend on the victor's whims. Neither Vespasian in victory nor Vitellius' followers in defeat would be able to endure his living on in retirement. And neither Vespasian, nor his friends, nor even his armies would have peace of mind so long as Vitellius' six-year-old son lived. When the Flavians had butchered Valens, Primus and Mucianus ("that template for Flavian policy") would be bound to execute the boy. Vitellius had to prove himself worthy of his ancestry and fight on, if only out of desperation. His troops were still loyal, the people were with him, and no worse fate awaited them than the one they faced. They must die whether they fought or surrendered, and death with honor was better than being slaughtered in disgrace.

Vitellius, however, was overwhelmed by self-pity, and by anxiety that continued fighting would lead to harsh treatment for his wife and children. So he called a public meeting on the morning of 18 December, and came down to the Forum in mourning dress. His household accompanied him, as dejected as he, and his son was carried in a litter "as if on the way to a funeral." The people's comments were ingratiating but untimely, the troops kept a menacing silence. But no person of discernment (no aristocrat in other words), once confronted with this sight, could remain unmoved by the spectacle. Here was the emperor of Rome, until yesterday the master of the world, abandoning his palace, his powers, and his city. Never had they seen the like, never had they heard of the like. Now, in a meeting he himself had called, surrounded by his own soldiers, "while even women looked on," Vitellius announced that he was giving up the throne for the sake of peace and the state, and asked his listeners only that they remember him well and show sympathy for his brother, his wife, and his innocent children. Finally, when tears overcame him, he tried to hand his dagger to Caecilius Simplex, as if giving up the symbol of his office. But the consul refused to take it, and so did every other person of consequence to whom he offered it. So he left the rostrum, intending to place the dagger in the temple of Concord and to make his way to his brother's house. But this time the crowd not only remonstrated energetically, they also blocked every other exit from the Forum, and so forced him to return to the palace.

Tacitus obviously devoted all his literary skills to the delineation of this scene, and rightly so. In a constitutional monarchy abdication is not a problem, no matter how sentimental or sordid the motives of the parties involved. With an emperor the situation was different, one reason why Augustus supposedly contemplated abdicating but dropped the idea at once as far too dangerous. There may be details that reflect poorly on Vitellius, for example, his having neither the presence nor the will to force his way through the crowd. But in no sense is this account mean-spirited, as is Suetonius' version (the latter finds nothing to pity in the affair). Moreover, the care Tacitus lavished on the literary aspects of this episode hardly proves his account less accurate than Suetonius'. The latter, in essence, assigns the first half of the scene to Vitellius' second attempt to lay down his powers, adding only that the emperor delivered his speech from a script. The handing off of the dagger and what follows from that he apportions to the third attempt, and he assigns this to a meeting called after the fall of the Capitol and Sabinus' death. But it is highly unlikely that Caecilius Simplex or any other senior official was still around then to decline the dagger.

Whatever the truth, Tacitus' account continues as if Sabinus was unprepared for Vitellius' announcement, or had not considered likely reactions to it, or again had concluded that his own presence in the Forum would seem inappropriate as well as inflammatory. At the time of the announcement he was certainly in his own house on the Quirinal Hill. So, "once the rumor that Vitellius was abdicating had begun to spread and Sabinus [in consequence] had sent instructions to the tribunes of the cohorts to keep their troops in check, the leading members of the senate, many members of the equestrian order, and all the men from the urban cohorts and the cohorts of the watch flocked to Sabinus' house, as if the entire state had dropped into Vespasian's lap." Then the news arrived that the people remained devoted to the emperor, and that the praetorian cohorts were refusing to take orders from anybody else. Sabinus having gone too far to pull back, the others present urged him to resort to force, for fear that otherwise Vitellius' followers would catch up with them "before they had organized and gathered their strength." But Sabinus continued to procrastinate, "and as happens in situations of this kind, everybody offered advice, few faced up to the danger."

This last comment is Tacitus' way of preparing for the next scene, still on 18 December. Sabinus must have been persuaded eventually that his best move was to make his way down to the Forum, to issue some kind of proclamation on Vespasian's behalf, or else up the Palatine Hill, to get Vitellius to quit the palace (Dio's account hints at this). He took an armed guard with him, of unknown size, and as his party was nearing the Forum, they ran into a group of determined Vitellians. Since the encounter was unexpected, only a skirmish followed, but the Vitellians won it. Panicked, Sabinus took the action that "looked safest in light of his predicament," and seized the peak of the Capitol with a mixture of soldiers, senators, and knights. It is not easy, says Tacitus dryly, to give the names of the prominent men who accompanied him, since so many claimed to have risked their lives for the Flavian cause once Vespasian had won. And perhaps to deride these men, he adds that some aristocratic women underwent the siege too, the best known of them Verulana Gratilla, "who had the claims of neither children nor relatives to attract her, only her love of danger." It is not the kind of tribute paid to a Roman woman in normal circumstances, but these were not normal circumstances and Verulana was daring, something Tacitus will not say of the one prominent man he names later, the consul Quinctius Atticus.

What Sabinus hoped to achieve by occupying the Capitol, and how long he expected to hold out are questions we cannot answer, and Sabinus may not have been able to either. But Tacitus reports that since the Vitellian soldiery at first threw only a loose cordon round the hill, Sabinus was able not only to summon his own children and his nephew Domitian to join him an hour or so before midnight (18/19 December), but also to get a message out to Antonius, to the effect that he was under siege and needed help. Tacitus seems to have regarded this as an illustration of Sabinus' incompetence and vainglory, since he adds that the rest of the night was so quiet that he could have slipped away easily. Bold as the Vitellian troops might be when facing danger, they had little taste for boring work like guard duty, and besides a sudden rainstorm made it difficult for them to see or hear anything.

At dawn on the next day (19 December) Sabinus decided to send a message to Vitellius before hostilities could start. His emissary was the senior centurion Cornelius Martialis, and he was instructed to present Sabinus as the injured innocent. Hence Tacitus gives him a message that is both highly disingenuous and openly threatening. Vitellius, he was to say, had made only a pretense of abdicating, this to deceive all the illustrious men who had rallied to Sabinus. Why after leaving the Forum had he not made for the family home on the Aventine? That would have been the conduct of a citizen determined to shun any claim to the throne.

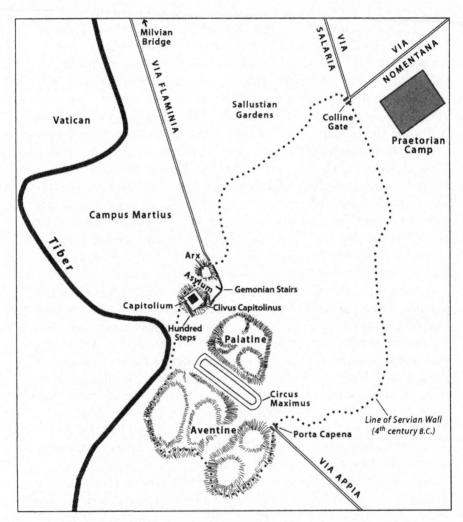

The Capitol and Its Environs

Instead, Vitellius had returned to the palace. From there an armed column had issued forth and had strewn one of the most crowded parts of the city with the corpses of innocent victims. And now not even the Capitol was being spared. Sabinus himself, as everyone knew, was a civilian and just one senator among many. Ever since the war between Vitellius and Vespasian had broken out, he had remained loyal to the emperor, even though Vespasian was his brother and was winning that war. It was Vitellius who had invited Sabinus to discuss terms for a surrender, terms that had value only for the vanquished. If Vitellius regretted the arrangements they had made, he would gain nothing by slaughtering an old man and a young boy. It was the enemy legions he should confront. That battle would decide the outcome.

Vitellius made only a brief reply in which he offered excuses for his conduct and placed blame on the zeal of troops he could not restrain. "Unable to issue orders or prohibitions, he was not now an emperor, only the cause for a war." Hence Martialis had hardly returned before a swarm of Vitellians launched a furious attack. Suetonius has no qualms about asserting not only that Vitellius had arranged the original attack on Sabinus, but that he ordered this assault as well, and watched the results from a dining room in the palace. This is spiteful rubbish, and there is no reason to prefer it to Tacitus' report that the Vitellians acted off their own bat. Charging through the Forum, they marched in column up the hill by way of the Clivus Capitolinus, till they reached the outer gates, that is, the gates in the wall that marked off the precinct in which the Temple of Jupiter Best and Greatest stood. In the old days, says Tacitus, there were porticos on the right-hand side of the road as you made your way up, and the defenders climbed out onto their roofs and began hurling tiles and rocks down on the attackers. As the Vitellians were armed only with swords and were too impatient to bring up artillery, they threw torches into one of the porticos and followed the flames. And they would have broken through the gates once these had caught fire, had not Sabinus made an impromptu barricade by tearing down the statues on every side, "the glorious memorials of our ancestors."

Thwarted, the Vitellians tried a two-pronged attack. One group moved round to the southwestern corner of the hill, where the "One Hundred Steps" were situated, while the other moved slightly north of the Clivus Capitolinus, and began an attack by way of the saddle between the Capitol's two peaks, an area known as the Asylum. "Both attacks were unexpected, but the one that began to develop through the Asylum was closer and more energetic." Here the attackers could not be halted, because they climbed up through the adjoining apartment buildings that, thanks to a long period of peace, had been allowed to rise so high that their roofs were level with the ground of the Capitol. Hence, says Tacitus with far more restraint than our other sources show, "it is uncertain whether the attackers threw firebrands into these buildings, or if it was the defenders (this is the commoner story) as they tried to dislodge those of the enemy who were climbing up and had reached the top." In either case, the fire spread from these buildings to the porticos attached to the temple of Jupiter Best and Greatest, and because the temple's "eagles," the gables or the pediments that supported the roof, were of ancient wood, they caught fire and the temple burned to the ground, "its doors closed, undefended, and unplundered."

At this point Tacitus halts to deplore the destruction of what was regarded as "the guarantee" of Rome's rule over the world—and not only by Romans. It was news of this disaster that spread Civilis' revolt to the Gallic tribes nearest the Rhine, since the tribesmen too believed that the end of the Capitol meant the end of Rome's empire. In the city the question of the responsibility for the fire was long to be a burning issue, and most of our sources take the easy way out. Two of them insist that the Vitellians burned down the temple (the Elder Pliny and Suetonius), and two more that they plundered it as well (Dio and Josephus). Likewise the restoration of the temple was one of the first subjects on the senate's agenda the moment Vitellius was dead. Tacitus ignores all this. Instead, he uses the destruction of the temple to justify his original claim that the consulship of Galba and Vinius was nearly the last year of Rome's existence. Conceding that this was not the first time the temple had been burnt down in a civil war, he distinguishes clearly—if speciously—between these conflagrations. The fire of July 83 B.C., he declares, was the work of an individual arsonist, a supporter of neither Sulla nor his Marian opponents. But the fire of 69 was a direct result of the crazed ambitions of emperors. Here Tacitus' rhetoric runs away with him. The entire passage is overdone, from the initial claim that Rome was fighting no foreign enemies at the time (his own survey of the empire has disproved that), to his failure to admit at the close that the replacement temple would last only ten years. (It burned down in an accident in 80.)

The fire frightened the defenders far more than the attackers. The Vitellians lacked neither skill nor determination, but the Flavian troops were panicky and their commander sluggish. At first, as if paralyzed mentally, Sabinus could not speak and he would not listen. Even when he pulled himself together, he countermanded orders he had just issued, and he ordered moves he had just forbidden. So, says Tacitus, everybody gave orders and nobody obeyed them, until at last the defenders began to throw away their arms and look for ways to escape. Once the Vitellians broke in, there was total chaos. A few military men of middling rank resisted bravely and were cut down, among them Cornelius Martialis, Sabinus' emissary to Vitellius earlier, and Aemilius Pacensis, once one of the commanders of Otho's maritime expedition. The Vitellians rounded up two of the most prominent men without difficulty, Sabinus himself, unarmed and rooted to the spot, and the consul Quinctius Atticus, who was a particular target because he had tossed leaflets from the hill in which he heaped praise on Vespasian and insults on Vitellius. Dio declares that Caecilius Simplex, the other consul, was present too. This is not unlikely, but if so, he must have been one of the men of rank who managed to escape. Some disguised themselves as slaves. Others slipped away and were smuggled out of the city hidden in the baggage of their clients. Still others, having overheard the Vitellians' password, got away by giving it to the enemy troops or even demanding it from them.

This said, Tacitus devotes a segment of narrative specifically to Domitian, Sabinus, and Quinctius Atticus, to bring out the three very different fates that awaited them. When the Vitellians broke in, Domitian hid in the quarters of the warden of Jupiter's temple (much as Piso had hidden with the sacristan of the temple of Vesta). Then, helped by a clever ex-slave, he put on the linen robes of a devotee of the Egyptian goddess Isis, and joined a procession of her worshippers who were passing through the neighborhood. (We can only conjecture what they were about, but there was a cult of Isis Capitolina.) In this disguise Domitian made his way to the house of a client of his father, and lay low until the fighting ended. Suetonius tells a slightly different story in his *Life* of Domitian, and much has been made of the supposed discrepancies between the two versions. But what concerns Tacitus is not Domitian's itinerary and his perhaps unheroic behavior, but the contrast between the debt he owed to Isis and the payment he made to Jupiter. In his father's reign, says Tacitus, Domitian demolished the sacristan's quarters and put up a small shrine to Jupiter the Life-Saver, its altar embellished with a marble relief that depicted his adventures. Once he was emperor, he dedicated a massive temple to Jupiter the Guardian and set a statue of himself sitting in the lap of the god's cult image. Truly important persons were not saved by foreign deities it seems. Rome's principal god took care of them personally.

Sabinus and Quinctius Atticus, on the other hand, were thrown in chains and taken to Vitellius. Although he was willing to treat them in kindly fashion, neither his troops nor those of the common people who had gathered around approved. The former grumbled noisily, wanting to round off their achievement with two more deaths, and the latter demanded Sabinus' execution with a mixture of threats and flattery. They had their way. Sabinus was decapitated and his headless trunk was dragged to the "Stairs of Lamentation" and exposed there, before being thrown in the Tiber, this being the punishment humble folk liked to see meted out to highborn criminals. "We have heard," says Tacitus, "that the death delighted Mucianus." To this he adds that many thought it in the state's best interests that Sabinus die, since that ended the rivalry between men, one of whom was too conscious of being the emperor's brother, the other too conscious that he had a potential coruler on his hands. The life of Quinctius Atticus was spared, however. Vitellius resisted the calls for his execution, "as if repaying a favor." When Atticus was questioned about the origin of the fire, he accepted the responsibility for it, and "by that confession, or perhaps it was a lie to suit the occasion, shifted the blame and the disgrace off the shoulders of the Vitellians."

While Aulus Vitellius' troops disposed of Sabinus, his brother Lucius took care of the desperadoes in Tarracina. Apinius Tiro had left with the urban cohort shortly before Lucius' attack (18/19 December), and was extorting money and supplies from neighboring towns. His efforts were not very successful, but this probably worried him not at all. The plunder was intended only to let him and his partners continue living high on the hog—as the other two were doing. Julianus, Apollinaris, and the mix of gladiators and marines they commanded were so busy enjoying themselves that the region echoed with their noisy parties, and war was something they discussed only over meals. Though Lucius could have made short work of such opponents anyway, a slave escaped from the town and promised that, if given a small force, he would seize the unguarded citadel and then open the main gates. So Lucius positioned the rest of his troops on the heights overlooking the town and, when the signal was given, "they ran down to a massacre rather than a battle." Caught off guard, the enemy panicked. Though a few gladiators fought bravely, everybody else ran for the ships, including the townsfolk, since the Vitellians were slaughtering them too. Six warships got away, Apollinaris on one of them. The rest were captured on shore or sank under the weight of the refugees who poured aboard. But Julianus was taken prisoner, dragged before Lucius Vitellius, and killed on the spot. Then, to individualize this particular sack, Tacitus adds: "some said that Lucius' wife Triaria put on a soldier's sword and stamped around the town in an arrogant and savage manner." There is no telling whether this is true, but Triaria almost certainly accompanied her husband south, and this is exactly the kind of behavior of which she was thought capable.

Lucius sent a dispatch to his brother to announce his success, but he also asked for instructions, uncertain whether to complete the suppression of the revolt in Campania or to return to Rome. To him it may not have looked as foolish an action as it does to us. The Capitol had fallen, after all, and Antonius' forces were still some way off. In fact, once they had completed their work at Narnia on 16 or 17 December, they advanced only another 12 Roman miles down the Flaminian Way to Ocriculum (Otricoli). This put them 44 miles from the city, and there they halted, in part at least to celebrate the Saturnalia, the Roman winter festival that began on 17 December and ran for five days. Though the festival was observed even by Roman armies, Tacitus declares that "they gave as their pretext for this improper delay that it was to wait for Mucianus." He expands on this by reporting that "some" alleged that Antonius was delaying on purpose, because he had received secret letters from Vitellius in which the latter kept on offering him a consulship, his own daughter in marriage, and a sizable dowry, if only he changed sides. "Others" declared this a fiction, created to ingratiate its originators with Mucianus. "Some more" asserted that the plan agreed on by all the generals was to make a show of force rather than an attack on Rome. To them it seemed likely that Vitellius would give up power, now that his bravest cohorts had changed sides and no other forces could intervene. But this plan was wrecked by Sabinus' rashness and incompetence.

Tacitus refuses to endorse any of these possibilities. Instead, he observes that "it is difficult to lay on any one individual the blame that attached to all." This he substantiates with three points. First, Mucianus kept trying to delay the army with his equivocal letters. Second, Antonius deserved censure, be it for his untimely decision to humor Mucianus or for claiming this as his motive in order to shift the opprobrium onto his rival. And third, all the other generals behaved as if the war was over and turned what should have been a glorious end to their campaign into a disaster. Even the impetuous Petillius Cerialis dawdled, although he was sent on ahead with 1,000 cavalry to make his way across country and reconnoiter the possibilities for entering Rome unopposed by the Salarian Way in the northeastern corner of the city. As a result, it was only the messages from Sabinus that spurred the Flavians into action.

Once they heard that the Capitol was under siege, Antonius marched the rest of his forces down the Flaminian Way at top speed. But as they had 44 miles to cover, they were able to reach only Saxa Rubra (Prima Porta), 9 miles short of their mark, when they learnt that the Capitol had been fired and Sabinus killed. This was not the only bad news. The common people and the slaves, they were told, were being armed to fight for Vitellius. And Petillius Cerialis' cavalry had suffered defeat earlier in the day. Anticipating no opposition as they moved down the Salarian Way, they had run into a force of foot and horse on ground short of the city. The area was a jumble of buildings, gardens, and narrow lanes better known to the Vitellians than to the attackers. Besides,

Cerialis' force included cavalrymen recruited from the Vitellians who had surrendered at Narnia. As a result, his men were routed, and the one thing that saved them was the Vitellians' breaking off the pursuit at Fidenae, 6 miles north of the city.

Though minor, this setback had a disproportionate effect on the morale of the common people in Rome. A few had the proper weaponry, the rest grabbed whatever they could find, and all demanded the signal to march forth to battle. So Vitellius sent them on their way on the morning of 20 December and then, being less sanguine about the likely outcome of their efforts, he called a senate meeting. This picked envoys to approach the enemy forces and urge a peaceful settlement. None of the envoys was treated with due respect, but their reception varied. Not surprisingly, those who went to Petillius Cerialis were handled very roughly. His men not only rejected a settlement out of hand, but also wounded the leader of the delegation, the praetor Arulenus Rusticus. This, says Tacitus, violated not only his status as a magistrate and an envoy, but also "the regard in which he was held as a man." Still, Rusticus was a stiff-necked defender of the senate's rights, selected for this mission probably because he was a partisan of neither Vitellius nor Vespasian. The lictor (attendant) standing next to him was killed when he dared to sweep the crowd aside, and the rest of Rusticus' companions were scattered. At this point, not before time, Cerialis intervened and gave the envoys safe conduct out. Tacitus has perhaps some justification for huffing and puffing that the immunity granted to envoys "even by barbarians" was *almost* violated outside the walls of Rome itself, so strong a hold had "the frenzy of civil strife" taken on the participants.

The envoys who made their way to Antonius were received more calmly, "not because his troops were better disciplined, but because they had more respect for their commander." Whether or not this qualifies as a distinction without a difference, a busybody had grafted himself onto this embassy, Musonius Rufus. A knight and a doctrinaire Stoic (his admirers still call him "the Roman Socrates"), he mingled with the troops and lectured armed men on the blessings of peace and the evils of war. Many thought him a joke, more a bore, but a few wanted to beat him up. They dropped this idea, however, when he abandoned his untimely philosophizing, "heeding the advice of the best behaved and the threats leveled by others." It may also have helped that these envoys were accompanied by the Vestal Virgins. Called upon to act as intermediaries in times of major crisis, they brought a letter from Vitellius to Antonius, asking that he consider a cease-fire for 24 hours. That way, the emperor said, everything could be arranged more easily. The Vestals were dismissed with respect, Vitellius' request was not. The answer given him was that the slaughter of Sabinus and the burning of the Capitol had made negotiations impossible.

Despite his firm answer to the envoys, Antonius called an assembly of his troops and argued that their best plan would be to encamp near the Milvian Bridge just outside the city boundary, and to enter Rome the following day (21 December). He reasoned that the troops were so exasperated that, if they were not given time to calm down, they would do grievous bodily harm to the senate and people, and plunder and burn down the temples and shrines of the gods. But the troops were suspicious that delay would get in the way of their victory, and they had already caught sight of the sun glinting on the standards behind which the common people were advancing. Since this created the impression that an enemy army was about to attack, Antonius was left with no choice but to prepare for battle at once.

He split his troops into three columns, forcing the Vitellians to do the like. The main body continued down the Flaminian Way and across the Milvian Bridge, dispersing the Vitellian "people's army" with a cavalry charge, perhaps at the bridge. Then they ran into the Vitellian column sent to oppose them, but Tacitus gives no details on this, remarking only that as a rule the Vitellians were out-generaled by the Flavians. Antonius' second column made off to the left (west) of the Flaminian Way, and advanced along the bank of the Tiber until it reached the Aurelian Gate. This gave them access to the Campus Martius in the northwest, and here the fighting was heavier, since the Vitellians made one desperate charge after another, and even when they were dislodged from this open ground, they rallied within the city. Antonius' third column took the heaviest casualties. This trekked eastward to the road Cerialis had followed, the Salarian Way, and advanced as far as the Colline Gate on the northeastern side of the city. This area was much more countrified. So the roads were narrow and slick, the Vitellians were able to take up position on top of garden walls, and they held back the attackers with showers of rocks and javelins. Only late in the day were they driven back, after being taken in the rear by a cavalry charge. Even then the surviving Vitellian praetorians from all three columns fell back to their fortified camp on the northeastern corner of the city.

Before Tacitus goes into the details on that, however, he indulges in another burst of rhetorical, even disingenuous, indignation. The common people, he asserts, watched the two sides as they fought their way through the city, and just as if they were at a gladiatorial show, they cheered and applauded first this side, then that, depending on who was winning. And when the defeated hid in shops or took refuge in houses, they demanded that they be dragged out and their throats cut. Then, while the soldiery were intent on slaughtering one another, the people appropriated the greater part of the plunder (this is the only aspect of the situation Dio mentions). Yet it was no more unusual in Roman times than it was in later ages for civilians to gather and watch a battle, though it may have been rare for the spectators to keep their vantage points when the fighting was so close. In any case, this is Tacitus' excuse for enlarging the size of the frame. Savage and grotesque scenes were to be witnessed all over the city, he avers. At one point there were battles and casualties, at another the taverns and baths were doing a roaring trade; at one point, the streets were covered with blood and corpses, at another they were the haunts of "prostitutes and their male counterparts." There were all the vices of a long and affluent peace, and all the outrages committed in taking a town. "In short, you would have thought that this one city was simultaneously maddened by war and drunk with pleasure."

The vividness of this description has induced some to believe that Tacitus witnessed these events. In fact, he is engaging in rhetorical trickery. As the fighting was limited by and large to the northern part of the city, there was no reason why life should not pursue its normal course in the regions untouched by the fighting. Without radio and television to inform them, many inhabitants may not have known or cared what was going on elsewhere, or have believed the reports they heard. And it was the Saturnalia, after all. This does not deter our author. As he puts it, there had been civil war battles in Rome before, three of them during the 80s B.C., and there had been no less cruelty then. But then "there had not been the unnatural indifference of a populace that abandoned its enjoyment not even for a second, as if civil war were one more amusement added to the festivities." Still, his posturing has a point. Belaboring the people's indifference creates the strongest possible contrast with the ferocity the two sides showed in the storming of the praetorian camp, and the high rhetoric devoted to the populace's diversions allows for similar flights to describe this final battle.

The fighting was intense. The fiercest of the Vitellians regarded holding the camp as their last hope, and that made the Flavians—especially Otho's one-time praetorians—still more determined to capture it. Using every means employed to take the strongest cities, siege-sheds, artillery, ramps, and firebrands, the attackers encouraged one other by shouting that capturing the camp would cap all the hard work and all the danger they had undergone. In an interesting mix of the inspirational and the practical, they supposedly told each other that they had restored the city to the senate and people of Rome, and the temples to the gods (thus carrying out Antonius' wishes). The camp was the soldier's crowning glory: this was his country, this his home. And if they failed to take it in the first assault, they would have to spend the night under arms. The Vitellians, on the other hand, were much inferior in numbers and luck, but they did all they could to mar the victory, delay the peace, and defile the barracks with blood and gore. Many fell fatally wounded in the turrets or breathed their last on the battlements of the camp. "When the attackers tore down the gates, the defenders still massed in the entryway and fought on, every one of them falling with his wounds in front and his face turned to the enemy. Even as they died, they were determined that their deaths be glorious."

Once the city had been taken (but before the camp was stormed), Vitellius slipped out of the back of the palace, and set off in a litter for the family's house on the Aventine (accompanied only by his baker and his cook, Suetonius tells us). He planned to stay hidden there until nightfall, and then to find refuge with his brother and the praetorian cohorts at Tarracina. But he changed his mind, seemingly almost at once, and—according to Tacitus—because he was in the kind of panic where everything frightened him but his current predicament terrified him most. So he returned to the palace. Though huge, it was completely deserted. Even the humblest of his slaves had run off or scuttled away rather than face him. The silence and the solitude unnerved him. He tried closed doors and shuddered at the emptiness of the rooms beyond. Finally, worn out by his wretchedness and his aimless wanderings, he concealed himself in "a shameful hiding place," and from this he was dragged by the tribune Julius Placidus (the man is otherwise unknown). "His hands were tied behind his back, his clothes were torn, and—a shameful spectacle— he was led through the streets. Many of the bystanders abused him, none pitied him. The ugliness of his end had destroyed all compassion. One of his German soldiers swung at him with his sword, but it is uncertain whether he did so in anger, or to put him out of his misery, or he may have been aiming at the tribune. He sliced off the tribune's ear and was promptly cut down himself."

Such is Tacitus' account of Vitellius' last hours, often discounted as fiction, because we cannot know what Vitellius was doing in the palace if there were no witnesses. This is silly. Obviously, Tacitus is giving us a historical reconstruction, but unless Vitellius simply curled up into a fetal ball, there was not much else he could have done, so long as he clung to life. Besides, Tacitus is trying to achieve an effect that occurs to neither Suetonius nor Dio, to view the situation through the emperor's eyes. Since Vitellius refused to commit suicide, a point Tacitus chooses not to bring up, he must have been truly terrified, and this helps explain, among other things, why the imperial palace grows so much in size at this point. The structure Tacitus describes is far closer to Nero's Golden

House than it is to the relatively poky affair the Julio-Claudians inherited from Augustus. Similarly, it is not the decorum of historiography alone that induces Tacitus to suppress the sordid details of the emperor's hiding place. According to Suetonius, Vitellius hid in a janitor's closet, pulling a bed and a mattress across the door; according to Dio it was a room where the watch dogs were kept, and one of them bit the emperor. So too with Tacitus' failure to report that the troops who entered the palace failed at first to recognize their ruler, another unflattering detail preserved by Suetonius and Dio. And so too, again, with his omitting the tale that Vitellius made a last attempt to wriggle out of trouble by claiming to possess "important information fit only for Vespasian's ears," yet another of Suetonius' touches. In fact, Tacitus demonstrates a compassion for the emperor shown neither by the bystanders at the time nor later by the other sources.

This same attitude informs the rest of his narrative, as emerges from the contrasting ways in which Tacitus and Dio tackle Vitellius' last minutes on earth. To judge by Xiphilinus' summary of Dio, and by Suetonius' slightly shorter and differently accentuated account, Dio followed the stock line and played up the theme how the mighty had fallen. "So they led down from the palace the Caesar who had lived there so luxuriously; along the Sacred Way they dragged the emperor who had often been carried past in his imperial litter, and to the Forum they took the Augustus who had often made speeches to the people there. Some struck at him, some pulled at his beard [Vitellius cannot have had time to shave]; all made fun of him, and insulted him, commenting especially on his prodigality since he had a pot belly. When he lowered his eyes in shame, the soldiers prodded him under the chin with their swords, to make him look up again." On this follows his version of the attack by the German soldier, to whom he attributes only a wish to put Vitellius out of his misery. In this account, as in Suetonius', Vitellius is the spectacle for everybody else to view. Tacitus' briefer version takes a different tack. Having already explored this theme in—or even relocated it to—his description of Vitellius' abdication, he has the soldiery make Vitellius raise his head to face the insults, to watch his statues being toppled, and to look again and again on the Rostra (where he had made his speech of abdication), or on the site of Galba's murder (which he had precipitated by his bid for power). Then they drag him to the Stairs of Lamentation where the headless corpse of Flavius Sabinus had been exposed. Having remarked earlier that this was indeed a shameful spectacle, Tacitus once again invites the reader to see the situation through Vitellius' eyes. The theme may be how the mighty are fallen, but his point is that no emperor, not even Vitellius, deserved to be treated like this.

Tacitus makes his approach explicit by recording the last comment Vitellius made before falling under a shower of blows. To a tribune who insulted him he replied, showing no ignoble spirit, that even so he had been the man's emperor. Dio, to be sure, tells this story in much the same way, but he undermines the effect by reporting that the troops cut off Vitellius' head and paraded it around the city, leaving his wife Galeria to give the remains proper burial. For his part, Suetonius knows nothing of any last words, and this is probably a deliberate omission, since he doted on collecting these remarks. Instead he has the body dragged on a hook to the Tiber and tossed in. Tacitus omits not only all such details but even this approach to the material. He sets up a contrast between an emperor who was capable of showing a not ignoble spirit and the mob that reviled Vitellius in death with the same viciousness with which they had fawned on him in life. It is a telling way of skewering both the malicious delight of the onlookers and the attitude of the earlier historians whose accounts Tacitus had criticized in his prologue.[7]

Just as the implication of all these remarks is that Vitellius did not deserve such treatment, so the theme of deserts holds together the obituary Tacitus devotes to him. The emperor gained his consulship, his priesthoods, and his place among the leading men of Rome through no efforts of his own, but by virtue of his father's distinction. He was offered the principate by men who did not know him. And few commanders of good character won the enthusiastic support of the armies to the degree Vitellius won it by his worthlessness. Yet he was open and generous, even if self-destructively so. Since he thought friendships were won by magnificent gifts rather than consistent behavior, he deserved rather than held onto them. It was undoubtedly in the state's best interests that he die, but those who betrayed Vitellius to Vespasian could not claim credit for their treachery, when they had deserted Galba for Vitellius. Vitellius should never have become emperor, but no more did he deserve so ignominious a death, even if it was in everybody's interest that he die. Despite all the criticism to which Tacitus has been subjected for his portrayal of Vitellius, it is a fair epitaph for a man whose death late on 20 December left Vespasian undisputed emperor of Rome.

Conclusion

The killing of Vitellius late on 20 December ended the war, but it did not bring peace. Tacitus remarks that Domitian emerged from hiding as soon as it was safe, was hailed "Caesar" by the victorious Flavian troops, and was escorted to his father's house. This merely underlines that what was safe for Domitian was not safe for others, whatever their rank. The magistrates were too scared even to call an emergency meeting of the senate. Flavian troops began roaming the city, hunting down the last Vitellians, killing innocent victims too, and, once they had sated their bloodlust, looting on the same grand scale as they had at Cremona. And ordinary citizens joined in, some of them—according to Dio—masquerading as Flavian soldiers in order to save their own skins. Dio's further claim that "the casualties during these days were as many as 50,000" is clearly an exaggeration, but not perhaps quite as flagrant as it looks.

The Flavian leaders did—maybe could do—little or nothing to control their men. Domitian was escorted to the palace the next day (21 December), but there he indulged in riotous parties celebrating his survival. The new, perhaps self-appointed prefect of the praetorian guard was Arrius Varus, and he was almost certainly too busy trying to reorganize the guard to have time to restore law and order outside the camp. And real power rested with Antonius, who allegedly spent his time helping himself to cash and slaves from the imperial household. The chaos began to abate only when news arrived that Lucius Vitellius was on his way back from Tarracina with his six cohorts. Unwilling to draw attention to the fact, or to the attendant irony, that here too Lucius did something to benefit Rome, Tacitus makes the Flavians' organizing themselves for battle the product of frenzied pleas from the city they were so busy terrorizing. The result was an anticlimax. Lucius surrendered without a fight, his praetorians were disarmed and led through the streets of Rome, and Lucius himself was put to death.

This did little to restore normal conditions. Yet the senate was able to persuade itself that peace was nigh: "now that the civil wars had worked their way through every province and every army from one end of the empire to the other, the entire world had been, as it were, cleansed of its madness." Safe in this delusion, says Tacitus, the members attended a meeting on 21 December, and quickly fell to quarreling amongst themselves with their customary gusto. Vespasian was recognized as the new emperor, naturally. Mucianus was voted triumphal ornaments for his success in Moesia, and the other Flavian leaders, Domitian included, were granted assorted distinctions. Then the senators passed a resolution to restore the Temple of Jupiter Best and Greatest. According to senatorial etiquette, matters affecting the gods were to be taken up first, but on this occasion the members were confronted with a letter from Vespasian, and prudence as well as self-interest dictated that it be put at the head of the agenda and discussed with a show of unanimity. Once they turned to the restoration of the temple, the stiff-necked Helvidius Priscus threw a wrench in the works. So was Rome robbed of any guidance, says Tacitus: the defeated Vitellians grumbled, the victorious Flavians got nothing done, and later senate meetings bogged down in petty quibbles and pointless recriminations. In Tacitus' words, "there was no emperor, and there were no laws."

What changed the situation was Mucianus' arrival with his army, in the first week of January 70 apparently. Within days he settled everybody's hash, acting throughout like a plenipotentiary. Dio asserts that he had a signet ring given him for the purpose by Vespasian, but he would probably have behaved this way with or without authorization. Domitian Mucianus neutralized him by taking him firmly under his own wing. Arrius Varus he switched from prefect of the guard to prefect of the grain supply, a demotion but not a marked one, since a man with energy to spare was needed to deal with the food shortages from which Rome was suffering as a result of all the extra military mouths to feed. And Antonius he took out of play, first by dangling before his eyes the prospect of becoming governor of Tarraconensis in place of Cluvius Rufus, and then by sending him off to Vespasian. Assorted other aristocrats were removed too, among them Piso Galerianus, a son of the Piso who had headed the conspiracy against Nero in 65. He was "taken for a ride" some 40 miles down the Appian Way and then "persuaded" to commit suicide, a move that amply fulfilled its programmatic intention of cowing the senate. And the troops who had been Antonius' foremost supporters were given their marching orders: III Gallica, which had been billeted for a while in Capua to punish the town for backing Vitellius, was returned to Syria without delay; VII Galbiana was sent back to Pannonia with the same dispatch; VIII Augusta, XI Claudia, and XIII Gemina were bundled off to Lower Germany, to form part of the huge army Petillius Cerialis was marshaling against the rebels under Julius Civilis. Thus, says Tacitus, "the laws regained their force, the magistrates their functions."

Vigorous as they were, these measures settled only the most pressing problems. Vespasian would announce presently that he needed 40,000 million sesterces to get the empire back on its feet, but he would not reach Rome for another ten months. (As best we can tell, he arrived between September and November 70.) By then Mucianus had taken care of much more dirty work, including the execution of Vitellius' son. His claim that the boy was a threat to peace looks specious, when we take into account the fact that Otho's nephew Cocceianus would live on into the early 90s, but Cocceianus was never proclaimed heir to the throne. Besides, Mucianus' removal of Vitellius' son left Vespasian free to present himself in a more merciful light, as he did by finding a dowry and a suitable husband for Vitellius' daughter. The first question we need to address, however, is whether the civil wars of 68/69 lived up to the billing Tacitus gives them, whether the year that opened with the consulship of Galba and Titus Vinius truly was "very nearly the last year of Rome's existence."

The general statements made by the literary sources suggest that every part of the empire suffered enormously during these upheavals. This is another exaggeration. There was scarcely a province untouched in some way by the fighting over the throne, and in many there was loss of life and destruction of property. But in most areas the damage was neither catastrophic nor irreparable. The province Africa, for example, suffered for a few months in 68 from the attentions of the legate Clodius Macer, a small-time tyrant as Tacitus calls him, and later there would be a miniwar between the rival cities of Lepcis Magna (Lebdah) and Oea (Tripoli). The two Mauretanian provinces witnessed the murder of their governor, Lucceius Albinus, while the inhabitants of Corsica participated in the forcible removal of theirs, Picarius Decumus. There was disorder in Britain, where the legionary legates drove out their governor and quarreled among themselves, a situation of which the Brigantes took advantage to throw off their allegiance to Rome. Yet little came of all this, and the campaigning that began in the island in 71 was carried out in areas north of the province's frontiers. There was Caecina's bloodthirsty march through the territory of the Helvetii in spring 69. There was the pseudo-Nero who managed to terrorize a single Aegean island, Cythnus, likewise in the early spring of 69. There was the uprising masterminded by Anicetus in Pontus that led to piratical activity along the southern coast of the Black Sea later in the year, and Josephus tells us that other pirates took advantage of the Jewish Revolt to operate out of Joppa. Finally, Syria and Asia Minor were subjected to Mucianus' money-raising efforts. But while most of this would likely not have happened, had the emperor in Rome not been distracted by the need to fight off another contender for the throne, none of it warrants talk of threats to Rome's existence.

From that perspective only four areas suffered major damage and serious loss of life, and we can take them in what the Romans would have considered an ascending order, from the least to the most serious. The Jewish Revolt, then, was obviously a catastrophe, albeit a catastrophe that was a distraction from rather than a result of the civil wars. As it happened, Vespasian swiftly forced the rebels to take refuge in this town or that, and proceeded methodically to capture those towns one by one. If the conflict lasted longer and caused more suffering than it need have done, that was due to the virtual cessation of military activity during 69. But though the fighting cost the Romans casualties, especially after Titus took command, and the destruction lost them revenues, there was never any doubt that the Romans would prevail.

In Moesia the situation probably looked less immediately worrying, but it was taken more seriously. Hence Otho's reaction to the victory gained over the Rhoxolani in the winter of 68/69, and the haste with which Antonius dispatched ex-Vitellian legions to the province after the sack of Cremona. After this came the incursion Mucianus had to beat off and the defeat of Fonteius Agrippa in the winter of 69/70. It matters little that different tribes mounted these raids across the Danube. The important consideration is that, whatever the cause for it, there was serious unrest among the peoples on the northern bank of the river. This was a danger that would force the Flavian emperors over time to switch their attention—and their legions—from the Rhine to the Danube line, and it was a danger that Trajan would decide eventually to remove by conquering Dacia in two costly, full-scale wars at the start of the second century.

In Gaul and the two Germanies, the military districts alongside the Rhine, the situation was manifestly much worse. Gaul suffered repeatedly, in fact, one area after another, and this was the wealthiest of Rome's western provinces. In 68 there was Vindex's unsuccessful siege of Lugdunum and the slaughter of Vesontio. In 69 the Riviera coast suffered from the attentions of Otho's maritime expedition and the Vitellian detachments sent to oppose them. Meanwhile, if we believe Tacitus' lurid account, there was the devastation Valens' march caused between Colonia Agrippinensis in the north and the Alps in the south. Perhaps as a side effect of all this there was the small-scale disturbance created by the Boian Mariccus, who raided the territory of the Aedui for a while. And northern Gaul, Belgica, the least developed area, suffered most when the situation got out of hand at the end of the year. Once the tribesmen

heard of the firing of the Capitol in December 69, they threw in with
Julius Civilis and his Batavians. This caused major devastation in the two
German districts as well, and led to the destruction of two Roman legions (I Germanica and XV Primigenia), and eventually to Vespasian's
cashiering two more (IV Macedonica and XVI), for all that he absorbed
some of the surviving Vitellians into two new legions (IV Flavia Felix
and XVI Flavia Firma). Besides this, the area was reduced only by hard
fighting, which had to be conducted by nine legions, divided between
Petillius Cerialis and the ex-Othonian Annius Gallus, and lasted all
through 70. After it was all over, no less than three legionary camps
along the Rhine had to be rebuilt, Novaesium (Neuss), Bonna (Bonn),
and Mogontiacum (Mainz), while a fourth, Vetera (Xanten), was not only
rebuilt but relocated too.

Finally, there was Italy, and another of Tacitus' reasons for confin-
ing his account largely to the events of 69. As he says apropos of Otho's
departure from Rome in March, it was the flooding of the Tiber, the
shortage of grain, and the tight money supply that first brought home
the seriousness of the situation to people in the city. Most of the strife in
68 they had been able to ignore because it took place in provinces;
Vindex's revolt could be passed off as a foreign war; and horrendous as it
must have been to witness, the massacre of the marines at the Milvian
Bridge could be discounted as an isolated incident. In 69, by contrast,
war not only came to Italy but stayed too.

South of Rome the damage seems to have been minor. Capua was
punished by having III Gallica billeted on it, but only for a few weeks.
Tarracina no doubt suffered more severely (Tacitus reports only that
the slave who had betrayed the town to Lucius Vitellius was crucified for
his pains), but it too recovered. North of Rome, on the other hand, not a
season passed without misfortune. In the spring, there was the damage
to towns along the western coast done by Otho's maritime expedition,
and Caecina's assault on Placentia. In the summer, when Vitellius relocated the defeated Othonians after Bedriacum, there was the firing of
part of Augusta Taurinorum (Turin), and the emperor's locustlike
progress from Bedriacum to Rome, not to mention the brief uproar created in the northeastern corner of the peninsula (Histria) by the runaway slave Geta. And in the fall there was the campaign by Antonius
Primus' troops, a campaign that must have damaged other towns before
as well as after the sack of Cremona. As for Cremona itself, Tacitus reports that the city was rebuilt thanks to the generosity of its leading citizens, but as Guy Chilver observed long ago, "the rebuilding . . . must
have been only nominal, since there are few remains and the scanty inscriptions are almost all of the period before A.D. 69."

As Tacitus says, Vespasian encouraged the Cremonans to rebuild their city, but gave them no financial assistance. In this, however, Vespasian was not merely exhibiting his tightfistedness. It looks as though he was also refusing to accept responsibility for the disaster, and he was certainly acting on the basis of a widespread conviction that the city's destruction was insignificant by comparison with the damage done in Rome. There, having survived both the praetorian mutiny and the natural disasters that coincided with Otho's departure in March, the people took his suicide with remarkable equanimity. It did not last. Vitellius billeted his army all over the city, and the people had but a brief respite when Caecina took most of the men north in September. In December there was the sack of the Capitol and the reappearance of soldiery in huge numbers, and this time there was fighting in the streets and looting everywhere. This is one reason why Vespasian and his sons launched an ambitious building program. Besides the restoration of the temple of Jupiter Best and Greatest (Vespasian himself took a prominent role in the initial stages), new structures were erected aplenty. It was no accident that one of the first was the Temple of Peace vowed in 71.

We can declare the Romans parochial for viewing the situation exclusively in terms of what happened in their own city, but the center of any self-respecting empire is supposed to enjoy the benefits provided by its dependencies, not to suffer from the ills its rule or misrule generates. Besides, speculative as such an inquiry may look, there is the question of how much psychological damage these wars did to the inhabitants of Rome. On a grand scale, so we could argue, the very fact that Augustus' dynasty had lasted for a century had created an impression of stability and order that the citizenry expected to last, if not forever, at least far into the future. They may not have cared to be ruled by an eccentric like Caligula or a degenerate like Nero, but even the worst excesses of the Julio-Claudians cannot have prepared them for the game of musical thrones that began in June 68. Small wonder that the senators in December 69 so happily embraced the idea that "now that the civil wars had worked their way through every province and every army from one end of the empire to the other, the entire world had been . . . cleansed of its madness."

Whether the "ordinary Roman in the street" would have thought in such terms is another matter. But it is probably unwise to assume that his everyday life proceeded normally throughout this period either. Suetonius declares that by the time Vespasian arrived in Rome, the courts were so clogged with unheard lawsuits that extraordinary measures were needed to clear the logjam. What neither he nor any other source mentions is the still more prosaic subject of criminal activity. Given that the praetorian and urban cohorts—the primary guarantors of civil order—were as often absent from Rome in 69 as they were present, there is no reason to think that, just because there was a war on, there was a cessation of "normal" criminal activity, as distinct from the political crimes on which emperors focused and the military crimes to which Tacitus gave space. Some 50 years later the satirist Juvenal derived considerable amusement from the fact that the Pontine Marshes south of Rome served as a kind of ancient Sherwood Forest, and that every time troops were sent to sweep the area, the "career criminals" migrated to Rome and exercised their skills there during the troops' absence. The to-ing and fro-ing of the armed forces in 69 should have made it a banner year for criminals. Those inclined to antisocial behavior could mask their activities as military operations when the troops were present, and conduct them unmolested when the troops were away. This cannot have encouraged a sense of security in citizens at any level of society in Rome.

Yet if Tacitus' verdict is to this extent less far-fetched than we might fancy, it does not justify our concluding that the Romans would be haunted for years by their suffering. The Romans had longer memories than we do, in good measure because they had to rely on them much more. But when the Flavians bent their every effort to convincing people that 68/69 had been only a momentary hiccup in Rome's glorious history, it is hardly surprising that the evidence does not support a number of themes stressed in the recent past. Consider, for a start, the phenomenon of which Tacitus himself was a beneficiary, the shake-up in the governing class that supposedly robbed the republican families of their hitherto unchallenged preeminence. It is one thing to observe of the social standing of the emperors thrown up in 68/69 that "the premium on ancestry fell sharply." It is quite another to translate this lapidary comment by Sir Ronald Syme into a sociopolitical revolution, in which the right to claim the throne shifted from the old republican aristocracy through the new Augustan nobility to arriviste Julio-Claudian functionaries. Though all the Julio-Claudian emperors could trace their ancestry back to republican families, there were few enough of them left when Augustus became master of the Roman world in 31 B.C., let alone when he died 44 years later. In this light the reign of Galba looks more like the last gasp of the republican aristocracy—and an excellent reason for ensuring that men like him and his heir, Piso Licinianus, were never given another chance to occupy the throne. Galba was an anachronism in more ways even than Tacitus thought.

It is no more significant that Otho and Vitellius came from the new nobility brought to the fore by the Augustan settlement. By 69 such men were probably the largest segment in the senatorial class, no matter what level they had reached inside the élite. Otho, however, was hamstrung by his inability to win the trust of his peers in the senate, thanks largely to the methods he had used to remove Galba. And if Vitellius was the least suited member of his generation to take the throne, his failings merely confirmed the lesson the Romans should have learnt from Galba, not to mention the four Julio-Claudians, that ancestry need not be synonymous with ability. Yet neither this nor Vitellius' inability to present Rome with a functioning, adult heir made it inevitable that his successor would come from a family whose nobility was freshly minted in the Julio-Claudian period. No ineluctable historical process put Vespasian on the throne. He became emperor because he was the last man standing, and he was the last man standing because so few took him seriously beforehand. As emperor, it is true, he delighted in his humble origins. Perhaps he was struck by the irony that once he had no more wanted to be a senator than Vitellius had wanted to be an emperor. More probably, he was so proud of his success, achieved against all the odds, that he thought it ridiculous to try at 60 years of age to pass himself off as what he was not. Either way, his accession still astonished Romans 50 years later, as is evidenced by the profuse apologies for the obscurity of those origins with which Suetonius prefaces his *Life*.

Now let us turn to the military aspects of the "secret of empire" of which Tacitus talks. This may seem a more promising theme, not only because this secret should have been harder to conceal again, once it had been revealed, but also because the danger should have become more acute after Vespasian legalized his seizure of power by making acclamation by the troops a constitutional principle in the final clause of the "Law on Vespasian's Powers." This way of thinking has prompted weighty pronouncements that the civil wars of 68/69 "gave warning that if once an army had broken its oath of loyalty to an emperor, it might make light of its engagements to all future rulers."[1] Such assertions cannot be taken seriously. Although major upheavals followed Commodus' murder in 192 and 50 years of near anarchy began with the assassination of Severus Alexander in 235, to see the upheavals of 68/69 as a precursor of these events plays fast and loose with the historical facts to a degree inexcusable even in the cliché-ridden "documentaries" on Rome that supposedly reputable television channels cannot resist airing. Conditions changed drastically in the intervening century or so, and this fact cannot be undermined by appealing to Tiberius' famous remark that "he was holding a wolf by the ears." It is irrelevant. The context in which Suetonius sets this dictum shows that Tiberius was talking, not about the armed forces specifically, but about running the empire, and not about the difficulties

of hanging onto power but those of abdicating it. It was abdication that
exposed an emperor to dangers on every side.[2]

So let us ask a very basic question: were the legionaries truly such
ferocious specimens that an emperor had cause to fear them, should they
escape from his control? Tacitus seems never to tire of portraying
Vitellius' legionaries as barbarians, either Germanic tribesmen or recruits who were no better than tribesmen. He draws similarly invidious
contrasts between Antonius' legionaries and the conduct of armies in
the republican period, most notably in the story of the soldier who killed
his brother and demanded a reward for it. These too are red herrings,
based on two interrelated claims, first, that (some) imperial legionaries
were so foreign that they qualified as barbarians with no awareness of
Roman values, and second, that whatever the troops' reasons for fighting, genuine devotion to Rome was not amongst them.

The legionaries of 68/69 were long-term professionals in an all-
volunteer force, and to that extent they stood apart from the rest of the
population. But no matter what precise level the recruits occupied in their
communities beforehand, many still came from Italy, and most of those
who did not were drawn—as inscriptions indicate—from the more civilized and settled areas of provinces like Spain, southern Gaul or Syria.
The troops stationed on the Rhine and Danube frontiers had little contact
with civilians, it is true, and so little awareness of or time for the usages of
polite society. But this was not, as Tacitus seems to believe, a function of
their being legionaries. After all, he depicts Mucianus' legionaries in Syria
as model citizens. Yet they were no more and no less Roman than the men
on the northern frontiers, even if their being billeted in the towns made
them more considerate of civilians. As for the legionaries' supposed lack of
devotion to Rome, the troops expressed their allegiance in much the same
way in republic and principate. In the early principate, from Tiberius'
reign on, the troops swore an oath to the emperor on 1 January every year.
But the troops had sworn allegiance to their generals in the republic too,
not to the state as such. It had been the loyalty of the general to the republic that had formed the link between troops and state. And just as the failure of that link had produced the warlordism that destroyed the republic,
so the failure of that link produced four emperors in 68/69. To us the
imperial legions may look more threatening than the short-term,
semimercenary forces of the late republic, because they formed a standing
army permanently on call. In fact, they were less of a threat—unless they
were both thoroughly discontented and given a strong lead by a dissident
legionary legate or general. Then, and only then, the disintegration of
their ordered world encouraged them to gratify their own transient, short-
term interests as well.

This is why there is no convincing evidence that the Flavian emperors—let alone their successors—were hagridden by fears that the legions would turn on them. The Flavians undeniably paid more attention and gave more consideration to the armed forces—legions and praetorian guard alike—than previous rulers had done, but this was as it should be.[3] It was no credit to Nero that one reason for Vitellius' being thought eager to become emperor lay in his showing unusual concern for the welfare of his officers and men. And it was no more credit to Galba that Otho was able so easily to suborn noncommissioned officers in the praetorian guard. The Flavians learnt the lesson. Not only did they restore discipline, they also took care to ensure that the troops had better quarters (sometimes of necessity, but not invariably so), that they had all the necessary equipment to carry out their duties, and that the number of troops in the ranks approximated the number on the rolls. Domitian even gave the legionaries a pay raise in 83, the first they had received since Julius Caesar's day.

It is no obstacle that there was a revolt against Domitian in 89. Although the evidence is scanty, it is reasonably certain that its instigator, Lucius Antonius Saturninus, governor of Upper Germany, took action because the emperor had denounced him publicly as a "queer" (*scortum*). The rebellion certainly never amounted to anything. When Saturninus came out into the open on 1 January 89, he was supported by only two of the four legions in his province, those stationed with him in Mogontiacum, and he as good as took them hostage by seizing the military chest that contained their savings. Furthermore, the revolt was crushed and Saturninus killed inside two weeks, and neither of the legions involved was punished severely. They may not even have fought hard for him in the first place. They undoubtedly continued as functioning units, even if they were shifted to the Danube frontier within a year or so.

The praetorians, the "flower of Italy's youth" as Otho calls them in two of his Tacitean speeches, are usually charged with venality, largely because Tacitus harps so relentlessly on their resentment at Galba's failure to pay the donative Nymphidius had promised. Again the picture is overdrawn. It was not the donative alone that induced the guard to abandon Nero, nor could they be persuaded to abandon Galba for Nymphidius. And if they ended up deserting Galba for Otho, Galba was hardly the innocent victim solely of a lust for cash. Otho paid no donative to the guard as a whole until after the mutiny a month or more into his reign. Vitellius never paid them one, though he compensated them in other ways. And Vespasian gave the guard only a minimal donative. By same token, fear did not lead Vespasian to reduce the guard to nine cohorts of 500 men, the establishment set up originally by Augustus. Had that been his motive, he would never have allowed any Vitellians to keep their membership in the new units, as inscriptions prove that he did, and no more would Domitian have added a tenth cohort. What animated Vespasian was an economy drive. When the annual pay of a praetorian before 83 was a minimum of 750 denarii (HS 3,000), reducing their numbers from 12,000 to 4,500 saved at least HS 22.5 million a year. This may have been a drop in the bucket compared to the 40,000 million sesterces Vespasian claimed to need to put the empire back on its feet, but it was a large drop, and it could be done quickly, whereas the empire-wide census he launched to uncover fresh sources of revenue took time to conduct.

This does not end the matter. Not only did the praetorian guard not cause trouble for Vespasian and his sons. They were neither involved in nor gratified by the palace intrigue that led to Domitian's murder in September 96. In fact, they wanted the assassins executed, but their two prefects took a different view. Whether they participated in the plot or merely gave it their blessing, they left the guardsmen leaderless. In October 97, however, Nerva appointed a new prefect, Casperius Aelianus, and he took the men's side. This produced a mutiny, in which the guard clamored for and at last secured the punishment of the conspirators. It also persuaded Nerva to adopt as his heir the nearest military commander, Trajan in Upper Germany. Understandably, these developments have been seen as a crisis that both revived memories of Nymphidius' antics in 68 and prompted Tacitus to compose the *Histories*. But no matter how attractive this scenario may look, it is unconvincing. Like Galba, Nerva was in his sixties, but since he was also a compromise—and compromised— emperor, his grip on power was much weaker. So his adopting Trajan was indeed part of a major power play, but that power play took place within the senatorial aristocracy. The mutiny was a sideshow, and there is no evidence that Nerva had to pay the guardsmen a donative to restore order or regain their loyalty.[4]

Too much, it seems clear, has been read into Tacitus' comment that "an emperor could be made elsewhere than in Rome." He was not asserting that emperors would be made elsewhere than in Rome on a regular basis, nor that they should be. So if we are to draw valid conclusions from the wars of 68/69, we might do better to consider another of his comments, that the reigns of Nerva and Trajan brought in an era when, for the first time in years, "you can think what you like, and say what you think." Fact or compliment, this statement highlights an altogether more significant theme, the servility of the senate under the emperors. It was, after all, from the senate that most of the senior officers and commanders of Rome's armed forces were drawn, and if these men had not the intestinal fortitude to stand up to their emperor, there was virtually no prospect that the rankers would.

Though the senate had never lacked for time-servers, right up to the last days of the republic senior members felt free to express their opinions on important matters. Although Octavian claimed repeatedly that Cleopatra, aided and abetted by the renegade Antony, was planning to establish a tyranny in Rome, for example, both consuls for 32 B.C. and some 200 senior men left the city to join these purported enemies of the state. After Actium, by contrast, senators proved more reluctant to voice their real thoughts even on trivialities. Their behavior so frustrated Augustus that he would flounce out of debates in a huff (or so Suetonius says), and led Tiberius sourly to declare the senate a body of men born to serve rather than to rule. The death of Nero and the end of the Julio-Claudian dynasty produced no change, as Tacitus demonstrates by devoting so much space in the *Histories* to the senate's showing signs of life mostly when an emperor was not present to breathe down its collective neck. In these interludes, as he also makes clear, senators indulged repeatedly in irresponsible, score-settling debates. This was just about all they did in the months between Nero's suicide and Galba's arrival in Rome, during Otho's absence in the north, between Otho's death and Vitellius' arrival in the city, and between Vitellius' execution and the arrival of Mucianus.

This is not to imply that there were no powerbrokers behind the scenes (Mucianus was a prime example in Vespasian's reign) or, for that matter, that the knights were any more enterprising: they just lacked an assembly in which to exhibit such foolishness. For our purposes, the important point is the effect this behavior pattern had on senators and knights when the emperor sent them off to govern provinces or entrusted them with military commands. Two tendencies emerged, both of them extreme. Most of these men never considered defying their emperor. Hence, for example, they readily turned over to the authorities the letters Vindex sent out in the winter of 67/68. But a handful went to the opposite extreme. No more hostile than their peers to the principate as institution, they sensed weaknesses they could exploit and, determined to become powerbrokers in their own right, they emerged as the loose cannons of their day. The majority, unsurprisingly, died in the attempt, among them Vindex, Titus Vinius, Fabius Valens, and Nymphidius Sabinus. But four survived. The risk-taking Cornelius Fuscus settled down and became prefect of the guard under Domitian. Helvidius Priscus resumed his career as the noisiest critic of every emperor from Nero on, until the otherwise equable Vespasian put him to death in 75. And Aulus

Caecina and Antonius Primus were sidelined. Vespasian may perhaps have made them members of his advisory council, the *consilium principis*, but if so, he acted probably on the adage that one should keep one's friends close but one's enemies closer. Like Verginius Rufus, no loose cannon but for all that a man who had once been thought worthy of the throne, they received no other employment. Caecina would last ten more years before being executed by Titus in 79, allegedly for involvement in a conspiracy against Vespasian in his last days. Antonius was living in retirement in his hometown of Tolosa (Toulouse) around the close of Domitian's reign. And it was Nerva who resurrected Verginius Rufus, and Tacitus who delivered the funeral oration over the man 30 years after his "15 minutes of fame."

Against this we have to set the fact that Vespasian and his sons promoted a slew of men whose records were no less suspect, but whose conduct was at least more submissive. Some owed their status to Nero, like Rubrius Gallus, who sold out Nero to Galba and Vitellius to Vespasian, and yet was given the command in Moesia after Fonteius Agrippa's death. Some had been brought to the fore by Galba, for example, the two "rich old men" Tampius Flavianus and Pompeius Silvanus. Neither emerged creditably from the upheavals of 68/69, but each received a second consulship. There were Othonians like Suedius Clemens, the commander of the maritime expedition. He was prefect of the camp (*praefectus castrorum*) to the two legions stationed in Egypt by November 79, as we know from a graffito scratched on the statue of Memnon at Thebes (Karnak). There were Vitellians like Caecina's co-conspirator, Lucilius Bassus, who was made not only a senator but governor of Judaea in 71. There were even close associates of Antonius, most notably his right-hand man, Arrius Varus. Varus would fall from grace, but it looks as if he was brought down by score settling on the part of the daughter of Corbulo, the general he had traduced in Nero's reign. Another formidable personality, Domitia Longina became Domitian's wife in 70. Even so, it seems clear that Vespasian thought he had found a much simpler, more practical solution to the problems of 68/69 than modern theoreticians care to embrace, namely, to ensure that important posts in the new regime were not given to manifest loose cannons or—in Verginius' case—to men who had ever been thought worthy of the throne. We lack the evidence to declare his diagnosis either wrong or even wrong-headed.

Appendix 1:
The Principal Sources for 68/69

Rather than clutter the main narrative with details on the background of the ancient literary sources for the Year of the Four Emperors, I have tried to include in this appendix enough material to enable readers to orient themselves, should they wish to pursue questions of fact or interpretation raised by my handling of these writers. The five surviving sources—Josephus, Plutarch, Tacitus, Suetonius, and Dio—are discussed in the chronological order in which they wrote. I have added brief remarks on two lost accounts, the so-called common source, and the memoir by Vipstanus Messalla.

Josephus

Most of our information on Joseph ben Matthias (Titus Flavius Josephus) derives from his own writings, and on sensitive issues they are as equivocal as was his behavior at the time. He was born in Jerusalem in 37/38, about a year after Tiberius recalled Pontius Pilate from Judaea. The son of a priest and, on his mother's side, of royal blood too, he was given a thorough grounding in his religion, at the end of which he threw in with the Pharisees. In 64 he traveled to Rome for the first time, to help some priests who had been sent for trial before Nero, but the main effect of his mission was to convince him of Rome's might. So when the Jewish Revolt broke out in 66, he tried at first to persuade his compatriots not to rebel and, when that failed, to take part in such a way as to control and guide their fanaticism (his words). Hence he commanded a rebel force in Galilee in the first half of 67. When Vespasian advanced, most of the troops deserted, and Josephus and the others willing to stand their ground took refuge in Jotapata. The town fell in July, after a 47-day siege, and Josephus was made prisoner. Taken before Vespasian, he prophesied that the Roman would "soon" become master of the world. The story appears also in Suetonius and Dio, but Josephus adds that Vespasian was unimpressed at first. Only after he had been proclaimed emperor in July

69 was Josephus set free. He witnessed Titus' sack of Jerusalem in September 70, and he accompanied him to Rome. There, as a Roman citizen and a Flavian pensioner, he devoted the rest of his life to literature, dying shortly after 100, early in the reign of Trajan.

Four of his works survive, all in Greek. The *Jewish War* (*Bellum Iudaicum*) was written originally in Aramaic and was published, with Vespasian's encouragement, soon after the events it described. The version we have is a second edition, written in Greek between 75 and 79 to reach a wider audience. He returned to the subject in the last part of his *Antiquities of the Jews* (*Antiquitates Iudaeorum*), a work in 20 books, the first edition of which appeared in 93/94, late in Domitian's reign. And on this there followed two apologetic works written around 100, a *Life* (*Vita*) in which he defended his role in the Jewish Revolt (this was attached to a second edition of the *Antiquities*); and the *Against Apion* (*Contra Apionem*, not his choice of title), which defended the Jewish religion against the anti-Semitism to which Greek rowdies were especially prone. No self-respecting Greek could deny that Greeks were the "chosen people," not Romans, and certainly not Jews.

The *Jewish War* takes seven books to cover events from the outbreak of the revolt in 66 through the fall of Masada in 73/74. Like Tacitus' *Histories*, it opens with a statement insisting that this was a truly formidable war, and that it had been described incompetently by all previous historians (*BJ* 1.1–2). The first two books cover the period before Vespasian's arrival, but they include an enormous speech against rebellion by Herod Agrippa II (*BJ* 2.345–401), and a laudatory appreciation of Roman military discipline (*BJ* 2.577–82; cf. also 3.71–75 and 107). Vespasian appears at the start of Book 3 and is treated forthwith to a fulsome eulogy (*BJ* 3.3–8). Then the work settles down to a more straightforward narrative. The references to contemporary events in Rome are sparse, brief, and usually incidental, but as Vespasian, Titus, and Josephus himself are pictured in the best possible light, there has been a widespread tendency to dismiss Josephus as a Flavian hack, and to invent a chimaera entitled "Flavian propaganda."

There are two difficulties in this approach. First, there is very little evidence that Vespasian or his sons pressured the writers active during their reigns to follow a "party line," even if a modicum of caution was advisable in Domitian's later years. If Josephus *was* a toady and a lickspittle, therefore, it was largely by choice. This as much as his vulnerability to charges of being a renegade, leveled at him by both Romans and Jews, would have opened him up to the attacks to which the *Life* and the *Against Apion* ultimately respond. Second, "Flavian propaganda" is invoked far too often as a cure-all. It is one thing to puncture the grandiose claims made by Vespasian and his followers before and after their victory. It is quite another to use "Flavian propaganda" as a way of rescuing Vitellius from the criticisms modern historians would rather not accept. Since Vitellius was hardly up to the job of being emperor, and his reign lasted less than a year, it is unlikely that systematic denigration was ever thought necessary, of him, or of his two predecessors for that matter. Neither Vespasian nor his adherents stood to gain from negative advertising about the past, and Vespasian even allowed senators to criticize him to his face.

The best and most straightforward assessments of Josephus in English are probably those by Tessa Rajak, *Josephus, the Historian and His Society* (Philadelphia 1984) and S. J. D. Cohen, *Josephus in Galilee and Rome. His Vita and Development as a Historian* (Leiden 1979).

Plutarch

Born only a few years later than Josephus, probably around 40, Plutarch came from a family prominent in Chaeronea, a small town in Boeotia, a heavily agricultural region in eastern Greece. His parents gave him the best education money could buy, including a thorough training in rhetoric. Not that he chose to advertise his expertise in this area, once he had decided to devote himself to philosophy, a decision he took in his early twenties—and yet to pair a Greek life with a Roman one is itself a rhetorical device, no matter what larger purpose it serves. In any event, Plutarch seems to have traveled fairly widely through the east during his formative years, spending time in Athens, Smyrna (Izmir), and Alexandria in Egypt. He visited Rome more than once, and since he had the wealth needed for equestrian status, he secured Roman citizenship through the efforts of Lucius Mestrius Florus. He also toured the battlefield of Bedriacum with Florus at some point before he wrote his *Lives* of Galba and Otho (*Otho* 14.2). And since Florus was one of the senators taken north by Otho early in 69 (under constraint, as he hastened to assure his protégé), it has been conjectured that Florus also provided Plutarch with reminiscences for his account. Even if this is correct, the material need not have been valuable: Florus was a politician and a pedant. In later life, Plutarch seldom moved far from his home town, and much effort has been devoted to proving that this decision to become "the sage of Chaeronea," or a big fish in a little pool, did not cut him off from contact with prominent Greeks and Romans or with the lastest trends in Hellenistic culture. But what we know is that he held various local magistracies and priesthoods, and when Trajan awarded him "consular ornaments," it was in recognition of his services to literature (Quintilian had received the same honor from Domitian).

Plutarch was a prolific writer. He specialized in moral-cum-philosophical essays (known collectively as the *Moralia*), which he churned out in enormous numbers from early life until his death as he was nearing his eightieth year. To moderns, however, he is better known for his paired or parallel *Lives of Noble Greeks and Romans*, one of the works Shakespeare plundered for his Roman plays. In these, written and published on and off between Nerva's accession in 96 and his own death around 120, he paired a Greek "hero," from mythological through Hellenistic times, with a Roman figure, drawn half the time from the city's first six centuries, and half the time from the last century of the republic. In one of the *Lives* he wrote early in the sequence he allows that he began reading Latin fluently only late in life (*Demosthenes* 2.2), and this has been used sometimes as a lever with which to undermine his reliability as a historical source. In fact, it is much less significant than his unrelenting preoccupation with ethics and philosophy. A conservative through and through, he had a low opinion of females in general but took as much delight in virtuous women as Tacitus derived from describing their "naughty" sisters. A firm defender of the "haves" against the "have-nots," he was a champion not only of law and order over individual liberty (anarchy in his estimation), but also of Rome's empire. As he put it, his fellow countrymen would do well to remember that the legions' boots were just above their heads.

The *Lives* of Galba and Otho are the only surviving items from a series that covered the eight emperors from Augustus through Vitellius. We know that Plutarch wrote them before he embarked on his *Lives of Noble Greeks and Romans*, but we cannot be certain how much earlier they were composed (as a rule they are set in the first half of the nineties, during Domitian's reign), nor whether we should engage in linear thinking and regard them as some kind of dry run for the *Parallel Lives*. Though little study has been devoted to these imperial *Lives*, it is enough here to stress two respects in which they differ significantly from the *Parallel Lives* (both points are discussed in more detail in Appendix 2). First, they are less unified, since Plutarch provides us with slices of history rather than with proper biographies. Second, he does not follow the principle he enunciates in one of the earliest of the *Parallel Lives* (*Cimon* 2.4), that a biographer—like a portrait painter—should neither suppress any blemishes in his subject nor draw attention to them. He is far too favorable to Galba, and far too harsh with Otho.

The best book on Plutarch the man is C. P. Jones, *Plutarch and Rome* (Oxford 1971). Scholarship on Plutarch the biographer has appeared mostly in scholarly articles, but there are two books the reader can consult with profit: T. A. Dorey (ed.), *Latin Biography* (Routledge 1967) and, much more up-to-date, Barbara Scardigli (ed.), *Essays on Plutarch's Lives* (Oxford 1995).

Tacitus

Tacitus brings up the details of his own life and career, as a rule, only to make some other point. It is generally agreed that his full name was Publius Cornelius Tacitus, that he was born around 59 (where is disputed), and that his father was the knight Cornelius Tacitus, mentioned by the Elder Pliny as the procurator of Belgica (*Natural History* 7.76). To back up his claims to impartiality, Tacitus declares in the preface to the *Histories* that he became a senator under Vespasian, was promoted by Titus, and was advanced much further by Domitian. In the *Annals* (11.11.1) he adds that when Domitian celebrated the Secular Games in 88, he participated as praetor and as a member of the *quindecimviri sacris faciundis* ("the board of fifteen priests for carrying out sacred rites"). It was probably to Domitian too that he owed his designation as consul for 97. But the main source for his term of office is a letter by the Younger Pliny, recording that as consul Tacitus—the foremost orator of his day—delivered the funeral speech over Verginius Rufus (*Epistles* 2.1.6). Finally, an inscription shows that around 112/113 Tacitus became proconsular governor of the province Asia, one of the two highest posts a senator could achieve. The date of his death is uncertain. Some scholars maintain that he predeceased Trajan (117), others that he lived into the reign of Hadrian, dying between 120 and 123. For the rest, he tells us in the *Agricola* (9.6) that "while still a young man," i.e., around 76, he married the daughter of Gnaeus Julius Agricola. This was a highly advantageous match since his new father-in-law had just reached the consulship. We do not know whether the couple had children, but the emperor Claudius Tacitus had no justification for claiming to be his descendant two centuries later.

To this outline a few details have been added recently by the reattribution to Tacitus of a fragmentary funerary inscription found long ago in Rome. This has sparked fresh conjectures to fill gaps in his career. In particular, as Theodor Mommsen once denounced Tacitus as "the most unmilitary of historians," much effort has been expended on finding him official posts where he could have gained military experience. So the inscription has been restored to suggest that he was a military tribune in a legion, possibly in Britain under Agricola, between 77 and

79. Similarly, his absence from Rome between 89/90 and 93 (*Agr.* 45.5) has long been taken to suggest that he was a legionary legate in some province. But no matter how much military experience Tacitus gained, the conventions of Latin literature would hardly have allowed him to write differently than he does. The best way to defend him against Mommsen, in fact, is to adopt a comment by M. L. W. Laistner, that the verdict is grossly unfair to Tacitus' predecessor Livy.

Before Tacitus embarked on his major historical works he composed three monographs. First came the *Agricola*, to all appearances a eulogistic biography of his father-in-law and a harsh denunciation of Domitian, the emperor who had refused to appreciate his merits. Published in 98, when Domitian was safely dead, this was devoted largely to Agricola's years as governor of Britain and, in good measure, conqueror of Scotland. On this there followed in that same year the *Germania*. It looks like an ethnography, but since it lacks a preface we cannot be sure of its purpose. The work falls into two halves. In the first Tacitus gives a general description of the origins of the many tribes beyond the Rhine and of the customs they had in common (sometimes contrasted favorably, sometimes unfavorably, with Roman behavior). The second half is a catalogue of the tribes, from those nearest to and best known to the Romans to those furthest away. Some hold that Tacitus was motivated by contemporary pressures, for example, the hope that the new emperor, Trajan, would undertake a war of conquest in Germany. But as ethnography was fashionable at the time (Seneca had written "On India"), this is not compelling. His final minor work was the *Dialogus* or *Dialogue on Oratory*, the dramatic date of which is set in 75, the sixth year of Vespasian's reign (*Dial.* 17.3). This and the very different, almost Ciceronian style in which it is written, used to be taken as evidence that the *Dialogus* was Tacitus' first foray into literature. In fact, it was composed around 102, and as its subject is the question whether there is a place for political oratory under the principate, a question that the work does not actually answer, it has been seen as his farewell to oratory before embarking on the writing of history on a grand scale.

Tacitus certainly turned next to a major undertaking, the *Histories*, an account of the period from 1 January 69 through the death of the last Flavian emperor, Domitian, on 18 September 96. This was composed either in 12 or in 14 books. (The manuscripts tell us that his two major works, the *Histories* and the *Annals*, added up to 30 books, but scholars still argue whether we should allocate 12 or 14 to the *Histories* and 18 or 16 to the *Annals*.) Only the first four and somewhere between a quarter and a third of the fifth book of the *Histories* survive. Together these carry the story from the start of Galba's second consulship to a point late in the year 70. So they cover the last two weeks of Galba's life, the entire reigns of Otho and Vitellius, and the opening months of Vespasian's ten-year stint as emperor. There is also a detailed account of much of the war against the rebellious German tribes sparked by Julius Civilis (this is the main theme of Book 4), and the surviving fragment of Book 5 is largely occupied with the Jewish Revolt and the siege of Jerusalem. How long it took Tacitus to compose the *Histories* is unknown, but the first three books had been published by 106. In that year Pliny the Younger sent Tacitus a letter that described the eruption of Vesuvius in 79 and the death in that disaster of his uncle, the Elder Pliny, purportedly because Tacitus had asked him for material to include in the *Histories* (*Epist.* 6.16).

In the preface to the *Histories* Tacitus announces also that he has set aside for his old age an account of the reigns of Nerva and Trajan, "a subject both richer in material and safer to handle, thanks to the rare happiness of times in which you can feel what you like and say what you feel." This is more than a conventional compliment to the two emperors who succeeded the supposedly tyrannical Domitian, but it cannot be taken literally. In essence, it explains only why Tacitus decided to write near-contemporary history and yet to stop before bringing the story down to his own day. He wanted, that is, to focus on a period when contemporary historians could not feel what they liked or say what they felt. So it is no real surprise that for his next work, the *Annals*, Tacitus decided to go back to the Julio-Claudian emperors, and to write an account of the reigns of Tiberius, Caligula, Claudius, and Nero. Once again, we have no idea when he began the work, whether he finished it, or—if he finished it—when he did so. What survives is most of the first six books, covering the reign of Tiberius (much of Book 5, on the years 29 to 31, is lost), and, in a separate manuscript that is our main source also for the *Histories*, Books 11–16. As the beginning of 11 and the conclusion of 16 are missing, what remains covers the latter half of Claudius' reign (47 to 54) and the first 12 years of Nero's principate (54 to 66).

Why Tacitus wrote the *Histories* and the *Annals* has been discussed almost endlessly. Until the 1950s it was customary to argue that he was so scarred by his own experiences—and those of his father-in-law Agricola—during the reign of Domitian that he undertook the *Histories* in an attempt to understand how such a monster could ever have become emperor. On this interpretation, Tacitus' study of the years between 69 and 96 must have failed to yield an adequate explanation (otherwise, supposedly, he would have gone ahead with his announced plan to write about Nerva and Trajan). So he resolved to carry his research back into the Julio-Claudian period, and there he found the prototype and the explanation for Domitian in the no less monstrous Tiberius. In 1958, however, Sir Ronald Syme published his massive two-volume study of Tacitus, as great a work of history as anything Tacitus ever wrote and—it must be added—just as self-willed. Syme set out to cut the ties between Tacitus and Domitian. He argued instead that Tacitus was responding to contemporary events. Thus the *Histories*, the opening books especially, constituted a meditation on what might have happened in 97, when a mutiny by the praetorian guard helped precipitate the aged Nerva's decision to adopt Trajan as his successor; and the *Annals* were prompted above all by events at the start of Hadrian's reign. Despite the enormous learning Syme deployed to make his case, he failed to persuade many other scholars on anything save the dating of the *Dialogus*. But he deserves full credit for disposing of the theory that Tacitus was disabled by a Domitianic trauma. To embrace that view was always to confuse rhetoric and reality. However pungently Tacitus expressed himself on the last of the Flavians, he had worked closely with Domitian.

If this leaves up in the air the question why Tacitus wrote the *Histories*, an answer these days can be found in more down-to-earth considerations. For a start, a senator might well give up a career as an orator, simply because being the foremost speaker of his day made inordinate demands on his time and energy. In such circumstances, it would be natural for him to turn to literature, the writing of history or of philosophy, these being the particular pursuits of elder statesmen. Since Tacitus had no patience with philosophers, history was bound to be the subject he chose. Next, there is the point that no matter how much Tacitus praised the republic when it suited his purposes, he was not just born under the empire but accepted the principate as an institution. His problem, insofar as he had a problem, was with the character and behavior patterns of individual emperors. And since he seems to have believed his own claim that he alone could write, without fear or favor, an accurate account of the Flavian dynasty, a dynasty that had risen and fallen within his own lifetime, there is no need to suppose that he was responding to anything other than his own familiarity with the period. As a member of the governing class for 20 of the Flavians' 27 years (76 to 96), he possessed an intimate knowledge of the era. He could revisit themes he had covered from different angles in the *Agricola*, the *Germania*, and the *Dialogus*. As the foremost orator of his day, he had the gifts needed to bring out the difficulties of a time dominated by a massive gap between appearances and realities. And he could write up the results in less time than would be required for the study of another period, and so make his mark as a historian that much sooner. If there is one thing clear about the *Histories*, it is that the work was intended literally to stun its immediate audience.

Modern readers are often stunned by another aspect of the work, its pessimism. This was to some degree a pose, forced on Tacitus by his criticism of the earlier historians whose works he meant to eclipse. As he points out, they had praised each emperor during his lifetime and vilified him after his death. In a rhetorical world, however, there can be no "heroes" if there are no "villains." The logical corollary is simply stated: when the living emperor was the hero, the senatorial class must then have been the villains, and when the dead emperor became the villain, the heroes then must have been the senators. This set Tacitus' predecessors on the same level as the urban mob that had fawned on Vitellius while he lived and turned against him the moment he was dead. No historian worth his salt could follow in their footsteps. Either he could think the best of everyone, as Livy had done when his material on the early republic gave him the opportunity—and Livy admitted in his Preface that this was escapism. Or he could think the worst of everybody, even the three emperors who had raised him to the highest level in the senate. This was Tacitus' choice, a pose perhaps, but logical in light of the subject matter, and probably congenial too.

The best modern monograph on Tacitus in English is R. H. Martin's *Tacitus* (Batsford 1981), and the latest study of the epigraphical evidence for his career is A. R. Birley, "The life and death of Cornelius Tacitus," *Historia* 49 (2000) 230–47.

Suetonius

Gaius Suetonius Tranquillus was born probably in the early 70s of an equestrian family, his father—Suetonius Laetus—having served as a military tribune in legion XIII Gemina at Bedriacum. Wherever Suetonius was born, he was educated in Rome, and there he was encouraged and supported in his earlier years by the Younger Pliny. The latter addressed four letters to him (1.18; 3.8; 4.10; 9.34), and wrote two more on his behalf (1.24; 10.94). Pliny paints a picture of a youngish man, uncertain in his career aims but inclined to scholarly pursuits and perhaps overly superstitious. Yet an honorary inscription set up to Suetonius in Hippo Regius (Annaba in Algeria) shows that he held not only an assortment of lower offices but also three high positions in the imperial secretariat, those of *a studiis*, *a bibliothecis*, and (this one we knew about before) *ab epistulis*. The first two belong probably in Trajan's reign, the third definitely in Hadrian's, because Hadrian fired him in 122, supposedly for insulting the emperor's wife. The date of his death is unknown. Those who imagine the *Lives of the Twelve Caesars* his crowning achievement tend to set it in the early 120s, soon after this work was completed. Those who reject a linear approach and allow him more time for his literary endeavors have argued for a date as late as 141.

Suetonius was another prolific writer, but the vast majority of his works have been lost. They included treatises on such diverse topics as clothing, the Roman calendar, grammatical matters, and punctuation. Indeed, the only work to have survived more or less intact (and it lacks its preface) is his *Lives of the Twelve Caesars*. This must have been started in the second decade of the second century, in Trajan's reign, when Julius Caesar's reputation was once more on the upswing. This is one reason why the *Julius* heads the list, although he was never emperor. The work was dedicated to Septicius Clarus, prefect of the praetorian guard from 119 until 122, when he too was fired by Hadrian. Suetonius, anyway, was interested primarily—like Plutarch—in what kind of man each of his 12 Caesars was, but he pursued a different line. Although the format varies from one *Life* to another, he tended first to take his emperor from birth to accession to the throne. (This makes him the key source for the earlier years of Galba, Otho, Vitellius, and Vespasian.) Once his emperor was firmly on the throne, he described his qualities or failings by category (*per species*), subdividing these into those shown in public life (his justice, for example, or his cruelty), and those exhibited in private life (sexual proclivities, for example, his physical appearance, and so on). And this he rounded out with an account of the emperor's last days, a quite extensive narrative in Nero's case. The format is clearer in the *Lives* of Galba and Vespasian than it is in those of Otho and Vitellius, but all the later *Lives* are significantly briefer than those devoted to Caesar and his descendants.

Since Suetonius remained a knight throughout his career, attempts have sometimes been made to argue that he preserves an "equestrian view" of the Roman world, but this is another will-o'-the-wisp. Nonetheless, his approach to his material produces an account that is not so much antihistorical as ahistorical. The tight focus on the emperor requires that he cut out all material in which his subject had no hand. This is particularly notable in his treatment of Nero's first years as emperor as well as in his report of Vitellius' revolt. Under each heading, again, he may list the examples of a given trait in chronological order, but he is just as likely to settle for a social categorization, one example of cruelty towards senators, one towards knights, and one towards common people. Then too, he is particularly interested in the omens and prodigies attending an emperor's birth, accession, and death. (These figure most prominently in the *Augustus* and the *Vespasian*, probably because each set up a dynasty, and the latter needed besides something to counter the obscurity of his origins.) But in this regard it may be the *Vitellius* that is most remarkable. For here the signs are used relentlessly to show that the emperor is destined to fall.

This raises the question of Suetonius' reliability, and on this opinions vary widely. It is too often forgotten by his critics that in biography even apocryphal anecdotes are valid illustrations of how an emperor was perceived, and this holds good even if, on occasion, Suetonius shows too great a readiness to generalize from gossip. On the other hand, his defenders have argued that, as a member of the imperial civil service, he should have had access to the palace archives. It is hard to make a convincing case for this. As best we can tell, most of the documents he quotes in the earlier *Lives* were in circulation before he put his accounts together. But he is remarkably scrupulous in researching the ancestry and the birthplace of his emperors, using even physical evidence like the name of a road or of the quarter of a town to prove his case.

What has misled Suetonius' readers most is his style. Though terse, it looks deceptively simple. This creates the impression that the material was assembled by a man of no great intellect. This impression is reinforced by his willingness to quote sayings or documents, in Greek or Latin, that preserve the wording and the style of their originators. (Tacitus would never have dreamt of doing this.) Described sometimes as a "chancery style," as if Suetonius had picked it up while serving as a bureaucrat, it is as mannered in its avoidance of obvious rhetorical tricks as is Tacitus' style for its delight in those techniques. In this way it masks two larger rhetorical tricks. First, it persuades the reader to accept his description of an emperor's behavior by categories as if it were the most natural thing in the world, when the categories are themselves products of a rhetorical scheme. And second, Suetonius' tendency to shun overt moralizing of the kind in which Plutarch indulged will induce some readers to imagine that he is impartial. This idea is disproved most clearly, once again, by the *Vitellius*. Suetonius picked his categories, he picked the examples for each category, and he decided which emperors to present as "good" and which as "evil." The majority are "evil."

Though Suetonius has always been a much-read author, the latest revival of interest in his *Caesars* was sparked in 1951 by Wolf Steidle's *Sueton und die antike Biographie*. Since then the best work has appeared in German, French, or Italian. There have been numerous editions of the *Lives* in English, but for Galba, Otho, and Vitellius the best despite—or perhaps because of—its age remains G. W. Mooney, *Suetoni Tranquilli De Vita Caesarum Libri VII–VIII* (Dublin 1930). This includes a text, a translation, and detailed notes.

Dio Cassius or Cassius Dio

With Cassius Dio Cocceianus we can deal more briefly, since what survives of his work has relatively little value for the Year of the Four Emperors. He was born ca. 164, of a Greek family that already possessed Roman citizenship and had long been prominent in Nicaea in Bithynia (modern Turkey). His father, Marcus Cassius Apronianus, had risen to the consulship, and Dio followed in his father's footsteps. He traveled to Rome around 180, entered the senate around 190, and was consul for the first time probably around 206. No military man, he still held an army command in Pannonia, probably between 226 and 228, and he returned from that to hold a second consulship in 229, as *ordinarius* with the emperor Severus Alexander. After this he retired to his homeland, but we have no idea when he died. He lived mainly in Italy down to 218, and he tells us that he had a country villa at Capua, to which he would retire to compose his *History* (76.2.1).

Dio has been described, justly, as "the supreme instance of a man who was at once a Greek and a Roman." When he set out to write in Greek a history of Rome from its foundations down to his own day, he intended from the start to compose it in the Roman annalistic mode. He declares that he spent 10 years assembling his materials and another 12 writing them up (72.23.5), this for a history that would run through the death of Septimius Severus in 211. These two processes are usually set between 201 and 223, but he continued the work into the reign of Severus Alexander, ultimately in 80 books. Assessments of Dio *qua* historian seldom rank him highly. He is often careless, with a penchant for setting events in the wrong year. He was himself prone to act on the basis of dreams, and includes numerous omens and portents in his narrative, though he may have been less inclined than Suetonius to draw conclusions from them. He puts long, turgid speeches in the mouths of his characters (Julius Vindex, for example), and not always with as good a reason as he has in Vindex's case. And his style is run-of-the-mill, partly because of the speed with which he wrote, partly because his was a less demanding audience than Roman senators.

What is unclear is the extent to which Dio's narrative of 68/69 was colored by his own experiences. Since he witnessed at close hand the reigns of the string of emperors from Commodus through Severus Alexander (180 to 235), a period when relations between emperor and senate were strained severely and military discipline was usually conspicuous by its absence, we might expect these themes to have dominated his narrative. But no matter what he does elsewhere, we lack evidence enough to justify speculation on this particular period. Books

64 and 65 survive only in fragments and summaries, and the summaries were made by two Byzantine monks with their own quirks. In the second half of the eleventh century Joannes Xiphilinus summarized Books 36 to 80 (from the age of Pompey and Caesar on). He excerpted huge chunks of material in Dio's own words (this is his principal virtue), but his choices often betray his own predilections. As has been pointed out, for example, he seems to have been obsessed with Nero's eunuch Sporus. In the first half of the twelfth century, conversely, Joannes Zonaras composed an *Epitome of History* that ran from the creation down to 1118. He used Dio for the period between Caesar's murder and the accession of Nerva in 96, but he produced a genuine abridgement of Dio's work. Hence his account preserves the layout, not the wording of the original. But he too decided which material to abridge and, as in the matter of Otho's suicide, how to spin it.

The best study of Dio the man and his career is Fergus Millar's *A Study of Cassius Dio* (Oxford 1964). There is no full-length study of Dio *qua* historian in English—it would be a formidable task anyway, given the timespan Dio covers. But a series of editions of his *History* is in progress and, on matters of detail, the reader will find helpful notes in the volume by C. L. Murison, *Rebellion and Reconstruction: Galba to Domitian. An Historical Commentary on Cassius Dio's Roman History Books 64–67* (Scholars Press 1999).

The "Common Source"

There can be no doubt that Plutarch, Tacitus, Suetonius, probably Dio, and perhaps Josephus took sizable quantities of material and, on occasion, even the phrasing of that material from an earlier Roman writer on the Year of the Four Emperors. The farcical details of the Nero-Poppaea-Otho triangle, for example, are reported in almost identical terms by the first three, and only in the *Annals* (13.45–46) does Tacitus provide a differently nuanced account. Still, the existence of this work is most easily proved by setting side by side the detailed accounts of the campaign between Otho and Vitellius that Plutarch and Tacitus provide. Both have clearly lifted large quantities of material, and sometimes the same wording, from this earlier writer.

It is impossible to identify the common source, first because he is nowhere given a name, and second, because Tacitus seems so thoroughly to have eclipsed every earlier historian on the periods he covers that not even small fragments of their works have survived to give us a basis for comparison. Three names have been suggested repeatedly, however, because Tacitus cites them all together in one passage on Nero's reign (*Annals* 13.20.2), and makes one separate reference to each of them, again for episodes in that reign. There is Fabius Rusticus (cf. *Annals* 15.61.3), a friend of Seneca and a historian whom Tacitus had already named in his discussion of Britain's shape (*Agricola* 10.3). Then there is Cluvius Rufus (cf. *Annals* 14.2.1), the man Galba installed as governor of Tarraconensis when he himself set out for Rome in 68, but Cluvius' work may not have gone beyond 68. And there is the Elder Pliny (cf. *Annals* 15.53.3). Besides the *Natural History*, which has survived, he wrote a work on the wars in Germany (*bella Germanica*), and a 31-book continuation of Aufidius Bassus' history (*a fine Aufidii Bassi*), for which the outside limits are 41–71. In the preface to the *Natural History* (§ 20) Pliny declares that he planned withholding publication of this history until after his own death, to avoid accusations of currying favor with the new dynasty. This gives us some idea of the line it took, and it could be the work for which Tacitus cites Pliny once in the *Histories* (3.28), on the sack of Cremona. This does not prove Pliny the common source, rather the opposite. Besides, Tacitus could easily have appropriated both the details he reports and the reference to Pliny from the common source. That sort of thing too was by no means unusual among ancient historians.

Speculation about the identity of the common source was fueled by the hope that solving this problem would enable us to form an idea of his reliability as a historian. As this has proved to be a dead end, all we can say for certain is that his narrative covered the reigns of Galba, Otho, and Vitellius, and did so more comprehensively than does Plutarch. The biographer manifestly edited out material in his account of the campaign between Otho and Vitellius. But how much Tacitus added to or modified the common source's account there is no telling. All we can say, again by comparing Plutarch's account with Tacitus', is that the latter clearly put a different interpretation on the material. And so we come to the irony of the situation, that since we cannot use the supposed reliability of the common source to "correct" Tacitus, it is his existence that has been used to achieve that end (see Appendix 2).

Vipstanus Messalla

For the opening stages of the campaign Antonius Primus launched against Vitellius, so it is generally agreed, Tacitus consulted an unusually precise, more or less contemporary author, Vipstanus Messalla. In his early twenties, Messalla was serving as a military tribune of legion VII Claudia in 69, but he became the unit's acting commander for September and

October, after Aponius Saturninus ran off its legate, Tettius Julianus. Tacitus cites Messalla twice for specific incidents early in the campaign, in a manner showing that he wrote a kind of memoir. Some fancy that it covered the entire campaign, but Messalla is much more likely to have described only the two months of his command. He was replaced by Plotius Grypus in early November.

Messalla must also have written the work soon after the actual events, while his memories were still fresh. For Tacitus describes him as "the possessor of a distinguished ancestry and outstanding personal gifts, the only man to bring good qualities to this campaign" (*Hist.* 3.9.3). If his father was Lucius Vipstanus Poplicola Messalla (*cos. ord.* 48), he was linked by birth to the Valerii Messallae, a family prominent in republican times. In the *Histories* (4.42) he wins high praise from Tacitus again, for defending his older half brother, the unscrupulous informer Aquilius Regulus, against his score-settling senatorial enemies early in 70, and he plays a large role in the *Dialogus* as a champion of "classical" oratory against the modernists. So it is reasonable to assume that Messalla would have secured swift advancement to high office under the Flavians, had he lived. Since there are no traces of this in the record, it looks as if he died young, perhaps as early as 76.

The memoir was clearly favorable to Antonius, Messalla's commander in chief. Even if Messalla had disapproved of Antonius as a demagogue and a troublemaker, it was neither gentlemanly to criticize one's superior, nor wise to do so when one had followed his orders. But this, unfortunately, has generated another hobbyhorse to bedevil scholarship on Tacitus' reliability, the temptation to carve Tacitus' portrait of Antonius into good and bad strands, to trace these back to favorable and unfavorable sources, and to identify Messalla as the former and the common source as the latter. It seems to have been no deterrent that this reduces Tacitus to the level of an incompetent clerk without a brain in his head, something he manifestly was not.

Appendix 2:
Characterizations of Galba and Otho

The most difficult problem faced by anybody attempting to reconstruct and interpret the events of 68/69 is that of determining how to view Otho. Assessing Galba is not much easier, and since there are grounds in one case at least for thinking the portrayals interlinked, both issues need discussion. To do this in the main narrative would have caused it to bog down on page after page. To gloss over the problem, however, or to make a choice without any attempt to set out the reasoning behind it, would be misleading as well as dishonest.

Three of our sources lie at the heart of the problem, Plutarch, Tacitus, and Suetonius. (Dio's account is too fragmentary to be helpful and Josephus does not concern himself much with either ruler.) Between them, nonetheless, they give us two different portraits of Galba and three of Otho. On Galba they divide into opposing camps. Plutarch admires the man, presenting him as a harsh but just, worthy, and misunderstood old man. Tacitus, by contrast, declares that Galba "did not so much possess virtues as lack vices," and the only redeeming quality Suetonius seems to have found in Galba was his not being a heavy drinker. On Otho the situation is more complicated. Here Plutarch stands at one extreme, presenting us with a panicky, effeminate, vicious weakling. Tacitus stands at the other, picturing Otho as a tough-minded, murderous usurper. And Suetonius pursues a middle course with Otho the impetuous risk taker. On the whole, Suetonius' account is, once again, closer to Tacitus' than it is to Plutarch's, as in the story that when Otho went ahead with his coup, he joked that it made no difference to him whether he fell beneath his creditors in the forum or beneath his enemies in battle. Nonetheless, Suetonius' picture *can* be accommodated to either of the other two, but not to both at once. So we must make a choice.

As if this were not complication enough, making that choice has become entangled in another conundrum. All our literary sources drew material from the so-called common source (see Appendix 1), and even though we cannot establish how reliable he was, his existence has been used as an argument to prove Plutarch more trustworthy than Tacitus on both emperors. The basic thesis is straightforward: the author who seems to follow the common source without deviation (that is, Plutarch) becomes by definition less manipulative than the author who recasts the material (that is, Tacitus). On this ground he is held to be the more reliable of the two in other areas as well, because less inclined to adjust the evidence to suit his own purposes, literary or otherwise.

It is easy to prove that Tacitus "massaged" the evidence from time to time. Consider, for example, the remark that those who contemplate treason are already traitors. This Plutarch attributes to Titus Vinius at the meeting in April 68 where he urged Galba to assume the leadership of the revolt against Nero. Tacitus uses it as the final argument advanced by Licinius Mucianus in August 69 to persuade Vespasian to take up arms against Vitellius. Clearly, Tacitus has recycled and relocated a noteworthy comment he could not otherwise have fit into his annalistic narrative.[1] It is hard to see how this proves distortion or bias, nonetheless. The remark is misattributed, to be sure, but it is set in much the same kind of context to much the same end, and it is hardly impossible that two different men at opposite ends of the Mediterranean should have had the same basic idea within 15 months of one another, when they found themselves in the same predicament. By our standards, Tacitus has played fast and loose with the evidence, but this case—and others like it—fail to prove either that he twisted or distorted that evidence, or that the common source did not.

So, to revert to the common source, the main support for the idea that he presented a more honest picture of the situation in 68/69 seems to spring from the way in which Plutarch constructs his *Lives* of Galba and Otho. They are not self-contained structures like his later *Lives of Noble Greeks and Romans* or, for that matter, Suetonius' *Lives* of the two emperors. Instead, they are slices of history. The *Galba*—after its obligatory preface—covers the period from Nero's fall in early June 68 to Galba's murder in mid-January 69. This is one reason both for the prominence given to Nymphidius Sabinus at the start of the work, and for the material on Otho and Vitellius that bulks it out. Similarly, the *Otho* covers the period between 15 January and 16 April 69, and includes all the historical events that Plutarch thought relevant within these limits. There is less extraneous matter than in the *Galba*, but Plutarch probably says more about Caecina and Valens than he needed to. And so we come to the real point behind—or the catch in—the argument. If Plutarch took the layout of his material and the facts he chose to report from the common source in as mechanical a manner as he appears to have done, he ought *ex hypothesi* to have taken over the common source's views on Galba and Otho just as mechanically. And since Tacitus, and Suetonius too for that matter, offer different assessments, we can accuse them of distorting the record from bias or malice, and dismiss their accounts out of hand.

This is an incredibly naive argument. Even if we take it on its own terms, it tells us only that Plutarch followed the common source more mechanically than did Tacitus, not that the common source's account was any less skewed in one direction than Tacitus' was in the other. And even slices of history are not immune to Al Smith's famous observation that "no matter how thin you slice it, it's still baloney." For a start, it is inherently improbable that any Roman writer, the common source or any other author one might care to name, composed a favorable account of Galba's principate after he was dead. Although Tacitus may exaggerate, he insists that each and every emperor had been vilified once he was dead. Then too, it is easy to show that Plutarch cleaned up Galba's image. He suppressed all reference to Galba's sexual tastes, a subject on which Suetonius waxed eloquent.[2] And rather than admit that Galba was manipulated by his three pedagogues, Plutarch pushed Laco and Icelus into the background and cast Titus Vinius as his evil genius, clearly to exculpate the emperor. Arguments as disingenuous as this were as easy to float in Roman times as they are today. But no Roman writer would have subscribed to the idea that an emperor could shrug off responsibility for his subordinates' misdeeds, not Tacitus, not Suetonius, and since he too wrote after Galba was dead, not the common source.

So Plutarch's characterization of Galba has to be largely his own work, and that hardly makes it more reliable than our other accounts. And it is not hard to see why he should have viewed the emperor so favorably. First, as is evident from remarks he makes in other works, Plutarch recognized as a Greek that Nero's philhellenism had benefited his countrymen, but as an inhabitant of the empire, he saw that the emperor's self-indulgence had nearly destroyed the established order. So a firmer, stricter ruler was much to be preferred. Second, the thesis on the evil soldiery adumbrated in the preface to the *Galba* required that Galba be presented as the relatively innocent victim of the machinations of Nymphidius Sabinus. Third, Roman citizen or not, Plutarch was an outsider, and his readiness to blame others shows that he was as willing to make excuses for a man he thought a good ruler as Russian serfs would be in later centuries to blame a czar's shortcomings on his evil ministers. And fourth, Plutarch admired old men. Later in life he would not only compose a treatise on the question whether the old should be put in charge of public affairs, but answer it affirmatively too.

This is important, because it gives us the means to undermine Plutarch's presentation of Otho as well. Not only is there the obvious point that if the biographer admired Galba so much, he would not have warmed to Galba's murderer. There is also a more telling point. As soon as we grant that Plutarch's interpretation of Galba is not derived from the common source, we are under no compulsion to hold that he drew his picture of Otho from that source either.

This is not conclusive, of course. But there is another line of argument that will confirm its essential accuracy, the way in which Plutarch, Tacitus, and Suetonius viewed a man's character. This is a very controversial subject, in good measure because ancient ideas of character differed significantly from ours. But though oversimplification is perilous, it seems fair to say that all three authors believed or, when it suited them, chose to operate on the principle that a man's character was a given or, if not that, at least predictable within limits. Usually, there would be a pattern behind his actions indicating that he was a certain "type" of person.[3] In its simplest form, this meant that somebody who was good was good from birth to death, and somebody who was born bad died bad, whether or not he also died badly. So Suetonius presents Nero as a bad emperor, both because his ancestors were vicious and because he manifested from the start a predisposition to do wrong. Tacitus' Tiberius is a man who did not look as evil at the start of his reign as he became by its end, and so must in his earlier years have hidden his vices behind a veil of hypocrisy. And in his *Lives of Noble Greeks and Romans* Plutarch regularly used as valid indications of an adult's predisposition incidents that took place at almost any point in his childhood.

This was never a rigid principle, however. It was more like a rule of thumb, and there was always wiggle room, some freedom to pick and choose when, where, and how to apply it. Had it not been so, Tacitus might have been hard put to declare Vespasian the first man to be improved by becoming emperor.[4] But the situation became far more problematical when an ancient author was confronted with a paradoxical character, a man who switched from good to bad, or from bad to good, on a grand scale, or throughout his life mixed virtues and vices not commonly associated with one another. Such "antitypes" were irresistible from a rhetorical point of view, since their conduct generated contrast after contrast, as in Dio's portrait of Caligula. But from a historical, biographical, or moralistic point of view, it could prove difficult to explain a sudden, marked change in a subject's patterns of behavior without invoking madness (as in Suetonius' portrait of Caligula), or to attribute a subject's mixing good and bad qualities to anything more than fate or sheer contrariness. And so we come back to Otho.

Otho obviously qualified as a paradoxical character. First, there was his murdering Galba to seize power for himself and his committing suicide in a vain attempt to end the slaughter. Second, there was the contradiction in his "type," an aspect the common source summed up in the statement that "Otho's mind was not effeminate like his body." This we know because it turns up in Plutarch, in Tacitus, and in Suetonius. Now, none of our three sources embraces the idea that the suicide canceled out the assassination, or that the suicide justified a reassessment of the murder. Suetonius comes fairly close, when he reports that some people claimed after Otho's death that he had assassinated Galba for the good of the state, but he himself still balks. So all three writers regarded Otho as a villain to one degree or another. Where they differed was in their explanations of how he became a villain, and what kind of villain he was. Hence all three picked up from the common source the proposition that "Otho's mind was not effeminate like his body," even though the distinction being made was not new in and of itself.[5]

Any modern assessment of Otho must obviously stand or fall on the question how we exploit this statement. But there can be no certainty about where in his narrative the common source set it, and what kind of significance he attached to it, since Plutarch, Tacitus, and Suetonius each use it differently. The one thing of which we can be reasonably sure is that Suetonius is most likely to have moved it to an entirely different context. The besetting vice of his Otho being impetuosity, even the decision to commit suicide is taken on the fly, as soon as Otho hears that his army has been defeated decisively at Bedriacum. But since Suetonius subscribes explicitly to the view that Otho killed himself in hopes of avoiding further bloodshed (an idea his own father no doubt drummed into him), he uses the statement as a way of creating the strongest possible contrast between Otho's previous conduct and his demeanor during the last 24 hours of his life. Hence his assertion that "the manner of Otho's death" was "entirely at odds with his way of life." There is also a literary consideration at work. In the *Otho*, Suetonius lays out his material in the same way as in the *Galba*, and switches from his subject's death to a description of his physical appearance. As the context shows, he thought the common source's dictum tailor-made to facilitate that transition.

This may seem to leave us with two possibilities, unless we merely throw up our hands in despair. The first is to accept Plutarch's placement and handling of the remark, even though he strips it of virtually all its significance. He sets the comment at the point in his narrative where Otho arrives in the Forum on the morning of 15 January to find that only 23 praetorian guardsmen have gathered there, and he buries it inside a sentence that undercuts its force: "though Otho's mind was not effeminate like his body, he was terrified by the smallness of the turnout." The other option is to follow Tacitus, who makes the comment the key to his interpretation, by setting it programmatically at the head of his narrative of the plan to assassinate Galba. After that, it underlies everything the Tacitean Otho does, up to and including his suicide. Hence the Tacitean Otho decides *before* Bedriacum that he will commit suicide, if the battle goes against him.

In fact, we can reach a kind of compromise between these options. There is good reason to think that the common source set his statement in more or less the same context as Plutarch places it. For one thing, Plutarch would have had far more difficulty sweeping the comment under the rug, had the common source made it the key to his interpretation of the emperor. And for another, Plutarch did indeed follow the common source more mechanically than did Tacitus. Yet it is wildly improbable that the common source would have buried an epigram powerful enough to impress our three surviving sources in a sentence that robbed it of its force. On the contrary, he would most likely have given it exactly the opposite spin, producing a sentence along the lines that though Otho was surprised by the smallness of the turnout, he did not lose his nerve, because. . . .

To explain why Plutarch disarmed the comment is relatively easy. Of our three authors he had the greatest difficulty in dealing with, and the least use for, a paradoxical "type." This is evident from his *Lives* of Lysander and Sulla, unless we engage in special pleading. Moreover, Plutarch tended anyway to flatten out idiosyncrasies. In Otho's case he seems to have gone still further, and to have rejected altogether the notion that his was a paradoxical character. Treating Otho as a "normal" personality, a man whose behavior could be seen always in one light, he could not refer back to his youth or education (a staple of the *Parallel Lives*, these topics do not appear in the *Galba* and the *Otho*). But he found the ammunition he needed to justify his preexisting determination to view Otho unfavorably in the latter's behavior as a courtier in Nero's reign. Not only had Otho been a boon companion of an emperor whose self-indulgence had nearly wrecked the empire. The bizarre details of the Otho-Poppaea-Nero triangle also "proved" his worthlessness, leading Plutarch to assert that Otho won fame first by marrying Poppaea, just as had Paris of Troy by marrying Helen. Plutarch does not recur to this motif, but it is clearly a vital element in his portrait of an emperor who, like his Homeric counterpart, was an effeminate, villainous weakling from start to finish.

Now come two related questions: why Tacitus took an incidental insight and turned it into a programmatic interpretation, and whether we are justified in following his lead. It is all very well to point out that Tacitus clearly revels in the contradiction created by an Otho whose every action is the result of cold, hard calculation when his physical appearance and his entire mode of life suggest that he is incapable of such behavior. Indeed, Tacitus' Otho personifies one of his *idées fixes*, that things are not always as they seem, and that realities need not match appearances any more than words correspond with deeds. It still does not follow that his portrait is the result solely, or even largely, of authorial caprice. Both Tacitus and the common source before him seem to have been as powerless to get over the enormity of Otho's assassinating Galba as the emperor's contemporaries. Both appear to have decided, that is, that such an outrage could be neither explained nor explained away by invoking emotions like impetuosity, disappointment, desperation, or effeminate spitefulness. So, at some point, a measure of iron must have entered Otho's soul, and the question was when. The common source placed it in Otho's encounter with the guardsmen in the Forum, because that was when he was first tested by an untoward turn of events. Tacitus backdated it to the point when Otho began planning Galba's assassination, since the planning of such an outrage required the same hard-headedness as the doing of the deed. Besides, Tacitus has presented Otho as a devotee of astrology and, more particularly, a firm believer in the prediction that he would become emperor. All in all, it adds up to a persuasive picture. Unlike Macbeth, Otho did not merely talk a good game. He delivered.

The Tacitean picture of Otho may be overdrawn, but that is not enough to invalidate it. We can complain that it is oversimplified, but even this will not justify our setting it aside in favor of the portraits drawn by Plutarch and Suetonius. All three authors hold that one key opens every door. To this extent it is legitimate to contend that the historical Otho was probably a far more complex personality, less consistent in his thinking and in his behavior patterns than our sources pretend. But unless or until fresh evidence emerges, we must make a choice. And this is not a case where we can argue plausibly that the outsider, Plutarch, saw more of the game. Even if it is only by default, our wisest option is to settle for the idea or—in more highfalutin' terms—the working hypothesis that the historical Otho combined in some measure the drives attributed to him by Tacitus and Suetonius.

Appendix 3:
Checklist of the Legions
Operational in 68/69

When Augustus set up the principate, he created a standing army whose backbone was constituted eventually by 28 legions of heavy infantry, each numbering supposedly about 5,000 men. Some of the legions traced their origins back to Julius Caesar (most obviously V Alaudae); some were raised in the triumviral period, when the Roman world was carved up by Marc Antony, Marcus Lepidus, and Octavian (Tacitus tells us that III Gallica had served with Antony). And some were new units formed by Augustus after he established the principate. Because of their different origins, and because of the importance the men attached to the records of their units, a consistent, consecutive numbering system was never applied. Numerals were often repeated, and legions with the same number were distinguished by title. So, for example, there were three third legions, one titled Augusta, one Cyrenaica, and one Gallica.

Since Augustus lost 3 legions in the Varian Disaster of 9 (XVII–XIX, numbers never used again), only 25 units remained when he died. By the time Vespasian was recognized as emperor by the senate in December 69 the total had risen to 30. Two new legions were created by Caligula (XV Primigenia and XXII Primigenia), 1 by Nero (I Italica), and 2 by Galba (I Adiutrix and VII Galbiana). There was 1 more unit (I Macriana Liberatrix), the work of Clodius Macer in Africa, but it lasted only for a few months in 68. As emperor, Vespasian disbanded 4 legions that had followed Vitellius (I Germanica, IV Macedonica, XV Primigenia, and XVI), though he incorporated some of the men into 2 new legions, IV Flavia Felix and XVI Flavia Firma (hence their numbering), and he regularized the creation of yet another legion (II Adiutrix), giving a total of 29. For the sake of convenience I have given a brief account of all the units except Vespasian's two new creations, since every one of them turns up sooner or later in the Year of the Four Emperors. Each entry is designedly self-contained, though this has led to some repetition, and where it seems appropriate, I have included specific citations of ancient evidence, especially the Tacitean references to the units or their officers in the *Histories* and those made by Josephus in his *War Against the Jews (BJ)*.

Although Augustus intended his legions to act as mobile forces, many units were kept for years in the same provinces, sometimes in the same camps. But assignments were reshuffled on a large scale three times before 69, and once more after the fighting had ended. The first set of reassignments accompanied Claudius' invasion of Britain. Four full legions took part in the expedition and were stationed in the island afterwards, and this required that other units be moved as well. A similar ripple effect resulted from the campaigns against the Parthians in Nero's reign. A third reshuffling was in process at the time of Nero's death, in part because he had laid plans for expeditions into Ethiopia and the Caucasus, in part because a major revolt broke out in Judaea in 66. And the fourth reshuffling was a mixture of ad hoc measures taken late in 69 and of a conscious attempt by Vespasian to tidy up the mess. Besides this, there were minor adjustments from time to time, and we cannot always fix the precise date at which any given legion was transferred from one base to another, or from one province to another. In a few cases we cannot even identify their bases.

I (GERMANICA):   though formed earlier, this legion spent almost its entire existence in the imperial period on the Rhine frontier. Originally (from 16 B.C.), it was stationed with V Alaudae in a double-camp at Ara or Oppidum Ubiorum (later Colonia Agrippinensis = Cologne) in Lower Germany, and was involved in the mutinies of 14. When this camp was dissolved in the 30s, the unit was moved upstream to Bonna (Bonn). If Fabius Valens was the legionary legate in 68/69 (as is usually assumed), Herennius Gallus must have taken over when Valens left for Italy (*Hist.* 4.19.2). Only a detachment accompanied Valens on his march south. It fought at Bedriacum, was taken by Caecina to Hostilia, and was defeated at Cremona. The bulk of the legion, left behind in Germany, ended up making up common cause with the rebellious tribesmen led by Julius Civilis, and it was one of the four legions cashiered by Vespasian after the revolt's suppression.

I ITALICA: raised by Nero in Italy for his planned expedition into the Caucasus (Suetonius, *Nero* 19.2; cf. Dio 55.24.2), almost certainly in 66. Still in Italy in early 68, it was sent north to counter the threat from Vindex and Galba. Though its role in what followed is unclear, it ended up at Lugdunum (*Hist.* 1.64.3). Added to Fabius Valens' force, it remained loyal to Vitellius through the battle of Cremona in October 69. Its legionary legate in early 69 was Manlius Valens, but how long he kept his post is unclear (*Hist.* 1.64.4). After Cremona the legion was assigned to the province Moesia.

I ADIUTRIX: was formed by Nero early in 68 from marines in the Misene fleet, but was constituted a regular legion (*iusta legio*) by Galba, probably in October 68. It made common cause with the praetorians against Galba, fought for Otho at Ad Castores and Bedriacum, was sent by Vitellius to Spain to cool off (*Hist.* 2.67.2), and was mainly responsible for swinging Spain behind Vespasian (*Hist.* 3.44). One of the eight units assigned to Petillius Cerialis for the suppression of Civilis' revolt in Lower Germany (*Hist.* 4.68.4), the legion was transferred to Annius Gallus in Upper Germany during the course of 70.

I MACRIANA LIBERATRIX: a unit raised, perhaps illegally, in Africa in 68 by Clodius Macer, the legionary legate of III Augusta. Galba disbanded it, but Vitellius tried to reactivate it in autumn 69 (*Hist.* 2.97.2). If it was reconstituted in fact, it must have been disbanded again by Vespasian.

II ADIUTRIX: this legion was formed from the marines of the Ravenna fleet by Vespasian after the civil wars were over (Dio 55.24.3). But it looks as if the unit was composed of marines incorporated by Antonius Primus into his own preexisting legions after the battle of Cremona (*Hist.* 3.50.3). One of the eight units assigned to Petillius Cerialis for the suppression of Civilis' revolt in Lower Germany (*Hist.* 4.68.4), II Adiutrix was stationed in Britain from 71 onward.

II AUGUSTA: stationed in Upper Germany in 14, this was one of the four legions moved to Britain when Claudius invaded the island, and it was still there in 69. The detachment of (probably) 2,600 men it sent to fight for Vitellius joined him after Bedriacum, and fought against Antonius Primus' forces at Cremona (*Hist.* 3.22.2). But Vespasian had commanded the unit as legionary legate during the conquest of Britain, and that supposedly induced the legion to join him, albeit only after Cremona (*Hist.* 3.44.1). Lucius Antistius Rusticus may have been acting legate at the time.

III AUGUSTA: stationed in Africa from Tiberius' reign through 69, for most of the time at Ammaedara. A detachment may have been present in Alexandria in 66 as part of the forces gathered for Nero's planned expeditions (Josephus, *BJ* 2.494), but it seems to have returned to Africa by 68. In that year the legionary legate was Clodius Macer. After his assassination, the legion was entrusted to Valerius Festus, a kinsman of Vitellius who declared for Vespasian (*Hist.* 2.98.1).

III CYRENAICA: one of the legions that could trace its origins to the triumviral period, III Cyrenaica seems to have been stationed in Egypt from the start of the principate. From 23 onward it occupied with XXII Deiotariana the double-camp at Nicopolis, just outside Alexandria. Its primary function was to keep the city's population under control (Josephus, *BJ* 2.385), but a detachment of unknown size served in Domitius Corbulo's campaigns against the Parthians in 63, and a detachment of 1,000 men joined Titus for the storming of Jerusalem in 70.

III GALLICA: established by Julius Caesar, the legion served under Antony in his Parthian expedition of 36 B.C. (*Hist.* 3.24.2), and was stationed in Syria after the battle of Actium. In Nero's reign it took part in Corbulo's campaigns against the Parthians, and inscriptions show that it was active in Armenia in 64/65. By the end of 66 it had become part of the garrison of Syria, and shortly before Nero's death it was relocated to Moesia, perhaps at Novae (Česava), to counter raids by the Rhoxolani. It destroyed the band that invaded the province in the winter of 68/69 (*Hist.* 1.79.1–4). The legionary legate between 64 and 69 was Aurelius Fulvus (*Hist.* 1.79.5), but at some point in 69 he was replaced by Gaius Dillius Aponianus (*Hist.* 3.10.1). The legion retained its ties with the forces in Syria and some Syrian customs (*Hist.* 3.24.3). After the Flavians' victory it was billeted for a time in Capua, south of Rome (*Hist.* 4.3.1), but it was returned to Syria as fast as possible, because Mucianus wanted to remove from Italy the troops especially loyal to Antonius Primus (*Hist.* 4.39.4).

IV MACEDONICA: raised by Julius Caesar, the legion was stationed in Spain in Augustus' reign. It was transferred to Upper Germany in 43, in the reshuffle accompanying Claudius' invasion of Britain, and was still there in 69, stationed with XXII Primigenia in the double-camp at Mogontiacum (Mainz). Caecina was probably its legionary legate, appointed by Galba in 68 (cf. *Hist.* 1.53). A detachment accompanied Caecina in his advance to Rome. The bulk of the legion, left behind in Germany, performed poorly during Civilis' revolt and was disbanded by Vespasian, though some survivors were incorporated into the replacement unit he created, IV Flavia Felix.

IV SCYTHICA: formed probably by Marc Antony, the legion was stationed at first in Macedonia, but was repositioned in Moesia perhaps as early as 29 B.C. The unit was moved to Syria, apparently in 58, and was still there in 69. It was disgraced in fall 62 at Rhandeia, when Caesennius Paetus surrendered to the Parthians. A detachment of perhaps 2,600 men accompanied Mucianus to Rome (*Hist.* 2.83.1).

V ALAUDAE: originally one of Caesar's legions, this unit was stationed in Lower Germany. Initially it shared with I Germanica the double-camp at Ara Ubiorum, and it was one of the prime movers in the mutinies of 14. When the camp was dissolved in the 30s, it was moved to Vetera (Xanten), which it shared with XV Primigenia in 69. Its legionary legate then may have been Cornelius Aquinus (cf. *Hist.* 1.7.1), but by the time of Cremona Fabius Fabullus held this post (*Hist.* 3.14). The bulk of the legion became the core of Fabius Valens' expeditionary force (*Hist.* 1.61.2). It fought at Bedriacum, took the lead in thwarting Caecina's attempt to change sides at Hostilia (*Hist.* 3.14), and fought again at Cremona. After the battle the survivors were made part of the garrison of Moesia, while the segment of the legion left behind at Vetera was massacred during Julius Civilis' revolt (*Hist.* 4.60).

V MACEDONICA: formed in the triumviral period, the legion was perhaps stationed in the East in Augustus' reign, but in 33/34 it was in Moesia. One of the three legions assigned to Caesennius Paetus for his campaigns against the Parthians, it was not involved in his surrender at Rhandeia in 62. We do not know where the legion was stationed after the conclusion of peace in 63, but in winter 66—along with X Fretensis— it was assembled at Antioch in Syria for Vespasian's campaign against the Jewish rebels (Josephus, *BJ* 3.29). A detachment accompanied Mucianus on his expedition to Italy. Between 67 and 69 the legionary legate was Sextus Vettulenus Cerealis (Josephus, *BJ* 3.310).

VI FERRATA: raised by Julius Caesar no later than 52 B.C., the legion seems to have been stationed in Syria from the very start of the principate. It participated in Corbulo's campaigns against the Parthians during Nero's reign. Though a detachment was involved in Cestius Gallus' defeat by the Jewish rebels in 66 (Josephus, *BJ* 2.544), the legion formed the core of Mucianus' expeditionary force to Italy in autumn 69 (*Hist.* 2.83.1). In the event, Mucianus decided to leave it in Moesia, to counter an incursion by Sarmatian tribesmen (*Hist.* 3.46.2), and from there it was returned presently to Syria.

VI VICTRIX: formed in the triumviral period, the legion was stationed in Spain in Tiberius' reign and was still there in 68. Galba left it there, forming a new unit, VII Galbiana, to escort him on his march to Italy. In early 68 the legionary legate was Titus Vinius (Suetonius, *Galba* 14.2), but who replaced him when he traveled to Rome with Galba is unknown. One of the eight units summoned to help Petillius Cerialis suppress Julius

Civilis' revolt in Lower Germany (*Hist.* 4.68.4), it was stationed later at Novaesium (Neuss).

VII CLAUDIA PIA FIDELIS [or CLAUDIANA]:   formed by Augustus and originally named Macedonica, the legion was stationed at Delminium in Dalmatia between 9 and 58. It won its name Claudia pia fidelis for assisting in the suppression of the revolt of Camillus Scribonianus in 42. Seemingly in 58/59 it was transferred to Moesia (as a result of IV Scythica's being attached to Caesennius Paetus' army), and it was still there in 69, stationed perhaps at Viminacium (Kostolač). The legionary legate in 69 was Tettius Julianus (*Hist.* 1.79.5), but when the governor, Aponius Saturninus, forced him out, Tettius fled to Vespasian (*Hist.* 2.85.2). The latter sent off a letter giving the command to Lucius Plotius Grypus (*Hist.* 3.52.3). In the interim, during the Cremona campaign, the unit was commanded by the military tribune Vipstanus Messalla (*Hist.* 3.9.3). It was transferred to Moesia at the start of 70, perhaps as a result of Fonteius Agrippa's defeat (chapter 10).

VII GALBIANA [later GEMINA]:   raised—allegedly from Roman citizens—in Spain by Galba from April 68 onward, it was constituted a regular legion on 10 June. The legion escorted Galba to Rome and "massacred" the marines at the Milvian Bridge in October. A month or so later Galba sent it off to Pannonia, probably to Carnuntum, a move that permitted the reassignment of X Gemina to Spain. At the same time Galba made Antonius Primus its legionary legate. The legion was returned to Pannonia in January 70 by Mucianus, because he wanted to move the units most devoted to Antonius Primus out of Italy (*Hist.* 4.39.4).

VIII AUGUSTA: set up originally by Caesar, the legion may have been stationed in Syria during Augustus' day, but it was in Pannonia at the start of Tiberius' reign, and took part in the mutinies of 14. Apart from a detachment that may have participated in the conquest of Britain, it remained there until some date between 46 and 57. Then it was shifted to Moesia. Originally, it may have been stationed at Novae (Česava), but in 69 it probably occupied the camp at Oescus (Gigen). Its legionary legate then was Numisius Lupus (*Hist.* 1.79.5; 3.10.1). One of the units that helped Petillius Cerialis suppress Civilis' revolt in Lower Germany (*Hist.* 4.68.4), it was transferred to Annius Gallus in Upper Germany during 70, and became the garrison of a new camp at Argentorate (Strasbourg).

IX HISPANA: of uncertain origins, the legion was stationed in Pannonia at the start of Tiberius' reign and took part in the mutinies of 14. It spent the years between 20 and 24 in Africa, contending with the rebel Tacfarinas, before being returned to Pannonia. One of the four legions used for Claudius' invasion of Britain, it suffered heavy losses in Boudicca's rebellion thanks to the rashness of its legate, Petillius Cerialis, but it was still in the island in 69. The detachment of (probably) 2,600 men it sent to fight for Vitellius joined the emperor after Bedriacum and fought at Cremona. The balance of the legion declared for Vespasian after Cremona (*Hist.* 3.44).

X FRETENSIS: raised perhaps by Octavian, the legion was stationed in Syria from the early principate through 66. It participated in Corbulo's campaigns against the Parthians. We do not know where it was based after the conclusion of peace in 63, but in winter 66—along with V Macedonica—it was assembled at Antioch in Syria for Vespasian's campaign against the Jewish rebels (Josephus, *BJ* 3.29). The bulk of the legion was kept in Judaea, but a detachment, perhaps of 2,600 men, accompanied Mucianus on his expedition to Italy. The legionary legate between 67 and 69 was M. Ulpius Traianus, father of the emperor Trajan (Josephus, *BJ* 3.289).

X GEMINA: created originally by Caesar, the legion was stationed in Spain from 30 B.C. onward. It was moved to Carnuntum in Pannonia for a brief period in Nero's reign (when XV Apollinaris was transferred from Pannonia to Syria), but it was returned to Spain by Galba, when he shifted VII Galbiana out of Rome to Pannonia, probably in November 68. The unit was added to the forces Cerialis was using against Civilis in Lower Germany, when XIV Gemina Martia Victrix was transferred to Annius Gallus in Upper Germany (*Hist.* 5.19.1), and ended up as the garrison of a new camp at Noviomagus (Nijmegen).

XI CLAUDIA PIA FIDELIS [or CLAUDIANA]: of uncertain origins, the legion was stationed at Burnum in Dalmatia from 9 onward, and there it remained. A detachment may have fought for Otho at Bedriacum or have turned up after the battle. In either case it was sent back to its quarters by Vitellius (*Hist.* 2.67). It was slow to join Antonius Primus, mainly because of the obstructionism of the province's governor, Marcus Pompeius Silvanus, but the legionary legate Annius Bassus got it moving after Cremona (*Hist.* 3.50, the only clear reference to the unit in the Flavian campaign). Assigned to the suppression of Civilis' revolt (*Hist.* 4.68.4), it ended up stationed at Vindonissa in Germania Superior (Windisch in Switzerland), its place in Dalmatia being taken by the new IV Flavia Felix.

XII FULMINATA: probably raised by Julius Caesar, the legion was stationed in Syria by at least the middle of Augustus' reign. Nothing is known of its history until the 60s, but in that decade it disgraced itself twice. It was involved along with IV Scythica in Caesennius Paetus' surrender to the Parthians at Rhandeia in autumn 62. And Suetonius reports that it lost its eagle in the opening stages of the Jewish Revolt in 66 (*Vespasian* 4.5; cf. Josephus, *BJ* 2.500 and 7.18). A detachment perhaps of 2,600 men accompanied Mucianus' expeditionary force to Italy.

XIII GEMINA: of uncertain origins, the legion was stationed at Vindonissa in Upper Germany (Windisch in Switzerland) between approximately 10 and 50. Then it was moved to Poetovio (Ptuj) in Pannonia because of disturbances there. After Otho summoned it to his aid in 69, the advance detachment fought at Ad Castores and was joined by the rest of the unit for Bedriacum. After that defeat it was kept in northern Italy for a time, building amphitheaters at Placentia and Cremona (*Hist.* 3.32), and then was ordered back to Poetovio. There Antonius Primus mobilized it once more. The legionary legate in 69 was Vedius Aquila (*Hist.* 3.7.1), and Suetonius' father was one of the tribunes (*Otho* 10.1). One of the eight units assigned to Petillius Cerialis for the suppression of Civilis' revolt in Lower Germany (*Hist.* 4.68.4), it was returned to Pannonia afterwards, being stationed initially at Poetovio yet again.

XIV GEMINA MARTIA VICTRIX: of uncertain origins, the legion was stationed in Upper Germany from 9 onward. One of the four full legions used by Claudius for the invasion of Britain in 43, it won its titles Martia Victrix for the suppression of Boudicca's revolt in a campaign commanded by Suetonius Paulinus (cf. *Hist.* 2.11.1 and 5.16.3). It was summoned back to Italy by Nero, probably in 66 for his planned eastern expeditions. Still there in early 68, it remained loyal to Nero, but was held in check by the eight Batavian cohorts attached to it (*Hist.* 2.27.2). Galba moved it to Dalmatia, and a detachment fought for Otho at Bedriacum. It was returned to Britain by Vitellius (*Hist.* 2.66), in part no doubt to compensate for the absence of the 8,000 men he had drawn from the three other legions in the province (II Augusta, IX Hispana, and XX Valeria Victrix). One of the eight legions assigned originally to Petillius Cerialis for the suppression of Civilis' revolt (*Hist.* 4.68.4), the unit was transferred to Annius Gallus' command in Upper Germany in the course of 70 (*Hist.* 5.19.1) and took up residence in Mogontiacum (Mainz).

XV APOLLINARIS: formed originally by Octavian, the legion was stationed in Pannonia at the start of Tiberius' reign and was involved in the mutinies of 14. It remained there, apparently, until shifted to Syria in 63 as a result of Caesennius Paetus' surrender at Rhandeia (Tacitus, *Ann.* 15.25.3, noting that the task was entrusted to Marius Celsus). In the winter of 66/67 it was one of the three units entrusted to Vespasian for the suppression of the Jewish revolt. Since he sent his son Titus, newly appointed the unit's legionary legate (Suetonius, *Vesp.* 4.6), to fetch the men from Alexandria (Josephus, *BJ* 3.64–65), it must have been earmarked for one of Nero's planned eastern expeditions. The bulk of the legion stayed in Judaea, but a detachment of perhaps 2,600 men was attached to Mucianus' expeditionary force. Eventually it was recalled from the east and sent to Carnuntum in Pannonia, taking the place of XXII Primigenia.

XV PRIMIGENIA: one of the two legions created by Caligula, probably in 39, it appears to have been stationed first at Bonna (Bonn) in Lower Germany. It was moved to Vetera (Xanten), also in Lower Germany, probably in 43 as part of the reshuffling that accompanied Claudius' invasion of Britain, and there it occupied a camp jointly with V Alaudae. A detachment accompanied Valens on his march to Rome. The balance of the legion was massacred at Vetera during Civilis' revolt (*Hist.* 4.60) and the unit was disbanded by Vespasian. In 69 Munius Lupercus was the legionary legate probably of XV Primigenia, possibly of XVI (*Hist.* 4.18.1).

XVI: formed originally by Octavian, the legion was stationed at Mogontiacum (Mainz) in Upper Germany in 23. It was transferred to Novaesium (Neuss) in Lower Germany in Claudius' reign, to replace XX Valeria Victrix, and it was still there in 69. A detachment accompanied Valens on his march to Rome. The balance of the legion was caught up in Civilis' revolt and was cashiered by Vespasian afterwards, though survivors may have been drafted into the new unit XVI Flavia Firma. The legionary legate in 69, if not Munius Lupercus, may have been Numisius Rufus (*Hist.* 4.22.1 and 59.1).

XX VALERIA VICTRIX: stationed originally in Spain, the legion was based in Lower Germany in 14 and was involved in the mutinies attending Tiberius' accession. One of the four legions moved to Britain when Claudius invaded, it was still there in 69, winning its title Valeria Victrix for its part in the suppression of Boudicca's revolt. The detachment of (probably) 2,600 men it sent to Vitellius joined him only after Bedriacum and fought at Cremona. The balance of the men proved the most reluctant of the troops in Britain to abandon Vitellius for Vespasian, but it is unclear whether they were following or defying their legionary legate,

Marcus Roscius Coelius (*Hist.* 1.60 and 3.44). In either case, Mucianus replaced Roscius in 70 with Tacitus' father-in-law, Agricola (*Agr.* 7.3).

XXI RAPAX: stationed in Lower Germany in the early principate, it was one of the prime movers in the mutinies of 14. The unit was shifted to Vindonissa in Upper Germany (Windisch in Switzerland), probably around 50, when XIII Gemina was transferred to Poetovio (Ptuj) in Pannonia. Although XXI Rapax played no clear part in Vitellius' elevation, it formed the core of Caecina's column (*Hist.* 1.61.2), fought at Bedriacum, and was sent with I Italica to hold Cremona against the forces of Antonius Primus (*Hist.* 2.100.3 and 3.18.1). Returned to Vindonissa immediately after Cremona's sack (cf. *Hist.* 3.35.1 and 4.70.2), it was one of the units used by Petillius Cerialis to suppress Civilis' revolt (*Hist.* 4.68.4), being stationed then at Bonna (Bonn) in Lower Germany.

XXII DEIOTARIANA: in origin a force raised and trained in the Roman manner by King Deiotarus of Galatia, it was incorporated as a regular legion when his kingdom was made a province in 25 B.C. By 8 B.C. it was stationed in Egypt, and from some point in Tiberius' reign through 69 it occupied the double camp at Nicopolis, outside Alexandria, with III Cyrenaica. As happened also with III Cyrenaica, a detachment of unknown size served under Corbulo in 63, and a detachment of 1,000 men joined Titus for the storming of Jerusalem in 70.

XXII PRIMIGENIA: one of the two legions created by Caligula, probably in 39. From the start, it seems, until 69 it was stationed with IV Macedonica in the double camp at Mogontiacum (Mainz) in Upper Germany. A detachment accompanied Caecina in his march on Rome and fought at Bedriacum. The rest of the legion escorted Vitellius to Italy (*Hist.* 2.89.1 and 100.1), marched with Caecina to Hostilia, and fought at Cremona (*Hist.* 3.22.2). Immediately after, it was sent to Carnuntum in Pannonia, replacing VII Galbiana as the garrison (cf. *Hist.* 3.35.1). The legionary legate in 69 was Gaius Dillius Vocula, but he remained behind in Germany (*Hist.* 4.24.1), and was murdered by a deserter during Civilis' revolt (*Hist.* 4.59.1). After the revolt it occupied the new camp at Vetera (Xanten) in Lower Germany, its place at Carnuntum being taken by XV Apollinaris.

Notes

Introduction

1. There is no valid way of setting up equivalencies between Roman and modern money, but I have attempted to convey orders of magnitude by converting every specific sum into sesterces (abbreviated *HS*). For sesterces the reader can substitute dollars, pounds, or euros to get the general effect.
2. Romans cut off the heads of prominent enemies for two reasons. First, there was identification. Before photography, this was the easiest way to ensure that the man in question had been killed. Hence Dio's story of the aristocrat who evaded the clutches of the emperor Commodus and was never found, "even though many heads said to be his were sent to Rome." Second, there was the humiliation of having one's corpse mutilated. This was redoubled if the victim's head became an object of sport, as happened not only to Galba. Gaius Trebonius was the first of the Liberators to be caught and killed by Julius Caesar's heirs. The soldiery cut off his head and "for amusement bowled it from one to another along the city streets like a ball, until it was wholly unrecognizable." Fabia's comment is taken from his paper "La journée du 15 janvier 69 à Rome," *Revue de Philologie* 36 (1912), 102–3.
3. For a striking example of the widespread failure to grasp what Tacitus is saying and how he says it see my "Greed for Power? Tacitus, Histories 1, 52, 2," *Philologus* 146 (2002), 339–49.
4. Many of the horrendous errors of fact in Suetonius' *Life* of Vitellius are the result of an attempt to arrange and present the material artistically. See Paola Venini, "Sulle vite svetoniane di Galba, Otone e Vitellio," *Rendiconti dell'Istituto Lombardo, classe di lettere* 108 (1974), 991–1014.

Chapter 1

1. Under the imperial system, the two consuls who took office on 1 January, still gave the year its name, no matter how briefly they served, and were known as *consules ordinarii*. The rest were *consules suffecti* (replacements). The evidence for the senate under the emperors has been assembled by R. J. A. Talbert, *The Senate of Imperial Rome* (Oxford: University Press, 1984).
2. On the seven cohorts of the watch (*cohortes vigilum*) see P. K. Baillie Reynolds, *The Vigiles of Imperial Rome* (London: Oxford University Press, 1926); J. S. Rainbird, "The Fire Stations of Imperial Rome," *Papers of the*

British School at Rome 54 (1986), 147–69. Paramilitary units, they played little part in the story of 69. But their commander, the *praefectus vigilum*, more than once moved up to become prefect of the praetorian guard.

3. For a fascinating discussion of the tensions created in the minds of senators able to distinguish between forest and trees, whether they accepted or opposed their ruler, see the introduction to V. Rudich, *Political Dissidence under Nero* (London and New York: Routledge, 1993). He may overestimate the number capable of such discernment.

4. By 68/69 the number of praetorian cohorts had risen to 12, the number of urban to six, and they were numbered sequentially. Three urban cohorts remained in Rome, but the other three were distributed between Ostia (*cohors XVII*: see chapter 5), Puteoli, and Lugdunum (*cohors XVIII*).

5. Assessment of Verginius' motives would be more difficult, if we were to accept Plutarch's claim that the troops proclaimed him emperor before Vesontio. But his account is muddled. Dio's statement that the proclamation followed the battle is far more plausible.

6. If, as J. P. V. D. Balsdon once suggested, Galba's four legions were XIII, XIV, XV Primigenia, and XVI, the case would work just as well. In 68/69 there would have been no anti-Galban legion in Upper Germany, since XXII Primigenia would not have been involved, but there would have been two in Lower Germany, XV and XVI, and it was in Lower Germany that one of the most persistent malcontents was stationed, Fabius Valens.

7. Plutarch, our main source for the donative (*Galba* 2.2), reports that not only were 7,500 denarii promised to individual guardsmen, but also that 1,250 denarii was the sum offered to "those outside" (τοῖς ἐκτός). This has been taken to denote the armed forces all over the empire. It more likely means "those forces in Rome outside the praetorian guard." First, Nymphidius engineered a coup and needed support only in Rome. Second, Tacitus limits complaints about the nonpayment of the donative to the praetorians, never bringing it up in relation to the Rhine legions, although they were equally aggrieved. And third, Polybius 36.2 uses the phrase in a similar context to mark the distinction between "those in the senate" and "those outside the senate but in Rome." See F. W. Walbank, *A Historical Commentary on Polybius*, vol. 3 (Oxford: University Press, 1979), 654.

Chapter 2

1. Macrobius preserves three jokes about Galba's father (*Saturnalia* 2.4.8 and 2.6.3–4). The most telling asserts that his physical disability put his audiences off so much that it ruined the effect his oratory might otherwise have had.

2. See the excellent discussion by T. P. Wiseman, "Legendary genealogies in late-republican Rome," *Greece & Rome* 21 (1974), 153–64.

3. Later, so Suetonius remarks, it was considered significant that Galba, consul ordinarius for 33, followed Gnaeus Domitius Ahenobarbus (Nero's father) as ordinarius for 32, and was himself followed by Lucius Salvius Otho (the father of his murderer) as suffectus for 33. He does not add that Aulus Vitellius, the emperor's uncle, and Lucius, his father, also appeared in the sequence, as suffectus in 32 and ordinarius in 34 respectively. That would

have ruined the effect. The pattern proves only that these men were all of the same generation, advancing at much the same pace.

4. Though exaggerated, the reports were not baseless. There was trouble in Rome (Nymphidius was fomenting it). Clodius Macer was withholding Africa's grain supplies. There was trouble in Germany. And until late in 68 Licinius Mucianus, governor of Syria, was feuding with Vespasian in Judaea (see chapter 8). But as this is one of the few chronological hints Plutarch provides, Nymphidius' dwelling on the mutinous state of the troops in Germany could perhaps be held to suggest that Galba had not yet made his way north from Narbo Martius.

5. These details help explain Galba's ordering the execution of Cingonius Varro, the senator who wrote the speech, and they underline Nymphidius' inferior status and capacities. A senator worth his salt did not get others to write his speeches, nor did he deliver them from a script, whether or not he had gotten the words by heart beforehand.

6. For this stimulus-response interpretation of emperors' activities see especially Fergus Millar, *The Emperor in the Roman World* (Ithaca, N.Y.: Cornell University Press, 1977); for the gaps in the surviving evidence, G. P. Burton, "The Roman Imperial State (A.D. 14–235): Evidence and reality," *Chiron* 32 (2002), 249–80. The former point may be illustrated by the new constitutions for the provinces Africa and Cappadocia that Otho put into effect. These could have been items inherited from Galba: Africa probably needed reorganization after the antics of Clodius Macer, and Galba reorganized Galatia and Pamphylia, a step likely to have affected arrangements in Cappadocia too. But if this is correct, Galba failed to carry out these "policies" before his murder.

7. Galba's ties with other senators are discussed by Ronald Syme, "Partisans of Galba," *Historia* 31 (1982), 460–83, reprinted in his *Roman Papers* 4 (Oxford: University Press, 1988), 115–39. As he admits, the evidence is slight and the links tenuous. It is arguable, for example, whether Marius Celsus was ever Galba's friend, even though he won fame for his loyalty to him as emperor.

8. Though marines were not allotted quarters in Rome before the Flavian era, detachments from the fleet at Misenum carried out assorted duties in and around the city in the Julio-Claudian period, for example, managing the awnings stretched over the theaters to shade the audience from the sun. Rome's deleterious effects on troops stationed there was a commonplace.

9. The basic work on the recruitment of legionaries is Giovanni Forni, *Il reclutamento delle legioni da Augusto a Diocleziano* (Milan and Rome: Fratelli Bocca, 1953), updated by his study "Estrazione etnica e sociale dei soldati delle legioni nei primi tre secoli del impero," *Aufstieg und Niedergang der römischen Welt*, vol. 2, part 1 (Berlin: De Gruyter, 1974), 339–91. The troops' diet is discussed by Roy W. Davies, "The Roman military diet," *Britannia* 2 (1971) 122–42, reprinted in his *Service in the Roman Army* (Edinburgh: University Press, 1989), 187–206.

10. This is discussed by Ramsey MacMullen, "The legion as a society," *Historia* 33 (1984), 440–56, reprinted in his *Changes in the Roman Empire* (Princeton: University Press, 1990), 225–35. He stresses the positive effects on unit cohesion, not the negative effects of isolation.

11. See chapter 4. Suetonius signals what he is doing by stating explicitly that "the troops took no account of the day or the time of day" (*Vitellius* 8.1). For the belief that the day following the first of the month was a "black" day, on which one should not start anything new, see Varro, *de lingua Latina* 6.29; Livy 6.1.12; Plutarch, *Quaestiones Romanae* 25; Aulus Gellius, *Noctes Atticae* 5.17.1–2; and Macrobius, *Saturnalia* 1.16.21. The idea that evenings were to be spent "off duty" is a commonplace: for two more examples see chapters 5 and 10.

Chapter 3

1. Tacitus and Suetonius report, each in his own way, that the people bandied about the name of a third possibility, Vespasian's elder son Titus. But both dismiss him as a genuine candidate. What occasioned the gossip was his being sent from Judaea to Rome in the winter of 68/69. He never reached Rome (see chapter 8).

2. Originally scouts, *speculatores* by the end of the republic were élite troops, attached closely to a general and used for special missions. In the praetorian guard 24 of them seem to have been carried on the roll of each cohort, though they were not regarded as actual members of the cohort.

3. According to Tacitus, "some believed" that Laco had pressed hard for Piso's adoption, having met and formed a friendship with him at the house of Rubellius Plautus. Given what we know about the characters of the two men (honesty was the one virtue they shared), the friendship seems unlikely. And those who told the story (as Tacitus also says) explained the lack of evidence by claiming that Laco never revealed this, craftily speaking in Piso's behalf as if the young man were unknown to him.

4. One Tacitean speech is demonstrably based on fact, Claudius' address to the senate in 48. We have a fragment of the original, on a bronze tablet found at Lyon in 1524. See E. Mary Smallwood, *Documents illustrating the Principates of Gaius, Claudius and Nero* (Cambridge: University Press, 1967), no. 369. Tacitus' version is much briefer and snappier (*Annals* 11.23–24).

5. Claudius had given the praetorians a donative when he declared Nero his heir in 50, but it is arguable whether this was customary yet (see below, chapter 7 and conclusion).

6. Vinius, ironically, seems not to have offered Otho money, only moral support and the hand of his daughter. Whether Otho wanted to marry her is moot. According to Suetonius (*Otho* 10.2), in his last days he was meditating a match with Statilia Messallina, previously Nero's third and final wife.

7. Tacitus has two terms for common soldiers: *gregarius miles* denotes a private pure and simple; *manipularis miles*, the term applied to Barbius and Veturius, refers to a ranker at any level up to centurion. So these two were noncoms. Suetonius tells a different story, interesting primarily for the specific figures he gives (probably unreliable): "initially the business was entrusted to five *speculatores*, then to ten others, two of whom were picked by each of the first five. To each of the 15 men 10,000 sesterces were paid cash down, and 50,000 more were promised." The annual pay of an ordinary soldier in the praetorian guard amounted to *HS* 3,000 before stoppages.

Chapter 4

1. There is one early Vitellian gold coin, an *aureus* struck in Spain, that honors "the Senate and People of Rome" (SENAT P Q ROMANVS), but this legend was almost certainly taken over from Galba's issues on the initiative of the local mint-master.

2. See especially Valerie A. Maxfield, *The Military Decorations of the Roman Army* (Berkeley and Los Angeles: University of California Press, 1981), chapter 4.

3. A detachment (*vexillatio*) drawn from a legion could vary in size. The four Balkan legions that Otho summoned to his assistance each sent on ahead a detachment of 2,000 men, and 1,000 and 2,000 were the standard numbers. But the detachments from the three British legions that joined Vitellius totaled 8,000 men, near enough to 2,600 men apiece. We could remedy this supposed anomaly by assuming that Tacitus thought Britain contained four legions at the time, but he also says explicitly that the detachments from the five eastern legions put under the command of Licinius Mucianus totaled 13,000 men, once again 2,600 men apiece.

4. It is often said that Tacitus overestimates the size of both forces by as much as a third, since he gives Valens 40,000 armed men altogether and Caecina 30,000. But German tribal contingents under their own chiefs (as distinct from auxiliary units officered by Romans) were attached to both columns. And both probably included large numbers of camp-followers, as well as soldiers' slaves. They too could be reckoned combatants. As is pointed out by M. P. Speidel, "The soldiers' servants," *Ancient Society* 20 (1989), 239–48, one of the slaves' tasks was to defend the camp when the troops marched out to give battle. So the numbers may not be greatly exaggerated.

Chapter 5

1. There is only one hint of this idea in Tacitus, in the speech he gives Otho just before his suicide, and that is discussed in chapter 7.

2. Suetonius' description of Augustus illustrates the point. He was short, "but this was concealed by the proportion and symmetry of his limbs, so that one recognized it only from the contrast with anyone who was taller."

3. Plutarch sets Sabinus' appointment as city prefect in mid-March, when Otho left Rome for the north. This is clearly an error, whether brought about by ignorance, or by a misunderstanding of the fact that Otho put his brother Titianus in charge of Rome then.

4. The chronology is difficult. These four issues, it is usually said, must have been minted before 9 March, because the emperor's titles on the obverse do not include Pontifex Maximus (conferred formally on that date), whereas the official celebrations for the victory in Moesia were staged only on 1 March. But the mint need not have stopped striking these issues on 9 March in favor of designs styling Otho Pontifex Maximus as well. Since this title is sometimes present on, and sometimes absent from, Galba's final bronze coinage, issued in the last few weeks of his life (C. H. V. Sutherland and R.

A. G. Carson, *The Roman Imperial Coinage*, vol. 1 [London: Spink, 1984], 223), Otho's practice may have been just as inconsistent.

5. See chapter 2, note 6.

6. This is the interpretation of G. E. F. Chilver, *A Historical Commentary on Tacitus' Histories I and II* (Oxford: University Press, 1979), 138–39. As he says, Otho could not have heard from all the Balkan legions in 11 days, but there are parallels showing that he could within that time have sent messages to and received replies from the legionary legates in Pannonia, Vedius Aquila in charge of XIII Gemina at Poetovio (Ptuj), some 550 miles from Rome, and Antonius Primus, with VII Galbiana at Carnuntum, 700 miles away. As Tacitus states that Antonius supported Otho enthusiastically at first, he may have assured the emperor that the other legions would respond similarly.

7. The view that Otho began his preparations only around 1 March rests on calculations that work back from the dates at which the Balkan legions arrived in Italy, and on the assumption that these forces traveled at the normal march rate (15–20 miles a day). Since Tacitus states explicitly that the legions did not make all appropriate speed, the argument is specious. It is better to contend that Otho sent orders to the Balkan legions at the same time as he made all his other arrangements, in the second half of February.

8. The squadron stationed at Forum Julii almost certainly decamped when the governor of Narbonensis switched his allegiance from Otho to Vitellius. The marines may have made for Misenum or for northern Italy (otherwise unidentified marines show up there too).

9. What happened to the Othonians after Vitellius' victory Tacitus does not report (see chapter 7). All we know is that Aemilius Pacensis was killed in the Vitellian attack on the Capitol in December 69 (chapter 10), and that Suedius Clemens survived into Vespasian's reign (conclusion).

10. Once again, the problem is chronological. Tacitus gives us the most detailed account and, immediately after reporting the celebrations attending the victory over the Rhoxolani, he remarks that "meanwhile" the praetorian mutiny began. Since we know that those celebrations took place on 1 March, it is sometimes held that the mutiny must belong in March. But the account of the celebrations is only a postscript to the campaign, and that occurred in January or February. As Tacitus uses "meanwhile" casually elsewhere, it is better to set the mutiny between campaign and celebrations, in February.

11. As has always been recognized, the main problem lies in the senselessness of summoning the cohort from Ostia to Rome while its weaponry was being loaded on wagons for some other (unspecified) destination. Hence my suggestion that there was to be a parade of some kind in Rome. The further idea that the destination was Ostia depends on Suetonius' cryptic reference to marines by whom "weaponry was to be loaded on ships and sent back." The "back" in "sent back" (*remitti*) makes a kind of sense if the destination was Ostia, the port from which the cohort had been summoned.

12. Though Tacitus' date is almost certainly confirmed by the evidence of inscriptions, Suetonius (*Otho* 8.3) sets the emperor's departure from Rome up to ten days later, partly to blame Otho for ignoring religious rites that

took place then, and partly to stress his rashness, by shortening to three weeks the time-lag between his leaving Rome and the decisive battle at Bedriacum.

Chapter 6

1. Most scholars identify Bedriacum with the modern village of Calvatone, but Wellesley argued repeatedly for Tornata, a village 2 miles further south. Since the Othonians marched only 19 or 20 miles once they had decided to give battle (below, note 8), even a difference of 2 miles plays havoc with attempts to fix the site of the battle.

2. The prefect of the camp (*praefectus castrorum*) was on the same level as the legionary legate, but was not in the main chain of command, partly because his functions were administrative, partly because he was often a man who had risen from the ranks (it was the highest position a ranker could hold). But unlike Alfenus Varus (of whom more later), Gratus must have been an officer, since his brother Fronto was a tribune who had been cashiered from the cohorts of the watch by Galba (chapter 3).

3. Plutarch has Paulinus assert that the Othonians were outnumbered from the start, but Tacitus rightly makes their numerical inferiority a result of Otho's taking a strong force to Brixellum with him after the meeting. See A. Passerini, "Le due battaglie presso Betriacum," *Studi di antichità classica offerti a Emanuele Ciaceri* (Genoa, Rome, Naples, Citta di Castello, 1940), 178–248.

4. Paulinus had fought successfully against tribes in the Atlas Mountains in 42 (Pliny, *Natural History* 5.14; Dio 60.9.1). For his record in Britain in 61, the conquest of Mona (Anglesey), and the defeat of Boudicca, see Tacitus, *Annals* 14.29–39.

5. The three legions from Moesia, III Gallica, VII Claudia, and VIII Augusta, never arrived (see below, chapter 9). The whereabouts of the other two, VII Galbiana and XI Claudia, cannot be fixed. The latter's advance guard may have turned up just after the battle, but VII Galbiana was perhaps held back by its commander, Antonius Primus (see, again, chapter 9). On the cavalry squadrons see below, note 11.

6. Plutarch's naming Celsus rather than Paulinus may have been determined by his awareness that Celsus urged surrender immediately after the battle. He appears not to have seen that it weakened his case.

7. The statement that Otho shut his eyes "like somebody leaping off a cliff" seems to have struck a chord especially with the two German scholars who championed this interpretation, Friedrich Klingner and Heinrich Heubner. So it is worth noting that both began their research in the interwar period. During World War I, German government circles had observed repeatedly that this policy or that, above all the resumption of unrestricted submarine warfare in February 1917, represented "a leap in the dark."

8. Much has been made of the disagreement between Tacitus and Plutarch on the distances the army marched on its last two days: Tacitus gives 4 miles for the first day and 16 for the second, Plutarch 6 and a quarter (50 stades) for the first and 12 and a half (100 stades) for the second. The total

is much the same, 19 or 20 miles, as was pointed out over a century ago by L. Valmaggi (ed.), *Cornelio Tacito: il libro secondo delle Storie* (Turin: Ermanno Loescher, 1897), 72–73.

9. There is no basis for assertions that the Othonians' aim was to cut lines of communication between Caecina and Valens and Vitellius beyond the Alps. There were no lines. As Titianus and Paulinus had recognized in the council of war, Caecina and Valens were on their own. There is no more to be said for the theory that the Othonians were trailing their coats to bring on an attack. Even if our sources overstate the chaos created in the Othonian ranks by the Vitellians' response, the Othonians had clearly made no serious preparations for a battle.

10. It is usually said that they must have come from the cohorts brigaded with the gladiators on the southern bank of the Po opposite Cremona, because officers from there could easily have slipped across the river unnoticed. But by now this force should have been brought across the river. Still, this force did fight poorly in the battle, perhaps because its officers held it back. This may even be Plutarch's justification for claiming that *all* the praetorians fought shamefully, fleeing the field before the enemy came to close quarters. Tacitus insists that the praetorians in the center of the Othonian line fought long and hard.

11. Tacitus does not identify these cavalry units in his account of the battle, but in a speech he attributes to Antonius Primus early in *Histories* 3, he has him assert that one Pannonian and one Moesian squadron were responsible.

12. Since axes were never part of legionary or praetorian equipment, it has been held that the fight on the causeway took place between auxiliary units. But it is inconceivable that either side would have entrusted the center of their lines to auxiliaries. Otho's praetorians at least could have grabbed axes from the baggage train with which they had been entangled.

Chapter 7

1. It is generally agreed that the battle fell on 15 April. What has been argued is whether Otho committed suicide at dawn on the first or the second day after the battle. Tacitus insists on the first day (16 April), before Otho learnt of the surrender at Bedriacum, and this is consistent with the accounts of Plutarch, Dio, and Josephus. The one ground for delaying his act until dawn on the second day (17 April) is Suetonius' assertion that Titianus was present when Otho died (*Otho* 10.2). Since Titianus was involved in the surrender at Bedriacum (as Plutarch tells us), this has been used to argue that we must insert another day between battle and suicide, to give him time to reach Brixellum. Suetonius is probably wrong, however. He appears deliberately to have added every relative he can think of, actual or potential, to the roster of kinfolk the emperor tried to console before killing himself.

2. Tacitus may not say explicitly that Otho could have won further battles, but no more does he say that Otho was bound to lose them. Like Plutarch and Suetonius, he allows the possibility that the tables could have been turned.

3. Even Plutarch does not reject this way of thinking. It forms the basis of the speech he credits to Celsus after the battle (chapter 6). But as he sees it, Otho did the right thing for the wrong reasons, out of weakness.

4. Tacitus' stating that Otho "spent a quiet and—so it is said—a dreamless night" has caused perplexity. But nobody knew whether Otho dreamt, since he talked to nobody the following morning. And the detail stresses Otho's calmness and firmness of purpose, separating this night from that following his assassination of Galba. Then, if we believe Suetonius and Dio-Xiphilinus, Otho had been tormented by nightmares.

5. Tacitus asserts that Blaesus' generosity was unwelcome to Vitellius (because he could not reciprocate), and that while he accepted these gifts with fulsome thanks, he conceived a strong hatred for his benefactor. This is possible, but Tacitus is also preparing for the emperor's being persuaded to kill Blaesus in October or November (below, chapter 10).

6. This elliptical reference to an all-night orgy is as close as Tacitus comes to the story in Suetonius (*Vitellius* 10.3), that Vitellius held an all-night festival (*pervigilium*) during his army's passage of the Apennines.

7. As we have seen already, Valens supposedly had started out with 40,000 men, Caecina with 30,000, while Vitellius collected another 25,000. Although this gives a total significantly higher than 60,000, the discrepancy is explicable, once we make allowance for casualties in battles, forces told off to watch Othonian units, reserves sent back to their homelands, and men let go the service.

8. Otho had planned for Marius Celsus and Arrius Antoninus to be consuls for July to September. For October he had designated Valerius Marinus and Pedanius Costa; Vitellius disregarded Costa because he had been hostile to Nero, and he postponed the term of office for Marinus, originally one of Galba's choices, writing him off as a nonentity. (Marinus would respond by decamping to Vespasian, a detail preserved by Pliny the Elder, because he made the sea journey from Puteoli to Alexandria in a record nine days.) For November and December, Otho had planned for Martius Macer to partner Quinctius Atticus.

9. Vitellius may have followed Augustus' practice, and have assumed "the powers of a consul" without holding the office itself. In that case, Vitellius was a third consul (for life), with the power of veto—if the need arose—over any other senator who held the office, for whatever length of time he held it.

10. The pay for auxiliaries varied, and the rates are controversial. See, e.g., M. A. Speidel, "Roman army pay scales," *Journal of Roman Studies* 82 (1992), 87–106, and R. Alston, "Roman military pay from Caesar to Diocletian," ibid. 84 (1994), 113–23.

11. Though Tacitus' account is tendentious, what has raised doubts about its accuracy is the ability of Flavius Sabinus to rally the urban cohorts against their emperor in December. See below, chapter 10, note 6.

12. For Caligula see Suetonius, *Gaius* 37.3 (Dio 59.2.6 gives the figures as 2,300 or 3,300 million and allows the emperor two years). For the shortfall Vespasian faced see Suetonius, *Vespasian* 16.3. All such figures must be treated with extreme caution (see W. Scheidel, "Finances, Figures and Fiction," *Classical Quarterly* 46 [1996], 222–38), but the rumor is not incredible in and of itself.

13. In Pliny's day (*Natural History* 3.66) there were 265 wards (*vici*), and unlikely as it may seem that gladiatorial shows could have been given in every one, Suetonius (*Augustus* 43.1) states that "sometimes Augustus gave games (*ludos*, not quite the same thing) in every ward." Though it makes some difference to the chronology whether we set Vitellius' birthday on 7 or 24 September (see chapter 4), my account has tried to allow for either possibility.

Chapter 8

1. The best discussion of Vespasian's brother is by Kristine Gilmartin Wallace, "The Flavii Sabini in Tacitus," *Historia* 36 (1987), 343–58.
2. Suetonius, *Titus* 2. The *metoposcopus* "read" the forehead of his victim. In the East the art was held in high esteem (Plutarch, *Sulla* 5.9), but not in Rome (Juvenal, *Satire* 6.582–84). This detail may help explain why Suetonius reports that the man was brought in by Claudius' freedman Narcissus.
3. Many discussions misstate Vespasian's position and powers, or sidestep the problem. As was recognized by P. Le Roux, "Galba et Tarraco: à propos de Suétone, *Galba*, XII, 1," *Pallas* 31 (1984), 115–16, Vespasian's province at first was almost certainly "the war against the Jews."
4. For Josephus' prediction see *Bellum Judaicum* 3.400–408. It is mentioned also by Suetonius, *Vespasian* 5.6, and Dio-Xiphilinus 66.1.4.
5. A legionary legateship could be regarded as a substitute for a praetorship anyway (cf. Tacitus, *Annals* 14.28.1), and Caecina had already been appointed a legionary legate by Galba without holding a praetorship.
6. To these reflections Tacitus adds one more clause: "but if Vespasian were to take over the state, those preparing for war would have to forget about prior insults." It may look as if Tacitus has anticipated events here, since Vespasian's decision to take on the winner of the struggle was made in Titus' absence (see below). The thought *could* still have occurred to Titus independently, as a logical extrapolation from his awareness of his father's unhappiness with Galba, and his own realization that Otho and Vitellius had weaker claims to the throne than the man they displaced.

Chapter 9

1. Tacitus says, not that Antonius wrote to Otho, only that he was believed to have done so. The second half of the sentence, a statement that "Antonius was of no use in the Othonian war," is more problematic, but it likely means that he took no part in the war.
2. For Fuscus' character see the discussion of Galba's partisans in chapter 4.
3. The government itself seems to have overlooked this backwater. A recently discovered military diploma of 8 September 79 shows that Sextilius was still procurator of Noricum ten years later.
4. Demosthenes' attack on Epipolae during the Athenian siege of Syracuse is the first large-scale night battle reported by a major historian, Thucydides (see W. K. Pritchett, *The Greek State at War*, Part II [Berkeley, Los Angeles, and London: University of California Press, 1974], 162–71). So it is

often held that he was the model for Tacitus' narrative. But Thucydides' account could have been refracted through Livy's lost version of a night action between Pompey and Mithridates of Pontus in 66 B.C. The surviving accounts (Plutarch, *Pompey* 32.4–7; Dio 36.49.6–8) offer the same clichés about the darkness, passwords, and so on.

5. Tacitus too has women from Cremona taking out food to the Vitellians, but he gives no hint that the latter shared it with the Flavians, probably because he sets the snippet in a different context.

6. See E. W. Marsden, *Greek and Roman Artillery: Historical Development* (Oxford: University Press, 1969), 86–98 and 187, for the ranges achievable with such weaponry and the soldiers' action respectively.

Chapter 10

1. As Caecina Tuscus was the son of Nero's nurse (Suetonius, *Nero* 35.5), he was of freedman origin, and no kin to Aulus Caecina. Made prefect of Egypt in September 63, he held the post perhaps until 66. Suetonius and Dio (63.18.1) report that he was exiled for bathing in baths built for Nero's intended visit to the country. He must have been recalled to Rome by Galba or Otho.

2. To "feast one's eyes" was a proverbial expression in Latin too, and to do so on the suffering or death of others was the mark of the consummate villain. But even if a cliché, it accords not only with the comments Vitellius made at Bedriacum and over Otho's tomb, but also (if we accept Tacitus' account) with his brother's having stressed that Blaesus was doing the same to him. Suetonius also attributes the remark to the emperor (*Vitellius* 14.2), but he sets it in a chapter full of wild allegations, and places it at the execution of a knight who had dunned Vitellius for debts he had run up before 69. There is no reason to believe this, when Dio states explicitly that Vitellius spared the lives of all his creditors, albeit in return for the cancellation of his debts.

3. The story is suspect, since it rests on two common themes. First, the tale of a spy's being granted the chance to inspect enemy dispositions goes back to Herodotus (of Xerxes), and reappears often in Roman history. Second, so far as concerns Agrestis, Suetonius, *Otho* 10.1 declares that his father spoke of a similar incident involving a ranker after Bedriacum, and that story reappears in Dio-Xiphilinus 64.11.1–2 and 14.2, albeit told of a cavalryman (see above, chapter 7).

4. Suetonius gives the timespan as ten years specifically, but he sets this step at the start of the reign, as an example of Vitellius' abuse of the constitution, in that the emperor at the same time took up a perpetual consulship himself (*Vit.* 11.2). If he is right, it is odd that the title (*COS PERP*) appears on no coins and only one inscription. Overall, Tacitus' interpretation is preferable.

5. It is just possible that Vitellius offered these terms, not to the people as Suetonius claims, but to the "legion" of marines he never mentions.

6. As the urban cohorts would back Sabinus in his coup, it has been suggested that Vitellius' overhaul of the city troops never got beyond the praetorians. Another possibility is that the slackers in his armies opted to serve in the

urban cohorts (the pay was good and the duty easy), and that they had less
enthusiasm for Vitellius' cause. The conduct of the cohort of which Apinius
Tiro took command at Tarracina certainly supports this idea.

7. It may be worth considering the possibility that this is why Tacitus makes
nothing of Vitellius' refusal to commit suicide, even though it is likely that
Vitellius' reasoning involved concern for his six-year-old son.

Conclusion

1. The quotation is taken from M. Cary and H. H. Scullard, *A History of
Rome* (London and New York: St. Martins, 1976), 408. It may look silly to
pick on a textbook, but they are widely read, and especially fertile in the
wild generalizations that distort the realities of specific situations.

2. Suetonius, *Tiberius* 25.1. The remark was proverbial (A. Otto, *Die
Sprichwörter und sprichwörtlichen Redensarten der Römer* [Leipzig: Teubner,
1890], 199), carrying the same force as our "riding on the back of a tiger."

3. I have limited comment to the legions and the praetorian guard, though
Henderson and other older writers held that widespread changes were
made in the regulation and postings of the auxiliary troops too. Since the
evidence is both complicated and questionable, I have left the *auxilia* out
of account. For one thing, the rambunctiousness of Civilis' Batavian cohorts was so exceptional that we cannot generalize from that. Again, so
long as the emperor controlled the legions, neither he nor his men had
real cause to fear the *auxilia*. And finally, the siting of legionary camps at
Noviomagus (Nijmegen) and Argentorate (Strasbourg) indicates that the
Flavians worried much more about tribesmen who were *not* enrolled in
the *auxilia*.

4. See Werner Eck, "An emperor is made: senatorial politics and Trajan's
adoption by Nerva in 97," in Gillian Clark and Tessa Rajak (eds.), *Philosophy and Power in the Graeco-Roman World: Essays in honour of Miriam Griffin*
(Oxford: University Press, 2002), 211–26. There may be numismatic evidence that Nerva paid the guard a donative on his accession: see G. R.
Watson, *The Roman Soldier* (London and Ithaca, N.Y.: Cornell University
Press, 1969), 196 note 321.

Appendix 2

1. Though the conclusions he reaches are unacceptable, G. B. Townend,
"Cluvius Rufus in the Histories of Tacitus," *American Journal of Philology*
85 (1964), 337–77, provides an extremely useful collection of examples.

2. This is not an isolated phenomenon. As is demonstrated by J. Beneker,
"No time for love: Plutarch's chaste Caesar," *Greek, Roman and Byzantine
Studies* 43 (2002/3), 13–29, Plutarch similarly ignores or suppresses most
of the stories about Julius Caesar's womanizing in order to improve the
parallels the biographer wants to draw between his subject and Alexander
the Great.

3. The Roman idea that an emperor's first act would be programmatic sprang
from a different way of thinking, but it no doubt reinforced this approach.

4. Some assert that Tacitus is talking of Vespasian's behavior patterns (*mores*), not his basic character (*ingenium*). Neither word appears in the original text (*Hist.* 1.50.4: *solusque omnium ante se principum in melius mutatus est*), and the preceding comments on Otho and Vitellius suggest that character is very much the issue.

5. For an early anecdote on the subject see Cicero, *De oratore* 2.277. To this it is worth adding that the question whether Otho was gay is not a major issue in any Roman sources except the satirists. Tacitus alludes to Otho's love for Poppaea *and* Nero (*Hist.* 1.78.2), and Suetonius reports an affair between Nero and Otho only as an allegation (*Otho* 2.2).

Index

Emperors are indexed—in capitals—under the names by which they are best known. Authors too appear under their usual names. But most of the actors in the events covered by the narrative are listed under their family names (*nomina*), e.g., *Fabius* Valens, *Flavius* Sabinus, *Licinius* Mucianus.

CPSIA information can be obtained
at www.ICGtesting.com
Printed in the USA
BVOW03s0553171117
500437BV00001B/30/P